Y0-CBZ-086

New Perspectives on the Cultural Revolution

Harvard Contemporary China Series 8

edited by
WILLIAM A. JOSEPH
CHRISTINE P. W. WONG
and DAVID ZWEIG

Published by
THE COUNCIL ON EAST ASIAN STUDIES/HARVARD UNIVERSITY
Distributed by Harvard University Press
Cambridge (Massachusetts) and London 1991
Publication of this book was substantially assisted by the An Wang Fund
for Research on China at the John K. Fairbank Center
for East Asian Research at Harvard University.

New Perspectives on the Cultural Revolution

© Copyright 1991 by the President and Fellows of Harvard College
Printed in the United States of America

Index by Margo Lavoie

The Council on East Asian Studies at Harvard University publishes a monograph series and, through the John King Fairbank Center for East Asian Research and the Edwin O. Reischauer Institute of Japanese Studies, administers research projects designed to further scholarly understanding of China, Japan, Korea, Vietnam, Inner Asia, and adjacent areas

Library of Congress Cataloging in Publication Data

New perspectives on the Cultural Revolution / edited by William A.
Joseph, Christine P. W. Wong, and David Zweig.
   p.   cm. — (Harvard contemporary China series ; 8)
Includes bibliographical references (p.   ) and index.
ISBN 0-674-61758-4 : $16.00 (paper)
ISBN 0-674-61757-6 : $35.00 (cloth)
   1. China—History—Cultural Revolution, 1966–1969.   2. China—
Politics and government—1949–1976.   3. China—Economic
conditions—1949–1976.   I. Joseph, William A.   II. Wong, Christine.
1950–   .   III. Zweig, David.   IV. Series.
DS778.7.N48   1991
951.05'6—dc20   90-20970
                                                              CIP

C O N T E N T S

ACKNOWLEDGMENTS

The essays in this volume are based on papers that were originally presented at a conference held in May 1987 at Harvard University under the auspices of the National Resource Center for East Asian Studies at Harvard, the John King Fairbank Center for East Asian Research, and the New England China Seminar. We should like to thank Merle Goldman, Roderick MacFarquhar, and Patrick Maddox for their encouragement and support in convening that conference. In addition to the authors of the papers that follow, many others contributed to the success of the conference; we should like to acknowledge Marc Blecher, Deborah Brautigam, William Byrd, Paul Clark, Victor Falkenheim, Edward Friedman, the late Hu Hua, Athar Hussain, Hong Yong Lee, Kenneth Lieberthal, Dwight Perkins, Enrica Colloti Pischel, Lucian Pye, Benjamin Schwartz, Wang Shaoguang, Ezra Vogel, James Watson, Ellen Widmer, Marilyn Young, and Zhuang Qubing. We should also like to thank Nancy Hearst for bibliographic support, Florence Trefethen for editorial guidance, and three anonymous outside reviewers for their very helpful comments.

William A. Joseph
Christine P. W. Wong
David Zweig

CONTRIBUTORS

LOWELL DITTMER, Professor of Political Science at the University of California, Berkeley, is the author of *Liu Shao-ch'i and the Chinese Cultural Revolution* (Center for Chinese Studies, University of California at Berkeley, 1974) and *China's Continuous Revolution* (University of California Press, 1986).

KEITH FORSTER is Research Fellow in the Contemporary China Center, Research School of Pacific Studies at the Australian National University. His most recent publication is *Rebellion and Factionalism in a Chinese Province: Zhejiang 1966–1976* (M. E. Sharpe, 1990). He is now working with a colleague on a book-length study of the Chinese tea industry.

WILLIAM A. JOSEPH teaches political science at Wellesley College. He is the author of *The Critique of Ultra-Leftism in China, 1958–1981* (Stanford University Press, 1984).

ELLEN R. JUDD is Associate Professor of Anthropology at the University of Manitoba. She has published widely on modern Chinese drama and is currently working on a project that examines the social and symbolic construction of gender in contemporary China.

RICHARD KING is Assistant Professor of Chinese at the University of Victoria. His present research is in the area of contemporary Chinese fiction, particularly the fiction of women writers.

RICHARD KRAUS, who teaches political science at the University of Oregon, is the author of two recent books: *Pianos and Politics in China: Middle-Class Ambitions and the Struggle over Western Music* (Oxford University Press, 1989) and *Brushes with Power: Modern Politics and the Chinese Art of Calligraphy* (to be published by the University of California Press in 1991).

BARRY NAUGHTON is Assistant Professor at the Graduate School of International Relations and Pacific Studies, University of California, San Diego. His current research focuses on macroeconomic policy and economic reform in China. He is now completing a book on Chinese economic reforms.

PENELOPE B. PRIME teaches in the Department of Economics, Georgia State University, and is a consultant to the China Branch of the Center for International Research, Bureau of the Census, Department of Commerce. Her current research on China concerns taxation and provincial industrialization patterns. Her scholarly papers include "The Study of the Chinese Economy" in *The American Study of Contemporary China*, soon to be published by The Wilson Center and Cambridge University Press.

CARL RISKIN is Professor of Economics at Queens College and the graduate Center of City University of New York, and Senior Research Scholar at Columbia University's East Asian institute. He is the author of *China's Political Economy: The Quest for Development since 1949* (Oxford University Press, 1987). His current research includes a collaborative study with the Economics Institute of the Chinese Academy of Social Sciences on China's income distribution and a study of the link between economic development and poverty in China.

ANDREW G. WALDER is Professor of Sociology at Harvard University and an associate of the Fairbank Center for East Asian Research. In addition to his ongoing interest in the popular movements of the Cultural Revolution, he is conducting research on social stratification in Chinese cities, the financing of local industry, and workers' involvement in the 1989 popular protests in Beijing.

LYNN T. WHITE III is at Princeton University in the Woodrow Wilson School, Politics Department, and East Asian Studies Program. He has published *Policies of Chaos* (Princeton University Press, 1989) and *Careers in Shanghai* (University of California Press, 1978). His recent research treats "reforms" as a social pattern, not just a result of high politicians' intentions.

CHRISTINE P. W. WONG is Associate Professor of Economics at the University of California, Santa Cruz, and has written widely on rural industrialization and problems of economic decentralization. She is co-editor, with Elizabeth J. Perry, of *The Political Economy of Reform in Post-Mao China* (Council on East Asian Studies, Harvard University, 1985) and has recently completed a manuscript called "Maoism and Development: Rural Industrialization in the People's Republic of China." Currently she is studying the role of local government in the post-Mao reform process.

DAVID ZWEIG is Associate Professor of International Politics, The Fletcher School of Law and Diplomacy, Tufts University, and a member of the Executive Committee of the Fairbank Center, Harvard University. He is co-director, with Roderick MacFarquhar, of the Wuxi County Collaborative Research Project, funded by the Luce Foundation, and author of *Agrarian Radicalism in China, 1968–1981* (Harvard University Press, 1989). His current research focuses on the domestic impact of China's open policy.

A B B R E V I A T I O N S   L I S T

CC	Central Committee
CCP	Chinese Communist Party
CR	Cultural Revolution
GLF	Great Leap Forward
NPC	National People's Congress
PLA	People's Liberation Army
PRC	People's Republic of China
R&R	replacement and renovation (funds)

Introduction: New Perspectives on the Cultural Revolution

WILLIAM A. JOSEPH, CHRISTINE P. W. WONG, and DAVID ZWEIG

Reassessing the Great Proletarian Cultural Revolution is a timely and important endeavor for China specialists and other scholars with an interest in comparative socialism and the political economy of development. It has been more than twenty years since the formal inception of the Cultural Revolution (CR) in May 1966 and over a decade since the arrest of the Gang of Four in October 1976. The latter is said to mark the conclusion of a movement that profoundly affected nearly every aspect of life for hundreds of millions of Chinese citizens, tore apart the Chinese Communist Party, fundamentally altered the organization of the economy, and propelled the People's Republic of China (PRC) into deeper international isolation. The passing of time alone is good enough reason for reexamining the cataclysm that shook China in 1966–1976 and whose legacies endure into the China of the 1990s. Like all momentous events in human history, the Cultural Revolution demands constant restudy, reinterpretation, and reflection.

But there is more than temporal distance and hindsight that can be brought to the task of reassessing the Cultural Revolution. The relative openness of post-Mao China has yielded new information that allows us to refine our ideas about some of the CR's key initiatives and to understand more fully the causal linkages between various facets and phases of the movement. Much of this new information is culled from the flood of statistics that emanate from China's modernization efforts; these data often contain time-series figures covering the CR decade.[1] Recently issued descriptive chronologies meant to set right the historical record also provide a rich source of facts about the CR years.[2] Some information comes from official and personal accounts that detail specific episodes, amplify the roles of certain individuals, and illuminate local variations of the national movement.[3] Opportunities for interviews with people who lived through the CR have also increased substantially.

Therefore analysis of many aspects of the Cultural Revolution can now be grounded more firmly in empirical research. This volume draws on new information and new conceptual approaches to present fresh perspectives on issues such as the political and economic environment in pre-Cultural Revolution China that shaped the way the movement unfolded; the relationship between theory and practice in the ideology, politics, economics, and cultural policies of the CR; and the enduring impact of the CR in the years after the movement was formally declared to have ended.

The best example of a part of the CR picture only now coming into focus as new information becomes available is the "Third Front" of 1964–1971, a crash program to build heavy industry in inland provinces away from the militarily vulnerable coastal and northeast areas. Although the Third Front strategy was conceived and implemented before the onset of the CR, it remained a major pillar of national economic policy for much of the CR decade. Until recently the secrecy surrounding Chinese military preparations prevented the release of substantive information on the Third Front. Only by piecing together recently published information can we understand how extensively the program dominated policymaking and absorbed the bulk of state resources through the early 1970s. While that task is performed by Barry Naughton, whose chapter examines the Third Front policy in detail, several other contributors to this book (Zweig,

Riskin, Wong, and Prime) also take account, in one way or another, of the pervasive influence of the Third Front on policymaking during the CR.

These new data, along with temporal and psychological distance, allow this volume to reassess some of the CR's most critical aspects. The Third Front and the CR were both motivated by a preoccupation with safeguarding Chinese socialism from what was perceived to be a mortal threat posed by its enemies. The Third Front was a response to perceived external dangers—from the United States in the south and the USSR in the north—whereas the CR was an assault against China's internal enemies.[4] Although scholars often talked of the impact of the external threat on Mao's antirevisionist tirade of the 1960s, it is now possible to analyze the concrete manifestations of this fear of external subversion. The Third Front's war footing contributed to the highly charged political environment of the CR, where "revisionists" and "capitalist roaders"—the targets of the CR—were seen as extensions of China's external enemies. Furthermore, both campaigns relied on mass mobilization—the Third Front largely of resources, the CR largely of people—to achieve their objectives.

In light of our new insight into the pervasive impact of the Third Front, it has become possible to gain a better understanding of "self-reliance," a central tenet of Maoist ideology. The view of self-reliance as principally a moral imperative must be reevaluated; in many ways self-reliance was an economic and strategic necessity that from the leadership's viewpoint involved the PRC's very survival. The strategic objective of the Third Front to build many "basically self-sufficient" regions capable of carrying out protracted resistance in the event of war was rooted in Mao's well-known (if somewhat ambivalent) aversion to concentrating authority at the center. During the CR this attitude led to the decentralization of economic management and a drive for autarkic development at every administrative level. In agriculture, provinces were expected to be self-sufficient in grain production and supply, whereas in industry, provinces and even subprovincial units were encouraged to build "relatively complete industrial systems." The excessive nature of regional autarky during the CR must be placed within the context of the Third Front campaign. Thus the Third Front and the CR have more in common than partial chronological overlap; they share much in the way of spirit, method, and policy.

This volume's analysis of the CR is multileveled. The chapters' points of departure range from specific individuals, single locales, and concrete policies to the realms of ideology and culture. Andrew G. Walder, Carl Riskin, and David Zweig examine pieces of the complicated, sometimes ambiguous, and often contradictory puzzle that made up the Maoism of the CR, but each relates his observations to the practical consequences of ideology. Richard Kraus does have his eye on the center of power in Beijing, but his dissection of the rise and fall of Culture Minister Yu Huiyong draws attention to the second rank of national leaders, who are often overlooked in studies of the CR.[5] Lynn T. White III is concerned with explanations of mass politics (especially the violence) and with the broader political culture that shaped mass behavior during the movement. Ellen R. Judd explores the model operas of the CR as an exercise in "myth creation" and cultural transformation, while Richard King analyzes how Chinese fiction in the 1970s reflected shifts in the political wind during various stages of the CR and its early aftermath. Keith Forster (factionalism in Zhejiang) and Penelope B. Prime (industrialization in Jiangsu) present provincial-level studies that illuminate the local impact of national politics and policies. Finally, the chapters in this book refute the argument that the countryside was relatively immune to the direct political machinations of the CR. The transformation of radical ideology into concrete policy (Zweig), the demands of the Third Front for rural self-sufficiency, and the rural industrialization program (Christine P. W. Wong) all greatly affected local politics, rural development, and the lives of 800 million peasants.

Several chapters sharpen our perspective on the periodization of the CR. Although the decade 1966–1976 marks the formal boundaries of the CR, some emendation of this time frame gives a clear sense of the movement's evolution. For example, the Third Front policy was set in motion as early as 1964. Likewise, Kraus notes that radical arts reforms were under way in 1962, well before 1966. Zweig describes efforts to mobilize peasants behind some principles of agrarian radicalism that had begun with the first Learn-from-Dazhai campaign in 1964 and that held sway over agricultural policy until 1978. Similarly Lowell Dittmer chronicles how Party leaders, such as Hua Guofeng and the proto-Maoist "Whatever" faction, sought to preserve the CR's legitimacy up to the Third Plenum in late 1978. The point is not simply that all great historical events have antecedent causes and enduring legacies; rather analysts must broaden their perspectives beyond the events that are usually taken as the historical landmarks of the beginning and the end of the decade of chaos—the 16 May Circular of 1966 and the arrest of the Gang of Four in October 1976—in charting the ebb and flow of the policies and politics of the CR.

Finally, this is not an effort to present a comprehensive reappraisal of the CR. Some crucial areas of inquiry about the movement are not directly addressed in the chapters that follow. High on the list is the analysis of elite politics during the CR. Many new accounts of the period have been published that may help explain the relationship between the supreme leader and other important actors at the center.[6] More work needs to be done on the Red Guards.[7] Our new perspectives raise important questions. For example, the extent of the Third Front suggests that China took the threat of a U.S. or Soviet incursion far more seriously than scholars previously believed. Given that, why did Mao place the entire nation at risk by beginning the CR, and why did military leaders let him do so? Similarly we need to understand more clearly the linkage between CR radicalism and the extremist policies of China's allies during the CR, such as the Indian Naxalites or the Khmer Rouge in Cambodia.[8] Much work remains to be done, but the purpose of this volume—together with the recent work of many scholars not represented here[9]—is to contribute to what, piece by piece, will become a more complete understanding of the CR in all its complexity.

GOALS AND OUTCOMES

The broadest theme of this volume is an assessment of the relationship between the goals and the outcomes of the Cultural Revolution. The CR aimed to transform state, society, and human nature. Class struggle, political turmoil, and ideological remolding would stem the tide of "revisionism" by returning the PRC to its revolutionary course, purifying its polity, and reinvigorating its economy. Bureaucracy, elitism, parochialism, inequality, and a host of other ills reflecting China's ideological degeneration would be vanquished, and a more equitable, more participatory, and ultimately more prosperous society would emerge.

Current Chinese orthodoxy holds that the realities of the Cultural Revolution fell far short of the movement's ideals; indeed, the prevailing line argues that the CR was an unmitigated disaster that caused enormous personal suffering and brought the country to the brink of ruin.[10] Dittmer's chapter lays out the convoluted and sometimes conflictual process that has led to the current Chinese view of the CR. He shows that the evaluation of the CR itself reflects as much the factional conflicts of the post-Mao era as it does the real events themselves. In the mid-1980s China's effort to come to terms with the meaning of the CR focused on a "total negation" of the CR and an attack on the "systemic roots" of the disaster. Although scholarly prudence cautions against simplistic judgments about very complex events, many of the data in this volume corroborate a negative assessment of the CR's impact.

In theory the Cultural Revolution was to be guided by the slogan "Grasp revolution, promote production!" This slogan conveyed the injunction that political struggle should not unduly interfere with economic activity; it also held out the promise that, properly conducted, the CR would become "a powerful motive force for the development of the social productive forces in our country."[11] Indeed, many CR innovations were production oriented—all schools were to emphasize "practical learning" by setting up their own factories and farms; many May Seventh cadre schools put equal emphasis on political education and agricultural work; and, at least in theory, the "mass line" called on factory leaders to encourage and adopt shop-floor innovations by workers. Although the economic impact of the CR is one area of inquiry that has been facilitated by the availability of new data, the total picture is far from clear.

On the one hand, the case can be made that economic production was not severely harmed by the Cultural Revolution.[12] Mindful of the economic disaster that followed the Great Leap Forward (GLF), Maoist leaders emphasized the importance of protecting production from excessive political disruption. Because of the centrality of food production, the Red Guards were forbidden to go to the countryside to spread the CR.[13] When the CR's political storm threatened to undermine production too severely, the army went into urban factories to restore order, confining significant industrial disruptions to 1966 and 1967. Without the massive institutional transformations or severe weather that combined to shatter the rural economy during the GLF, no major dislocations in agricultural production occurred during the CR. Unlike the GLF, major changes in rural policy—such as the shift to brigade-level accounting or restrictions on private plots and free markets—were not uniformly implemented,[14] and innovations such as rural industry were introduced gradually and on a relatively sound technological base. Finally, war preparation, as embodied in the Third Front, also made it imperative to keep the economy going. Imposing military control in many counties facilitated that process.[15]

On the other hand, although short-term disruptions were less severe than expected, the CR did have very adverse cumulative effects on the economy because of its lengthy duration and the destructive influence of some of its specific policies. Closing rural markets, underpricing agricultural outputs, and implementing policies limiting off-farm activities and the distribution of collective income to peasants severely restricted rural income growth. The resulting incentive problems led to slow growth that thwarted the goal of national self-sufficiency in food production. By 1978 China not only had become the world's largest importer of vegetable oils and cotton, but it also depended on imports for 40 percent of its urban grain supplies. Growing shortages in the mid-1970s led to serious diet deterioration in some regions;[16] Chinese officials estimate that by 1979 more than 100 million peasants had "insufficient amounts of food grains."[17]

Industry grew at a very respectable 8 percent annual rate from 1966 to 1976[18] but was financed with investment rates that had risen to levels unsurpassed except during the Great Leap Forward—between 31 and 34 percent of national income in 1970–1976.[19] These investment rates masked deteriorating efficiency and adversely affected living standards by depressing consumption. Under inappropriate investment policies, growth decelerated amid increasing sectoral imbalances and a secular decline in capital productivity.[20] Naughton argues that the most important source of waste was the Third Front, which built immense factories that produced little. The regional-autarky policy also created waste by mandating duplication of basic industries at provincial and sometimes subprovincial levels. Wong's study of rural industrialization shows that decentralization failed to improve management because local governments had little incentive to prevent the construction of uneconomical projects or to operate local plants efficiently. Without effective coordinating mechanisms, Mao's strategy of intensified resource mobilization led to rising investment rates, but the massive misallocation of resources sapped the economy's growth momentum, resulting in "austerity socialism" without the prospect of an accelerated transition to communism. Owing to sectoral imbalances, for example, shortages of and bottlenecks in supplies caused an estimated 20–30 percent of industrial capacity to be idled during 1975–1977, costing 75 billion yuan in output forgone.[21] Individual productivity was to be unleashed by ideological liberation, yet long-term austerity and anti-incentivist measures created serious motivational problems within the work force that were compounded by chronic shortages of foodstuffs and consumer goods. As a result economic performance deteriorated and popular discontent mounted.

The political and social destructiveness of the CR has been extensively and graphically documented, although it does not lend itself to statistical "proof" as readily as do the movement's economic consequences.[22] Mao's instructions that there could be "no construction without destruction" and "to put destruction first" expressed both the theory and the reality of the CR;[23] but little that was constructed proved durable. Mass violence, physical and psychological brutalization, elite intrigue, organizational chaos, cultural tyranny, and military suppression are just some of the terms that come to mind when describing the political milieu of the CR, whereas CR catchwords like proletarian democracy, revolutionary committees, worker-peasant-soldier students, three-in-one combinations, and other "newborn socialist things" are but fragments of a Maoist world that never really jelled.

Just as CR economic policies seriously harmed China's economy, the movement had deleterious effects on China's political system beyond the intense chaos of the Red Guard years and the militarization of politics during Lin Biao's heydays in power. Forster shows how local political animosities generated in 1966–1968 led to continuing instability, with major disruptions resurfacing in 1975 and 1976. Conflict between the Gang of Four and their opponents disrupted elite politics until the Gang was purged in 1976.[24] The continuing succession crisis and struggle over the official interpretation of the CR led to the Tiananmen Incident of April 1976 and the temporary fall of Deng Xiaoping. The result was two years of instability that culminated in Deng's ultimate triumph over those—specifically the "Whatever" faction and Hua Guofeng—who had serious misgivings about a thorough repudiation of the CR and the Maoist legacy. Dittmer shows how the struggle over defining the nature of the CR persisted into the early 1980s and colored much of the elite politics of that time.

The studies in this volume validate a critical assessment of the CR; they also help us understand the negative consequences of the CR and the reasons for the profound gap between ideal and reality. Riskin notes the failure of the CR to unleash "genuine popular initiative" and to uproot bureaucratism in economic organization and decision making. Naughton describes the "retardation of growth" that resulted from the industrial investment strategy of the CR. Wong analyzes how rural industrialization—"a central pillar of Mao's development strategy"—fell far short of the idealized models of such enterprises; by and large, rural industries never lived up to CR expectations in terms of self-reliance and resource mobilization, to say nothing of more conventional economic criteria such as productivity and efficiency.

The poorest peasants and localities—in theory the beneficiaries of the Maoist line—were, according to Zweig, often materially disadvantaged by the policies of agrarian radicalism during the CR; also CR models of both the "Dazhai peasant" and the revolutionary rural cadres were figments of the Maoist imagination, bearing little relation to the realities of either mass or elite behavior. Elsewhere Zweig has shown how the gap between "form" and "reality" in policy implementation let cadres manipulate radical policies to their own advantage and ensure that outcomes differed dramatically from the radical goals.[25] For Forster, factionalism in Zhejiang that was motivated not by idealism but by "a blatant grab for power" prohibited the emergence of revolutionary unity in the latter years of the CR, leaving most actors little moral reason for political involvement.

Most ironic was the fact documented by Kraus that arts policy of the times resulted not in the vibrant proletarian culture that was the titular objective of the Great Proletarian Cultural Revolution, but in a "cultural famine" in which the quantity of art produced was extremely limited because of onerous political restrictions on form and content. For Judd the model operas were a dramatization of ideals meant to motivate a social movement—a cultural vehicle for "winning the hearts and minds of the people" by showcasing the power of human will. But in practice the course of the CR proved that such ideals have a "limited potential for realization." Similarly, post-Mao "exposure literature," according to King, is "an admission that the moral certainty of the Cultural Revolution was a cruel illusion." This reference to the exaggerated morality of Chinese fiction during the CR could serve as a fitting epigraph for every aspect of life in China in which Maoist ideals proved hollow.

Both Walder and White address one of the most disturbing questions about the CR: Why did a movement based on seemingly noble ideals turn so brutal? Mao never believed the CR would be "a dinner party."

He knew there would be great resistance and often remarked that some chaos and disturbance would be inevitable; yet he appeared surprised and anguished that the violence became so aimless and endemic.[26]

Walder links the violence to the very purpose and rationale of the CR—to ferret out and destroy the enemies of socialism in China. For Walder an "image of conspiracy," not the pursuit of virtuous ends, lay at the heart of the CR; thus "the political viciousness so often presented as an unfortunate but unintended consequence appears instead as a direct expression of the Maoist political mentality" that motivated the CR. White describes the political "climate" that made violence inevitable once the movement began. His analysis focuses on three attributes of PRC politics as it evolved from the 1950s through the mid-1960s: the practice of "labeling" groups and individuals according to loaded political values; the pervasiveness of "bossism" as the main style of local politics; and the use of "campaigns" as an administrative technique for problem solving and policy implementation. These facts of political life in Mao's China exacerbated factionalism and antagonism in Chinese politics and were "the ingredients of the bomb" that was ignited by elite conflict and exploded into the social violence of the CR. Thus White posits a connection between the pre-CR political system and the violence of the movement, while Walder amplifies this link by describing the Maoist variant of Stalinism that provided ideological legitimacy for the vengeful viciousness that marked both elite and mass struggles in the CR. Together the two authors offer insights on how structure and ideology can combine to create wanton violence, such as that witnessed in the CR.

CONTRADICTIONS AND AMBIGUITIES

To understand why the CR's results were often contrary to its stated ideals, many of the authors in this volume stress the inherent contradictions and ambiguities of the movement's goals, methods, and motives, showing how the CR contained the seeds of its own destruction. Walder and Riskin analyze the unstable combination of ingredients that made up the ideology of the CR. Walder describes this ideology as Maoist in its exultation of mass mobilization, but Stalinist in its emphasis on "conspiracy and national betrayal" by enemies bent on subverting the revolution. The result was "doctrinal incoherence" that fostered deep divisions among Red Guard factions that "could only be resolved by force." Riskin argues that the economic policies of the CR combined the "odd couple" of Maoist self-reliance and central planning so that neither functioned effectively. Radical ideas were undercut by bureaucratic interference, yet radicalism paralyzed the bureaucracy; as a result "China seemed by the mid-1970s to have arrived at the worst of both worlds."

The fundamental contradictions of the CR revolved around issues of power, decision making, and control. In theory, the CR sought to wrest control of decision making from bureaucrats and give it to the masses and to imbue localities with prerogatives formerly controlled by the center. In practice, powerholders at all levels showed little willingness to share power with the people unless forced to do so.[27] Thus while decentralization of power, in terms of the central-local axis, may have occurred, there was no automatic redistribution of power from the bureaucracy to society.

In terms of economic power, Wong, Naughton, and Prime deal empirically with the relationships between centralization and decentralization in CR policymaking, each by focusing on a different part of the economy. Wong and Naughton discover a dysfunctional tension between seeking self-reliance and a consistent and pervasive reluctance on the part of the central authorities to decentralize economic power in any real sense. Wong shows that rural industrialization, which "was to be based largely on local resources and local initiative," in fact was "a program initiated from the top, which determined the scope and objectives" of the program and provided many resources for its implementation. This fact, she concludes, provides a "clear illustration of the contradictory impulses that motivated Maoist economic policies"; the inability to resolve conflicting demands of central control and local participation doomed the program. Naughton shows that, although the Third Front absorbed an enormous proportion of the PRC's economic resources during 1964–1971, the program's purpose and impact had little to do with some of the core economic principles of the CR. "The Third Front was a massive centrally directed investment program, and it was carried out in a highly centralized manner." Factories were relocated, but power was not devolved and local needs were not given priority.

In contrast, Prime finds that the central-local balancing act worked well in Jiangsu, where the effects of self-sufficiency on the provincial economy were consistent with both local industrialization and the maintenance of central control over resources. She portrays a province prospering under self-reliance, expanding provincially controlled resources, with provincial industrial growth surpassing the national average.

The three authors come to somewhat different conclusions about the balance of power between the central and local governments at the end of the CR. While concluding that overzealous local investment contributed to macroeconomic imbalances that eventually "worsened enough to cause crisis at the center," Prime uses provincial budgetary data from Jiangsu to show that decentralization through the 1970s was "not significant enough to alter fundamentally the central-provincial balance of power as reflected in [revenue] flows." In contrast, Wong extrapolates from rural industrial finances to argue that decentralization policies had seriously eroded central control over the pace of local industrialization, with localities taking advantage of lax financial regulations and generous provisions for local control of output to expand control over key resources. Naughton's chapter shows that the first half of the CR period (1964–1971) was dominated by the massive, centrally controlled Third Front program, in which "decentralization and local initiative played no role." But beginning in 1972 the parallel program of decentralization forced the central government to set aside its national development program and cut large-scale projects to make way for continuing Third Front projects and growing local investment. All three authors agree that robust local industrialization posed a growing problem for maintaining macroeconomic balance, and the failure to coordinate development of the national and local economies was a principal factor behind the deterioration of the CR economy. The different conclusions reflect differing approaches to central-local relations.

In politics and culture, ideals of popular power and mass spontaneity were much espoused during the CR, but the reality was the strangulation of popular will. Walder characterizes the CR as a "peculiar rebellion" because of the contradiction between its call for the masses to seize power and its doctrinal rigidity and deification of the leader; his discussion of ideological differences within the Red Guard movement reminds us of the suppression of the "dissident radicals" who fundamentally challenged the Leninist system and sought to replace it with a government based on principles of proletarian democracy. Zweig suggests that the radical rural policies of the CR never really displaced the "state-centric model" of development despite the oft-stated ideological commitment to build "a decentralized economic and political system based on mass participation and widespread political participation." However, while power did not devolve to the masses, as earlier analysts had argued,[28] the weakening of the local monitoring system allowed many local cadres to adjust policies to their own benefit, creating a new class of rural leaders who used their control over productive resources to dominate local politics.

Kraus reiterates this theme, pointing out how radicals in charge of arts policy during the CR kept a tight rein on the production of cultural works, despite insisting that art be made by and for the masses. "The leaders of the Cultural Revolution were ultimately fearful of what mass participation in the creation of a new culture might unleash." Just as the contradictory tendencies in CR economic policy contributed to the shortage of consumer goods and widespread popular resentment, the CR's arts policy created a dearth of cultural "goods" that bred substantial discontent. Judd's study also probes the "internal tension between autonomy and hierarchy" in the style and symbolism of heroism in the CR's model operas. The activism and accomplishments of these heroes reflected "the populist vision of the early Cultural Revolution"; yet the organizational context (usually the Party or the army) that legitimized the heroes' actions, the heroes' "lack of individuality," and the "fixed" nature of the art form in which such heroism was expressed carried a powerful countermessage of control. This contradiction not only pervaded the culture of the CR period but, as Judd observes, also "embod[ied] the central tensions of their time." Maoism itself was embodied in the paradox that Mao wanted people to act voluntarily exactly as he wanted them to, without quite trusting that they would do so.

LEFTISM AND LEGACIES

This volume clarifies much about the ultraleftism that gripped Chinese politics for two decades. Chronological linkages and conceptual continuities emerge between the CR and earlier instances of leftism. For White the antirightist campaign of 1957 is "the most important watershed in recent Chinese history" in exacerbating the political practices and techniques that culminated in the CR storm—particularly the use of negative class labels, which reached a high point during that period. Riskin treats the GLF of 1958–1960 as a precursor of CR economic policies, while Zweig observes that in agricultural policy "vestiges of the Great Leap mentality persisted into the 1960s and 1970s." Wong's study of rural industry points out echoes of GLF self-reliance in the CR reformulation of the program, while Naughton sees the ambitious goals and mobilization methods of the Third Front as another instance of "leaping forward" in economic planning. The seeds of the CR were sown in the ultraleftist excesses of the late 1950s and what Joseph has called the "incomplete critique" of the ultraleftist policies of the Chinese communist Party.[29]

Yet the studies reveal telling nuances within the phenomenon of ultraleftism. Walder distinguishes among types of CR radicalism that profoundly affected the movement's fate. Wong shows that the implementation of rural industrialization was more gradual, central supervision more firm, and technology more sound in the CR than in the GLF. Kraus argues that the "cultural famine" of the CR had no parallel in the arts of the GLF, which were characterized by a "vigorous profusion of amateur poems, songs, painting, and dances." Elsewhere Edwin A. Winckler differentiates between "party radicals"—such as the Gang of Four—and "military radicals" of the Lin Biao type, and argues that, because their "pure policy tendencies" differed greatly on a variety of issues, policy outcomes when they held power varied as well.[30] Leftism was not the single-minded, undifferentiated monster that current Chinese portrayals of the Maoist era suggest.[31]

Finally, this volume addresses the question of the legacies of the Cultural Revolution in post-Mao China. The CR has left its mark on nearly every aspect of the politics, economics, and culture of the PRC in the reform era. As Elizabeth J. Perry and Christine P. W. Wong observed in an earlier volume in this series, "The origins of the reforms are found in the combination of poor economic performance and disruptive political upheavals resulting from the Cultural Revolution and its aftermath."[32] Walder's conclusion that the excesses of the CR created "a firm foundation for the reformist sentiments that repudiate Maoism and inspire a renewed search for an alternative to the 'Soviet model' " underscores this point, as does Dittmer's observation that since 1976 "the CR has dominated the Chinese political landscape, forming a conceptual backdrop against which the policies of the day are legitimized."

The economic impact of the Cultural Revolution is still felt in many ways. The massive dislocations of the Third Front continue to plague the Chinese economy (Naughton). The failure of the egalitarianism of the CR to motivate higher levels of productivity underlay the resurgence of elite and mass support for "letting a few people get rich first," an approach to economic development that encourages the strategy of comparative advantage and tolerates significant individual, regional, and sectoral inequalities. The roots of rural decollectivization lie in the abortive efforts to reradicalize the countryside during the CR decade (Zweig) and in the inability of Maoist agricultural policies to provide adequate material incentives to China's peasants. The CR's assault on central planning (Riskin, Naughton) and its emphasis on decentralization and self-reliance (Prime, Wong) have greatly facilitated the introduction of market reforms and the transfer of substantial political and economic authority into local hands. It should be noted, however, that these recent reforms have also generated problems where local governments empowered by the CR often actively resist attempts to force them to transfer decision-making authority to enterprises and production units.[33]

Several of the chapters in this volume also point out the concrete ways in which the legacy of the CR strongly influences the politics and culture of present-day China: memories of the factional conflicts of the CR still shape the politics of the Zhejiang (Forster); one strain of the Red Guard movement gave birth to the democratic activists who have been among the most outspoken (and now repressed) proponents of political reform (Walder); and a certain genre of recent Chinese fiction exposes the reality of painful experiences like the rustication program that dispatched millions of urban youths to the rural areas (King). Roderick MacFarquhar has observed elsewhere that the Tiananmen crisis of June 1989 occurred within "the dark penumbra of the Cultural Revolution." Deng Xiaoping and the other aged leaders who ultimately made the decision to end the protests with violent repression were partly motivated by haunting memories of their own sufferings at the hands of the Red Guards, while the demonstrators were emboldened by the Cultural Revolution precedent of a mass challenge to established authority and by the Party's tarnished legitimacy that is largely the result of the events of 1966–1976.[34]

Thus much that now happens in the PRC should be seen as a reaction against the memory of the Cultural Revolution as well as a reflection of the commitment to new goals. Dittmer points out how the official post-Mao critique of the CR has been a process of the type of "cultural learning" that often follows a national trauma. But despite the desire to learn the "lessons" of the CR so that such a catastrophe can be avoided in the future, he cautions that "residual support of the CR survives in some quarters" and that "the concerns that animated Mao and the original CR sponsors have not entirely dissipated." Likewise, White suggests that, since some of the practices that contributed to the virulence of the Cultural Revolution persist, "the danger of another CR cannot be absolutely dismissed." Indeed there were signs during and after the tragic spring of 1989 that lend credence to such cautionary views. Political labeling and the evaluation of people's involvement in the "counterrevolutionary rebellion" according to a nineteen-point scale show the revival of CR administrative techniques.[35] Jiang Zemin's attack in his 1989 National Day speech on the "unfairly wide gaps in social distribution" that have resulted from the process of economic reform can be seen as an effort to mobilize mass support on the basis of ideological appeals similar to those that motivated the CR.[36]

As both a living memory of a painful past and a warning about the future, the Cultural Revolution is very much a part of the Chinese present. The editors of this volume hope that the studies that follow will provide some important new perspectives on a pivotal decade in China's recent political history and heighten awareness of the need for further research on this period, for a better understanding of the Cultural Revolution will help us to understand better the China of today.

PART ONE

Politics

Learning from Trauma: The Cultural Revolution in Post-Mao Politics

LOWELL DITTMER

*They pushed one of the tables aside, and under it there was really a gravestone. . . . This
was what it said: "Here rests the old Commandant. His adherents, who now must be nameless,
have dug this grave and set up this stone. There is a prophecy that after a certain number of
years the Commandant will rise again and lead his adherents from this house to recover the
colony. Have faith and wait!"*

—*Franz Kafka*, The Penal Colony

National cultures that undergo a particularly devastating formative experience often seek to draw some redeeming "lesson" from it. Usually
the impact of such a lesson is limited to the elites responsible for guiding
future national policy. Thus Munich became a lesson that influenced
Western diplomatic behavior in dealing with international aggression from
World War II through Vietnam, and Vietnam taught its own lessons for
subsequent policymakers to observe or refute. This phenomenon might

be termed "learning from political experience." Only rarely have such experiences been deemed compelling enough for their lessons to be propagated intensively among all members of the national political culture. When this is the case, the phenomenon might be referred to as "cultural learning." The impact of the Nazi Holocaust on the Jewish community is of course the paradigm case, though its implications transcend that particular subculture to pose challenges to German, Arab, and other consciences as well. The Germans and Japanese experienced similar cultural learning after their defeats in World War II, however externally superimposed the lessons may have been by the victorious occupation forces.

Chinese efforts since 1976 to review and reassess the Cultural Revolution experience—a trauma its survivors have compared to the Holocaust[1]—fit into this category of cultural learning. Because the post-Mao reform movement has been guided less by an overall theory than by an effort to rectify past abuses and has permitted (at times encouraged) a general lapse of interest in ideology in favor of task-specific pragmatism, China seems unusually susceptible to this sort of reflexive learning. Yet the indirect and sometimes inconsistent way in which political lessons are drawn from the experience for collective commemoration tends to obscure its impact on the collective consciousness. My aim here is to lift this fog: Have the Chinese "learned a lesson"? If so, what was it?

The reevaluation of the CR in the post-CR era proceeded according to two essentially different logics. Cognitively the trend was defined by the need for *incremental deepening and broadening of the focus* of criticism, beginning with the Gang of Four, expanding to include Lin Biao and his co-conspirators, more hesitantly to include Mao Zedong, then to embrace the "ten years of catastrophe," and finally taking on traditional Chinese culture *tout court* for fostering "feudal despotism." Politically the logic was dictated by expediency, giving rise to waves of cyclical advance and retreat between two well-entrenched official rhetorical lines. Both lines deplored the CR, but one focused on its chaotic, anarchistic character, the other on its tendencies toward totalitarian thought control and individual tyranny. Although the former was embraced by a factional network supporting policies that from a Marxist-Leninist perspective are deemed "leftist," the latter by a faction supporting "rightist" policies, the strictly *cultural* perspective used here views the former as "conservative," the latter as "liberal." In addition to these officially sponsored rhetorical positions, there is some indication of popular support for other lines—for example, one that still champions the CR—but there is no direct evidence, making corroboration or further description difficult. The timing, issue focus, perhaps even the political outcomes of the periodic emergence of these lines is set by the policy agenda at the time. For example, rhetorical competition tends to intensify prior to major conferences, such as the Chinese Communist Party (CCP) congresses and Central Committee (CC) plenums or National People's Congress (NPC) sessions. Ceremonial occasions also provide a forum for rhetoric that may diverge to unveil factional cleavages. Funerals or anniversaries of the deaths of symbolic political figures (Mao, Zhou Enlai, Lei Feng, Hu Yaobang), the thirtieth anniversary of the founding of the PRC, the anniversary of the launching of the CR or the Hundred Flowers, the anniversary of the Japanese invasion of Manchuria—any occasion that provides a pretext for public gathering and speechmaking is a potential political flashpoint, particularly concerning issues symbolically linked to the occasion being commemorated.

Inasmuch as the interaction between these two "logics of disclosure" has been complex and unpredictable, the following periodization amounts to a rough approximation. (1) The Hua Guofeng period, from 1976 to 1978, was marked by *tacit discontinuation and overt defense* of the CR.[2] (2) The 1978–1980 period was characterized by *explicit discontinuation and implicit critique* of the CR. (3) The 1980–1983 period was one of *explicit repudiation and implicit exoneration* of the CR, followed by a (not fully successful) attempt to close the issue. (4) In 1985 and 1986 a *search for the roots* (that is, feudal tradition, the revolutionary experience) of the CR was launched with the aim of "total negation," following discovery that pro-CR sentiment was more deeply entrenched than previously suspected. Throughout much of this period the CR dominated the Chinese political landscape, forming a conceptual backdrop against which the policies of the day were legitimized.

TACIT DISCONTINUATION, OVERT DEFENSE

The Hua Guofeng period was characterized by the overt defense and tacit discontinuation of the CR. During its initial phase, from the arrest of the Gang of Four to the Eleventh Party Congress in September 1977, this consisted of rhetorically reaffirming the CR and its underlying theoretical rationale while simultaneously laboring to reconcile relatively moderate policy initiatives with these slogans. For example, class struggle in the form of factional recriminations against bureaucratic revisionism was in fact suppressed during this period on behalf of "great unity under heaven"; highest priority was placed on economic recovery from the difficulties raised by strikes and earthquakes in 1976 rather than on new initiatives toward greater ideological purity; and most radical factional networks were crushed (for suspected complicity with the Gang). Of course the central anomaly from the point of view of maintaining the revolutionary tradition was the arrest of the Gang of Four and their followers, who had made seminal contributions to the theory if not the practice of revolution, and whose close association with Mao was difficult to gainsay. If Hua wished his legitimacy to rest on anything more firm than the fact that he had seen his chance and seized it, he needed to shore up the reputation of the revolutionary helmsman whose chosen successor he claimed to be ("With you in charge, I am at ease"). Thus on 7 February 1977 Wang Dongxing (with Chairman Hua's putative approval) authorized publication of an editorial in the three most authoritative publications (*Hongqi* [Red flag], *Renmin ribao* [People's daily], *Jiefang junbao* [People's Liberation Army daily]) proclaiming the "Two Whatevers" ("Whatever decisions Chairman Mao made, we firmly support, and whatever Chairman Mao instructed, we unwaveringly follow"). In due course he also reasserted the validity of "the theory of continuing revolution under the dictatorship of the proletariat," class struggle as "the key link," the validity of the CR, and its conceivable future revival.

Hua's attempt to perpetuate the ideology of cultural revolution was, however, undermined, beginning in the fall of 1977 and with increasing effectiveness in the spring and summer of 1978. Subsequent events were to demonstrate that, by undermining Hua's legitimating ideology, his opponents stripped him of political armor, leading soon to his political demise. For the first time in CCP history, a sitting leader was divested of power without some disabling political catastrophe (true, the "foreign leap forward" of 1977–78 was abortive, but so were many subsequent reforms, and in any case the program was based on Deng's 1975 Four Modernizations documents). That the manipulation of political and ideological levers whereby this feat was achieved was exceedingly adroit goes without saying. Without taking the time to recount this slow coup in detail, I will focus on two of the reasons for its outcome.

First, Hua's political position necessitated decoupling theory and practice, meaning that CR ideology had no policy base to sustain it. Ideology rests not upon economics, as Marx assumed, but upon political power, which is enhanced by the successful implementation of policy. Hua reaffirmed CR ideology at the abstract level while deemphasizing or even vitiating it at the concrete level, giving rise to a widespread sense of theoretical incoherence. The Four Modernizations took pride of place, shifting priority from politics to economics and legitimating many of the concrete policies previously associated with "revisionism": differentiated material incentives, bureaucratic "regularization," and cost accounting. These new policies provided a vehicle on which survivors and even opponents of the CR could ride back into power. And, beginning with the rehabilitation of Deng in July 1977, they did so with accelerating momentum, as their cases were reversed either through rehabilitation *(pingfan, fanan, gaizheng)*, which implied that the original verdict was in error, or through rectification *(zhai mao)*, which implied that the original verdict may have been correct, but the wrong had been righted.

In the course of the year, Peng Dehuai and the "right opportunists" *(youqing fenzi)* purged in 1959 were rehabilitated, followed by Ma Yinchu and several hundred thousand other "rightists" *(youpai)* who had fallen in the 1957 antirightist movement. This process allowed a steady stream of steadfast opponents of CR slogans to return to high position, while the ongoing purge of radicals depleted the ranks of the defending army. Given the growing hiatus between ideology and policy in Hua's modernization program, to insist on dogmatic adherence to "whatever" Mao had said begged too many questions. Far more consonant with actual practice was the reformers' proposal to admit a discrepancy between the two, or even explicitly to adjust theory to political reality ("practice as the sole criterion of truth"). Hua's dogmatic legitimating ideology was at odds with his own pragmatic application.

Second, serious inconsistencies existed at the theoretical level. To some extent these were inherent in Mao Zedong Thought, but Hua seemed unable to resolve them—though not for want of trying. Hua immediately placed himself in charge of the committee to edit Mao's *Selected Works,* thereby claiming the mantle of ideological high priest, and the volume that was so expeditiously produced carefully stopped short of the CR, with no additional volume in view. Those selections that were given wider circulation in the mass media, such as "The Ten Great Relationships," also eschewed revolutionary sloganeering. Yet Mao's identification with the CR was so salient and so recent as to prove indelible, and as the Hua-Deng relationship polarized in 1978, the "Maoists" inclined to revert to the Chairman's more radical pronouncements.

But radicalism was anathema in the wake of a decade of incessant, inconclusive mass movements, particularly among the army of movement-scarred cadres now ascendant. With considerable tactical shrewdness, Deng exploited this antipathy in the context of the campaign against the Gang. Account after graphic account of the wounds inflicted by the Gang was articulated, often without mention of the movement in which they occurred—but everyone knew. The models selected for emulation during this period were usually martyrs who had died in opposition to the Four, such as Zhang Zhixin, a Party member whose throat was cut prior to execution to prevent her from expressing her loyalty to the revolution, or Chen Xinwen, the pilot allegedly killed by Lin Biao in the course of the latter's abortive escape attempt.

The ongoing rehabilitation of Gang victims was linked to demands for reversal of Mao's verdict damning the 5 April 1976 Tiananmen demonstration, now conceived as a courageous act of spontaneous protest. By supporting such demands, Deng Xiaoping, a fellow victim of Mao's verdict (for his alleged complicity in the April 1976 riots, he was again purged of all leadership positions), quickly won a mass base. After the Four Greats (big-character posters, great blooming, great contending, and great debates) were reaffirmed (consistent with Hua's basic pro-CR stance) at the First Session of the Fifth NPC in February 1978, those calling for a reversal of the Tiananmen verdict took to the streets, and grievances proliferated around this central theme. Han Zhixiong, a pro-"revisionist" CCP member who had been arrested at Tiananmen, was released in November 1978. Finally, on December 1, just before convocation of the Third Plenum, the verdict was officially reversed and the incident deemed to be "highly revolutionary."[3] Roundly condemning the Gang for fomenting havoc, separating revolution from production, practicing fascist dictatorship, turning Mao's Thought into a religious dogma, and reviving feudal thinking, the decision absolved the Tiananmen rioters of their excesses in valiantly opposing the Gang, now discerned to be a renegade faction without any connection to the CCP or to its leadership.

EXPLICIT DISCONTINUATION, IMPLICIT CRITIQUE

While the Third Plenum of the Eleventh CC (December 1978) defined the principles and rules of Chinese politics for most of the reform period, as far as the CR is concerned this meeting marked a shift from *tacit* to *explicit* discontinuation (shifting priority to economic modernization), accompanied by implicit criticism. Many resolutions undertaken at the plenum were direct reversals of policies or principles associated with the CR.[4] Yet the CR itself was still approached very gingerly, in effect tabling the issue pending further study:

> The session holds that the great CR should also be viewed historically, scientifically, and in a down-to-earth way. Comrade Mao Zedong initiated this great revolution primarily in the light of the fact that the Soviet Union had turned revisionist and for the purpose of opposing revisionism and preventing its occurrence. As for the shortcomings and mistakes in the actual course of the revolution, they should be summed up at the appropriate time.[5]

For the rest of 1979 and until the serious reappraisal of the position of Mao Zedong in the summer of 1980, the official attitude toward the CR remained within the mold defined by the Third Plenum. Its main evil was seen to abide in factional indiscipline, requiring institutionalization and consolidation of the Leninist Party structure. Creation of a Central Disciplinary Inspection Committee, under the leadership of Chen Yun, provided an articulate sounding board for this viewpoint.[6] Coexisting with this institutional analysis, however, was an older propensity for simplistic moralism: somehow bad people had wormed their way into the leading Party organs, "usurped" power, and inflicted great mischief. The implied solution was a purge and intense vigilance in the recruitment of new members:

> The most important lesson that the great CR has taught us is that the leading body—the Central Cultural Revolution Group—in this movement let its leadership be controlled by a number of renegades, secret agents, conspirators, careerists, counterrevolutionary doubledealers and elements who usurped Party and state power. . . . By using the portion of power they had usurped, they imposed fascist dictatorship from central organs to localities.[7]

Meanwhile rehabilitation of old members, most of whom had been disgraced during the CR, assumed floodgate proportions, as Hu Yaobang took charge of the CC Organization Department. Aging or posthumous officials from the Three Family Village group, Lu Dingyi and the former Propaganda Department, leaders of the "February adverse current," Tao Zhu, Yang Chengwu, Fu Chongbi, Yang Yufu, Yu Lijin, the Li Yizhe trio, Tiananmen victims—the list ran like a chronology of CR villains. New heroes were found who had stalwartly resisted the Gang, such as the CCP martyr Xu Yunfeng and Yu Luoke, brother of Yu Luojin and hero of her first novel (also martyred).

The Third Plenum made a major conceptual shift that permitted an intensification of criticism of the Gang, despite continuing restraint in dealing with the CR. This was the decision that the errors of the Gang of Four were not, as hitherto decreed, "apparently 'left' but actually right,"[8] but rather "ultraleftist and idealist."[9] A shift of this magnitude made it legitimate to attack the Gang from a more openly rightist position than previously permissible. Thus the slogan "Grasp revolution, promote production," or the critique of the "theory of the primacy of productive forces" now suddenly became vulnerable.[10] Ideology tended to be equated with "dogma" and was therewith discounted. In March 1979 Lu Dingyi broke new ground by (tacitly) implicating Mao in Peng Dehuai's purge: "It is now very clear that comrade Peng Dehuai's proposals at the Lushan meeting in 1959 were correct. It was not comrade Peng Dehuai but the opposition to him that was wrong."[11] Lu's conclusion was perhaps implicit when the verdict on Peng was reversed in December 1978, but not until March 1979 was it possible to say so. Yet on the very next day an article appeared in the same paper denying any criticism of Mao.[12] An editorial the following week evinced similar discomfort lest deviation from CR precepts go too far.[13] These conflicting signals may have been repercussions of a major internal debate on agricultural policy that took place in March 1979, leading to implementation of the household responsibility system (*bao chan dao hu*). Weakening Mao's status undermined Hua and other CR victors such as Chen Yonggui and Ji Dengkui, who continued to oppose extensive decollectivization.[14]

The general trend nonetheless seemed to be one of slowly gathering courage in criticism of once sacrosanct ideals and symbols. "Any criticism, no matter how sharp, must be welcomed so long as it helps advance the cause of socialism and Chinese modernization."[15] To be sure, most of the criticism was still far from "sharp." It continued to be focused on the Gang of Four, generally conceived to be isolated from the rest of the Party leadership, with Mao as their passive tool. The Gang had "transformed the leader of a proletarian political Party into a supreme being, an omnipotent god who could create everything."[16] This begged the question of how the masses could be so easily hoodwinked. There was a good deal of plaintive soul-searching on this issue. "How could Lin Biao and the 'Gang of Four' commit crimes and run amok for as long as ten years?"[17]

Slowly the answer came forth: the Chinese masses had been habituated by years of feudal superstition to obey authority blindly. Thanks to the Gang, "a situation emerged in which superstition was rampant and people's thinking became stuck."[18] They "desperately pushed an idealistic theory of genius in order to attain their criminal goal . . . [of] turning the scientific system of Mao Zedong Thought into a rigid dogma that was divorced from revolutionary practice."[19] The masses were mired in superstition and wishful thinking, enshrined as doctrine. The evident solution, unless the masses were to shift simply from one dogma to another, was that we "emancipate our minds," and exercise more critical, "scientific" thinking, independent of political prescriptions and taboos. "There are no forbidden areas in science."[20] As Hua Guofeng himself put it, "Our country has a long feudal tradition and is relatively backward economically and culturally. . . . In these circumstances, autocracy, bureaucracy, love of privilege, the patriarchal style of work and anarchism are apt to spread."[21]

Not only must critical thinking be strengthened; a socialist democracy and a socialist legal system should be implanted, to ensure that a "Gang of Four" phenomenon (that is, a CR) does not recur.[22] The interest in democracy was not expressed in positive statements (except in the most general form) but rather in criticism of the tyranny imposed by the Gang and, implicitly, of Mao. Criticism of the latter manifested itself in attacks on the personality cult, or on the *yi yan tang* (lit. "one-voice hall") of strictly regimented public opinion. Law was also emphasized, coinciding with the beginnings of the codification of law under Peng Zhen's legal group (at the Second Session of the Fifth NPC, 18 June– 2 July 1979); it was hoped in this connection that China's intellectuals might be more adequately protected than they had been under the Gang of Four: "We must never convict anyone simply on the basis of one's thinking or theoretical viewpoint as reactionary. . . . They should be allowed to put forth different views on certain questions and have certain reservations on current policies so that leading comrades . . . can 'hear concurrently opinions from all sides, and avoid making avoidable mistakes.' "[23] Considerable debate (unresolved) also arose on whether there should be a shift to the "presumption of innocence" in Chinese courts.

The most authoritative statement concerning the CR and its attendant issues during this period was Ye Jianying's National Day speech on the thirtieth anniversary of the PRC's founding. This statement (the product of a writing team reportedly led by Hu Yaobang) maintained a basically positive evaluation of the CR that for the first time was qualified by certain criticisms:

> The CR was launched with the aim of preventing and combatting revisionism. For a proletarian party in power, it is of course necessary to be on guard against going down the revisionist road characterized by oppression of people at home and pursuit of hegemony abroad. But the point is that when the CR was launched the estimate made of the situation within the Party and the country ran counter to reality, no accurate definition was given of revisionism, and erroneous policies and methods of struggle were adopted, deviating from the principle of democratic centralism.[24]

With regard to Mao Zedong, again the verdict was basically positive, to the point of disingenuousness: "The CC of the Party headed by comrade Mao Zedong led the whole Party and the people in exposing and smashing the counterrevolutionary clique of Lin Biao and in criticizing and combatting the Gang of Four." But for the first time Mao Zedong Thought was divorced from the man himself. The former was seen to be "the crystallization of the universal truths of Marxism-Leninism with the concrete practice of the Chinese revolution," whereas the latter, though not criticized in this speech, was clearly all too human. This opened the way for a more thorough critique of the Gang than ever before without fear of implicating Mao: "Their conspiratorial activities were entirely different from the errors committed by our Party." Chief among their crimes were:

> 1. In the sphere of ideology, they . . . preached the theory that men of genius 'decide everything' and treated revolutionary leaders as omniscient and omnipotent deities whose every word is truth. . . . They denied that it is the people who make history.
> 2. In the sphere of politics, they concocted the theory of 'new changes in class relations,' loudly asserting that a bourgeois class had been formed inside the Party.
> 3. In the sphere of economics, they were against developing the productive forces and wanted to supplant production with their so-called "class struggle."
> 4. In the sphere of culture, they engaged in large-scale disruptive activities under the banner of CR . . . willfully destroying our historical and cultural heritage.

5. In the sphere of organization, they dished up the reactionary slogan of 'kicking aside the Party committee to make revolution." . . . They incited factionalism . . . beating, smashing, and grabbing and large-scale armed clashes.[25]

The abuses Ye Jianying mentioned in his speech covered almost every area of Chinese political and social life, and he went into relative detail about the abuses. His speech seemed to prompt increasing willingness in the fall of 1979 to discuss the excesses of the CR. The focus of most of these criticisms was anarchism rather than tyranny.[26] This marked a subsidence from the positivist leitmotif of seeking truth from facts, allowing free criticism, and "emancipation of the mind" that had informed critical rhetoric earlier in the year. Keenly aware of the danger of a spontaneous uprising on the first anniversary of the Democracy Wall movement, the CCP leadership also arranged to have one of its most celebrated veterans, Wei Jingshen, tried and harshly sentenced at this time, "killing chickens to scare monkeys."

EXPLICIT REPUDIATION, IMPLICIT EXONERATION

The crackdown on Democracy Wall activists was harsh, its chilling effect transcending its target. In January 1980 the first mention of a "crisis of faith" arose among China's youth, who complained of a "generation gap" *(daigou)*. In May 1980 a female student named Pan Xiao wrote a letter to *Zhongguo qingnian* asking, What is the meaning of life?—which touched off a freshet of letters to the editor by other young people with similar concerns. Either out of consideration for youthful despair or simply because the liberals rallied to the defense of nascent ideals under challenge, somewhat more emphasis was placed on democracy in early 1980. Democracy was not "the root of all chaos"; *au contraire*, "There can be no solid foundation for stability and unity without socialist democracy."[27] Still, others differed: "It can be said that without stability and unity everything would be lost under present circumstances, including democracy, the policy of 'letting 100 flowers bloom and 100 schools of thought contend,' and liveliness."[28]

The issue lurking behind this "Yes, but" quasi debate was finally exposed on 29 February 1980 when the Fifth Plenum of the Eleventh CC deleted the Four Greats from Article 45 of the Constitution.[29] Ideological discipline, not freedom, was the appropriate response to youthful anomie. The Fifth Plenum also revived the CC Secretariat; elected (relatively) young reformers Hu Yaobang and Zhao Ziyang to the standing committee of the Politburo; accepted the resignations of "Whateverists" Wang Dongxing, Ji Dengui, Wu De, and Chen Xilian; exonerated former CR bête noire Liu Shaoqi; and adopted "Guiding principles for inner-Party political life" (designed to rectify the factionalism instilled by the CR and restore inner-Party life). Although no adverse verdict was yet rendered on Mao or the CR, the rehabilitation of Liu Shaoqi from "the biggest frameup the CCP has ever known in its history, which had been created out of thin air by fabricating materials, forging evidence, extorting confessions, withholding testimony,"[30] and the accompanying verdict that "it is now clear that the danger of so-called right revisionism did not actually appear in our Party before 1966"[31] certainly impugned both the CR and Mao's judgment.

The ouster of the "small gang of four" and concurrent promotion of Hu and Zhao strengthened Deng's hand, and he now forged ahead, his desire to eliminate Hua Guofeng reinforcing his animus against Mao and the CR. The critique of the cult of personality (later to become a leading charge against Hua) became particularly intense.[32] A new watershed was reached in the summer of 1980, when it was finally decided that (1) the CR was a mistake, and (2) Mao was to blame for it. This verdict first surfaced in a Harrison Salisbury interview with Li Xiannian on 28 July, in which Li described the CR as "ten years of disaster" and placed responsibility for it squarely on Mao's shoulders. The Great Leap Forward, he said, had been a joint mistake, but the CR had been Mao's decision; the "wrong" ideas embraced by the aging leader had opened the way to the excesses of the Gang of Four.[33] Deng Xiaoping, in an interview with Oriana Fallaci later that fall, amplified this indictment.[34] Some expressed a certain unease at this verdict,[35] but a vast majority of the August–September wave of articles on the personality cult were harshly critical. One particularly pungent piece ridiculed one of Mao's most famous allegories, the "Foolish old man who moved the mountains," as a fairy tale, while another pointedly attacked the notion that a leader could select his own successor.[36]

In the last week of July and first week of August, most portraits of Mao in public places were removed, no doubt to preempt any possible resurgence of support for these symbols on the fourth anniversary of his death (it was scarcely observed). The campaign reached a climax at the Third Session of the Fifth NPC in September 1980, where Hua Guofeng resigned his premiership, yielding to Zhao Ziyang, and the decision was made to try the Gang of Four along with surviving members of the Lin Biao clique.[37] Coincident with this meeting, the press started bracketing the term *Cultural Revolution* with quotation marks, thereby divesting it of any conceivable validity.

The "Gang of Ten," it was emphasized throughout the trial, was being tried only for its criminal activities (framing people, plotting to assassinate Mao and engineer a coup d'état), and not for its political mistakes (for example, its leftist line),[38] a distinction that separated their case from that of Mao Zedong. Although the Gang was obviously presumed guilty in the press from the outset, the proceedings were not as tightly controlled as in the Stalinist purge trials, and the trial lasted longer than planned and even permitted the accused a spirited defense. Nevertheless, the trial led to the posthumous eviction of Kang Sheng and Xie Fuzhi from the CCP and further denigrated Mao's reputation.[39]

Although clearly one purpose of this escalating critique was to eradicate the residual political roots of Maoism, the movement was also effectively linked to a series of positive political reforms. The most radical version of the household responsibility system swept the countryside during these years; the transfer of accountability to enterprise management was generalized from the Sichuan model; and Deng Xiaoping made his famous Gengshen speech in August, unleashing the first wave of proposals for structural reform.[40] In many ways 1980 set a high-water mark of reformist optimism. This was, however, dispelled in the fall of that year. Devolution of financial accountability to enterprises and lower-level governmental units resulted in a loss of fiscal control and in runaway investment. The introduction of multiple-choice candidacies in district elections allowed a resurgence of what the leadership disdainfully considered CR-style mobilizational practices. There was a pronounced retrenchment, a shift from "reform" to "adjustment," and the first modifications were introduced in the new electoral laws to permit the Party to maintain firmer control.

This policy shift chastened the reformers and revived the beleagured conservatives. Hua Guofeng, who had been receding from the scene with apparent grace, dug in his heels, with the apparent support of Ye Jianying.[41] The political representatives of the People's Liberation Army (PLA) launched a preemptive attack against the liberal playwright Bai Hua, inducing the Party to follow suit. A Learn-from-Lei Feng campaign was launched in the army from February through May, the first major article on socialist spiritual civilization appeared,[42] and the criticism of Bai Hua mushroomed into a campaign against "bourgeois liberalization" that would continue (at varying levels of intensity) through much of the next three years. The reform literature continued to appear but stressed the promotion of centralism and democracy, discipline and freedom, and deemphasized the emancipation of the mind (minds were now to be emancipated only within ill-defined but strictly enforced limits).[43]

Yet this reversal of fortune was not sufficient to revive the flagging reputation of the CR. At the Sixth Plenum of the Eleventh CC in June 1981, Hua Guofeng's resignation as Party chairman was accepted (he managed to retain a vice-chairmanship for the time being), and a "Resolution on certain questions in the history of our Party since the founding of the People's Republic of China" was approved, which contained an authoritative indictment of the CR.[44] The CR is depicted essentially as an ultraleftist disaster, responsibility for which is placed primarily with Mao. His errors, however, were aggravated by the Party's lack of appreciation of the need to shift to economic construction in the post-Liberation period, by China's long feudal tradition, and of course by the villainous depradations of the Jiang-Lin counterrevolutionary clique. The main points of criticism against the CR were (1) it contained no valid definition of "revisionism," (2) it confused the two types of contradictions (antagonistic and nonantagonistic), (3) it attacked the Party, and (4) it could not finally come up with any constructive program. Evidently Mao's evaluation was still a delicate issue. Although in the section "The decade of Cultural Revolution" his mistakes are not really glossed over, another whole section of the document is devoted to (1) listing all of Mao's positive contributions to China, most of which were of course made during the revolution, but some (for example, the exposure of Lin Biao, the opening to the West) during the CR; and (2) expounding the "heart" of Mao Zedong Thought (as understood by Deng Xiaoping), which remains valid: namely, seek truth from facts, the mass line, and independence (formerly known as self-reliance).

Publication of the "Resolution" prompted renewed interest in the CR, including a series of *Red Flag* articles on this topic, which essentially elaborated on foregone conclusions. Thereafter the leadership seemed to consider the issue closed. Owing to the embarrassing tendency for CR criticism to trespass into a critique of the contemporary political scene—or, even more broadly, of the forced pace of land reform, the regimentation of public opinion, and other basic features of post-Liberation socialism—further criticism was more or less suspended. Although the CR was still occasionally evoked, this was usually prefatory to more current concerns and did little more than reiterate old points and summarize the conclusions of the Eleventh Plenum. Vigorous reforms continued in the economic realm, but in the ideological realm the position of the Party was middle-of-the-road, as Hu Yaobang saw it, bounded by the CR, on the one hand (the leftist tendency), and by "bourgeois liberalization" (the rightist tendency), on the other.[45]

THE SEARCH FOR ROOTS

The two major events initiated by the Second Plenum of the Twelfth CC in the fall of 1983—the Spiritual Pollution campaign and the Party Rectification movement—did revive interest in the CR, albeit without generating new perspectives or lines of discussion. The Spiritual Pollution campaign seemed to many intellectuals disturbingly redolent of CR tactics, with its attacks against high-heeled shoes, permanent waves, and even growing flowers. Even for Deng Liqun, Hu Qiaomu, and its other sponsors, the CR was an embarrassing precedent with which they sought to avoid comparison.[46] They certainly made no attempt to reverse negative verdicts on the CR; the best they could do was claim that fighting against rightist deviation was just as important as struggling against leftist deviation when "emancipating the mind."[47] The conservative ideologue Hu Qiaomu, in attacking Wang Ruoshui's use of the concept of alienation to criticize Chinese socialism, did not exonerate Mao's personality cult, though he did consider it an individual deviation rather than a structural flaw in the system ("ideological alienation").[48] Thus whereas the campaign against the CR had not prevented the Spiritual Pollution campaign from occurring at all, it did attenuate it.

The Party Rectification movement, on the other hand, was aimed at eradicating the roots of the CR. The CR was seen to have had a "pernicious influence" in the form of a generally low political and ideological education level throughout the Party and in the existence of the "three types of people." All three of these "types," as it turns out, were identifiably CR veterans:

[The] first type, those who rose to prominence during the "CR," refers to those persons who closely followed Lin Biao, Jiang Qing and their ilk, formed factions and cliques, seized political power in "rebellion," rose to high positions and committed evil with serious consequences. The second type, those who are seriously factionalist in their ideas, refers to those who, in the "CR" period, vigorously publicized the reactionary ideology of the Lin Biao and Jiang Qing counterrevolutionary cliques and formed cliques for doing evil. . . . The third type, those who indulged in beating, smashing, and looting during the "CR" period, refers to those who framed and persecuted cadres and masses, extorted confessions by torture and seriously ruined their victims' health; it also refers to those chief elements and those behind the scenes responsible for the smashing of institutions, the seizure of files by force and the damaging of both public and private property.[49]

Although the instructions for implementation of the Rectification movement emphasized that relegation of Party members to one or another type should be based on individual records and not on factional affiliation during the CR, subsequent media discussions of the campaign suggest that the designation of the three types stirred up a hornets' nest of recriminatory factionalism.[50] Many used CR tactics (such as "living exhibitions") in a campaign designed to eradicate CR vestiges.[51] Even more surprising (after eight years of incessant anti-CR propaganda) was how the Rectification movement provoked defenders of the CR among those accused of being "three types of person." Sources of the most frequent reports suggest that residual support for the CR was strongest in the PLA and in certain outlying provinces (such as Guangxi and Yunnan). As one of the most thorough expositions of the "total negation" drive put it: "Some people argue that the 'CR' should not be regarded as devoid of any merit; some people contend that the 'CR' did play a positive role in 'opposing and preventing revisionism'; and still others maintain that the achievements of the 'CR' must be affirmed even though its mistakes should be repudiated. . . . This is not true."[52]

The appearance of such second thoughts and excuses apparently shocked the CCP leadership. Having based the legitimacy of the reform regime on the repudiation of the CR and all it stood for, and having perhaps not previously heard such views through their controlled media, the leadership reacted with self-righteous fury, launching a major campaign (generally unnoticed in the West) in 1984–85 to "totally negate" the CR.[53] "While many things have their merits and demerits after being analyzed, others do not. . . . A mistake is a mistake. . . . Counterrevolutionary cliques are counterrevolutionary cliques."[54] Without going into divisive specifics, all factionalism (not this faction or that faction), all leftist radicalism (even the "three supports and two militaries" that had justified PLA intervention in the CR), all "extensive democracy" and "mass criticism," and all legitimating principles of the CR must be completely discredited:

We must not quibble over specific issues, because what actually happened in various units during the "CR" was quite complex: and if the right and wrong of every situation has to be debated, not only will we fail to discredit thoroughly the "CR," but we will also compel some comrades to fight to justify their stand without heeding the principles.[55]

As the campaign to "totally negate" the CR ground on, it gradually became clear that, whereas CR symbolism had become thoroughly integrated into CCP folklore as a touchstone of evil, any attempt to resolve all the issues it had raised in specific times and places was like reopening Pandora's box. The movement was quietly abandoned in the spring of 1985.

Despite subsequent attempts by the authorities to close the issue, the traumatic impact of the CR continued to make it an attractive (indeed, almost inevitable) symbol in Chinese mobilizational politics. Thus during the summer of 1986, as the nation commemorated three anniversaries—the launching of the first Hundred Flowers movement, the Eleventh Plenum of the Eighth CC (which inaugurated the CR), and the death of Mao (which ended it)—the CR and the Hundred Flowers became pedagogic antitheses, in which the repercussions of the former functioned to legitimate the latter. Jiang Qing was lampooned in this connection as a would-be radical cultural czarina: "There was actually a famous saying during that period: Letting a hundred schools of thought contend, but only one school to have the final say and it was Jiang Qing who made the final decision!"[56] This sort of Procrustean cultural regimentation, it was argued, had contributed to the "oversimplification and vulgarization of Marxism" that made the ideology look ridiculous, ultimately leading people to question whether "Marxism has lost its validity"— a theoretical crisis to which Hu Yaobang and other CCP leaders also alluded. A realistic response to this crisis would require not the compulsive reincantation of a "stagnant and closed theoretical system," but the adaptation of Marxism to current problems and policies.[57] This perceived need to develop and adapt theory to changing practice, in the context of a more fully realized "double-hundred" policy, released the torrent of new ideas and proposals articulated in the first eleven months of 1986.

This attempt to rethink the CR also pointed to a more thorough critique of the past, to an attempt to go beyond the simple juxtaposition of "ten years" of disaster after "seventeen years" of socialist bliss (in which the former emerges *ex nihilo* as an evil aberration), and to *xun gen fan ci* (review the past and seek the deep roots). For the first time since the CR, articles began to suggest that all was not right with the seventeen years, that there were also "dark tendencies" in the period that made something like the CR unavoidable, perhaps even necessary.[58] Thus Zhou Enlai, to cite one unassailable example, could be excused for cooperating with Mao in promoting the CR, because "it could really help overcome and eliminate certain real shortcomings and the dark side that existed in the Party and government organs."[59]

But rather than looking more deeply into the disconcertingly sensitive antecedents of the CR during the seventeen years, most searchers after CR roots chose to dig deeper, joining in the 1986 "cultural wave" *(wenhua re)*, aspiring to "penetrate our minds and negate something deeply buried there—to analyze and critically examine the feudal ideals lurking at the bottom of the national character, that is, the deep-rooted bad national habits."[60] The concept of culture had been out of bounds for academic discussion since the early 1950s, but it now rose from the ashes. "National character," the "collective unconsciousness of the nation," and "cultural psychology" came into vogue, and there was even revived interest in Confucianism.[61] The central polemical thrust of such comparisons was of course on parallels (and imputed causal links) between traditional feudal and contemporary radical dispositions, such as the strong focus on hierarchy and unquestioning obedience and on the cult of the emperor (thereby disregarding the radical interest in egalitarianism), or the Confucian emphasis on blood ties as it resurfaced in the Red Guard's (and CCP's) focus on "family backgrounds" *(jiating chushen).*[62] Some people mixed psychocultural analysis with a more political approach, pointing to the impact of a small-peasant economy, hierarchical class relations, and a social structure historically closed to the outside world.[63] Others discussed in the summer and fall of 1986 how to handle residual cultural artifacts of the CR: there was a proposal to build a CR museum, and at the same time a fairly intense debate about reviving Jiang Qing's model operas *(yangbanxi).*[64]

The political implications of this renascent concern with culture seemed innocuous, diffusing guilt from particular scapegoats to the entire system: in the words of Liu Zaifu, *quan min gong chan hui*—"We are all guilty." But as Wang Ruoshui pointed out, if Chinese feudal culture was at fault, this precluded blaming capitalism. For Wang "the greatest disaster of the past thirty years was the 'Great CR,' which was an outcome of the evil influence of feudalism. Therefore, feudalist ideas are much more harmful than bourgeois ideas."[65] Freely translated, this implied an intropunitive rather than an extrapunitive solution to China's problems with modernization.[66]

The notion that the origins of China's great holocaust could be found at home rather than abroad may have offended the nationalist sensitivities of the conservatives, for at the Sixth Plenum of the Twelfth CC in September 1986, the resolution on building a socialist spiritual civilization dropped all mention of feudalism and repudiated "bourgeois liberalism." It was subsequently revealed that, in the face of liberal protest, Deng Xiaoping himself had insisted on this plank. After the December 1986 student demonstrations in favor of democracy and reform triggered an elite backlash in January–February 1987, the stock "conservative" line on the CR was resuscitated, censuring the CR for unleashing "extensive democracy" and chaos.[67] The CR could not plausibly be traced to spiritual pollution from the West or to domestic revisionism, so the question of its roots was quietly shelved.

To conclude, we return to the questions posed at the outset: Have the Chinese "learned a lesson"? And if so, what was it? Inasmuch as the first question presupposes an answer to the second, we take the latter up first.

What was the lesson? Every critique of the CR seems to bear its own grievance. Yet two general themes have consistently held pride of place. First, the CR stands for anarchy, chaos, factionalism, a complete breakdown of institutional order, and a relapse to pervasive suspicion in which only primordial ties (blood ties, or *quanxi*) offer possible refuge. Second, the CR is equated with "feudal (or oriental) despotism," ideological totalism, and the extension of egalitarianism to intellectual expression and even to thinking.

These two critical foci are not necessarily mutually exclusive, and in fact both are accurate characterizations of prominent features of the CR. Yet their political implications lead in quite different directions. The critique of anarchy usually prefaces a call for "unity and discipline," institutionalized order bolstered by law and respect for Party authority, and often restoration of a classic Leninist Party-state. Whether a Leninist "golden age" ever really existed, and if so when—pre-CR? pre–Great

Leap? during the Eighth Party Congress in 1956, in the brief hiatus between the completion of socialization of the means of production and the Great Leap?—remains open to question, but the ideal is appealing to many. The critique of "feudal" despotism, in contrast, is less devoted to any pre-CR utopia, more radical in its demands on the post-CR political order, and still more vague concerning the positive reform program, although a number of specific proposals emerged during the 1986 reprise of the "double hundred."

Unfortunately these two lines of thematic critical emphasis and their respective political supporters are ultimately on a collision course. Exclusive focus on the restoration of stability and unity has promoted the same tendency toward ideological totalism that discredited the Gang of Four, whereas excessive emphasis on "emancipation of the mind" has consistently resulted in the outbreak of intolerable anarchistic tendencies. The search for the roots of the CR cannot credibly lead to capitalism (which was of course the touchstone of evil for CR theorists), but finding these roots in Chinese tradition tends to induce intellectuals to look outward, to the West, for enlightenment, which flies against domestic ideological inhibitions. At this writing the Chinese are precariously poised once again between two diverging lines, each of which logically originates in the holocaust they both repudiate. The emphasis on the repression of anarchy must be said to hold the balance of power at present.

In view of the ambiguous, Protean character of the CR lesson, it becomes problematic to determine what the Chinese have learned. To the extent that learning one's lesson involves the acknowledgment that a given experience was aversive and that one does not wish to repeat it, the Chinese may probably be said to have "learned a lesson." Certainly since 1976 prodigious amount of publicity of every conceivable variety has been dedicated to demonstrating that proposition. If publicity praising the CR dominated Chinese airwaves and print media for ten years (1966–1976), publicity damning the experience has now prevailed for an even longer period. Yet many of the problems that precipitated the CR endure.

Still, pervasive censorship obscures the fact that residual support for the CR survives in some quarters, as became clear in 1984–85. The campaigns against bourgeois liberalization and spiritual pollution that emerged in the post-CR era demonstrate that the concerns that animated the original CR sponsors have not entirely dissipated. The ideal of self-sacrificial dedication to the collective interest (*da gong wu si*) that was carried to such extremes during the CR has made a strong comeback, after a somewhat uneasy flirtation with the notion that "to get rich is glorious." The policy of opening to the outside world continues to be upheld but incites ambivalence concerning its cultural externalities and spinoffs. The CR-style approach to mass mobilization, with its "breakthrough" mentality, resort to big-character posters, and anonymous character assassination, has persistently reemerged during periods of "thaw," much to the embarrassment of the reformers. Even the "personality cult" has been more easily dealt with in terms of formal organization (that is, by dividing legislative power among four assemblies, and executive power among at least three) than in terms of the underlying cultural predispositions (namely, reverence for seniority, factional loyalty). Why else was Deng able to purge his nominal superior in January 1987 and again in June 1989? Why was the Central Advisory Committee (and other senior cadres without even that portfolio) able to exert such power without votes in the CC?

These problems, however, have endured not because of but *despite* their obvious similarity to "late-Maoist" concerns. They have endured because the problems the CR was launched to solve (albeit unsuccessfully) are real and will remain real for as long as there is residual commitment to the "Maoist" values of self-reliance, egalitarianism, ideological unity, revolutionary revitalization, and so forth. The reform course essentially contradicts these values. This is why the secular trend toward the broadening and deepening of the anti-CR critique is recurrently frustrated by a short-term cyclical zigzag pattern between defendants and critics of what are essentially CR values.

Yet if the critique of the CR has not entirely eradicated residual loyalty to CR values, it has devalued and inconvenienced such loyalty. At no time is it conceded that concern with bourgeois liberalization or spiritual pollution bears any affinity with CR concerns, and any apparent similarity between the CR and subsequent campaigns has been deemed acutely embarrassing to sponsors of the latter. It is perhaps a tribute to the impact of the long anti-CR polemic that, although campaigns evocative of CR values have recurrently been launched since then, none of these has yet succeeded in generating sustained momentum. Whereas there are recurrent objections to overlearning the CR "lesson" by those with a perceived stake in the status quo of the bureaucratic centrally planned economy, the experience has emerged as perhaps the most potent symbolic weapon in the hands of China's liberal reformers.

Cultural Revolution Radicalism: Variations on a Stalinist Theme

ANDREW G. WALDER

The experiment was approved by the Leader, his Deputies, his Assistants, and by everybody else—except for a few holding mistaken opinions. The aim of the experiment was to detect those who did not approve of its being carried out and take appropriate steps.
                    —Alexander Zinoviev, The Yawning Heights

Zinoviev's Swiftian barb, aimed at the official rationale for Stalin's great purges, strikes an eerily familiar chord for those familiar with China's Cultural Revolution. Familiar, because the primary public justification for its initiation in the field of literature and art as well as its later intensification into a mass movement, and its most common type of political activity, was to unmask capitalist roaders and other hidden enemies who opposed the Cultural Revolution and the line for which it stood. Eerily, because Zinoviev's satire fits perfectly a Maoist mentality usually presumed to be a radical departure from Soviet Stalinism.

Mao's Cultural Revolution represented itself, and has been understood outside China, as a militant repudiation of the "Soviet model." During the upheaval of 1966–1969 and its aftermath in the early to mid-1970s, what most struck outside observers was the startlingly unorthodox nature of its doctrine. The supreme leader of a stable Leninist regime turned political structures and social institutions inside out in order, he claimed, to root out a new bourgeois ruling class that had consolidated its power in the bureaucracy and educational system. Bureaucrats and intellectuals were sent to perform manual labor and transform their elitist attitudes. Material incentives and other corrupting privileges were to be abolished. The masses were to participate directly in the supervision of their work units and government.

In these doctrines outside observers found hints of Djilas and Trotsky, a return to Marx's original writings on the Paris Commune, and parallels with Russian populism.[1] Others found in the CR the perennial Chinese struggle to infuse Western technique (in this case Leninism) with Chinese substance (in this case the historical Chinese understanding of leadership as a moral project).[2] However illuminating these varied comparisons and parallels, they share a common tendency to search for the origins of Cultural Revolution Maoism in traditions other than that of the Soviet Union itself—precisely the tradition that the CR appeared so emphatically to repudiate.

After Mao's death a stream of personal memoirs and monographs based on retrospective interviews has greatly altered perceptions of Cultural Revolution radicalism. As experienced by participants, bystanders, and victims alike, it is now commonly understood not as a pursuit of abstract ideals, but for what it turned out to be: an unprecedented wave of state-instigated persecution, torture, gang warfare, and mindless violence.[3] To be sure, all the themes highlighted in earlier studies of Maoist doctrine are also present in these memoirs and studies: anti-elitism, the impulse to remold people's thinking, the dismantling of bureaucratic institutions. Yet at the grass roots, the ways in which these themes are expressed changed them virtually beyond recognition.

There appears to be a massive contradiction between the lofty principles clarified in earlier studies of Maoist doctrine and the ugly realities of Cultural Revolution politics. At conferences and other scholarly meetings in the 1980s, I have heard it argued that the Cultural Revolution suffered from a contradiction between means and ends: despite good intentions, unforeseen social forces turned the CR into something unanticipated and unwanted. I have also heard it argued that every great modern revolution, beginning with the French, unfortunately entails regrettable excesses. In this chapter I argue that both these ideas are wide of the mark: the realities of the Cultural Revolution were directly in line with its doctrine, if we give the single most important political tenet of this doctrine the emphasis it deserves.

This political tenet dominates all the post-Mao memoirs and interview studies, forcing us to recognize its centrality: hidden enemies and traitors within Chinese intellectual circles and within the Party—right up to its highest reaches—were claimed to have conspired to overthrow Communist political power and restore capitalism. While there are surely populist and egalitarian strands in the reigning ideology of the period, these values are invariably expressed within the framework of this conspiracy theory. The ubiquitous theme of conspiracy has too long been discounted. It deserves attention, not simply in order to restore some balance to our interpretations, but for a more important reason: a populist and egalitarian movement inspired by a theory of conspiracy and national betrayal is fundamentally different from one that is not. Just as important, if we recognize the centrality of the theme of conspiracy and betrayal, we are led inevitably to a doctrinal source for the Cultural Revolution that is central to the political tradition that Maoists have long been understood to repudiate. For the theme of hidden conspiracy, as expressed during the CR, is borrowed directly, with only minor emendations, from the Stalinist political culture of the era of mass liquidations and show trials.[4]

Stalin's atrocities were also committed in the name of political and ethical ideals. Stalin justified his actions in the name of the grand experiment of building socialism in one country. His novel brief for "continuing the revolution" in the mid-1930s is easily mistaken for Mao's in the mid-1960s. As socialism approached, he claimed, class struggle would become more acute. Hidden remnants of exploiting classes would spring out of their hiding places just as the victory of socialism seemed assured, and they would take advantage of the fact that remnants of bourgeois ideas still lingered in the minds of some Party members. Cooperating with encircling imperialist powers that were seeking to subvert socialism, and using traitors and agents hidden within the ranks of the Party, these class forces sought to restore capitalism. Stalin smashed these bourgeois plots and kept the Soviet Union on the road of socialist construction.[5] Having settled with these "enemies of the people," the Soviet dictator later proclaimed the "complete democratization of the electoral system" and "greater control by the masses over the organs of Soviet power."[6] Stalin's apologia for the great terror of the 1930s not only expressed the same historical outlook as that used to justify the Cultural Revolution; in many places it does so in virtually identical language.

Although in later decades Soviet leaders did not hesitate to use the language of conspiracy and betrayal regarding dissent, real or imagined, they considered their 1930s victory over class enemies to be final. As Stalinism evolved into an essentially conservative doctrine, the history of this struggle became part of a heroic mythology.[7] Mao resurrected this old class-based conspiracy theory, on an equally grand but more dramatic scale, some years after other Communist parties had declared it, and the atrocities to which it gave rise, to be regrettable errors in the history of socialism.

According to the Maoist view that developed in the early 1960s, the forces of conspiracy were still afoot throughout the world, fostered by imperialist powers and by dark forces within the socialist bloc. These forces had first revealed themselves in the betrayal of Yugoslavia's Tito and in a series of reactionary outbursts in Eastern Europe, culminating in the open Hungarian counterrevolution of 1956.[8] Now they were quietly eating away at the foundations of socialism in the Soviet Union itself. Chinese traitors, posing as good Communists and in concert with remnants of old exploiting classes, revisionist Soviets, and Western imperialists, were plotting in the same manner to subvert socialism in China. These traitors could be recognized by their failure to adhere to Mao's vision. Their class consciousness was expressed in revisionist ideas that attacked the dictatorship of the proletariat and the "basically correct" revolutionary line still followed in the Soviet Union when Stalin was alive.[9] The proclaimed purpose of the Cultural Revolution was to unmask these hidden traitors, drag them out of their hiding places, and save socialism from domestic and international forces of subversion. This aim, and its rationale, was laid out more clearly than allied notions about organizational reform or wage equalization—ideas that so dominate much of our writings about the CR "experiment."

Viewed with this in mind, the political viciousness sometimes presented as an unfortunate but unintended consequence appears instead as a direct expression of the Maoist political mentality. The ubiquitous charges made in the official press and Red Guard tabloids, the violent and incoherent factionalism, the endless accusations made in struggle sessions, the countless confessions extracted from prisoners held in isolation, often under extreme mental and physical torture, all were inspired directly by this image of conspiracy.

That this conspiracy theory was central to the official rationale for the Cultural Revolution, and that it was an integral part of the world view of many of the radical groups that arose in these years, is of course widely "known." It is there in seemingly every newspaper editorial and Red Guard tabloid. Quite properly, scholars have not taken such utterances at face value; but neither have they taken them seriously. It is as if these charges were seen as mere rhetoric that obscures what these documents must *really* be telling us. After all, how could such obviously unreal notions have inspired such political forces?

We have, as a result, fashioned a partial view of CR radicalism, filtering out the seemingly irrational and rhetorical, and magnifying the apparently rational and goal-directed.[10] We see this in two of the most influential strains of interpretation. In the first, the Cultural Revolution is seen as a contest over policy or principle, with those who hew to Soviet practices on one side, and the innovative Mao on the other. Sometimes this is presented rather bloodlessly as a policy difference between Mao and Liu Shaoqi over education, incentives, leadership practices, or other subjects.[11] At other times it has been presented more grandly as an experiment that rejects the premises of the "Soviet model" and seeks to fashion a more egalitarian, nonelitist, and participatory socialism.[12] These varied efforts to make sense of the CR share a common characteristic: they extract evidence from scattered sources and reconstruct a rationale for the CR that is more complete and coherent than the ones we will find in any Chinese source. While these interpretations have shed considerable light on the rationale behind the CR, they inadvertently purge from the record all the things that appear to be exaggerated, rhetorical, or nonsensical.

In the second strain of interpretation, the conspiracy theory is acknowledged directly but is viewed as a rhetorical tool useful in defeating opponents in political struggle or as a mask for the forwarding of interest-group demands. In this view the "conspirators" have a different identity depending on the elite or mass faction wielding the rhetoric. Students from "red" class backgrounds, especially the children of high officials, saw the conspiracy as springing from remnants of old exploiting classes. Students with other than red heritage saw the conspiracy as stemming from the privileged bureaucrats and their children. Temporary workers saw the conspiracy as residing in a bureaucracy that denied them permanent employment and state pensions. Inflated rhetoric, in other words, is manipulated to serve essentially rational, self-interested ends.[13]

Because we have so often drained the radicals' political language of its original meaning, we have fashioned explanations of what the Cultural Revolution was "really" all about that leave us with little choice but to view the violence and incoherence of the ensuing movement as somehow unexpected and unintended, foreign to the conception that inspired it. But if the CR was "really" an idealistic quest for equality and democracy or a dispute over national policy, why did it take the form of a search for hidden traitors and enemies? If CR radicalism was a rhetorical mask for rational interest-group activity, why did these rational actors appear to take their rhetoric so seriously and routinely kidnap, humiliate, and physically abuse in public rituals, torture, and murder accused traitors, and fight wars of annihilation against other radical workers and students?

This neglect to take seriously what CR radicals of all stripes were saying, and how they said it, has prevented us from seeing the Cultural Revolution whole, as it really was. It has led us to ask questions about the ignoble consequences of noble ends, questions that are premised on an interpretation of intentions that has been purged of messy realities. It has obscured from us a partial answer to the question of "how such things could have happened" that has been right in front of us all along. This rhetoric, and the political mentality it expresses, should not be purged from our understanding of Chinese radicalism in those years—it should be put in its proper place, at the center of our interpretations. For this mentality blamed the problems of socialism on a hidden conspiracy of traitors, and it is entirely consistent with the intolerance and viciousness that has become so painfully clear to us in the revelations of the past decade.

CULTURAL REVOLUTION MAOISM AS REACTIVE EXTREMISM

Once we place this conspiracy theory back at the center of attention, we need to interpret it. What kind of political mentality is it that opposes the revision of fundamental doctrines and traditions, that warns against corruption and imminent subversion, and that calls for revolutionary action by the masses in the form of a hunt for ill-defined traitors located variously among the masses and among the ruling oligarchy itself? We must try to locate this mentality in relation to other kinds of political orientations—not only in relation to conservative and reformist tendencies in the socialist countries, but in relation to such ideologies as fascism and Stalinism with which Maoism has at times been contrasted and compared.

Maoism in its Cultural Revolution manifestation is obviously "radical" and arguably "revolutionary." But the precise nature of this radicalism is difficult to untangle. Was it radical and revolutionary in the sense of the most militant wings of European fascist movements, or more in the sense of Communist parties before they succeeded in seizing political power? [14] Many interpretations of Maoism implicitly accept the Maoist self-image of a forward-looking, progressive vanguard, seeking to push China forward into a new stage of history. Yet the neglected side of Maoism, in particular its theory of conspiracy and its doctrine of mass action against hidden traitors, is strongly reminiscent of those varieties of fascism that called for true patriots to seize power from subversive intellectuals and corrupt bourgeois who controlled society's leading institutions and were weakening the nation.

Our task is therefore fraught with multiple ambiguities. The doctrine itself was ambiguous, as are the orienting categories we use to understand it. We shall understand Maoism better by highlighting this ambiguity than by seeking to resolve it and make Maoism consistent and rational. For Maoism was a doctrine that defies easy classification: it sanctioned attacks against the establishment and the virtual destruction of China's existing government; yet it had its roots in conservative opposition to de-Stalinizing change. The conspiracy theory at the core of its political mentality was resurrected from the early Stalinist canon, but the doctrine was implemented in a very un-Stalinist way, by small paramilitary organizations more reminiscent of interwar fascism or contemporary Islamic fundamentalism. It encouraged one to "dare to rebel," but only on the premise of even more slavish conformity to a single doctrine and worshiped leader.

Conservatives, Reformers, and Maoists

Karl Mannheim's discussion of conservative and progressive ideologies reminds us of the difference between conservative and reformer in the Leninist regimes during the first two decades after Stalin's death. Both conservative and progressive orientations, he reminds us, are actively concerned with shaping the future. They differ only in the sources of their inspiration and ideals. Whereas the conservative seeks to preserve what was valuable in the past, revitalize it in the present, and make it relevant for the future, the progressive seeks a future that is rationally conceivable yet has not heretofore been approximated in reality. What the conservative fears is that the values of the nation and people will be lost, that the community will degenerate and decline. What the progressive fears is that prejudice, inertia, and short-sighted attachment to an idealized past will prevent humankind from reaching its true potential.[15]

In communist regimes, these same tendencies are apparent in the contention between proponents of orthodoxy and of reform. Both sides, as Mannheim stressed, contend over their appraisal of their movement's tradition and its relevance for the future. Conservatives seek their inspiration, inevitably, in the glorious accomplishments of the revolutionary era. Both Stephen Cohen and Moshe Lewin emphasize that in the Soviet Union this tradition is identified with the "positive accomplishments" of the Stalin period. Conservatives speak the language of deviation, degeneration, and orthodoxy. Reformers, on the other hand, seek another source of tradition that fosters their desire for rational and open-ended experimentations beyond the strictures imposed on communist theory and practice in the Stalin era. In the Soviet Union and eastern Europe in the 1950s and 1960s, this was found in the alternatives to Stalinism debated and practiced partially in the 1920s, during the New Economic Policy. This era serves to legitimize the kind of innovation and openness that reformers seek to introduce.[16]

Conservatives and reformers define differently the fundamentals of socialism. In every country that has adopted political and economic structures of the Soviet type, the central point of contention is how to evaluate the defining features that emerged from Stalin's rule and were implemented to a considerable degree in all the socialist countries in the late 1940s and early 1950s. This legacy included rule by "proletarian dictatorship": a Party membership pressured by demands for political discipline and conformity enforced through periodic purges, and an attitude toward dissent wherever it existed or was imagined to exist, quick to attribute it to subversive intrigues of spies, foreign agents, or class enemies. In the economic realm the legacy was central planning through physical indicators; overemphasis on investment, especially in heavy industry, at the expense of consumers; administered prices and planned allocation of producers' goods and commodities; and collective farming with private plots and petty trade tightly restricted.[17]

The point of contention is not whether these features should be changed, but what kind of change should be made and how much. Conservatives held that, although some mistakes and excesses certainly occurred in the Party's work, proletarian dictatorship by a disciplined party and central planning are *the* defining features of socialism, and anything that serves to undermine rather than improve or revitalize them subverts socialism. Thus conservatives may agree to greater scope for discussion within the Party (and greater physical and career security for Party members) and an end to the terrorization of the population through purges and repression campaigns. But conservatives typically balk at reforms that institutionalize internal democracy or popular checks on Party authority, fearing excessive weakening of Party leadership. And while conservatives may agree that the economic mechanism needs revitalizing, and even that limited experiments with profit and market mechanisms are acceptable, they tend to view such experiments as temporary expedients.

Progressive "reformers," on the other hand, argue that the political institutions represented by "proletarian dictatorship" and central planning had been frozen prematurely into orthodoxy during the Stalin era (or in the corresponding period in their own country), and by no means represented "socialism" for all times and places. Reformers view changes in political and economic institutions, not as a consolidation and improvement of proletarian dictatorship and central planning, but as part of an experiment designed to define a new model of socialism that bursts through the constraints of the old dogmas.[18]

The mutual characterizations that accompany political debate also have a common form. In their criticisms of "the cult of the individual" that glorified the genius of the Great Leader, progressives point to the dogmatism, arbitrariness, and mindless loyalty typical of the Party in the past, and to unnecessary repressions against largely imaginary enemies and loyal Communists. Attacks on the Stalinist past imply that the conservatives are unwilling to let go of the institutions responsible for these excesses and in fact may be guilty of the same errors. Progressives also attacked the conservatives' "subjectivist errors" in economic policy: pushing forward agricultural collectivization too far and too fast, damaging peasant initiative and weakening agriculture; pushing forward the pace of heavy industrial growth too rapidly, sacrificing resources at the expense of consumers' goods and wages and damaging work incentives; and suppressing private trade and services before the state is able to step into the gap. In their harsh criticism of the traditional system, progressives imply that their most conservative opponents are politically repressive dogmatists, responsible for retarding the economy and harming the welfare of the people.[19]

Conservatives brandished a very different set of themes. The first is the violation of orthodoxy: extensive reform threatens to undermine the political and economic institutions that are synonymous with socialism and were responsible for the great victories of the past. Reform represents an improper deviation, or revision, of the "basically" correct path laid down earlier. The second theme is fear of a loss of control. Programs for political and economic reform threaten to create instability in the form of popular resistance, dissent, inflation, and unemployment. The third theme is the danger of subversion: extensive reform will weaken the Party's dictatorship and ideological unity, making the nation susceptible to more subversive ideas from abroad, possibly aiding the activities of class enemies and imperialist agents.[20]

A fourth, more inflammatory conservative theme lay just beneath the surface: that reforms threaten to restore capitalism. All of the conservatives' objections to reform hint that there is something subversive about reformers' ideas. As a Hungarian conservative wrote in response to attacks on Stalinism in his own country shortly after Khrushchev's "secret speech" in 1956, "Could the reader not easily be induced to think that those who expect a radical change in the country's economic and political life mean by this the liquidation of the dictatorship of the proletariat . . . and the restoration of bourgeois rule?"[21] This rhetorical question became a militant charge in the increasingly radical Maoist reaction against the world tide of de-Stalinization from the late 1950s through the early 1960s.[22] The betrayal of "revisionists" and the danger of the restoration of capitalism were the themes that Maoists rode into the Cultural Revolution.

From Conservative Fears to Reactive Extremism

China's Maoists shared the conservative distrust of many aspects of de-Stalinization and their alarm at the idea of reform. They also shared the fundamental rationale for this opposition: that it threatened to deviate from the fundamental institutions of socialism—a planned economy that precluded markets, and the proletarian dictatorship—established for the first time in the USSR under Stalin. But Maoists were not politically conservative. The conservative argues within party circles against too rapid and extreme change, opposes the appointment of reformers to important positions, seeks to thwart the implementation of reform when such measures are adopted as party policy, and uses the trump card of "revisionism" primarily in debate. But by the mid-1960s Maoists had concluded that the Party itself had become corrupted by an ongoing, massive, yet largely hidden conspiracy of reactionary social classes and revisionist traitors who were consciously embarked on a plot to restore capitalism and who needed to be dragged out by the mass action of Chairman Mao's militant loyalists.

The groundwork for this position was elaborated as early as 1964 in the polemics against the Soviet Union. The famous "Ninth Commentary" summarized a world view that would shortly spawn the radicalism of the Cultural Revolution. Here are reasserted all the distinguishing elements of Stalinist political culture, beginning with the paranoiac view of external encirclement, internal subversion, and pervasive treachery: "In socialist society, the overthrown bourgeoisie and other reactionary classes remain strong for quite a long time. . . . They have a thousand and one links with the international bourgeoisie. They are not reconciled to their defeat." These enemies "conduct open and hidden struggles against the proletariat in every field." Posing as loyal Marxist-Leninists, "they work to undermine socialism and restore capitalism . . . sneak into the government organs, public organizations, economic departments, and cultural and educational institutions so as to resist or usurp the leadership of the proletariat."[23]

To this familiar Stalinist suspicion of ubiquitous subversion we find added new Maoist elements. There was nothing new in the Maoist assertion that through some vague process of contagion the hidden bourgeois that have insinuated themselves into the Party and government begin to turn proletarian Communists to their traitorous cause. Their secret activities have "corrupting effects in the political, economic, ideological, and cultural and educational fields." What *was* new was the assertion that a new bourgeoisie was forming within the Party and government—something that Soviet Stalinists had not claimed in their class-conspiracy theory. This creeping corruption of orthodox Marxism-Leninism "constantly breeds political degenerates in the ranks of the working class and the Party and government organizations, new bourgeois elements and embezzlers and grafters in state enterprises . . . and new bourgeois intellectuals in the cultural and educational institutions and intellectual circles."[24]

Here we find the distinctive Maoist contribution to Stalinist political culture. Class struggle did not die in the Soviet Union because of the handiwork of Stalin's mass liquidations (nor, by implication, did China's many persecution campaigns do the job either). Instead, members of old exploiting classes are *still* out there, secretly corrupting the ranks of the proletariat, giving rise to a "newly arisen bourgeoisie." There subsequently arises a subversive coalition between these "old" and "new bourgeois elements," who coordinate their activities to attack socialism. The greatest danger comes from hidden agents in leading positions: "The political degenerates entrenched in the leading organs are particularly dangerous, for they support and shield the bourgeois elements in organs at the lower levels."[25]

This is not the innovative class analysis that some Western interpreters have claimed. Up to the point where the traitors are labeled a "new bourgeoisie," the analysis is barely distinguishable from 1930s vintage Stalinism. Were this a class analysis, it would have analyzed a mode of production and sought the roots of the "new bourgeoisie" in the political and economic institutions inherited from the Stalin era. Moreover, it would have found, as some of the more radical revisionists—notably Milovan Djilas in the mid-1950s—were also finding, that the sources of the "new class" were inherent in the concept of "proletarian dictatorship" and the system of distribution characteristic of central planning.[26] This was far from their intention, since Maoists had always viewed such ideas as "bourgeois."

As early as 1956 Mao's party had answered Tito's suggestion that Stalin's bureaucratic system must be dismantled with the following argument: Stalin, despite his mistakes, correctly established a socialist system, and "Once we have the right system, the main question is whether we can make the right use of it; whether we have the right policies, and right methods and style of work."[27] For the Maoist argument was that the new bourgeoisie arose from ideological subversion spread from old class enemies to the ranks of the proletarian communists themselves. There was nothing wrong with the Stalinist premises of that system.

Since the class position of hidden "degenerates" was virtually identical to that of loyal Maoists—that is, they enjoyed precisely the same ranks and privileges—how can they be distinguished from the politically pure?

By their "revisionist" ideas. If Khrushchev is the world's leading revisionist in a Soviet Union that is reverting to capitalism, what, after all, is he seeking to revise? The essential truths handed down by Stalin, who, despite his "mistakes," still established the fundamental truths of Marxism-Leninism.[28]

Of particular alarm to China's leaders in 1964 was Khrushchev's call for more openness and democracy in the Soviet system. They argued that this violated Stalin's revolutionary repudiation of the hypocritical trappings of bourgeois democracy and his recognition of the necessity to exercise harsh dictatorship over class enemies "for a long period of time."

On the pretext of "combatting the personality cult," Khrushchev has defamed the dictatorship of the proletariat and the socialist system and thus paved the way for the restoration of capitalism. . . . He has in fact negated Marxism-Leninism which was upheld by Stalin . . . peddling bourgeois ideology, bourgeois liberty, equality, fraternity, and humanity, inculcating bourgeois idealism and metaphysics and the reactionary ideas of bourgeois individualism, humanism, and pacifism . . . and debasing socialist morality."[29]

In response, China's leaders reiterated the Stalinist formula: "The more thoroughly bourgeois democracy is eliminated"—that is, through persecution campaigns against "rightists"—"the more will proletarian democracy flourish." This "fundamental thesis" of Marxism-Leninism is distorted by revisionists, who "hold that so long as enemies are subjected to dictatorship there is no democracy and that the only way to develop democracy is to abolish the dictatorship over enemies, stop suppressing them, and institute 'democracy for the whole people.' "[30]

Here we find expressed, in classic form, the characteristic Stalinist evasion. Like their Soviet predecessors, Maoists entirely evaded the question that would be opened as soon as they passed from the political scene: whether "dictatorship" had primarily been exercised *correctly* over *real* enemies, or whether such dictatorship was an arbitrary excess that has no place in modern socialism.[31] By the early 1960s Maoists felt compelled to repudiate criticisms of Stalinism even more thoroughly than in 1956 and 1957. By this time Mao and his followers were responsible for the antirightist campaign, the Great Leap Forward and resulting three-year depression and famine, and the Peng Dehuai affair. Soviet criticisms of the "cult of the individual," of the "exaggeration of the suppression of counterrevolutionaries," of the trampling of socialist democracy and collective leadership, and of rashly subjective economic policies that harmed the welfare of the people now stung the Maoists even more than in 1956. The essential arbitrariness of the Maoist position, like the older Stalinist one it echoed, was that anyone who opposed Mao's "correct" line was a counterrevolutionary, no matter what blunders that line had inspired or what that critic's past contribution to the revolution may have been.

That Maoists were simultaneously critical of "bureaucracy" did not make them so innovative as some interpreters have imagined. Criticism of arbitrary political repression, a lack of "close ties with the masses," excessive centralization, bureaucratism, and corruption and self-seeking within the Party—these had long been themes promoted by reformers in Eastern Europe and the USSR, and Maoists deserve no credit for initiating them. Some observers of China have implicitly identified Maoism with reformist and anti-Stalinist thought in Eastern Europe because of the common antibureaucratic themes. But Maoism in fact arose as a reaction against reformist critics. Like the conservatives, Maoists insisted that these problems must be remedied not by reform but by *revitalizing* and *rectifying,* returning to a purer version of the *original* system. Maoists shared with conservatives the notion that these problems were *not* systemic in nature.[32] That is, they were not due to Party dictatorship and central planning; they were due to ideological laxity, slackening discipline and commitment, the moral degeneration of individuals, and the subversion of enemies.

What *did* set Maoists apart from reformer, conservative, and their Stalinist forebears alike is that they felt the solution to these problems must lie in a kind of fundamentalism: a moral regeneration and political cleansing spearheaded by a movement in which the mobilized masses would seize power.[33] It was a peculiar rebellion, however, one marked by exaggerated loyalty and worship of a deified leader, demanding heightened discipline, conformity with his doctrine, and, indeed, worship of his person. Even in their most radical departure from historical Stalinism, Maoists betrayed their Stalinist heritage.

MASS RADICALISM: VARIATIONS ON A THEME

Maoist doctrine had another distinguishing feature: ambiguity bordering on incoherence. Who were the enemies and traitors who sought to restore capitalism in China? Remnants of old exploiting classes and former associates of the Nationalists? Corrupt officials, regardless of their past? Past critics of Party policy? All who enjoyed a privileged lifestyle? In

Mao's writings and the official media one may find each of these criteria, with no logical ordering or priority.[34] How does one recognize "capitalist roaders," since by all outward appearances they may look like loyal Communists? There simply was no clear guide to be found in the elusive doctrine itself.

This ambiguity gave Cultural Revolution radicals license to shape their own interpretations and political orientations out of the Maoist mélange. Our standard interpretation of the radical movements during these years is that radicals everywhere divided into two groups, "conservatives" and "rebels," according to the extent of change they wished to bring about. This two-part factional division, however, refers not primarily to political orientation and belief but to a practical or situational orientation with regard to powerholders in a specific work unit or locality. If you opposed whoever happened to seize power in a locality or unit first, you were a rebel; if you supported them, you were a conservative. It was not unusual to find a group considered "radical" in its unit allied with a "conservative" organization of a province or a city.[35] The labels were relative and depended on the local political situation.

Among those groups that articulated a political mentality to guide their action in the tumultuous years of 1966 and 1967, one may detect three distinctive subvarieties of the Maoist theory of conspiracy and subversion. The first, orthodox radicalism, emphasized the subversion of old political and class enemies and their offspring, and especially of disloyal intellectuals. The second, heterodox radicalism, emphasized the perfidy of degenerate elements in leading Party positions who had been corrupted by bourgeois ideas. The third, dissident radicalism, emphasized the idea that the Party system had itself become degenerate, necessitating the removal not of individuals but of the entire class of degenerate Party officials and the creation of new revolutionary organizations.[36] When we speak of Cultural Revolution radicalism, we refer not only to official Maoist doctrine but to these varied interpretations as well.

Orthodox Radicalism

Orthodox radicalism is "orthodox" because its mentality is descended unchanged from the old Stalinist class theory. Threats to the revolution, and to the dictatorship of the proletariat, must come from *outside* the revolutionary ranks. In this conception the ranks of the real revolutionaries are being infiltrated by old exploiting classes, historical counterrevolutionaries, and former adherents of the Nationalist Party, as well as by people with links to foreign countries, either through past residence, association with foreign organizations, having received a Western education, or having overseas relatives. These radicals ignored that innovative part of Maoist theory that claimed a new bourgeoisie was forming within the Party. Nor is there any trace of the idea that the Communist Party system, and the positions of privilege and power it gives cadres, is itself responsible for a falling away from loyalty to revolutionary ideals. Instead, the system is being corrupted, literally polluted, by outsiders, and this corruption reaches into the Party, educational institutions, the press, and the arts via alien elements who have wormed their way into trusted positions.

This variety is "radical" because, unlike conservatism, it advocates mass action to search out and eliminate hidden traitors. True to its guiding conception, these activists focused their activities, initially, onto targets that symbolized anything foreign to the revolutionary spirit and tradition of the Party. Attacks on historical relics, museums and temples, examples of foreign architecture, old street names, and individuals with foreign hair styles and clothing were one common type of activity. When these groups took to attacks on individuals, they typically raided the homes of former capitalists and landlords, rightists, former Nationalists, intellectuals with foreign degrees or Western training, and people with overseas relatives. They roughed up and intimidated the inhabitants, carted off family possessions, and burned books.[37]

For orthodox radicals these relatively powerless individuals—bourgeois intellectuals, people of "bad class" background or family history—were the real threat to the revolution. These were the people they later imprisoned and subjected to interrogations, struggle sessions, and often torture. They also singled out Party cadres for attacks, but only if they also fitted into one of these other categories and therefore could be said to have "wormed into" the leadership. It was the Party and its loyal cadres, after all, that these radicals sought to protect from corrupting influences. The people who had been the habitual targets of past persecution campaigns were logical carriers of this contagion.[38]

This orientation appears to have had a clearly identifiable social basis—those who had been most closely associated with the Party organizations in their units. It drew from among the ranks of the students from "good class" background, especially those who were the children of high-level cadres. Some of these students—for example, United Action (*Lian-*

dong) in Beijing—developed a "blood-line theory" whereby the children of revolutionary classes were "naturally red" and thereby trusted members of the proletariat.[39] In work units this orientation was rooted in the active membership of the Youth League, among Party members who had not yet taken up office, and among the most junior cadres.[40] These groups, trusted by the Party organization and destined for privileged positions within it, logically adopted a form of radicalism oriented toward staving off infiltration from without.

Heterodox Radicalism

Heterodox radicals advocated a definition of loyalty shorn of the ascriptive markers that orthodox radicals stressed. Parentage, family political history, and membership in the Party and Youth League were not relevant in determining who might be a true revolutionary and who might be a revisionist and traitor. In fact, to many of these radicals, who saw existing institutions as riddled with degenerates, membership in these organizations could make one suspect. Not unlike Reformation Protestantism's attitude toward the Church, these radicals sought to separate the body of the Party and its worldly existence from the spirit that sanctified it—Mao's teachings—and to use Mao's teachings to criticize respected *members* and established custom in the Party itself. Faith alone, adherence to Mao's thought in word and deed, was the standard by which to measure whether someone was a member of the revolutionary fold.

Unlike their orthodox rivals, heterodox radicals did not divert attacks from the Party organization and onto the perennial victims of persecution campaigns. They went directly after the leading cadres of their schools or work units and later of their local governments. They demystified the sanctified Party by profaning its members. Like the orthodox radicals, theirs was an intensely personal and vindictive form of politics. Anything about a cadre's past might be seized upon and turned into an accusation—corruption, past persecution of individuals in the unit, involvement in extramarital affairs, privileged lifestyle. The accused were commonly placed in solitary confinement, paraded in the streets, and subjected to violent public struggle sessions and long private interrogations, often accompanied by torture. Violence and murder were fueled by the fact that the radicals were often former victims of the persecuted official.

Heterodox radicals neglected that part of Maoist theory that stressed the origins of degeneration in old class forces. To their minds the Party was not being subverted from without; it was rotting from within. Corrupt and degenerate cadres were everywhere to be found. *Anyone* was potentially subject to accusation and interrogation. As in the witch hunts of late medieval Europe and early colonial America, one accusation quickly led to a wave of confirming ones, rapidly establishing the accusation as a social fact.[41] Radical attacks on individual cadres were often based on extracted confessions and unfounded accusations, but had not the Maoists said that revisionists and traitors were hiding everywhere, that they appeared on the surface to be loyal Communists, and that class vigilance was necessary so that not a single enemy should escape? The aim was to seize power and replace the subversives with young leaders of mass factions who demonstrated their loyalty to Mao in the militance and ruthlessness of their hunt for hidden enemies.

The membership of heterodox radical groups is not so easily described as that of the orthodox radicals. The earliest heterodox radicals were apparently students of middle-class origins and sometimes of working-class background, people who had resented the inherent privileges and the claims to natural redness of the students from cadre background.[42] In work units the earliest heterodox radicals were often young activists frustrated with their progress within the unit, activists or young cadres who had been disciplined by the Party organization in a recent campaign, and "intellectual" youths in menial positions who had never gotten along with culturally backward leaders.[43] As the Cultural Revolution progressed, however, the social characteristics of these groups became less distinctive. Members of orthodox radical groups joined after their orientation was officially repudiated, or they simply reoriented their activity toward heterodox principles. As the mass movement progressed, "conservative" and "rebel" factions practiced essentially the same variety of heterodox radicalism and could be distinguished only by their allegiance to one or another faction of local political leaders.

Dissident Radicalism·

Dissident radicals were descended from heterodox radical groups that came to dissent from the officially defined orientation of the Cultural Revolution: to "drag out" individual cadres and "seize power" in units on behalf of a small sect. These radicals developed a *systemic* critique that did not place the blame on degenerate individuals within the Party, whether they were seen as rising up within it or sneaking in from without. They argued that the purpose of the Cultural Revolution should not be a "great exchange of cadres," simply placing "pure" individuals in place of corrupted ones. Rather, there was something about the Party system that encouraged this degeneration, and so the system of power and privilege must be restructured in order to prevent similar degeneration in the future.

These people should not be confused with the heterodox radicals who survived to take up positions as "mass representatives" on revolutionary committees created by military units. Dissident radicals viewed these people as lackeys of the victorious faction of cadres within the system, and they viewed the revolutionary committees as a way to impose order without substantially realigning power and privilege.[44] Dissident radicals, instead, were the diehard opposition to the formation of revolutionary committees under army control. They bore the brunt of military repression, imprisonment, and execution and were choice targets in the military-directed campaigns to "cleanse the class ranks" and remove "May 16 elements" in the years 1968 to 1970.[45]

Dissident radicals appear to have emerged from a certain kind of political situation, not from any clearly defined group in the population. Many radical groups clashed with soldiers sent to reimpose order beginning in 1967 and suffered suppression as a result. In this political context it was becoming apparent that many months of rebellion, violence, and death were going to lead to little more than a militarized society under the tutelage of military control committees. Some radical groups, in the course of this resistance, began to reflect on the reasons for their rebellion and articulate their ultimate aims in a way that clashed sharply with the intentions of leading Maoists in Beijing. The most famous is the position expressed in documents put out by the Provincial Proletarian Alliance (Shengwulian) in Changsha. These radicals styled themselves Marxist revolutionaries: their purpose was to overthrow the "red bourgeoisie" of the People's Republic and replace it with a self-governing organization, which they likened to the Paris Commune.[46]

As it evolved into an articulate position, dissident radicalism would reject that part of the Maoist canon that blamed class enemies for corrupting the Party from without. And it gave only lip service to the notion that the Party was filled with bourgeois degenerates who must be replaced with Maoist loyalists—the reigning official view at the end of the period of mass turmoil. In taking class analysis more seriously than did leading Maoists, dissident radicals departed from the ambiguous

premises of official Maoism and approached a position not unlike reformers, but expressed in radical Marxist-Leninist language. Some dissident
radicals, when they later became leaders of China's democracy movement
of the 1970s, would make their break with Maoism clear in a way they
did not in the 1960s. Two members of the Li Yizhe group in Canton
were in the faction that had opposed military dictatorship. By 1974 they
had developed a dissident critique of the Lin Biao system that reflected
the mentality of the Hunan group some six years earlier. Wang Xizhe
further developed his dissident democratic-Marxist position from 1978
to 1980, which is the point at which dissident radicalism of the Cultural
Revolution repudiates its heritage and evolves into democratic reformism
of the post-Mao era.[47]

Had this variety of radicalism not been so severely repressed by the
military, and had it been allowed to link up with "interest-group radicals" that articulated the interests not simply of marginal groups like
temporary workers but of broader categories of workers, students, and
intellectuals, China's Cultural Revolution would have been a popular antibureaucratic movement. That this did not even come close to happening shows the dominance of the Stalinist heritage and the wide gulf
between it and democratic movements in Eastern Europe. This gulf was
not bridged until the late 1970s, when dissident radicals would repudiate
Maoism along with the Stalinist heritage and explore varieties of human-
ist Marxism and liberalism.

The three different varieties of Maoism highlight its contradictory faces:
the old Stalinist theory of subversion, degeneration, and betrayal; the
Maoist emphasis, in contrast to Stalin and his successors, that such dangers have a class basis that never subsides; and the distinctive Maoist
notion that a new bourgeoisie somehow emerges within the Party, and
that only a mass movement to seize power can root it out. One may
argue that none of the three varieties of radicalism developed in quite the
way that Mao had intended, but they are nonetheless rooted in the fundamental ambiguities and inconsistencies of the doctrine itself. During
the mass movements of 1966–1968, Maoists tried to extricate themselves from the consequences of doctrinal incoherence by issuing a continuous stream of directives and switching sharply from one interpretation to another as factional conflicts played themselves out in the capital,
in the provinces, and even in the camp of Maoist officials. Finally, the
contradictions could be resolved only by force, in a series of harsh persecution campaigns run by the army from 1968 to 1970.

In the long run the Maoists' radical reassertion of what they saw as the fundamentals of Marxism-Leninism, despite a decade of criticism by socialist reformers and de-Stalinizers in many countries, prevented them from developing a political alternative that would avoid the "excesses" of Stalinism. To emphasize the ubiquity of subversive class forces, and to demand thereby *more intense* loyalty to a "correct" doctrine, effectively precluded any serious attempt to undermine the privilege or arbitrary power of bureaucrats. To implement "mass democracy" under these conditions generated heightened ritual and deference and provided surviving bureaucrats with even more arbitrary power over the people under them.[48] Furthermore, to preclude as "bourgeois" markets in any form ruled out the only existing alternative to bureaucratic allocation; mobilization campaigns only changed bureaucrats' behavior for a limited time.[49] Finally, to glorify austerity with homilies about proletarian lifestyle and revolutionary sacrifice is simply to make a virtue of the worst features of Stalinist forced-draft industrialization, which enforced sacrifices from the population for wasteful overinvestment in a heavy-industrial base.[50] In their radical reassertion of the virtues of proletarian dictatorship and an economy purged of markets and profit incentive, Maoists reproduced some of the worst excesses of Stalinist rule in a new form. In so doing, they laid a firm foundation for the reformist sentiments that repudiate Maoism and inspire a renewed search for an alternative to "the Soviet model."

To underline the Stalinist premises of the Cultural Revolution is not to suggest that there is some essential identity between the two. We are already aware of the many and obvious ways in which Maoism departs from Soviet Stalinism. It *is* to suggest, however, that in order to see Cultural Revolution radicalism *whole,* we need to recognize that its innovations and iconoclasm, its excesses and failures, were firmly grounded in a sadly familiar political mentality. If we place this radicalism in its proper perspective, we see it as a form of reactive extremism whose defining premises were descended directly from the rationale for Stalin's mass murders. If we take seriously the political mentalities expressed in its often extravagant rhetoric, it no longer makes sense to pose questions about the unintended outcomes of an idealistic quest. For what actually happened in China during the Cultural Revolution—the inquisitions, witch hunts, cruel and vindictive persecution of individuals, unprincipled and often incoherent factionalism—were inherent in the doctrine and mentality that inspired it.

Agrarian Radicalism as a Rural Development Strategy, 1968–1978

DAVID ZWEIG

While mainstream scholarship on the Cultural Revolution has long argued that this political eruption in China had only a minimal impact on the countryside,[1] Mao's radical vision of carrying out a "great leap into communism" was one of the driving forces behind agricultural policy during the decade of the CR. Mao and his radical associates believed that by transforming peasant ideology, eradicating all vestiges of the private sector, building new institutions with a larger scope of collective ownership, and mobilizing massive amounts of peasant labor to increase the level of productive forces in the countryside, China's impoverished rural areas could be swiftly transformed into a prosperous, thriving socialist countryside.

Although the earlier attempt to introduce this "agrarian radicalism" into the countryside during the Great Leap Forward (1957–1959) had

failed, Mao revolted against the reformist policies of the early and mid-
1960s engineered by Liu Shaoqi and Deng Xiaoping. As power shifted
back into his hands, he began to reintroduce his radical policies into
China's rural areas. The first effort arose in 1964, at the time of the first
Learn-from-Dazhai campaign and the Four Cleans campaign. Thanks to
Barry Naughton's contribution to this volume, we now better understand
the political and economic environment—that is, the massive state investments in the construction of the Third Front—that necessitated the
imposition of self-reliant policies on the countryside in the mid-1960s.
Nevertheless, Mao's concern that "revisionism," as well as a rural "capitalist restoration" led by local cadres, was taking root in rural areas also
explains the renewed effort to introduce agrarian radicalism into the
countryside.

Beginning in 1968 and continuing to early 1978,[2] supporters of agrarian
radicalism were able, through a variety of techniques, to introduce their
policies into many parts of rural China.[3] Although they almost always
confronted more conservative opponents who resisted the implementation
of the entire agrarian radical program and who posited a more moderate
strategy,[4] the radical development strategy had a major impact on the
rural areas. That program, and an evaluation of it, form the core of this
chapter.

As with other policies of the CR, agrarian radicalism suffered from a
dramatic dichotomy between ideology and reality. This gap arose in three
ways. First, owing to the heavily utopian nature of this radical vision
and to the fact that the anti-incentivism in these policies was anathema
to peasant interests, little spontaneous support for this policy line developed among the Chinese masses.[5] Thus normative aspects of the strategy
were supplemented, if not at times totally replaced, by heavily coercive
tactics to frighten the peasants into acquiescing to the radical policies.
Second, the propaganda of the period, with its portrayal of rapid economic development and popular support under this line, was simply a
lie. And third, popular resistance and cadre manipulations of many radical policies to suit the cadres' own interests meant that policy outcomes
in the rural areas varied greatly from locality to locality and as a result
differed from the radical vision that was agrarian radicalism.

Finally, agrarian radicalism contained its own inherent contradiction.
Although it was to be based on local spontaneity and local self-reliance,
the radicals mistrusted most local cadres and peasants. Left to their own
devices, they were more likely to return to the revisionist policies of the

early 1960s, if not to the policies of the early 1950s. Instead, the radicals favored centrally controlled "spontaneity." As Carl Riskin has pointed out in his contribution to this volume, the result was the worst of both worlds, as peasants were prevented from adopting more market-oriented policies by the antimarket nature of the radical line, while at the same time the radicals undermined the planning system. The result—often irrational national policies that overemphasized grain production at the expense of cash crops—impoverished the collective sector and forced peasants to rely on marginal and surreptitious efforts to expand the private sector as a meager supplement to the low collective incomes. Although statistics demonstrate continued economic growth during this era, the outcome was continued poverty for most Chinese peasants.

AGRARIAN RADICALISM AS A DEVELOPMENT STRATEGY

The radicals faced many difficulties in transforming their theoretical and ideological perspective into appropriate policy proposals, and at no time after the Great Leap Forward was this policy package implemented in its totality. Moreover, since radical leaders spoke infrequently on rural policy after the GLF, they may not have possessed a systematic perspective on rural development. Nevertheless, drawing on the writings and policies advocated by radical elites during this era, one can delineate the basic contours of their program, their vision for the rural areas, and the concrete policies they advocated as they practically tried to build utopia in the Chinese countryside.

The "basic line" of agrarian radicalism was Mao's "theory of the continuing revolution under the dictatorship of the proletariat," as applied to the rural areas.[6] The development strategy that evolved from this basic line involved a highly integrated program whose general policies may be divided into four broad categories:[7] (1) a political-organizational component, comprising concrete changes in rural political and economic structures; (2) an ideological-moral component, which was to bring about changes in the peasants' attitudes toward those structures and toward work in general, as well as create support for eliminating "bourgeois" values and narrowing class, income, and status inequalities; (3) an economic component, involving an improvement in the level of rural technology and standard of living; and (4) a mobilizational component, which defined the techniques by which the general and specific policies were to be implemented.

One caveat is in order. The developmental model presented here of a practical attempt to build communism in the countryside may represent to some little more than a framework in which national elites maximized their ability to extract resources, particularly grain, from the countryside while minimizing the input costs to agriculture. Although this perspective has merit, especially in light of the Third Front development program, the radicals remained motivated primarily by an ideological desire to narrow the scope of the private sector and expand the collective sector to prevent revisionism in the Chinese countryside. Their attitude toward the state bureaucracy was highly suspect; one of the last articles written by the radicals' theoretical group at Beijing University before the arrest of the Gang of Four in October 1976 argued that state bureaucrats had already become the new ruling class in China.[8] Moreover, although Mao's actions created a highly centralized bureaucratic state, his and the radicals' purpose was to develop a decentralized economic and political system based on mass mobilization and widespread mass political participation. To this extent, one must recognize the importance of ideology in agrarian radicalism and accept the argument that the state-centric model was more of an outcome than a goal of this development strategy.[9]

The Political-Organizational Component

Radical elites desired to change basic rural organizational structures and expand the scope of collective, party, and state control in the countryside. They tried to transfer administrative authority from private to collective organizations, from lower to higher levels of the rural collective structure, or from collective to state control. Key policies included establishing brigade accounting, unifying production teams, placing supply and marketing co-ops under collective control, and developing the brigade and commune economy.

Foremost among these policies was shifting control over economic activity and the ownership of the means of production to higher levels in the structural hierarchy—a structural transition to higher stages of socialism. Both Soviet and Chinese Marxism posit that the transition from socialism to communism involves transforming the collective-property system into a higher form of social ownership. For the radicals, state ownership—ownership by "all the people"—was more socialized than collective ownership by units who could respond to more parochial local interests.[10] Thus the transition to communist society depended on the vertical integration of the rural organizational framework.

During the Great Leap Forward, establishing people's communes with ownership and accounting at the commune level signified to some Chinese that China was on the verge of entering the communist utopia.[11] Even after the GLF was abandoned, people's communes were seen as a vehicle for the transition to a single ownership system.[12] Vestiges of the GLF mentality in the 1960s and 1970s made the size of the unit an indicator of progress and a measure for cadre success.[13] However, the GLF's precipitous and disastrous shift to commune ownership showed that a premature transition to higher levels of socialism and ensuing declines in agricultural output could supply opponents with political ammunition. Slower steps to higher levels of socialism, rather than the GLF's jump to commune ownership, were necessary.

Amalgamating production teams into larger production and management units was another contentious policy. Between 1958 and the 1980s, the number of teams in the countryside rose and fell with the political winds. Whereas the number of teams decreased by 12.3 percent in 1959–60, their number increased by 76.6 percent during the rectification of the following two years. Similarly, the number of teams decreased by almost 20 percent between 1965 and 1970 but increased by 5.6 percent over the following five years.[14] In the late 1960s and 1970s, supporters of merging teams focused on two functions played by the team: its role as the basic labor-organization unit and its job as the basic accounting unit. According to Xu Dixin, its former function was of particular interest to those, such as Lin Biao, who sought to mobilize the peasants for capital construction projects.[15] When brigade accounting could not be implemented, however, merging teams was a valuable expedient: interteam inequality could be reduced more gradually; two teams with different income levels could be united more easily than a whole brigade; and the smaller number of teams simplified the eventual transition to brigade accounting.[16]

Amalgamating teams and shifting to brigade accounting, while affected by the degree of interteam equality, also offered a shortcut to equality by readjusting the value of a work point in the amalgamated teams. The value of a day's work in the poorer teams would rise; in the richer teams it might drop. Similarly, enlarging units increased the economies of scale, particularly for rural capital construction work, which was an important part of this development strategy.

Brigade and commune enterprises helped establish the economic basis for transitions to higher stages of socialism. Although peasants could develop loyalty to their production teams,[17] loyalty to the brigade was more elusive and could occur only if the brigade's economy provided peasants with material benefits. Otherwise, according to one study:

This narrow sphere of team collective ownership can limit the vision of commune members and cause some commune members to always see only the interests of the small collective and be unable to see the big one, the more distant one, that which belongs to the complete and total interest, which does not benefit the development of the large socialist agriculture.[18]

Brigade factories could overcome the conflict between social consciousness and the desired level of economic organization.[19] Thus in 1975 Zhang Chunqiao extolled the fact that over a one-year period the brigade's share of total collective assets in suburban Shanghai had increased by one or two percentage points, while Hua Guofeng, quoting Mao, referred to brigade and commune enterprises as the "great bright hope" of Chinese socialism.[20] Speaking at the Second Dazhai Conference of 1976, Chen Yonggui called for the continued growth of the economy at the commune and brigade levels "so as to create conditions for the gradual transition."[21] Where interteam inequality created opposition to brigade accounting, developing the brigade economy could resolve that conflict by narrowing inequality. If one team was poor owing to a labor surplus, collective factories could siphon off some of the excess labor. Also, if a team needed money, the brigade could use factory profits to fund the team's projects. In this way collective enterprises permitted brigades to consciously narrow interteam inequality and create the conditions for a successful ownership transition.[22]

Another organizational change involved transferring control over supply and marketing cooperatives from peasants to the commune, in essence, from true collectives—peasants had bought shares in these co-ops in the 1950s—to bureaucratic control. This change, which began during the Four Cleans campaign of 1964–65 and was completed in 1968–69 during the CR, transferred management authority over restaurants, shops, and local hotels from peasants' private hands into the hands of commune officials. Formal pronouncements declared that the poor and lower-middle peasants had taken control.[23] But, as with many aspects of the CR, peasant control was nominal; commune officials, under the leadership of the county supply and marketing organization, managed these firms. Restricting private marketing and forcing peasants to sell to a commune-dominated supply and marketing cooperative gave local officials a monopsony, which also strengthened their ability to control the types of crops peasants planted.[24]

Moving the level of ownership to the brigade transferred decision-making authority on distribution and accumulation of both grain and capital out of the hands of peasants and team leaders whom peasants could influence and into the hands of the lowest level of Party organization in the countryside, the brigade Party branch and its leader, the brigade Party secretary. In the continuing struggle among peasants, the collective, and the state over control and distribution of the product of the peasants' labor, brigade ownership represented increased Party control and decreased peasant influence over decisions directly affecting peasant livelihood and collective capital formation.[25]

The Ideological-Moral Component

To be successful, agrarian radicalism had to generate moral and political support among peasants for collectivist values and policies that transcended their individual interests and persuade family-oriented peasants to strengthen the state and build a communist society. To this extent they had to create a "positive morality" in support of agrarian radicalism. At the same time, as William Joseph has pointed out, they also had to impose a form of "negative morality," whereby peasants would be convinced of the evils of material incentives and the pursuit of private wealth. While it would be difficult enough to inculcate these values in a prosperous socialist society—peasants might accept restrictions on private activities if collectives fulfilled their economic aspirations—the poverty of rural China and the weakness of the national economy in the late 1960s and 1970s compounded these problems. Following the 1968 Soviet invasion of Czechoslovakia, national security imperatives for rapid industrialization financed by extractions from the rural areas left radicals with few financial incentives with which to generate rural political support. Instead they relied above all on political mobilization and the creation of a "moral incentive economy."[26] As James A. Malloy explains:

From a purely economic point of view, the combination of mobilization and moral stimuli could be viewed as a functional adaptation to the realities of an economy that had to restrict its consumption and increase its production; a policy designed for a situation of scarcity in which material incentives are no longer available or are considered too expensive.[27]

Given Mao's belief that attitudes could change before the economy developed and that these changed attitudes could precipitate economic and organizational changes, raising the political consciousness of peasants became a critical component of the radical development strategy.[28] In 1965, during the 1968–69 Three Loyalties campaign, and throughout much of the 1970s, the radicals tried to imbue peasants with a Maoist-collectivist ideology. From 1968 to 1970, PLA-organized Mao Thought propaganda teams tried to replace traditional Confucian values and habits with Marxist-Leninist Mao Zedong Thought.[29] From 1968 until Lin Biao's death in 1971, peasants in many localities attended regular political study sessions. From 1973 to 1977, during the Line Education campaign, work teams again descended into the villages to mobilize peasants to follow the Party's basic line. Political study and "class struggle" campaigns were to teach peasants the evil of following the private road to prosperity.

Focusing on Marx's concept of "bourgeois right" as the means by which bourgeois values could be resurrected and inequalities, left over from the old society, could be expanded under socialism, the radicals sought to prevent the development of an alternative and more materially oriented morality than that inherent in agrarian radicalism. Thus the radicals advocated restricting opportunities for any expansion of the inequalities derived from bourgeois right. Since peasants with special skills or larger families could produce marketable commodities at home and get richer than their neighbors, it became necessary to cut back, if not eradicate, these vestiges of the "small producer's economy."[30] Private plots, which created opportunities for private gain while maintaining the peasants' attachment to private property, had to be restricted or collectivized or both. Even in the mid-1970s, some radicals still believed that the old exploiting classes had strong ties to the private sector and preferred to see its expansion. For the radicals, according to a 1976 study, privaate plots were "the remnant of the peasants' small-ownership system [and] . . . the soil for capitalism. But because some rich peasants take advantage of this tendency, we must limit private plots' negative utilities in order to protect the development of the socialist economy."[31]

To support this contention, the study presented a purported 100-household survey in Guangxi Province showing that poor and lower-middle peasants earned 59 percent of their income from collective work and 37.9 percent from private endeavors, while new- and old-middle peasants earned 45.2 percent of their income from the collective and 53.5 percent from private endeavors.[32] Such findings reinforced the radicals' ideological preconceptions that, if they did not constantly restrict private plots, rural "bad class elements" would use these opportunities to reassert capitalism in the countryside.

Rural artisans, prohibited from practicing their trades, and peasants who traditionally had entered the cities for part- or full-time labor were all forced to return and work in the collective. Some radical leaders devised schemes for controlling rural trade fairs, "the clearest manifestation of bourgeois right,"[33] and replacing them with "big socialist markets" (*shehuizhuyi da ji*), where peasants were cajoled into selling all private produce to the supply and marketing co-ops.[34] From the radical perspective, markets taught "capitalist" values and skills and allowed peasants to turn privately produced goods into commodities through which they improved their economic status vis-à-vis less productive peasants. Some articles during the CR argued that the market itself was the critical locus for the creation of polarization in the countryside.[35]

Finally, restrictions on growing economic crops, imposed on collectives, sought to limit these units' comparative advantage and prevent the development of interregional inequalities.[36] Some production teams that expanded collective sideline activity were accused of following the road of "collective capitalism."

On the other hand, the radicals sought to increase the ideological level of rural inhabitants by rewarding those who demonstrated a positive attitude toward collectivization. Rather than pay peasants for work performed, which permitted the stronger to get richer and households with more workers to prosper faster than those with fewer workers, the radicals supported Dazhai's income-distribution system of "self-assessment and public discussion." Hard workers who demonstrated a strong commitment to the socialist revolution, regardless of their concrete contribution, could receive a financial reward equivalent to that of the strongest workers.[37] Public determination of individual work values, which created group pressures to reward everyone equally, generated income leveling, the essence of a moral-incentive economy.[38]

The transition from socialism to communism involved ameliorating and finally eradicating the "three great differences" (*san da chabie*)—between mental and manual labor, workers and peasants, and town and country—that had developed under capitalism and persisted under socialism.[39] To prevent alienation and the creation of class differences between "mental laborers" (rural cadres) and "manual laborers" (peasants), rural officials were admonished to participate in physical labor. Cadre participation in labor was part of the 1962 "Sixty Articles on Agriculture,"[40] but the radical guidelines of the Dazhai movement exceeded the more conservative demands of the "Sixty Articles." Brigade cadres were expected to work 300 days a year in the fields doing physical labor.[41] Cadre education was also critical, because the voluntaristic nature of agrarian radicalism dictated that cadre consciousness, not the socioeconomic base, determine the direction of development.[42] If cadres were not imbued with Marxist-Leninist values, the entire development pattern could go askew. To further ensure that political authority in the production unit did not become class authority, peasants were to participate in political decision making and monitor cadre behavior.

To resolve the difference between rural factory workers, who were free of the drudgery of agricultural labor, and those peasants still working in the fields, workers received work points, and their salaries were used to supplement the team's year-end distribution fund. With their incomes relying on the team's agricultural output, workers had an incentive to help in the busy season. Moreover, including these salaries in the team's year-end distribution increased the field workers' incomes, giving them a reason to support collective enterprises even if they themselves did not get a factory job. Rural industries also were to bring the socialized values of an industrialized workplace (that is, proletarian consciousness) to the countryside and help modernize rural inhabitants' values, whereas sending urban youth to the countryside was expected to help peasants learn to read and introduce technical knowhow into the countryside.[43]

Finally, moral exhortation and participation in interunit field construction projects were to imbue peasants with a "communist spirit" of self-sacrifice and concern for neighboring units, whereby they were to help their neighbors for free or resist taking advantage of their neighbors' plights to make quick profits. This emphasis on mutual concern may have diluted conflicts over resources and water.[44]

The Economic Component

Although Mao believed that will could transform reality, changes in the material conditions of society reinforced political consciousness and generated strong support for higher levels of socialism. Therefore advocates of agrarian radicalism developed their own specific policies to generate economic development.

They created a "cellular" economy, emphasizing regional, if not local, self-sufficiency in food and resource development.[45] Units nationwide were compelled to become self-reliant in cereal production.[46] Grazing land and land previously targeted for economic crops were plowed up, as the second half of the slogan "Take grain as the key link, seek all-round development" (*yi liang wei gang, quanmian fazhan*) went unheeded. Because quotas were distributed down through the bureaucracy, the unit of cereal self-sufficiency often became the production team, not the county.[47] Restrictions on markets and rural trade fairs intensified this cellular economy as peasants and production teams had to grow all the foods they needed to consume. Horizontal exchanges of goods between units and across administrative boundaries died on the vine of self-sufficiency.[48]

Agrarian radicals also placed great emphasis on capital formation and tight restrictions on personal consumption. Although China in the 1950s had set a 5-percent ceiling for cooperative accumulation,[49] agrarian radicals tried to limit the peasants' income and level of consumption, thereby ensuring that any economic surplus would go to strengthen the collective economy.[50] Wealthy units able to distribute more than 1.50 yuan per day—the level set in Dazhai—were forbidden to do so on the grounds that, "if units surpassed Dazhai, how could they learn from Dazhai?" (*chaoguo Dazhai, zenme xue Dazhai?*). And although the percentage of collective income going to state taxes dropped during this era, the surplus went to increase the level of collective income, not peasant income.[51] Data from several communes in Jiangsu Province show 1976 as the peak year for collective accumulation,[52] while in Da He Commune in Hebei Province, accumulation peaked during the Cultural Revolution and began to drop in the 1970s.[53] A similar pattern occurred in Cuba during the 1968–1970 "Revolutionary Offensive."[54]

Another economic aspect was to create a "guerriilla" economy. Based on the "big production movement" of 1943, in which labor mobilization was employed to overcome impending famine in Yan'an, Mao and other post-1949 leaders advocated organizing large groups of peasants to transform the face of rural China.[55] Particularly during the winter slack season, these capital construction campaigns, whereby peasants dug reservoirs, rivers, and canals and terraced and leveled fields, became a regular part of the rhythm of peasant life. Only since 1979 have they slowed down. These projects aimed at taking advantage of the idle time of able-bodied peasants, which during the years of private farming before 1949 was estimated to be 1.7 months a year, with 80 percent occurring in December/January.[56] Slack time expanded under collectivization, so unless labor was mobilized for collective, rural capital construction projects, peasants could turn to private endeavors. Peasants who previously had gone to the cities, and cadres, who were now to participate regularly in labor, took part in these projects.

Besides improving the rural economy, facilitating the use of modern technology, such as tractors and fertilizer, and making hillside land into paddy fields, large- and medium-scale rural capital construction projects could create a psychological interdependence and spirit of mutual assistance and concern among neighboring villages and rural inhabitants that would replace marketing and other forms of commercial interaction. Socialist cooperation would replace capitalist relations of exchange as the major medium of interpersonal and interunit exchanges. According to Hua Guofeng, "In the course of farmland capital construction, the collective concept and sense of organization and discipline of the peasants are greatly enhanced, and they think more of the collective and show greater zeal in building socialism."[57] Also, through these projects wealthy teams helped poorer teams catch up. In this way the "swarming" that was characteristic of the guerrilla economy could further strengthen the psychological-moral component of the development strategy.

Finally, agrarian radicalism recognized the need for introducing new technologies, such as tractors and diesel pumps, which would mold peasant consciousness and promote the "productive forces."[58] Land leveling facilitated the introduction of this technology, and high rates of capital formation supplied funds for localities to buy equipment. While the most extreme proponents of the radical strategy emphasized labor mobilization rather than mechanization, Hua Guofeng's functional responsibility for promoting agricultural mechanization, begun in 1971, influenced his ideological perspective; his brand of radicalism included mechanizing agriculture. At the 1975 First National Conference on Dazhai, Hua stressed the basic mechanization of agriculture, and in fact, during most of the 1968–1978 period, some counties built factories for small tractors. Still, from an economic perspective the main line of agrarian radicalism emphasized labor mobilization and labor accumulation more than the inculcation of new technologies.

The Mobilization Component

As with all Chinese rural campaigns before 1978, introducing agrarian radicalism was based on mass mobilization of peasants and local cadres. As mentioned earlier, however, the radicals faced a major dilemma in trying to implement this development strategy in the countryside. At no time, excluding perhaps 1976–77, did proponents of the radical line totally dominate the CCP's formal policymaking institutions. Their policies remained "informal," without the imprimatur of Central Party or State Council documents, making them unable to use formal party channels for policy implementation. Instead, radicals relied on informal channels, or "policy winds," to spread information to the grass roots about the content of their policies.[59] Through a variety of techniques—articles in the national and local press, test points *(shidian)*, model units and organized visits to these localities, personal networks of radical supporters, work teams, and the linking of campaigns—they introduced these policies into the rural setting. Moreover, to preempt local cadres' choices about whether or not to introduce these informal policies, the radicals whipped up a "radical environment" at the national and particularly the local levels.

This environment of radicalism turned economic policy decisions into political ones. During the Three Loyalties campaign of 1968–69, giving up private plots to the collective became a benchmark of a peasant's or cadre's loyalty to Chairman Mao.[60] During the Dazhai campaigns, local cadres were told that resisting brigade accounting showed they opposed Dazhai and stood on the wrong side of the "two-line struggle."[61] Cadres who remembered the anti–rightist campaign that in 1959 followed the Great Leap knew the cost of resisting leftist policies. Whereas excessive support for leftism was merely an error of "leadership style" *(zuofeng wenti)*, rightist errors were "political errors" *(zhengzhi cuowu)* and reflections of the "class struggle" in the party and the countryside. Cadres who fell on the wrong side of this line demonstrated an incorrect "political standpoint" *(zhengzhi lichang)* and became targets for censure. Similarly, in the late 1960s conservative cadres were often replaced by more radical local leaders whose world view was more in line with the radical strategy and who cared less about the peasants' standard of living than about demonstrating support for the radical line. Under these conditions many local cadres ignored peasant opposition, and by publicly accusing, abusing, or

beating the remnants of the old exploiting classes in their villages—
"killing chickens to scare monkeys"—they frightened peasants into acquiescing to these policies, which often harmed their economic well-
being. In this way the radicals inculcated many of their policies at the
local level.

EVALUATING THE DEVELOPMENT STRATEGY

The radicals possessed a rather comprehensive and integrated rural development strategy with simultaneous movements on three fronts—organizational, ideological, and economic—that were mutually reinforcing.
Raising peasant political consciousness might increase peasant support for
higher levels of socialist organization. Heightened consciousness, as well
as more tightly integrated rural organizations, could reinforce and facilitate the chosen pattern of economic development: the reliance on labor
mobilization and high levels of capital formation.

Problems, however, developed for several reasons. Establishing brigade accounting and management and merging teams did centralize capital; but hostility developed among amalgamated units, particularly when
income levels differed or if the new institutional boundaries extended
beyond the natural lineal boundaries.[62] As many teams were united, split,
united and split again, agricultural development suffered. Also, few
economies of scale exist in wet-rice cultivation, so enlarging units merely
complicated management and undermined incentives. Finally, because
these organizational changes were to increase capital formation, particularly for building rural factories, funds could have been centralized without brigade accounting, as they often were.

Restricting the private sector was to narrow inequalities that grew out
of bourgeois right. But did private plots really increase inequality? In
1980 the relationship between collective and noncollective income per
laborer in ninety-five households in three brigades in Four Families Brigade, Jiangning Commune, Jiangning County, Jiangsu Province, is neg-
ligible when all three teams are analyzed together.[63] A statistically strong
relationship existed in only one team (.483, $p < .01$), and a strong but
insignificant relationship held in another. Only in this one team was
inequality exacerbated by noncollective income. So although restricting
private plots in this one team could have increased interhousehold equality, it simply made everyone poorer in the other teams.

The key factor in determining income differences among households was not old social class, as the radicals argued, but the dependency ratio—the ratio of laborers to nonlaborers in each household—as well as the variation in the number of laborers among households. For Four Families Brigade the relationship between number of laborers and collective income, when correlated collectively and within each team, is very high (.860). Therefore, to the extent that income was determined by the collective sector, households with few laborers were poorer.[64] And to the extent that income was determined by the collective sector, smaller households with more dependents were poorer. But the importance of the private sector to total household income is not the same for all families. In Four Families Brigade, households with fewer than three laborers relied more on the noncollective sector for their total income.[65] For the households in Four Families Brigade, the correlation between the number of laborers and noncollective income as a percentage of total income was −.603 ($p<.01$).[66] Hence in this location, restricting the private sector hurt the families with fewer than three laborers more than it hurt larger families. And since larger families already made more money from the collective, restricting private plots further disadvantaged families at the bottom of the income scale. Since these data were collected in a wealthy area where brigade- and commune-run industries played an extremely important role in determining family income, they suggest that, in areas with strong collectives, restricting private plots may have increased the gap between rich and poor households rather than narrowed it as the radicals had planned. And to the extent that this relationship holds across the country, restricting the private sector simply made the already poor even poorer.

Little need be said about the extent to which the radicals were able to destroy "bourgeois right" in the countryside. No doubt, in areas where collective enterprises doled out money to team accumulation funds, peasants did develop ties to the collective economy.[67] The hesitancy with which peasants in wealthy areas accepted the decollectivization of the 1980s demonstrates a further tie to the collective economy.[68] But the speed with which many parts of rural China responded in the 1980s to opportunities for expanding the private sector and rural markets shows that little headway had been made in expunging these "tails of capitalism" from the peasants' world view.

Moral exhortation as a motivating force has severe limitations. Eventually moral suasion, especially appeals for self-sacrifice and self-denial, must give way to some material incentives. Otherwise the result is a high degree of coercion, which has its own economic limitations. Moreover, according to Richard Madsen, the carefully constructed balance between peasant Confucian morality and Maoist morality, introduced during the 1964–65 Socialist Education movement and the 1968–69 Three Loyalties campaign, broke down in the chaos of the Cultural Revolution decade.[69] The utilitarian morality that, Madsen argues, emerged in the 1970s undermined the radicals' reliance on the moral-incentive economy. Yet the weak economy left local cadres few material incentives to offer; the final outcome was in fact a deepening dependence on coercion and fear, which increased in 1969 with the Cleansing Class Ranks campaign and continued through most of the 1970s.

Numerous dilemmas in the radical strategy ran counter to various laws of economic development. The emphasis on universal self-sufficiency in grain flew in the face of comparative advantage, which undermined the economy in parts of Fujian, Shandong, and Guangdong provinces.[70] One informant argued that the price of bananas rose precipitously in Canton in the 1970s because of the local grain policy. Nicholas P. Lardy's critique of this aspect of the development strategy since the mid-1960s is devastating. In Jiangsu Province as well, accountants complained that triple-cropping of rice, with its added production costs, increased total output but bankrupted the collective.[71] Moreover, trade restrictions and the emphasis on cellularity slowed economic growth.[72] Also, analysts of local organizations who see the voluntary formation of rural organizations as essential ingredients in successful rural development would bemoan limits on horizontal interaction and horizontal linkages among local organizations.[73] And replacing market relations with a "communist spirit" of mutual aid to pressure peasants to help their neighbors for free allowed local officials to expropriate collective resources and transfer them to higher levels of the rural collective hierarchy.[74]

Finally, efforts to build the rural economy through guerrilla-style swarming had more negative effects than positive ones.[75] According to Dwight Perkins and Shahid Yusuf, labor mobilization significantly increased agricultural inputs in China, but "the organization required for this achievement (such as communes, mass campaigns, and so forth) played such havoc with management and incentives that many of the benefits of increased inputs, both modern and traditional, were lost."[76] In a brigade south of Nanjing, projects carried out in the 1960s were well planned and improved local irrigation. However, nationwide terracing of fields that resulted from the emulation of Dazhai eroded soil and wasted capital and peasant leisure time.

As with other aspects of the CR, the rural development strategy suffered from a wide gap between the ideological vision of what the movement was supposed to do and the reality of both the world in which the policies were implemented and their outcome. The vision of the future society—of a peasantry transformed into a rural proletariat, tilling land owned by all the Chinese people, possessing high revolutionary consciousness, and surrounded by a vibrant and nurturing collective—was a glorified picture of the Chinese peasant of the 1960s and 1970s that reflected the "Dazhai peasant" as he existed in the propaganda of that era, rather than a true picture of how peasants were indeed behaving.

The reality of peasant life was much harsher and the attitudes of peasants differed dramatically from what the radicals believed or hoped they could be. Throughout these ten years the level of economic development remained quite low. Restricting the private sector merely made a poor peasantry poorer, as even collectives whose wealth increased kept that surplus for continued investment; little of the surplus was shared with the peasants directly. Only rural capital construction projects brought elements of economic security to the peasantry. Yet most of the economic rents that were buried in the improved soil and irrigation systems had to await the "responsibility system" before they could play their full role in increasing peasant livelihood. As a result, most Chinese peasants remained tied to their household economy and their shrinking private plots and were concerned with the collective economy only to the extent that its output determined their income. Outside wealthy areas, little loyalty for collective organizations above the team level could be generated, as peasants jealously guarded the income of their collective unit.

A similar gap developed between the local cadre and the extant local officialdom. The portrait of local elites—totally unselfish; serving short terms without perquisites; closely tied to the masses through regular participation in physical labor; and, because of close interaction with self-assertive peasants, not desirous of becoming a new ruling class—was also divorced from reality. Cadres used the CR's violent political culture to stop peasants from pursuing their private interests, even as the cadres tried to build stronger collectives that they could dominate. Some of the peasants' winter spare-time labor went into building useless projects or

increasing the resources under collective cadre control. Some rural officials, especially county and commune ones, utilized the ideological policies of this era to expand the scope of their control over the politics and
economics of rural China, becoming in essence a new ruling class, precisely the outcome Mao and the radicals had most feared. Finally, the
radical economic vision—of a cellular economy composed of self-sufficient
villages, with limited or no market relations among them, and rapid
economic growth based on guerrilla-style labor mobilization—although
reflecting the pattern of economic behavior, did not move many areas of
rural China closer to prosperity.

The irony of this entire period is best indicated by the success of the
subsequent rural reforms. Collective enterprises have developed far more
rapidly under the reforms than they did under a policy line aimed specifically at strengthening the collectives. Fairer prices and easier access
for peasants to urban markets did a better job of narrowing the rural-
urban gap than policies that sought to narrow that gap through attacks
on bourgeois right. Even decollectivization, which has allowed many cadres
to use their preferred position to profit, has created a new competitive,
entrepreneurial peasant cohort that has challenged local leadership in many
localities. The reforms, not imposed radical guidelines, have forced sub-
township cadres back into the fields, while higher-ranking local leaders
have also begun to work harder at developing the economy through managerial techniques and by personally opening businesses. Liberation of
the peasantry, the ultimate goal of the revolution, has progressed more
rapidly under a more open market economy and the "second land reform," rather than under radical policies designed to impose a Maoist
vision of liberation.

Nevertheless, the reforms have not resolved many critical issues the
radicals held so close to their hearts. An immense ideological vacuum
remains in the countryside, as the search for profits, and profiteering, has
become the major goal of most peasants. Whereas agrarian radicalism
placed too much stress on capital formation, inadequate reinvestment by
individual households under the responsibility system has become a major problem that resists a solution. Field and irrigation construction, a
priority in China's unpredictable economic environment, has declined under
decentralization. Poorer and smaller families, which were somewhat protected under the collectives, are falling behind larger and stronger neighbors, and medical care in the countryside appears to be suffering. Finally,
efforts to introduce true collectives under the reforms have met with only

limited success. Economic associations *(jingji lianheti)* remain highly unstable, while the supply and marketing system, now bolstered by peasant shareholders, resists democratization and remains dominated by county and township cadres who are formally appointed to their posts and who confront only formalistic elections.

No single rural development strategy has brought benefits without problems. No strategy has avoided externalities that harm economic and political development. Future difficulties will unfold in the rural reforms. But compared with this current alternative, agrarian radicalism served the peasants, as well as the national economy and polity, poorly. Although in the future peasants may remember positive aspects of the radical era, with its egalitarian vision and secure "rice bowl," most are far more likely to prefer an economic development strategy that has filled their rice bowls and brought dramatic improvements in personal income and freedoms.

The Cultural Revolution as an Unintended Result of Administrative Policies

LYNN T. WHITE III

Because the Cultural Revolution wounded so many patriotic Chinese, the question of its cause haunts current politics. Its violence—including widespread physical attacks against intellectuals and local leaders—was its most unusual aspect, the thing that calls for explanation, the experience that tends to overwhelm other memories of 1966–1968 in many Chinese minds. This aspect of the Cultural Revolution has become its main definition for both current reformers and current conservatives. Like the legacy of Stalin's penultimate years in Russia, the legacy of Mao's in China provides a litmus test of political attitudes toward present change or continuity.[1] When Chinese leaders stress that the CR became violent because of repression, they argue for a new and free system. When they emphasize that the CR became violent because of anarchy, they speak for more socialist planning and order.

Questions about the cause of the Cultural Revolution also haunt many urban Chinese personally. The novelist Ba Jin, who lost his wife to the Cultural Revolution, frames the issue in moral terms: "I am sure it would be impossible that anyone who did not experience the Cultural Revolution directly or has never been forced to dig deep into his soul and reveal all the ugliness that he found could understand what actually happened."[2] Yet he does not tell why the CR occurred. The Cultural Revolution obviously tapped frightening parts of the human soul. But just saying *"hic dragones"*[3] is not enough to show why the dragons stay in their caves most of the time, or why they came out in 1966. The People's Republic before that time had suffered bouts of brutality, but none so widespread or directed at so many kinds of victims at so many levels of society. The particularly extensive and loosely organized tumult of the CR calls for an explanation that goes beyond the motives of a few people. Ba Jin eloquently shows the urgency of the problem, but he does not claim to solve it. Many who suffered in the CR are understandably wary of glib efforts to explain any tragedy that is so large.

Scholars may nonetheless usefully document the scope of the trauma.[4] Foreigners can offer consolation from the fact that other countries have undergone similar spasms of physical violence in their own revolutions and reactions. More comparative and systematic thinking could help build a framework strong enough to answer the most obvious questions about the CR: Why did so many urban Chinese ostracize and attack each other after 1965? What can be done to obviate the chance this could happen again?

•

POLITICAL INTENTIONS, UNEXPECTED CONSEQUENCES, AND CULTURAL REVOLUTION

The main roots of the Cultural Revolution's violence lie in previous measures undertaken by the state. From 1949 to 1966 three administrative policies—which can be summed up in the words *labeling, monitoring,* and *campaigning*—influenced Chinese urbanites' attitudes toward each other and toward their local leaders. Strong stress on the importance of official names, designated bosses, and fearful campaigns were all *measures by which an understaffed Party saved short-term costs* in seeking revolutionary goals. The greater long-term costs of these policies emerged only in the Cultural Revolution. In other words, three specific short-run implementing habits of the Chinese bureaucracy caused widespread social anxiety that was tinder for widespread violence.

First, rules cumulated slowly after 1949 to give practical meaning to political names (for example, "capitalist," "rightist," "bad element" *or* "worker," "dependent of revolutionary martyr," "cadre"). Such categories differentiated whole families for access to unionized jobs, good education, urban housing, rights to remain in cities, even health care and food rations.[5] Those labels designated status groups, not classes (with political and administrative, not "substructural," significance by the mid-1960s). Urban people acquired group interests in making sure this system would be used to their benefit, not to their harm. By 1966 some were eager to destroy the status quo, when for very transient reasons they could begin to organize for that purpose—while others were ready to defend it.

Second, policies also cumulated to make individuals in work units *(danwei)* increasingly dependent on local Party bosses—and to close alternative channels by which individuals could improve their livelihoods. Their futures depended on obeying their official monitors. By the mid-1960s many ordinary urbanites were ready to follow orders for "class struggle," which came through either the unit leaders or those leaders' local rivals. Individuals supported their officially designated bosses if they and their families had benefited from the previous system—or attacked the leaders if they had met discrimination from their designated monitors.

Third, public campaigns were yet another administrative technique, a policy for implementing more substantive policies. The official use of threats and activists in campaigns, directed against targets specified by the government, grew over time. The CCP came to use campaigns habitually, because it had huge social goals but relatively few members who were both loyal and expert at working toward these goals. Tactics such as "killing chickens to scare monkeys" stirred fear during campaigns, raising the rate of compliance to all Party directives. Like measures for official labels and monitoring by bosses, the policy of periodic public threatening must have seemed inexpensive, considering its big effect on compliance during each short-term movement before 1966.

These three policies became standard operating procedures whenever the government decided to manipulate people for short-run ends. There may well be longstanding Chinese cultural tendencies to stress the importance of group names, of individuals' dependence on wise patrons, and of fearing official coercion. But these cultural tendencies in China have not always led to cultural revolutions. The effective cause of the widespread havoc in 1966 should be more specific than all of Chinese (or communist, or other) culture, because "culture" by any hardy definition offers a thick array of inconsistent options.[6] No culture is a consistent set of traits from which social scientists might deduce fixed reasons for behavior. For the people who share it, any culture or ideology must be more useful and flexible than that. Many explanations of the CR thus seem too broad, unable to show why specific cultural or ideological options became more important in 1966 and first in cities than in other times and places. Some aspects of the Cultural Revolution extended after 1966–1968 and outside of cities, but this analysis focuses on why the violence began in the first period and in the urban centers.

The cause of the CR may also be less narrow than the ideas or psychoses of a single individual, even those of Mao. The intensity of the Mao cult, like that of the CR as a whole, requires some explanation that refers to his diverse worshipers. The CR can account for the cult, as much as the cult can account for the CR. Mao used people at that time, but many used Mao's vague legitimation of rebellion for their own ends too. The problem of the CR extends beyond a few men. *All* top Party leaders from 1949 to 1966 saw political labeling, appointing bosses for each unit, and scary campaigns as administratively necessary. Differences among them on these organizational measures, used outside the Party, were temporary and minor. Mao's cult was also important, but the task of explaining its popularity is probably identical to the task of explaining the CR. Mao abetted this faith, but he could not (even with the help of a few friends) have created it alone. Some precipitating factors of the CR undoubtedly lie in Beijing disputes and inspirations, but something beyond this is needed to show why the popular response on the streets was so forceful.

Broad, culture-centered exegeses of the CR explain too much, even though they give a sense of the underlying predispositions that may sometimes but not always lead people to violence. Narrow, elite-centered understandings, on the other hand, explain too little. They show that Mao and his comrades had ideas and disputes, but not why millions rose up so ardently. Beijing disputes alone cannot explain so much unusual mass behavior, and Chinese or communist cultures alone cannot explain its occurrence. Comprehending the Cultural Revolution as an outbreak of widespread violence requires an explanation that reaches for middle factors that structured the lives of Chinese by the mid-1960s. The three administrative policies mentioned above affected many city folk deeply over a long period, and they are candidate causes for the explanatory task at hand.

To use all three, we need also to employ diverse logics of action. Reasoning from group consciousness created by labels, from hierarchal patron-client links, and from legitimate opportunities for violent or compliant behavior are fundamentally different types of analysis. But if these analytic types are all useful for understanding, there is no substantive objection to using them together. These categories are the same in a more concrete sense; they all result from state policies.

This chapter is about the harshness and tumult of the Cultural Revolution, not about the CR as conceived separately from that essential aspect of it. Nonetheless, scholarly writings on other aspects of the movement need to be assessed here for their bearing on this treatment, either because they are relevant or because they are widely perceived to have relevance. What is the link between the violence of the CR—which was central to most of its victims—and more usual discussions about Liu and Mao? The approach here (in other words, this specification of what to ask about the CR) should allow a better definition of the role Mao actually played. Beijing power struggle were an immediate precipitating factor in the event, and Chinese or communist cultures surely contributed in underlying or probable ways; but none of these shows sufficient causes of the widespread tragedy.

SKETCH OF THE EVIDENCE: PRE-1966 LABELS, BOSSES, AND CAMPAIGNS

There is no space here for the 1949–1966 history that is needed to back fully the ideas suggested above.[7] Some highlights of the long cumulation of popular ire from administrative policies before the CR may nonetheless be mentioned. The "suppression of counterrevolutionaries" and the Five-Anti campaign's "tiger hunting" began to challenge a few local urban leaders in the early 1950s. The "Common Program" of Liberation and the mobilization of bourgeois patriots for the Korean War were also important at this early time in changing local authority patterns. The violence of the first national campaigns, especially land reform, gave most urban non-Communist elites as much incentive to cooperate with the Party as to resent it. Some people were recruited on patriotic grounds into land reform or aid-Korea work teams. Comprehensive urban labeling was introduced rather innocuously on a comprehensive basis only in the 1953 census. For most citizens (not including some notables from the Guomindang, churches, and newspapers), the movements of the next several years did not involve major violence in cities; they concentrated on the reorganization of economic and cultural life. Many city folk were at first affected by such campaigns only in minor ways, partly because the CCP depended on a great variety of people in these early years to keep the economy going. The Party's supply of experts was minimal in most fields relevant to urban management, and so it relied largely on "retained personnel" from the old regime.

The year 1957 may be the most important watershed in recent Chinese political history. Large numbers of "rightists" were dubbed then, and this sharply derogatory title greatly extended the importance of political and class-background labeling. This period strengthened the power of Party bosses who had been put in economic and educational institutions during earlier movements, because many alternative leaders were now declared illegitimate. Labels were not new in 1957, and job recruitment before that year had increasingly involved Party approvals. But the "administrative streamlining" and repression of rightists in 1957 gave political force to the claims of new local leaders against old ones.

By 1958 the Party still lacked enough reliable "red and expert" personnel to staff its new institutions. The use of secret files *(dang'an)* and the arbitrariness of label assignments had frightened many people into dependent compliance and hard work to prove their loyalty. "Killing chickens to scare monkeys" *(sha ji jing hou)* became normal policy for increasing compliance. This was temporarily effective in each campaign and helped the Party reduce dissent, at least for a while. Use of fear became an administrative habit.

The main effect of the Great Leap Forward, making individuals still more dependent on their bosses, came from its unintended and ironic result: an economic depression. As goods of all types, including food and factory materials, became scarce after 1959, economic organizations alternative to the Party's main system could seldom obtain resources or sell products. Noncontrolled firms increased for a while, as there were still some products to sell on black markets. By 1961, however, many had gone bankrupt because of shortages even for illegal enterprises. As the economy revived after 1962, resources were channeled more exclusively than before through Party-controlled units. Union membership came to mean even more to workers than in the 1950s, both because new jobs were scarcer and because alternative sources of benefits were reduced. Admission to universities was restricted, after 1961 on academic criteria and after 1963 according to family labels. The dependence of individuals on Party bureaucrats' decisions rose sharply. Economic disaster, by ending nonstate alternatives, put the cadres thoroughly in control of Chinese cities' supplies.[8] The plans to put resources almost totally under bureaucratic direction, as envisaged in the 1956 Transition to Socialism, were generally realized only because of the unplanned post-Leap depression.

Ambiguity about the legitimacy of the roles of different kinds of local leaders—even inside the Party—was institutionalized after 1963. People with different roles were often separated organizationally. At very high levels in Shanghai, for example, Zhang Chunqiao was charged with propagating a radical style in organizations concerned with cultural work; and at the same time, Cao Diqiu led economic organizations with technocratic tasks. For a while the two did not conflict because each stuck to his own job.[9] Sometimes this ambiguity was institutionalized regionally; the Beijing-Shanghai divisions are most famous. To some extent it was institutionalized by generations.[10] Youth camps under the army expanded after 1963, while older people ran a prospering economy with very different norms. Conflicting sets of agricultural and industrial policies emerged from Beijing, although these well-known disagreements among a few top leaders affected most basic-level leaders less than the ambiguous politics they symbolized. In 1965 large numbers were admitted to the Young Communist League,[11] and even to the Party. To what social role were these talented people being recruited? It was officially unclear, at this time, what kind of local leaders were supposed to rule China's cities. Labeling, monitoring, and campaigning had reached surreal heights by the mid-1960s. They were established habits that had by then become common tools of controversy. By 1966–1968 many kinds of local leaders would in turn use these measures to further their own aims.

Various sorts of urban people were anxious about their careers by 1966, after years of increasing state influence over their individual and family prospects. Some could join together in good family-background groups. Others could hope their talent, work, and loyalty would make their lives secure. But for many the oppression had become sharp—and when the state apparatus temporarily weakened (for reasons that originated in Beijing), the local reaction was more enthusiastic, violent, and uncontrolled than anyone had predicted. The growing conflict of top leaders catalyzed the 1966 explosion, but the ingredients of the bomb were mixed local motives created by longstanding organizational policies to categorize, monitor, and frighten people.

COMPARING THE POLICY-RESULT THESIS
WITH USUAL ALTERNATIVES

Most Chinese and Western views of the CR treat it essentially as a conflict of high (not local) elites, as a response to the concerns of a few people (not of many). This chapter suggests an alternative conception, and several steps can be taken to elaborate it. First, various causes of the Cultural Revolution proposed by other writers need to be examined; second, links should be sought between other definitions of the event and the main one here; third and last, various views may be compatible if they suggest different factors as important in playing different but consistent roles in the start of the Cultural Revolution.

Many explanations of this event fall into four types, relating it to (1) Chairman Mao's personality and cultural or political habits, (2) power struggle among high leaders, (3) ideal policies for radical development in an impoverished society, or (4) basic-level conflicts, induced by previous policies, of the sort suggested above. Let us examine these in order.

Mao's Personality and Chinese or Leninist Political Culture

Did Mao Zedong cause all the violence? Did his personality, and the cult of it, interact so powerfully with the authoritarian or feudal culture common locally in China that it could motivate all the tumult of the CR? This is the official explanation in the 1981 *Resolution on CCP History*—and in different forms it is also held by most dissidents and foreign scholars. It is no doubt partly correct. How does it relate to the explanation concerning local reactions to long-term administrative manipulation that is outlined above? For what might each of these views account? Do they play different roles, or show different aspects of the CR? Which is more important?

Chairman Mao penned the May 16 Circular of 1966—an inspirational polemic that legitimized criticism of many kinds. The Sixteen Points of August 1966, which were approved at Mao's instigation, kept police from preventing new political groups that, before then, would have been routinely suppressed.[12] This August decision, and others by Mao, were crucial to the development of the campaign—even though they do not fully tell us why it unleased so much mass political energy. What gave the Mao cult its power? Mao's sayings were often vague, and people interpreted his words in many ways. The Mao cult is too much like the CR to have started it. Can things so similar or inseparable be said to cause each other? Mao Zedong was a necessary but insufficient condition of the Cultural Revolution.

Mao inspired followers, and those who suffered in the CR blame him readily. He tried to control his environment "through behavior determined by intra-psychic needs no longer in touch with the actualities of the world."[13] He became willful, "lost all collegial sense," ending with a "fractured vision."[14] But it may be easier to think about Mao's own motives than to link his goals with those of the millions of Chinese who praised his words but fought each other while doing so. Explanations of the CR that rely too heavily on Mao are in danger of understating the extent to which his name was used by others.

The Central Committee's *Resolution on CCP History* notes that "Comrade Mao Zedong's prestige reached a peak and he began to get arrogant. . . . He gradually divorced himself from practice and from the masses, acting more and more arbitrarily and subjectively, and increasingly put himself above the Central Committee of the Party."[15] To its credit, the *Resolution* quickly goes on to say that "blaming this on only one person or on only a handful of people will not provide a deep lesson for the whole Party or enable it to find practical ways to change the situation." Instead, it blames the "evil ideological and political influence of centuries of feudal autocracy," which created conditions "for the overconcentration of Party power in individuals and for the development of an arbitrary individual rule and the personality cult in the Party."[16]

Men of affairs in China, like many who have written from outside,[17] stress Mao's leadership style as an important contributing factor to the Cultural Revolution. Mao said, "It is right to rebel." This sense of a need for havoc seems understandable, or healthy, as a rejection of rigid cultural traditions of authority and compliance in small units. Some scholars treat these traditions as largely Leninist rather than particularly Chinese. One promising line of investigation, pursued by Andrew Walder and Jean Oi especially, stresses the importance of "clientelism" in communist states.[18] Tight authority relations are normal in many Chinese work units,[19] so rebellion against them may be a natural reaction for members who feel oppressed. But patron-client bonds are only some of the political links that affect urban Chinese. Local rebellion against patrons was a frequent event in the CR, but not all members of conflict groups had suffered under the same boss. Labeling groups and campaigning in a totalist style share a big similarity with designating patrons: all three are administrative policies.

Another cultural explanation of the CR is Marxist. Wang Xizhe, one of China's most distinguished dissidents, published a 1980 essay entitled "Mao Zedong and the Cultural Revolution."[20] This says that Mao after 1956 was a Stalinist, a supporter of coercive bureaucratic rule in the imperial mold—with himself as the violent and arbitrary emperor. Mao's occasional antibureaucratic statements are seen as purely tactical politics to gain popular support. In the tradition of Marx's *Eighteenth Brumaire of Louis Bonaparte,* Wang Xizhe claims that a majority of Chinese (the peasants) were willing to support a dictatorship that was "fascist" despite its communist trappings. Wang emphasizes the importance of Chinese tradition and Mao's ability to capitalize on peasants' propensity to adulate a leader.

The shortcomings and powers of Wang's theory are typical of those found in many culturalist explanations. Rural authority relations are based largely on traditional "communities"[21]—but the CR began in the most modern Chinese cities such as Shanghai, where politics is also crucially based on specialized functions and "society." Wang's approach points to the rural-egalitarian bases of Mao's dictatorship, but it does not explain why specific modern urban groups (not peasants) responded first and most powerfully. Like other ideas that stress political culture, Wang's thesis does not specify why there was an uprising in cities first, or why the relevant years began in 1966.

As a serious Marxist, Wang is limited by an inability to conceive any pressing "social contradiction" except between classes, economically generated.[22] But he offhandedly admits, in an afterthought to his main analysis, "If we try to understand the Cultural Revolution from a different perspective, by taking Mao Zedong's Cultural Revolution as being in opposition to the people's Cultural Revolution, and then say that the Cultural Revolution was a product of sharpening contradictions within Chinese society, this makes some sense."[23] Such an admission is inconsistent with a stress on the causal importance of Mao's motives separate from his opportunities, and it does not account for Mao's reactions to his environment. Nonetheless, Wang's analysis is the most searching to have emerged from China—and especially because he is so powerfully inspired by Marx, it is ironic that he has been put in a Chinese jail for expressing his ideas.

Many scholars with interests different from Wang's are nonetheless like him in focusing on the question, "Why did Mao act as he did?" These often imply explanations of the social violence, without explicitly closing on that question. For example, Harold Hinton writes:

> The origins of the Cultural Revolution can hardly be attributed, as some analysts propose, to basic sociological causes, such as discontent among students and industrial workers over inadequate job opportunities and rule by the Party apparatus. . . . The inspiration and leadership of the Cultural Revolution were Mao's, and without his initiative there would have been no Cultural Revolution. [24]

Mao's personal role in encouraging the Cultural Revolution—especially in relaxing police controls during August 1966, and also in stirring Red Guards or soldiers to seize power—was a necessary condition of the whole event. But while the CR could indeed not have taken place without Mao's instigation, the Chairman provides an insufficient answer to the question, "Why did the CR grow so large and so violent?" Politics that widely invade personal and family life, as Robert C. Tucker has pointed out, flourish best under a totalitarian, a Hitler or Stalin or Mao. [25] But scholars oversimplify their task and define what is to be explained too narrowly when they imply the CR arose only at Mao's call, not from motives in vastly wider constituencies. [26] Hitler or Stalin surely would have considered Mao's national organization in 1966–1968 to be too disorganized. Despite his flashy personal style, Mao alone did not contribute as much to the CR's violence as most explanations aver.

Power Struggle as an Explanation

The CR was partly a power struggle among leaders in Beijing. Did not the chaos at low levels simply reflect these conflicts at the top? This is the main presumption with which most journalists and political scientists first reacted to the event. The best book on these *Origins of the Cultural Revolution,* by Roderick MacFarquhar, gives new and detailed information along these lines. It concerns "the thinking, actions, and interaction of the Chinese leaders [especially] Mao Tse-tung, who made the Cultural Revolution, Liu Shao-ch'i, who was cast as its Lucifer, and Chou En-lai, who survived it and its subsequent reverberations." [27]

This kind of explanation is convincing insofar as we want to know about Mao and a few of his colleagues. They had remarkable passions and provided examples of leadership that are interesting, to say the least. But as everyone knows, China contains more than four or five people. This most usual, top-elite explanation of the Cultural Revolution throws light on some of the precipitating causes of the movement as a national one, but it begs important questions about other aspects of the history: Why did motives of violence grow so luxuriantly in China's big cities after 1965? If the radical seed germinated first in the minds of some national leaders, how could they scatter it with such signal success, so widely and quickly? What was in China's ground, by the mid-1960s, to make it flourish? In what ways were the goals of these urbanites similar then, and can these be understood in terms of the lives they led? Were the policies dividing Beijing's elite the same as those most affecting the masses who actually "made" the Cultural Revolution?

As Roderick MacFarquhar and Parris Chang have shown, even Mao Zedong often had to cooperate with leaders having different policy preferences, in a complex process of "conflict and consensus-building."[28] Lowell Dittmer gives evidence that Mao was reconciled to Liu Shaoqi as late as October 1966—long after the CR had begun—and only later changed his mind.[29] Mao's intentions were so unclear and hidden, so full of options for himself, that irresolvable conflict among top leaders may well have come later than mass conflict in the streets.

It is doubtful that disagreements within the Beijing elite—for example, differences over agricultural policy since the Leap—can fully motivate the CR, which began in cities and rapidly involved basic-level leaders. Elite factions often tried to organize support groups in Beijing and other cities, but local struggles continued fiercely, long after Maoists controlled central and municipal governments. The "top" did not quickly garner enough means to control the "bottom." The CR was a power struggle, but it was not tightly coordinated and was not mainly in Beijing.

Radical Ideals and Modernizing Exercise as Motives for Cultural Revolution

Why not ask the CR participants why they made this campaign? They were articulate at that time, and they spoke about a kind of modernization. Many Westerners found their explanations credible then. William

Hinton wrote that CR policies would transform people, until finally no social classes would exist.[30] K. S. Karol extolled the communist purposes of the CR.[31] Richard Pfeffer said the CR was an "authentic" revolution, because Mao's goal was to create a new governing superstructure.[32] The Committee of Concerned Asian Scholars declared, "The Great Proletarian Cultural Revolution was . . . the struggle to determine which line China would follow," especially in terms of policy aims such as equality, community, national independence, and passing the torch of revolution across a generation gap.[33] Leo Huberman and Paul Sweezy rejected the idea that the CR arose from either mass or elite power struggles; they echoed contemporary Chinese statements that its purpose was to lead China into communism.[34]

A distantly similar kind of explanation could be put in the more dispassionate language of political development. "Red" styles of work were seen as useful for coordination in a huge "new state" with bad communications. "Expert," "instrumental" values were also needed. But because these two kinds of norms conflict, Richard Baum saw a zigzag alternation of emphases on the one, then on the other.[35] So the CR mainly continued the politics of earlier movements, especially the Socialist Education campaign. A. Doak Barnett, Michel Oksenberg, and others at first interpreted even the violent early events of the CR in modernization terms.[36] Mao's "revolutionary pragmatism" condoned violence for the purpose of "unfreezing" China's bureaucracy.[37] Other writers in this volume, such as Andrew Walder, David Zweig, and Carl Riskin, also take sensible and functional approaches to CR ideology, linking it with political and economic development goals. This view of the problem may cover the movement's explicit hopes better than its concrete aspects. The participants nonetheless spoke in these terms.

One Red Guard interrupted the poster writing of another to ask, "How did you get to be so dedicated and enthusiastic?" The reply was general, all about personality: "I want to exercise myself. I want to collect experience. Supporting the Great Cultural Revolution is a great chance for us young people to develop ourselves."[38] Michael Walzer, studying the "zealous, systematic, sustained politics" of violent radicalism in early revolutionary Europe, shows it flourished especially among "masterless men," whose interests went far beyond material benefits. Radicalism— in its Puritan form, for example—was not a phenomenon of impoverished groups. It grew among merchants and gentlemen. This early radicalism combined, as Mao did, an interest in personal exercise with a crusading, war-loving spirit. As the Huguenot enthusiast de Mournay put it, "Peace is a great evil, war is a great good. . . . Peace is proper to the miscreant; but war, to the true believer."[39] But does the moral verve of such a quasi-religious choice show, by itself, why this kind of existential selection (rather than a calmer one) is made by many people all at once? Symbols alone do not explain how they get used.

Contrasts between passive flight and violent activism, between blackness and light (especially the sun), between secret procedures and open ones, between dirt and purity—this Manichaean syntactic structure was inherent to the style of the CR. A symbolist approach to the movement can be tightly structured.[40] Even if it only indirectly gets at the causes of action in the campaign, it has the advantage of using the notions of the participants themselves.

By 1966 sharp ironies between ideals and actions were obvious. Many bourgeois-labeled people joined workers to create an ostensibly "Great Proletarian" Cultural Revolution. To live down their pasts, as well as to have revenge on the bureaucrats who repressed them, ex-bourgeois citizens often joined the most radical, ostensibly antibourgeois conflict groups.[41] Bureaucrats (many of whom were not from worker or peasant families) defended "the proletariat," referring in practice to themselves. But poor and contract workers (mostly real proletarians) were common in "rebel" factions that attacked labor-allocating bureaucrats.[42] The methods of many radical conflict groups at this time, especially those with army backing, were often indistinguishable from police conservatism.[43]

Could there have been such a sharp divergence between the rhetoric of a movement and the impulses behind it? There could have been and indeed was. Bourgeois intellectuals have often been radical before; and worker leaders, conservative.[44] Extreme radicalism is usually a phenomenon of well-to-do groups at times of revolution, even in preindustrial societies. It remained so in China.[45]

Explanations in Policy and Local Leadership Resources

The major questions to be answered remain: Why did people ostracize each other within their daily work units, and why did they so readily use all forms of violence to attack their neighbors? Ostracism, isolation, and humiliation were often harder for victims of the CR to bear than even the instances of torture.[46] What inspired such incivility in a civilized country, and often turned it into a rage? Why did so many people at that time—as most of them now admit—go politically crazy?

An answer can be found in the accumulated effects of policies for labels, bosses, and campaigns. School admissions, good jobs, avoidance of rural work assignments, rights of association, housing, food, and much else became subject to official rationing partly on the basis of "class" labels (such as "capitalist" or "worker") and other political labels (such as "rightist" or "model"). Second, because Chinese workplaces, educational institutions, and residential areas were increasingly centralized, with a few leaders controlling most of the resources people needed for leading happy lives, individuals had no choice except to confirm tight, local authority structures by obeying the designated leaders. Third, the habit of campaigns legitimized violence for both group and individual needs.

Interviews give evidence on the importance of political labels for people's lives, and so do recent Chinese fiction and many autobiographical accounts.[47] Individuals' consciousness about their labels was tinged with uncertainty because of the secrecy of files. "Class" designations, even in the household registers *(huji bu),* did not label people according to current links with economic production but on official status grounds.[48] This system created mass groups that were originally unorganized (although clubs of proletarian-labeled people could form). Labels such as "rightist" *(youpai fenzi)* or "bad element" *(huai fenzi)* were often affixed to people who did not know the evidence on which these were based.[49] Applicants for jobs in state organizations filled out forms indicating "class" and other particulars—which officials might later check by investigation or annotate in the secret files.[50] Labels largely determined individuals' life chances in urban China throughout the third quarter of this century.

Discontent among bad-labeled people threatened a bureaucracy that accorded benefits to officially designated proletarian and cadre families, some of which were actually ex-bourgeois. Thus cadres with real worker backgrounds developed an interest in "cleansing the ranks" of local leaders who had successfully hidden nonproletarian origins. They feared they might otherwise lose advantages that were well established in affirmative action programs by the mid-1960s. They also joined attacks against officials whose corruption was obvious enough to weaken the system that helped them. And they led the battle against disapproved intellectuals and "rightists," their potential rivals who might have become the local leaders in their stead.

In most cities two loose coalitions of Red Guard factions emerged—

and made war on each other. One type, popularly named the "protect emperors clique" *(baohuang pai)*, defended the previous regime, insofar as this was feasible. This first coalition included many of the earliest-formed Red Guard groups, whose members had proletarian or cadre backgrounds. The other coalition, the "rebel clique" *(zaofan pai)*, was generally more radical, because its members wanted more changes of previous bureaucrats. A PRC appraisal uses the same distinction when it refers to "the two types of factional organization in the Cultural Revolution," one of which "rebelled against leading cadres and the other protected leading cadres." [51]

Shanghai thus had its radical "Red Revolutionaries" and the more conservative "Scarlet Guards." Wuhan had its "Workers' General Headquarters" and the "Million Heroes." In Canton radical "Red Flags" conflicted with more proestablishment "East Winds." Beijing had its "Earth Faction" and "Heaven Faction" (the latter, named for an aviation institute, opposed old Party leaders less virulently than the former, named for a geology school). Even Wuzhou in Guangxi Province had an iconoclastic "Revolutionary Rebel Grand Army" and an "Alliance Command" that attacked Party authorities less. One of these was always relatively radical and willing to criticize local CCP leaders, whereas the other was more inclined to attack deputy leaders or scapegoats—at least until top leaders' positions became untenable because of past institutionalized mistreatment of too many groups or individuals.

Evidence in the scholarly literature to link this aspect of the CR with previous policies of "class" labeling is now fairly complete. The CR at first led analysts to correlate political positions with occupational groups. [52] Others then gathered data about the cleavage between the main coalitions in Canton, from which Hong Yung Lee drew the following conclusions: The radical group was diverse, comprising many youths and even pedicab drivers, as well as many who were seriously discontented with the regime. Radical publications were more numerous, and Canton's "Red Flags" communicated with their allies in other provinces more than did their rivals. They sometimes upheld "factionalism" as a trend that had revolutionary potential. They expressed criticism of "powerholders taking the capitalist road in the Party" (whereas "East Winds" more often attacked "monsters and freaks," especially intellectuals who had capitalist class labels). Radical publications more often conflicted with army policy and opposed the "Great Alliance and Three-in-One Combination" that sporadically gave the military more influence in civilian affairs. The radicals more often criticized head Party secretaries, especially those having openly political functions, whereas the East Winds sought targets among deputy heads and specialists.[53] Radical journals more often launched broadsides against whole Party committees, not just individual scapegoats. Stanley Rosen found that about three-quarters of the radical "Red Flag" members came from families with "middle" and "bad" labels. Four-fifths of the conservative "East Wind" Red Guards were from the families of workers, soldiers, and officials.[54] Marc Blecher and Gordon White, studying CR politics in a technical unit, found that over two-thirds of the employees with "proletarian" class labels joined the conservative group, whereas a similar portion of the employees with "bad" or "mediocre" class backgrounds joined the radicals.[55]

Officially labeled "workers" joined both coalitions (though the conservative groups usually contained more of them), because there were big differences between less-favored contract workers and more-favored unionized workers, and because some nonproletarian people had managed to get this good label.[56] But many conflicts were openly between groups of people having different labels. In Canton a conservative Red Guard newspaper described a more radical, less proletarian faction as follows: "When they were oppressed, to effect their own liberation they displayed a definite quality of resistance, objectively a definite revolutionary quality. But they rebelled out of selfishness (even to the point of acting to benefit the interests of their own reactionary class)."[57] Thus even the offspring of real workers sometimes had to give the children of bourgeois credit for revolutionary enthusiasm.

Radical groups commandeered trains more often than conservatives, partly for politics, partly for the fun of "revolutionary tourism," and partly to move away from their dossiers at a time of "class struggle."[58] When radical Red Guards from Shanghai and elsewhere came to Beijing, they met protests from conservatives. As a handbill written by local Beijing people put it:

Like a swarm of wasps, you sons and daughters of landlords, rich peasants, counter-revolutionaries, bad elements, and rightists have descended on the capital with great pomp and speed! Let us tell you, we allow only the children of the five red categories to come. . . . Some of you have the family background of capitalists; your uncles have spent a number of years in the people's prisons, and some of your uncles were historically counterrevolutionaries. . . . You, a bunch of bad eggs, the Red Guards and the five-red category children of Peking do not welcome you. We want you to get out of here, and at once.[59]

Not just "capitalists" unable to shed their labels, but also contract workers and other proletarians and intellectuals with grudges against bureaucrats were numerous in the most radical groups.

Yet every government needs some administrative classifications. There would be no way to concoct rules without them, despite the dangers they pose.[60] Especially when a government's staff is short of people who can muster real authority, a continuous reviewing of labels is prohibitively expensive. But fixed labels bear no clear relation to behavior. Labeling that seems a short-term administrative necessity can create long-term problems.

Bossism, as a pattern, likewise saves short-term costs. If an organization has big plans but few loyal and competent personnel, it may spread its resources thinly over the population it is trying to influence. "Line authority"[61] gives local cadres freedom to do their work. Such leaders' hands are strengthened if subordinates cannot expect to change to another patron. The short-term administrative benefits of such a system can hide long-term costs, which arise because institutionalized dependence hinders flows of information and fosters lethargy among lower employees who become craven, angry, or disaffected and thus do not put much effort into the organization's work.

By 1966 clientelist patterns had become somewhat muddled, because "political departments" and "socialist education work teams" for the previous two or three years had investigated many local cadres who had assumed their posts in the 1950s. Especially in large state organizations that confederated separate shops, patrons in many localities did not fully trust one another by 1966. Deputy leaders or second secretaries often proved, in the CR, to be at odds with top leaders or first secretaries—even though they had all usually supported the policies that had manipulated their common underlings earlier. Conflict groups in the CR were formed not just because of anxieties among individuals but also because of mutual complaints among local leaders. After August 1966 these grievances were expressed through all the means the state itself had previously legitimized.

Violence, as in campaigns, has been seen as a potential servant of order by thinkers ranging from Li Si to Machiavelli.[62] The habit of campaigns became a cause of the Cultural Revolution, because violence was officially legitimate for social ends in China by 1966. This legitimation was expressed then by Mao, but it also had been voiced and used systematically for more than a decade by the whole CCP. If the Party employed fear to achieve goals, it became natural for others to do the same. Yet the currency of this style of action may not explain the reasons for which it was adopted—which were based both on label-group interests (even articulated ones) and on individuals' patron-client bonds (official and not just traditional, either friendly or hostile). Violence as a standard administrative measure bred further violence, even after the administration broke down.

Campaigns (like bosses and labels) affected the Party's recurrent problem of lack of forceful staff; when the bureaucracy was in danger of ossification, a campaign mobilized both fears and ambitions to move it toward action. Designating official bosses solved a logically later plight; after a campaign caused chaos, channeling resources through official monitors was a way to restore order. Yet the "independent kingdoms" of petty tyrants that came to dominate many work units, because of this recurring administrative need, created yet a third typical quandary: local cadres' power had to be governed by larger, national rules, which inevitably involved labeling categories of people who were to receive specified rights and sanctions. In time, the labels created interests, and only a new campaign (of which the Cultural Revolution became the largest example) could change a label's meaning; so the cycle continued.[63]

The three organizational needs served by these policies (campaigns to inspire action, monitors to control action, and labels to coordinate it) never fully disappear as administrative demands, though at particular times one or the other of them is most prominent. Nor do the political constituencies of groups and individuals affected by them ever fully disappear. Yet in the modern revolutionary effort to specialize these functions over time, the concurrent need for all of them became unusually obscured in policy making.

China suffered from a lack of balance between the resources for state-led change and the hopes of the leaders. The resource infrastructure can best be presented in social terms and the hopes in cultural ones. The need to cover both together, for the sake of understanding these politics, arises because we naturally seek future lessons from an event like the Cultural Revolution. We want to know the unintended cause of such a tragedy, just as we also want to know the intentions that could have driven it.[64] Systems theorists argue for the importance of unconscious relations and causes; culturalists argue for the importance of conscious ideas. Accounting for the CR will require both, and the difficulties of explaining causation need not prevent us from trying to show what this experience means for China's future and for other countries.

In conclusion, the language of the CR had an intensity that shows the extent of mass anxiety in urban China by the mid-1960s. But the articulated ideals of that time fail to describe accurately its main political constituencies in cities, and they do not throw much light on who used force at the local level, or why. The main object here is not to show why certain ideals became popular, how official lines rose and fell in Beijing, or how Mao defeated his high rivals. It is, instead, to see why the CR's violence arose. An analysis with that aim must look at concrete interests as well as ideal passions.

An explanation of the CR in terms of very local leaders and their members' motives and resources can complement the usual emphases on Mao's totalitarianism, power struggle, or voluntarist ideology in explaining what happened. All these factors were important, and the linked situations and motives of many local leaders in cities were even more important in setting the movement's tone. These ecologies and norms were crucially determined by longstanding policies of the whole CCP top leadership, especially the policies for labels, designated patrons, and fearsome campaigns. Specific actions by Mao Zedong in August 1966 were necessary for the Cultural Revolution to begin, but the force of this movement arose from administrative habits that had been consensual in the Party since 1949 at least and that had manipulated many people.

As the campaign developed after 1966, immediate local factors also became important. Various kinds of factories, schools, and neighborhoods produced distinctive kinds of groups, differently at various times.[65] But the climate for Cultural Revolution emerged among tens of millions of urban Chinese during the whole decade of the 1950s and the first half of the 1960s.

Such violence is not unique in history. Since the first modern revolution, England's Puritan one, there has been a record of attacking traditions, smashing idols, renaming places, and killing counterrevolutionaries. France had its guillotines. The early revolutionary United States had tar-and-featherings. In China, as in other countries, the movement will fitfully wind down, as local leaders come to believe the costs of acrimony outweigh the benefits for their groups. As elites sporadically come to terms with each other, China's upheaval may develop a pattern close to that of the earliest revolutions and wind down at least as quickly as has the one in Russia.[66]

This conclusion is hopeful in two senses. First, the high tide of violence between large social groups in China's revolution may well now be finished, even though (as we have seen) the state still can use military violence against such groups. Largely because the CCP brought that tide to a very underdeveloped country, the possibilities of nurturing talent from old elite families was not completely destroyed there. Because Mao was less thorough than Stalin in creating a united elite at local levels, China has to wait less long after Mao than Russia did after Stalin, before reforms become so extensive that the state cannot stop them.

Second, if the policies of labeling, dependence, and campaigning become less important, conditions that made for mass uncertainty and violence in the mid-1960s can also be lessened. These policies are still in force to some extent, but the Deng Xiaoping era until mid-1989 saw a removal of the worst labels (especially in the 1979 rehabilitation of rightists). Even then, the PRC central state's ability to mobilize its society had fallen far below the levels that its old leaders recalled from the first fifteen years of their republic. The dependence of individuals on unit bosses has also been partially reduced in some kinds of work units, even though old local Party leaders are unsurprisingly reluctant to admit that their personal repression of subordinates was a major cause of the CR. Campaigns went somewhat out of style, although the old top leaders were often reluctant to admit how ineffective such movements had become. The Four Modernizations could be named to sound like a campaign, but editorials pointed out that reforms would have to be steady, for many decades, to have a real effect. In 1983 the Campaign Against Spiritual Pollution fizzled after a fearsome start.[67] By 1987 the Criticism of the Bourgeois Liberal Thought Tide[68] was not even called a campaign (*yundong*). By 1989 there was a revival that took the army's bullets to make it fearsome. The old style could hardly be made permanently effective, because of the use of these means.

As long as the Party is mainly an "organizational weapon," a system legitimized by "practical ideology" that justifies invading the social environment rather than adapting to it,[69] the danger of another CR cannot be absolutely dismissed. Lenin's doctrines lent legitimacy to the administrative use of violence. But this does not inculpate all socialism, which comes in many forms. Nor does it blame general traditions of either exemplary authority or moral rebellion in either Chinese or communist cultures.

The suddenness and scope of violence in 1966 came as a surprise to practically everyone. A dam broke; a raincloud thundered and poured; a spark ignited a wildfire. Physical analogies may still provide a means of trying to come to terms with such cataclysmic events. But that does not require they be inevitable. China is not fated surely to suffer spasms of totalism and anarchy forever. Chinese will decide on measures to allow or disallow a cumulation of heavy social malaise such as broke loose in 1966. Better policies—to reduce group labeling, personal dependencies, and harsh campaigns—could have prevented the past Cultural Revolution and can prevent a recurrence.

Factional Politics in Zhejiang, 1973–1976

KEITH FORSTER

Between 1972 and 1976 a struggle for succession to the aging and en-feebled Mao Zedong and the terminally ill Zhou Enlai erupted within the upper echelons of the Chinese Communist Party. With the disgrace of the central military leaders grouped around Lin Biao and their subor-dinates within provincial administrations in 1971–72, followed by the transfer of entrenched regional commanders from their bailiwicks on the eve of 1974, the dominance of the People's Liberation Army within the CCP was somewhat attenuated. This demilitarization of the Party at the central and provincial levels left two coalitions of political groups in contention for political hegemony. The first consisted of veteran civil-ian cadres who looked to Zhou Enlai and increasingly, after his return to office in April 1973, to Deng Xiaoping to rehabilitate victims of the Cultural Revolution and normalize political life by restoring pre–Cul-tural Revolution administrative practices and decision-making processes.

The other group comprised the rump of the Cultural Revolution group—civilian radical mobilizers who had gained their power and positions by their active engagement in and leadership over the chaotic mass movement of the years 1966–1969.

In the fluctuating battle for ascendancy that characterized the last four years of the Maoist era, Mao Zedong tended to maintain somewhat of an Olympian aloofness. Ideologically and no doubt sentimentally he identified himself with the concerns expressed by the radicals that the reforms initiated in the CR merited preservation and continuation and that to dilute or abandon them would bring into question the wisdom of initiating the campaign. He also realized, and gave sporadic and cryptic expression to the thought, that practical policies and sound administration were also required. Experienced cadres and accommodating politicians would balance and check the ideologically pure guardians of CR values.

The veterans possessed far greater political resources than their rivals. They had experience, honor, and glory by association with the revolutionary history of the CCP; informal relationships and contacts; and institutional bases conferring authority right through the system. By contrast, their opponents were disadvantaged by their relative arriviste standing within the Party and by what Lowell Dittmer has described as the shallow and narrow nature of their political base.[1] Lacking the institutional means and secure bureaucratic foundation to propel their cause, the radical mobilizers were forced to resort to the tactics they had previously employed with some success between 1966 and 1968, that is, to reconstitute what remained of their 1960 mass constituency across the country in order to disrupt the endeavors of their enemies within the system to carry on orderly administration.[2]

Yet the political strategy and factional activities of this period were not merely a rerun of the events of the late 1960s. At the beginning of the Cultural Revolution, semi-autonomous mass organizations had sprung up across China. Although they were sensitive to and often dependent on signs of partiality from Beijing, these organizations were not subject to the tight, centralized discipline that had until then characterized the relationship between superior and subordinate within the political system. The leaders of the mass organizations in many cases had no prior active experience or institutional standing in this system. They were for the most part political novitiates and as such were treated with a mixture of condescension, wariness, and frightened stupefaction by their civilian and military cadre colleagues in the revolutionary committees established to share the political spoils.

By the mid-1970s these mass organizations for the main part no longer existed. But in the intervening period, those leaders and activists who had neither fallen victim to the savage purges conducted against so-called May 16 elements[3] nor been consigned to some far-flung spot in the *xia-xiang* (Down-to-the-village) movement initiated at the end of 1968 had matured and learned through experience a great deal about the working of institutions on which they had previously expended so much energy to destroy. Many had joined the CCP. Many, particularly in the reconstitution of the pre–Cultural Revolution mass organizations in 1973, had obtained semiexecutive positions to supplement their membership on revolutionary and Party committees.

Yet the circumstances surrounding their initiation into the system, the brevity of their tenure, and the continuing conflict and controversy that surrounded them at their posts all contributed to an ambivalence about the values and procedures that had become implicitly accepted by those who had previously occupied these positions. Additionally they maintained a strong attachment to and a belief in the validity of the central tenets of rebellion that had brought them onto the political stage. Although the mass organization had been disbanded, links and networks were maintained and developed. Relations that had been established with civilian cadres and military leaders served as useful protective devices when required. The remobilization of this powerful force in 1973 would result in serious consequences for the operation of political institutions and normal administration in at least one province in China.

This study contends that the mid-1970s witnessed the transformation and reemergence of these mass organizations and their leaders. It argues that they, on the one hand, continued to espouse and practice the political style displayed by mass mobilization rebels in the 1960s and, on the other hand, operated within the system from various institutional positions as disruptive spoilers and ambitious officeseekers. The study garners evidence from the eastern China province of Zhejiang to substantiate its case.

To my knowledge no comparable case study of any other province in China exists for this period. In fact, the early 1970s are a largely neglected area of research at the subnational level. Generalizations made about the period 1966–1968—based largely on conclusions drawn from Guangdong Province, which, with its proximity to Hong Kong and well-known history of aversion to central authority, may not reflect trends elsewhere in China—tend to be applied indiscriminately to the country as a whole and projected onto the later years of the Cultural Revolution. Any deviation from the Guangdong experience, then, tends to be dismissed as incorrect or lacking in substantiation. This chapter, and the larger study from which it is drawn,[4] make the case for a reappraisal of this period particularly in relation to the political influence exerted by worker and student rebel leaders in provincial affairs.

Because of the paucity of comparative studies, it is difficult to assess whether the events herein described were unique to Zhejiang or typical of trends in other provinces. Certainly the influence of nearby Shanghai, stronghold of the civilian radicals, was always potent in Zhejiang, as it must have been in other eastern provinces such as Jiangsu and Anhui. Further, Zhejiang had no comparable politician with the regional and national status of Xu Shiyou in Jiangsu to deflect or mitigate radical demands placed on the administration. Virtually the whole of its pre–Cultural Revolution leadership had been removed in 1967. The CR regime, led by junior field officers and commissars of field armies loyal to the Lin Biao–dominated central military organization, lacked both experience in administering civilian affairs and familiarity with local conditions. It also proved unable or unwilling to eradicate politically or physically mass organization leaders and activists, a course of action that provincial leaders elsewhere did not hesitate to adopt.[5]

Through an examination of the structure and linkages of the factional network in Zhejiang over the years 1963–1976, I point to the organizational strength and political clout of the radicals. Their ability to obtain and use official positions and officially sanctioned organizations to undermine and even eclipse the top provincial leaders is thereby highlighted. For the veteran cadres in Zhejiang, the attempts by the radical mobilizers and their supporters to launch a "second Cultural Revolution" in 1974 were to have consequences that, given the official constraints under which the rebels were operating, almost equaled those of 1967.

FACTIONALISM OF THE MID-1970S

During 1975 Deng Xiaoping, in his capacity as acting premier for the hospitalized Zhou Enlai and as overseer of the day-to-day running of the CCP Central Committee and Politburo, inspired and launched an open attack on bourgeois factionalism *(zichanjieji paixing)*,[6] the code name for his opponents, Wang Hongwen in particular.[7] Deng could not have opened this campaign without the tacit support of Mao, who, several times in 1974 and 1975 at meetings of the Politburo and directly to Wang Hongwen's face, criticized the "Shanghai Gang," or Gang of Four, for factional activities.[8] In a major programmatic document drawn up under Deng's direction, bourgeois factionalism was equated with capitalism and revisionism.[9] What did Deng and his supporters mean by the term, apart from using it as a weapon of abuse, and did they view this factionalism as being of a different kind than that of the years 1966–1968?

Deng partially, and somewhat cryptically, answered these questions in a speech of 4 July 1975. Addressing a study class in Beijing, he remarked, in a scathing indictment of bourgeois factionalism, that, "if we say that the two factions which appeared in the early stages of the Cultural Revolution were likewise formed naturally *(ziran xingcheng de)* [here Deng was using a historical analogy to refer to the formation of mountain strongholds as a result of scattered revolutionary base areas before 1949], then their continuation now would be of quite a different nature *(xingzhi jiu butong le)*"[10]

Leading provincial officials and local newspaper commentaries echoed Deng's sentiments in the following months. For example, Liao Zhiguo, first secretary of the Fujian Provincial Committee, stated in an August address to sportsmen in Fuzhou that bourgeois factionalism opposed Party leadership and served Lin Biao's revisionist line. In words that were most probably a direct repetition of Deng's, Liao stated that "it is no longer in the form of small groups as it first appeared during the great Cultural Revolution. In short, bourgeois factionalism has been essentially changed."[11]

Describing the struggle against bourgeois factionalism as a line struggle, Liao was thereby viewing it as an antagonistic contradiction that, by definition, demanded suppression by dictatorial means. By implication, then, the factionalism of mass organizations in the 1960s had been a matter of contradictions among the people to be handled by means of education and persuasion.

An ideological commentary from Heilongjiang in the same month stated that "the factionalism we are fighting against now is essentially different from that which formed spontaneously between the two mass organizations in the early stage of the great proletarian cultural revolution."[12] Those people "afflicted" with the "illness," including leading cadres and "leaders of various groups," demanded independence from the

Party while simultaneously fighting for leadership. Although most suf-
ferers of the disease fell into the category of nonantagonistic contradictions, they were warned to desist or face serious consequences. In graphic
words, bourgeois factionalism was portrayed as "an illness that is hard to
cure. Bourgeois factionalism is latent, changeable and obstinate in nature. If you retreat an inch . . . it demands a yard from you. Confronted
with criticism [it] steps back and lays low; after a certain period of time,
when the conditions are favorable, it may stage a comeback. 'Bourgeois
factionalism is a spring which yields only to power.' "

In Zhejiang a *Zhejiang Daily* editorial of 23 August 1975 detailed the
following features of bourgeois factionalism as they had appeared in the
province: [13]

• Establishing groups and mountain strongholds, recognizing factions and not the
Party, using factions to suppress the Party and stir up independence from it, setting
up many centers, riding roughshod over Party committees, weakening, breaking
away from, and opposing Party leadership;

• Differentiating between "legalist" *(fajia dang)* and "Confucian" *(rujia dang)* groups
within the Party and dividing the revolutionary ranks into "innovators" *(gexinpai)*
and "restorationists" *(fubipai)* to split the Party and the masses and sabotage stability
and unity;

• Drawing lines according to factions and preaching that "rebellion has merit,
joining the Party pays off" *(zaofan you gong, ru dang you fen)*, or "whoever goes against
the tide can join the Party and become a cadre," stirring up the bourgeois wind of
struggling for fame and advantage, exchanging flattery and favors, promising high
posts and other perks, thus creating various impurities within the Party's organization and cadre ranks;

• Preaching the view that at present the principal contradiction is "the contradiction between new and old cadres," "the contradiction between this and that faction,"
and advocating such strange theories as "You can't be wrong if you direct your attack
at the leadership";

• Sermonizing about relying on some "faction" and that "we must use revolutionary intellectuals to reform the cadre ranks"[14] to sabotage the Party's class line of
relying on the working class and uniting with other laboring people in the cities,
and in the country relying on the poor and lower-middle peasants and uniting with
middle peasants;

• Acting hypocritically by verbally expressing support for the Party's leadership
and the implementation of Party directives while behind the scenes spreading rumors
and slander, attacking and opposing the Party's leadership, resisting Party directives,
and pursuing a set of vulgar things in the manner of bourgeois politicians *(gao zichanjieji zhengke de na yitao yongsu de dongxi);*

• Advocating the reactionary fallacy of "Don't work for the wrong line," and
smearing those cadres and masses who persist in grasping revolution and production

as "lambs" *(xiao mianyang)* and "mediocrities who don't understand politics" *(bu wen zhengzhi de yongren)*;

* Shielding the class enemy, thus allowing capitalism to spread unchecked;
* And finally, and of particular note, bourgeois factionalism continues to operate surreptitiously in an attempt to block the implementation of the July directives of the central authorities.[15]

Certain Chinese leaders thus viewed the factionalism of the 1970s as being different in nature and in form from the factionalism of the 1960s. It was hinted that these new groups, rather than being spontaneous, were organized, directed, and even manipulated from above. What form they now assumed was not specified, but the blunt warnings to cadres and other individuals to desist illustrated the seriousness with which factionalism was viewed.[16]

Factionalism, pointed out other articles in the press, seemed to have afflicted industrial enterprises in particular. A *Fujian Daily* editorial of 13 July 1975 castigated attempts to establish factions within the working class as "a counter-revolutionary plot engineered by Lin Biao and company to split the Party and the revolutionary ranks."[17] The editorial differentiated between veteran workers, who, with their experience and longer exposure to Party education, were presumably less susceptible to the attraction of factional alignments, and their younger, less socialized, and more impressionable comrades. A lengthy article in *Zhejiang Daily* of 30 September 1975 described the impact of some of the manifestations of factionalism at the Hangzhou Silk Printing and Dyeing Complex, the largest mill in the city's textile industry.[18] Production had suffered badly over a prolonged period, and relations on the shop floor had become tense and antagonistic as workmates joined rival factions.

From these revealing articles we gain an impression, even allowing for hyperbole, of rampant factionalism operating both inside the Party and among the working class and posing a major threat to Party unity and industrial harmony. Reports from other provinces demonstrated that factionalism within the working class was a widespread phenomenon.[19] With the State Council and its subordinate departments drawing up a new five-year plan to commence in 1976, these signs of instability were disturbing indeed.

What Chinese leaders and publications were referring to when they described this mysterious new manifestation of factionalism requires further elaboration. Both contemporary observers[20] and analysts writing somewhat later noted the qualitative difference in the political approach, organizational capacities, and posture of the radical mobilizers during this time as compared with their activities five or so years previously. Frederick Teiwes, for one, has described the attempts made by the central radicals to place their followers in the bureaucracy, where they spied on their opponents, sabotaged directives, and set up their own secret communications network that operated outside the formal channels controlled by the "old guard."[21]

Dittmer has outlined the efforts by the radicals to pursue conventional techniques of constituency recruitment through the revival, in 1973, of pre–Cultural Revolution mass organizations such as the Trade Union Council, the Communist Youth League, and the Women's Federation, as well as the establishment of urban militia commands, independent of PLA control, in major cities. According to Dittmer, the failure of this endeavor caused the central radicals, by 1975, to adopt spoilers' tactics, similar to those outlined above by Teiwes. Additionally they attempted to revive and remobilize their mass constituency, which had been rusticated and dispersed in 1968–1969. Despite their apparent inability to make real inroads into formal executive positions, the radicals, in Dittmer's view, did manage to infiltrate followers into "staff or legislative positions throughout the hierarchy."

The radicals may have, in Dittmer's words, "continued to assume a public posture of principled opposition to the informal rules of exchange on which bureaucratic politics was based" and thereby harmed their prospects for advancement, but their actions, as detailed above, seem to suggest that they were not averse to manipulating the system for their own benefit. As Dittmer observes, factionalism spread down through the hierarchy as subordinate officials sought protection in informal groups connected to officials in superordinate positions.[22]

Yet, from a study of factional politics in Zhejiang for the years 1973–1976, it is clear that the radicals' actual power was greater than generalizations about national politics would suggest. They may not have obtained formal positions of authority within the provincial and municipal leaderships, but at a time when ad hoc bodies were set up regularly to direct political campaigns and remnant officially recognized mass organizations of the 1960s continued to operate, the locus of power was to some extent dispersed and in a state of flux. The informal nature of the political processes worked to the advantage of those who paid little heed to formal bureaucratic procedures or even to tacitly accepted rules.

In my view it was precisely these trends that prompted Deng and his colleagues to warn of the dangers of bourgeois factionalism. By 1973 the rebel mass leaders of the 1960s had matured politically and gained valuable experience for their forthcoming test of strength with Party authorities. They were no longer the "ignorant children" of 1966[23] who had rushed onto the streets to seize power. Their opponents, by contrast, although better prepared than they had been in 1966, suffered from the constraints that Mao's legitimation of rebellion had placed on their powers of suppression. The history of factional politics in Zhejiang from 1973 to 1976 illustrates the power that these rebel charismatics and their followers could acquire and exercise.

FACTIONALISM IN ZHEJIANG, 1973 TO 1976

Before embarking on a schematic analysis of the leadership, organizational structure, and linkages of factional networks in Zhejiang from 1973 to 1976,[24] a brief background chronology is in order. Between the Tenth CCP National Congress of August 1973 and the arrest of the Gang of Four three years later, Zhejiang experienced a period of great political and economic turbulence. During the anti–Lin Biao, Anti-Confucius campaign in the first half of 1974, power appeared to pass out of the hands of the provincial Party leadership and into the hands of worker and Red Guard rebel leaders who had been prominent in the upheavals of 1967–1969. The administration lost the initiative and was completely outwitted and outmaneuvered by the rebels, who utilized mass campaign tactics to humiliate the Party leaders in public and also exerted pressure behind the scenes in a series of unorthodox moves to induct supporters into the CCP and place them in key bureaucratic posts. Additionally they mobilized existing and newly formed officially sanctioned organizations to press their claims for recognition, status, and power. Provincial Party leaders could only watch helplessly as production stalled, social order deteriorated, and government became further factionalized and subsequently paralyzed.

In July 1974 the Central Committee acted to bring the anti–Lin Biao/ anti-Confucius campaign to an end before the economy suffered even greater damage. The Zhejiang authorities took considerable time to rein in the destructive activities of the rebels, but they had achieved some initial success by September. Yet the situation remained highly volatile, forcing Beijing to call both its representatives and the factional leaders in Zhejiang to a conference in the capital starting in November.

The reassertion of central control over Zhejiang, coupled with the backing for the provincial authorities against those who sought to overthrow it, dominated the political agenda for the next six months. While a series of provincial conferences was held on such subjects as industry,[25] and agriculture, these were overshadowed by yet another destabilizing national campaign on the study of the dictatorship of the proletariat and the leadership's efforts to grapple with the effects of factionalism.

It appears as if a decision to disband organizations used for factional purposes was taken early in 1975 so as to remove a major source of instability from the Zhejiang political scene. The peasant leader and Politburo member Chen Yonggui came to Hangzhou in April to address a provincial meeting on agriculture. In his speech Chen uttered some stern words about the dangers of continuing factionalism. However, normalization had clearly not returned when, at the end of June, the central leadership dispatched two senior members of the Politburo, Vice-Chairman Wang Hongwen and Ji Dengkui, to resolve matters. They brought with them a high-powered delegation from CC Organization Department and two central ministries.

After a three-week investigation the two central leaders decided on recommendations that were submitted to the Politburo. This body made three major decisions that were then relayed back to Zhejiang for implementation. First, a major reshuffle of the provincial and municipal Party leadership and of the military district was announced. Cadres who had been compromised by their involvement in factional disturbances were demoted or transferred. Replacements were brought in from other provinces to assume leading positions. The rebel leaders and their supporters were banished, sent to the countryside, or enrolled in study classes to review their mistakes and receive ideological and political reeducation.

Second, the central leadership decided on sending at least 10,000 soldiers of the three services into the factories of Hangzhou to pacify workers and supervise the resumption of normal production. Outside troops, uninvolved in the lengthy and bitter local squabbles, were brought in. This was probably the largest mobilization of troops in China to quell domestic violence since the famous Wuhan Incident of July 1967.

Third, the investigation of industrial problems in Hangzhou resulted in the propagation of an intensive emulation campaign. Known as the "Eight Factories' Experience," it set guidelines for the restoration of order in the factories and for the criticism and discipline of unruly workers.

But despite the compromises that the leadership in Beijing had made to rescue the authority of the Zhejiang leadership, the decisions of July 1975 contained the seeds of their own destruction. Military occupation of factories was only a short-term solution to the unrest, and the new leadership installed in Zhejiang was at best an interim group, comprised as it was of representatives of different factional groupings. When the Gang of Four launched its counterattack on Deng Xiaoping at the end of 1975, his supporters in Zhejiang came under renewed pressure. The correctness of the decisions made under Deng's aegis had therefore been questioned and openly challenged by the time Mao died in September 1976. Renewed factional upheavals in 1976 only ended with the arrest of the Gang of Four in October. Its followers in Zhejiang were dismissed and the rebel leaders arrested and jailed.

The origins of this chronic factionalism in Zhejiang appear to go back to 1969. In May of that year the two major mass organizations of the Cultural Revolution, the Zhejiang Provincial Revolutionary Rebel United Headquarters (Zhejiang Sheng Geming Zaofan Lianhe Zong Zhihuibu) and its bitter rival, the Red Storm Provisional Headquarters (Hongse Baodongpai Linshi Zhihuibu), known, respectively, as United Headquarters (Lianzong) and Red Storm (Hongbao), finally signed a "great alliance" and formally dissolved their organizations.[26] But evidently, although the organizations outwardly disbanded, some members of the United Headquarters continued to meet surreptitiously *(dao qi, pai bu san)* and formed a tight circle intent on pursuing the goal of "rebels becoming officials."[27] Undoubtedly, committed activists of Red Storm acted in similar fashion, although they had not previously enjoyed the patronage of the military leaders who formed the nucleus of the provincial revolutionary committee established in March 1968.

"Revolutionary leading cadres" who had gained posts in the revolutionary committees were expected to look favorably on the efforts of these former rebels to become officials. In return they would be excused from their previous commitments to their favored mass organizations. These commitments had extended as far as becoming members or backstage backers of rival groups. According to post-Mao newspaper articles, these steps signaled initial moves for the formation of an "underground command center" *(dixia zhihui zhongxin)* stationed in Hangzhou, which would both operate as a clandestine power base and, through the official positions its members held in legitimate organizations, seek to exercise control over these organizations in the interests of the faction. Thus the strategy of working both from within and outside officially recognized organizations was mapped out.

A chain of command linked Hangzhou with subordinate centers located in districts, municipalities, and counties and in industrial enterprises and educational institutions across Zhejiang. The command center allegedly maintained contact with the central radicals through a "secret liaison office" in Beijing. Wang Hongwen seems to have played a major role by linking up with certain individual members of the underground command center and encouraging and supporting their campaign to destabilize and ultimately overthrow the provincial authorities.

Wang appeared on the scene in Zhejiang in January 1973 to remobilize the Cultural Revolution mass organization leaders after they had experienced several years of relative political inactivity. In 1972, during the campaign to ferret out provincial supporters of the Lin Biao group, these former rebels had been held to account and punished for violent incidents that had taken place in 1967 and 1968. Wang's arrival heralded a favorable turn in their fortunes.

Mao Zedong had arranged for Wang to move from his base in Shanghai to the national arena in September 1972.[28] In December of that year Mao, at the urging of central radical theorists such as Zhang Chunqiao, had redefined Lin Biao as a rightist. Mao's decision, which uncoupled and protected the Cultural Revolution and its reforms in various spheres from its leading promoter and beneficiary, Lin Biao, put an abrupt end to Zhou Enlai's tentative moves to launch a systematic critique of ultraleftism.[29] Perhaps as one of the first assignments intended to groom him for future responsibilities, Wang was dispatched to Zhejiang in January 1973, probably to explain Mao's change of mind to bemused provincial officials.

During his stay in Hangzhou, Wang met two prominent leaders of the former United Headquarters organization, Zhang Yongsheng and Weng Senhe. He encouraged them to resume the struggle they had started in 1966–1967 and be prepared to withstand enormous pressure to attain their goals.[30] Wang's words undoubtedly emboldened the two men, who, secure in the knowledge that they had a powerful backer, launched a new phase in their political careers. In the following three years Wang was to intervene again at crucial times. He was evidently entrusted with formal responsibility for Party affairs in Zhejiang, if not in all of eastern China, especially after his elevation to the post of CCP vice-chairman in August

1973.[31] After Zhou Enlai's hospitalization in June 1974, Wang was placed in charge of the daily affairs of the Central Committee, as the Chairman further tested his abilities for a possible future succession.[32]

Zhang Chunqiao also took an interest in the affairs of Zhejiang and the career of Weng Senhe.[33] Not only was he a standing committee member of the Politburo, Zhang was also the senior Party official in Shanghai as well as the first political commissar of the Nanjing Military Region under whose jurisdiction the Zhejiang Provincial Military District (ZPMD) came. In fact Shanghai, as a major supplier of industrial and consumer goods, as a recipient of raw materials such as cotton, jute, silk, and fresh food, and as a large metropolis contiguous to Zhejiang, exercised a strong influence, both economically and politically, on the province. During the Cultural Revolution the rebels of Zhejiang had looked to Shanghai for inspiration and guidance.

With the promotion of the city, under the leadership of Zhang Chunqiao, Yao Wenyuan, and Wang Hongwen, as a bastion of radicalism and a constant reminder of the legitimacy and success of rebellion, the authorities in Zhejiang often looked there as much as to far-away Beijing for signs of political initiatives or changes in direction. One sign was the reopening in 1973 of the Zhejiang government office in Shanghai. Like its counterpart in the national capital, it had been closed in 1967, but the Beijing office was not reopened until 1981.[34] Presumably it was considered more important and politically more rewarding in Zhejiang to have a representative on the ground in the nearer metropolis.

In 1973 Shanghai took the lead in reconstituting its Trade Union Council (April) and Communist Youth League (February) and establishing an urban militia command (September) led by the municipal trade union (under Wang Hongwen) and directly responsible to the local Party authorities rather than to the PLA. The model that the Shanghai urban militia presented directly influenced the Zhejiang rebels when they established the Hangzhou command in February 1974. In September 1973 the Shanghai authorities also launched a new journal, *Study and Criticism,* based at Fudan University, to present their views on ideological, political, historical, economic, and policy issues that they could not necessarily publish in central journals such as *Red Flag.*

Nevertheless, there were countervailing pressures and influences on Zhejiang to those emanating from Shanghai. The commander of the Nanjing Military Region, Xu Shiyou, had personally taken charge of the removal of Lin Biao's followers within the Zhejiang hierarchy early in

1972.[35] He had also overseen the selection of replacements. They included Tie Ying, political commissar of Zhoushan Island troops, who in May 1972 became the second most senior Party, government, and military official in the province. Until his transfer to Guangzhou in December 1973, Xu provided strong support for the Zhejiang leadership. After Xu's departure from Nanjing, Tie and a deputy political commissar of the ZPMD who had been transferred to Zhejiang in December 1970 came under a concerted attack from the rebels for their association with him.

The quiescent Cultural Revolution mass organization, which Wang Hongwen had reactivated, possessed, according to accounts of its activities published in 1977–78, its own advisers, general staff, armed forces (the Hangzhou urban militia), publications, writing groups, school (the Zhejiang Workers' Political School, which opened in June 1974), intelligence network, underground printing facilities, and logistics groups. It divided its work into functional divisions such as organization, propaganda, urban and rural affairs, and electronic communications (*dianxun lianluo*). According to the article that detailed these operations, "This was a counter-revolutionary clique concealed in the revolutionary camp with a program, a line and an organization."[36]

The Hangzhou-based underground command center seems to have resembled Andrew Nathan's model of a complex faction that fastens onto officially sanctioned organizations and bureaucratic institutions, using them as a "trellis . . . to extend its own informal personal loyalties and relations."[37]

Its commander, a senior cadre of the CCP Hangzhou Municipal Committee (HMC), could pass on highly confidential information to the group and thus cause acute embarrassment to, and undercut the solidarity of, the provincial and municipal authorities. An example of such disloyalty occurred in November 1973 when this person leaked the contents of a telephone call from Wang Hongwen to Tan Qilong, first secretary of the CCP Zhejiang Provincial Committee (ZPC), in which Wang had requested that Tan and his colleagues make a self-criticism for their past mistreatment of and prejudice toward "rebel cadres." Tan's evident refusal was then disseminated as an act of subordination to "Vice-Chairman Wang."[38]

Another senior member of the CCP HMC, known within the committee, as the other agent (*daili ren*) of the Gang of Four, circulated part of a private conversation that he had conducted with Tan Qilong while on tour in Fuyang County in June 1972, which, taken out of context, suggested that Tan was denigrating the achievements in agriculture of the previous eighteen years.[39] These words were produced in November 1973 at a most untimely moment for Tan, when he was under great pressure from the remobilized rebels. In February 1974 the same "agent" played a major role in opening up a large department under the CCP HMC to youthful cadres who were nominated by the rebel supporters of Weng Senhe and Zhang Yongsheng.[40]

Additionally the underground command center maintained relations with the first and second secretaries of the CCP HMC. These two leaders either failed to resist factional assaults on Party authority or turned a blind eye to activities they probably preferred not to know were happening. In return they received the praise and gratitude of the rebel forces.[41] Given the extent of the reshuffle of the CCP HMC standing committee in July 1975, it is likely that other members had been seriously compromised by their own association with factionalism.

Within the ranks of the CCP ZPC leadership, "bourgeois factionalism" also cultivated supporters who reciprocated favors. Lai Keke and Luo Yi, whom Wang Hongwen appointed in 1976 to lead the ZPC during the campaign against the provincial supporters of Deng Xiaoping, were later denounced and vilified as agents of the Gang of Four. Late in 1973 Lai allegedly responded positively to Wang's exhortation to the Zhejiang leadership to support his slogan of "going against the tide." After Mao's death, Lai publicly threw in his lot with the central radicals by publishing a speech he had delivered at a meeting to repudiate Deng. Lai openly identified himself with the "proletarian revolutionary faction" and offered support for the "revolutionary rebels" who, he asserted, had suffered at the hands of the capitalist roader Deng. He rejected the criticism of bourgeois factionalism that the ZPC had conducted between August and October of 1975 and blamed the ZPC, or in effect Tan Qilong and Tie Ying, for the influence that the "revisionist line" had exerted in the province.[42]

Luo Yi was a newcomer to Zhejiang, having been transferred there from Shanghai in the leadership shake-up of July 1975. For the position that he adopted in the Cultural Revolution, Luo had secured praise from Zhang Chunqiao. Tangible manifestation of his standing was evidenced by his membership on the standing committee of the Shanghai Municipal Revolutionary Committee and his leadership of that body's culture and education group. After his promotion as deputy-secretary of the CCP

ZPC, he evidently provided Wang Hongwen with information regarding his superiors in Zhejiang and their relations with central political leaders. Later, in 1976, he criticized the persecution of rebels that had occurred as a result of the July 1975 decision and expressed understanding for the rebels' political aspirations. Luo was undoubtedly viewed as a stalking-horse for the central radicals and provided a sympathetic ear for the beleaguered local rebels.[43]

Another powerful member of the political elite in Zhejiang who associated himself with members of the command center was Shen Ce, head of the ZPC's political work group *(zhenggong zu)*, the powerful superdepartment that had replaced the pre–Cultural Revolution propaganda and organization departments. Shen had his hands on the levers of appointment. He used this authority to appoint Weng Senhe a member of the political work group and chairman of the office of the Mao Zedong Thought propaganda team *(gong xuan ban)*. Weng thereby seized the opportunities that arose to visit campuses where these teams were stationed and promote the rebels' cause.[44] Shen had sponsored Zhang Yongsheng's application to join the CCP and in 1974 appointed him Party secretary of Zhang's alma mater, the Zhejiang Fine Arts College. With his powers to dispense patronage, Shen was a most useful ally, and he allegedly assisted Weng Senhe in his plans to rush-recruit Party members and rush-appoint cadres in 1974, *(tuji ru dang, tuji ti gan* or *shuang tu*—"the two rushes"—for short).[45]

Shen was one of the members of the ZPC Standing Committee who was transferred or dismissed in the July 1975 shake-up. But the central radicals did not lose out altogether in these personnel arrangements. Lai Keke was promoted to full secretary of the ZPC and Luo Yi brought in from Shanghai as deputy-secretary. Kang Sheng's son Zhang Zishi, a prominent Shandong Cultural Revolution rebel, was also appointed to this body and, in addition, became first secretary of the Hangzhou Party Committee. The command center may have lost some of its contacts with and influence over the provincial and municipal leaderships and, temporarily at least, suffered a setback, but with Tan Qilong's semiretirement late in 1975, together with the disappearance of Tie Ying from the political scene, the faction's stocks rose again in 1976.

Evidence of factional alignment is more difficult to uncover concerning the Zhejiang Military District and main-force PLA units stationed in Zhejiang. What emerges from the available material, however, is evidence that, during the 1974 campaign against Lin Biao and Confucius, the ZPMD political commissars Tan Qilong, Tie Ying, and Xia Qi—especially the latter two—were singled out by the rebels for harsh treatment, including the application of physical pressure.[46] It is clear that the rebels felt keenly their lack of influence over the military. Weng Senhe, sensing the urgency of the need to rectify this situation, apparently stated, "We must knock them [PLA leaders] out with one blow and get power into our hands before they have time to come around."[47]

Evidence that troop involvement in factional activities did take place is provided by the transfer of the Twentieth Army from the province in April 1975.[48] It seems as if this unit, which had been dispatched to Zhejiang early in 1967 to "support the left," had become too compromised by its lengthy involvement in civilian politics to act as a reliable instrument when the military was ordered to occupy the factories of Hangzhou. The departure of the Twentieth Army coincided with the disappearance of several military members of the ZPC Standing Committee from the provincial scene. The leadership reshuffle of 1975 saw a reduction in military representation on this body from eight to three in an unambiguous expression of the desire to civilianize the provincial adminstration.[49]

The driving force within the underground command center was provided by three Cultural Revolution rebels, Zhang Yongsheng, Weng Senhe, and He Xianchun. They were known, respectively, as "the brains" *(bitou)*, "the mouthpiece" *(shetou)*, and "the muscle" *(quantou)* of the organization. Zhang's prominence as a Red Guard leader and his position as head of United Headquarters in the Cultural Revolution had led to his appointment as vice-chairman of the Zhejiang Provincial Revolutionary Committee (ZPRC) in 1968. Jiang Qing had granted him the honor of a personal reception in that same year, an occasion he commemorated in a written pledge *(juexin shu)* on the sixth anniversary in 1974. Zhang does not appear to have held any formal posts in addition to his Party position at the Fine Arts College other than that of responsible person in the provincial "revolution-in-education" group.

Wang Hongwen intervened in July 1975 to prevent the CCP ZPC from sending Zhang down to the countryside to undergo forced labor as punishment for his involvement in the tumultuous events of the previous eighteen months. Instead, he was sent far away to a model production brigade in Hebei Province. When a further radical upsurge commenced in 1976, Zhang was recalled first to Tianjin and then to Beijing, where he was received by Wang, Jiang Qing, and Zhang Chunqiao. For the next eight months until the arrest of the Gang of Four in October, Zhang conferred with visiting emissaries from Zhejiang and issued instructions to his followers back in Hangzhou.[50]

Of the rebel trio, it was Weng Senhe who appears to have had the most charisma and dynamism.[51] That he was arrested on the direct orders from Vice-Premier Ji Dengkui in July 1975, the worst fate that befell any of the rebel activists, indicates that the authorities greatly feared his capacity to cause trouble and the hold that he apparently maintained over large sections of the younger workers of Hangzhou. Hua Guofeng singled out Weng, together with the Liaoning "student" Zhang Tiesheng, for special mention as "new-born counter-revolutionaries" in the first major public speech he delivered after his assumption of power.[52]

Weng's operational base was the Hangzhou silk complex, where he held the post of revolutionary committee vice-chairman. Weng joined the CCP in 1970. In 1973 he was elected a vice-chairman of the Zhejiang Provincial Trade Union Council. Weng and his confederates Zhang and He toured factories in Hangzhou and other provincial cities late in 1973 to mobilize workers and recruit members for the urban militia Weng and He Xianchun would establish in 1974. Only about three years younger than Wang Hongwen, Weng may have noted with envy his fellow rebel's rise to national prominence and compared it unfavorably with the limited progress of his own career. He saw the campaign against Lin Biao and Confucius as an opportunity to rectify the situation. After hearing Zhang Chunqiao state that the rebels must not only fight but should hold power, Weng is said to have remarked that it "was like the ultimate pleasure gained from eating an icy-pole on a summer's day. I thought of holding power while walking, eating, attending meetings, and I even dreamt of it."[53]

Weng rewarded supporters for their loyalty by placing them in important posts. To use his colorful language, it was like a hen laying brood after brood of chickens.[54] Weng's closest confidant was Huang Yintang, a fellow employee at the silk complex, whom he had installed as the mill's Party secretary. In 1974 Huang gained the positions of deputy-director of the Hangzhou public security bureau, deputy Party secretary of the city's militia headquarters, and vice-chairman of the detective office (*zhenpo bangongshi*) established in April 1974 to coordinate criminal investigation work conducted jointly by the public security bureau and the militia. Weng placed another factional ally as first deputy Party secretary of the silk complex and then forced the secretary out of office. From his headquarters at the trade union's sanitorium on Three-Step Mountain (San tai shan) in the hills to the west of Hangzhou's West Lake, Weng directed a series of operations in 1974 that involved the mobilization of young worker militia onto the streets of the city to fight against his factional opponents.[55]

The third member of the triumvirate was He Xianchun, a former worker. During the Cultural Revolution, He had commanded a detachment of workers, soldiers, and security police known as the social security headquarters *(shehui zhian zhihuibu)*, which enforced order in conjunction with the PLA. In 1974, by virtue of his chairmanship of the Hangzhou Workers' Congress (Gongdaihui), he became commander of the city militia headquarters. He was also a vice-chairman of the Hangzhou Municipal Revolutionary Committee and of the Provincial Trade Union Council, along with Weng Senhe. It was the rebels' control of the Workers' Congress that gave them the authority to mobilize workers at official rallies that were held to launch the campaign against Lin Biao and Confucius. This organization was arguably the most powerful institutional base from which the underground command center could initiate its attempt to challenge the Party's hegemony over political life, while simultaneously striving to place its members in key Party posts. It is little wonder that Beijing ordered the closure of both the Workers' Congress and the militia headquarters in July 1975 as factional organizations.

He Xianchun worked closely with Xia Genfa, a worker rebel from the Hangzhou Oxygen Generator Plant, who became his deputy in the urban militia and was also appointed deputy leader of the HMC production command group in 1974. Like his two associates, Zhang and Weng, He was punished for his involvement in the events of 1973–1975 and sent to labor at a production brigade in Ningbo District. Unlike Zhang and Weng, however, He did return to a brief stint of active political life in Hangzhou, only to accompany Weng into jail after the arrest of the Gang of Four.[56]

During the 1974 campaign against Lin Biao and Confucius,[57] a small group *(shuangpi xiaozu)* was established to direct the movement. The names of the group's members were not published, but the provincial Party First Secretary Tan Qilong was group leader. A provincial deputy Party secretary, Hangzhou Party Committee Second Secretary Wang Xing, and Weng Seneh were deputy leaders, and He Xianchun a member, of this group. The importance of the organization, provisional in nature though it may have been, can hardly be overemphasized. It is claimed that Zhang Yongsheng personally chose the group's members.[58] Certainly, from February to July 1974, Zhang, Weng, and He gained prominence and public exposure at meetings held by the CCP ZPC and officially sanctioned mass organizations that their comparatively lowly ranking as provincial officials would not otherwise have justified. Tie Ying later claimed that the ultimate power of this group derived from the authority of Tan Qilong. He used a classical Chinese phrase from the period of the late Zhou dynasty to assert that the three rebel leaders had ordered the provincial leaders to obey their directives in the name of the captured emperor (xie tianzi yi ling zhuhou).[59] Their status in the campaign allowed Wang Hongwen to direct the ZPC leaders to admit their surely unwelcome presence at standing committee meetings of the provincial Party committee.[60] And while the official campaign gave the rebel leaders a public forum at which they could express their views and build up their public image, behind the scenes a prolonged and bitter struggle was unfolding at a four-month joint plenum of the ZPC, ZPRC, and ZPMD Party Committee (san quan hui). Here, Tie Ying and Xia Qi in particular were interrogated, as representatives of the PLA, for their part in suppressing the rebels in the wake of Lin Biao's fall. Truly the time for revenge had come, and Zhang, Weng, and He were determined to repay the military in full for their sufferings at its hands.[61]

It is difficult to estimate the size of the mass constituency that the rebels were able to mobilize at this time. The urban militia headquarters in Hangzhou commanded 50,000 militiamen in a city whose population numbered less than 1 million. Factories such as the Hangzhou Silk Printing and Dyeing Complex (although 65 percent of its 4,700 workers were female), Hangzhou Oxygen Generator Plant (5,000 employees in 1978), and Hangzhou Iron and Steel Works (12,619 employees in 1978) seem to have provided the core members. In return for their service the militiamen were given extra food rations, time off with pay, and escape from the drudgery of their working lives to drive around in trucks armed with steel clubs. At Weng's silk complex, membership of the militia was allegedly restricted to those workers who were not third-generation proletarians, did not belong to the CCP, and did not have a full work attendance record since 1966.[62] Whether these stipulatioins excluded any worker is debatable. Nevertheless, Weng did not want as members of the militia workers who were obedient to the Party, who were conscientious in their jobs, or who accepted the system's social and political norms. He preferred those who had less of a stake in the system and would therefore be less hesitant in flouting accepted principles of behavior.

This coalition of rebel leaders with their mass support, organizational bases, Party sympathizers, and advisers was known as the "On-the-Mountain" (Shenshang pai) faction. In late 1973 Zhang, Weng, and He had openly rebelled *(fan'an)* against the provincial leadership and occupied *(anying zhazhi)* Mount Pinfeng, site of the ZPC standing-committee meetings on the outskirts of Hangzhou. The 300 or so participants in the rebellion were all rewarded for their services and became prime candidates for the "two rushes."[63] This faction operated under orders from the clandestine underground command center.

Grouped against "bourgeois factionalism" was the "Foot-of-the-Mountain" (Shangxia pai) group,[64] which was apparently composed of ex-rebels of United Headquarters who had not joined the 1973 rebellion, as well as former opponents of Zhang, Weng, and He from Red Storm. It evidently gained control of the original factory-based militia structure that came under the leadership of the PLA. In 1974 the group utilized this organization as their fighting force to join battle with the urban militia.[65] One of the leaders of this Foot-of-the-Mountain faction was Guo Zhisong, a vice-chairman of the Provincial Trade Union Council and a worker at the Zhejiang Construction Company. Other redoubtable opponents of Weng and He from the industrial system included Zhang Jifa,[66] a demobilized soldier and Party cadre at the Iron and Steel Works who had important contacts in Beijing; Liang Maomao,[67] a group leader at the Oxygen Generator Plant; and Qiu Honggen,[68] a former activist in Red Storm who had refused to accept the "revolutionary great alliance" of 1969 and spent the following seven years, apart from 1973, in prison. The Hangzhou Gear-Box Plant, sited in Xiaoshan, a county town east of Hangzhou, proved a model unit in resisting the influence of "bourgeois factionalism",[69] while the iron and steel mill probably witnessed the most serious factional clashes among its work force.[70]

From the predictable silence on the subject, it is difficult to ascertain what links the anti-Weng faction maintained with Party leaders in the province. Undoubtedly they existed. In 1976 Zhang Tiancheng, a senior Party leader within the Zhejiang Bureau of Agriculture and Forestry, was hauled before a mass rally in Hangzhou with other people to face accusations connected with the Qingming festival disturbances.[71] The Zhang-

Weng-He faction apparently tried every means, including combing records kept by the military, to prove the undoubted links between Tie Ying and Xia Qi and between Xu Shiyou and Zhou Enlai.

While the power and influence of the rebel cadres in Zhejiang is not open to doubt, its limitations were apparent. While Zhang, Weng, and He, thanks to Wang Hongwen, acquired observer status at meetings of the ZPC standing committee, they were unable to convert it into membership in that body. The *pilin pikong* (anti–Lin Biao, anti-Confucius) small group and the *sanquanhui* (triple plenum) remained in existence only as long as the campaign they oversaw and were thus merely transitory bodies. Because of their blatant use for factional ends, both the militia headquarters and the Workers' Congress were dissolved by mid-1975. At the end of the day the rebels, heavily reliant for their success on patron support and the opportunities provided by mobilization politics, could not sustain their assault on the provincial leadership and were forced to yield.

The detailed evidence assembled in this study points to the gradual evolution after 1969, in particular, of a series of clientelist ties[72] in Zhejiang that, taken in their totality, combined to create a powerful and dangerous threat to the provincial administration. Given impetus and direction from above by Wang Hongwen, the factional setup spread its tentacles into the bureaucratic structure and formal organizations across the province. While Nathan's model as a whole does not apply to Zhejiang, certain aspects of it help throw light on the structure and behavior of factionalism in Zhejiang in the period under discussion. The flexibility that Nathan attributes to factions was certainly evident in Zhejiang. For example, early in 1974 He Xianchun's militia encircled a group of its opponents in two downtown hostels in Hangzhou. Sympathetic leading cadres in the municipal administration ordered the besieged to surrender, factional members at the telephone exchange blocked all lines out of the buildings to isolate those inside, and the militia then stormed the hostels.

The difficulties in communications that Nathan believes characterize relations between members of factions were largely overcome by the formal organizational features of the underground command center and the high public profile of its leaders. Certainly the rebel faction in Zhejiang proved capable of intermittent but persistent functioning. The dissolution of the Workers' Congress and militia headquarters in 1975 seriously curtailed its activities. Yet in 1976 activities were resumed, although, as Dittmer has written of this period,[73] mass apathy and membership disillusionment had set in, which contributed to the decline of the group. The principal reason was, according to Nathan, the loss of key leaders. The "bourgeois faction" of Zhejiang seemed to have several leaders of roughly equal standing. Their removal and dispersal in July 1975 was a body blow to its existence. Even Zhang Yongsheng, installed in a guest house in Beijing, could only fulminate against his opponents and try to rally the sagging morale of his followers.[74]

The desperation with which the faction pursued all avenues to secure Weng Senhe's release is further evidence of the threat to the faction's continued functioning that his loss represented. Wang Hongwen had hoped to placate the antagonism that provincial and central leaders clearly felt toward Weng by excusing his behavior on the grounds of inexperience. Then, after Weng's arrest, Wang lamented the fall of his "old comrade-in-arms" and tried to dissociate himself from responsibility for Weng's fate.[75] In March 1976 Weng's wife wrote to the ZPC asking it to review her husband's case. Lai Keke and Luo Yi evidently procrastinated. They were very aware of the high passions that Weng's name evoked in Zhejiang.[76]

Nathan[77] groups fifteen characteristics of factional politics under three sets of propositions concerning the modes of conflict within such a system, the clientelist basis of factions, and the system's relationship to the general political environment. Of these, several relate directly to Zhejiang in the years 1973–1976. First, there may have been a "code of civility" that circumscribed the severity of the punishment meted out to Party cadres implicated in the upheavals of 1973–1975. No such code applied to rebel cadres such as Weng Senhe or, arguably, Zhang Yongsheng and He Xianchun. The harshness of their penalties related precisely to the fact, as Nathan has pointed out in his propositions 1 and 12, that these men were perceived as threats to the factional system itself. The rebel trio ignored, or treated with impunity, the rules of conflict; they blatantly flouted Party statutes concerning the admission of new CCP members; they disdainfully broke codes of convention regarding the appointment and promotion of cadres. They published an open letter of rebellion against the provincial authorities and could thus be treated more like counterrevolutionary criminals than political deviants. Even Wang Hongwen was forced to accept Weng's arrest, and Zhang Chunqiao admitted in February 1976, while offering extenuating circumstances, that Weng had committed grave mistakes. This important factor lay at the heart of the case against Weng and his colleagues. They had committed assaults on the political system while at the same time attempting to seize control over its key institutions from within. More gravely, they had defied orders from Beijing to discontinue such activities.

Three other characteristics of factional politics relate to the consensus form of decision making within the system. To settle the "problem of Zhejiang" required a series of meetings and the application of a great deal of pressure to arrive at a consensus in Beijing in July 1975. The decision arrived at by the central authorities reflected this compromise.[78] The personnel arrangements did likewise.[79] Nathan's cycle of consensus formation and decline was apparent in the maneuvers that lasted from late 1974 (crisis) to July 1975 (action) and into the next cycle of conflict (December 1975 onward). Wang Hongwen, in his efforts to break with the consensus of July, was hampered by the fact that he had been one of its principal mediators during his mission to Hangzhou with Ji Dengkui. Although Zhou Enlai and Deng Xiaoping had most probably masterminded the intervention, Wang was cleverly locked into a firm commitment to it.

A final point relating to factionalism in Zhejiang between 1973 and 1976 derives from observations made by Tang Tsou[80] about the relationship of formal organizations and political institutions to informal groups. In Tsou's view the former bodies, to the extent of their size and legitimacy, can positively constrain the activities of the latter. Conversely, the size and capability of informal groups can undermine the constraint exercised by formal structures. Zhejiang in the years 1973–1976 provides a good example of weak and discredited structures and institutions attempting, with little success, to exercise authority over strong and high-risk-taking informal groups. Even subordinate formal organizations seemed to treat directives from superior bodies with disdain.

The Zhejiang provincial administration survived the intense factional struggles of the mid-1970s, but the legacy, as became apparent once again in the 1984 campaign to repudiate the Cultural Revolution,[81] has remained. In the intervening period the vast majority of the principal participants have departed the political stage. In 1984 Weng Senhe and Zhang Yongsheng were sentenced to permanent internal exile on a labor farm in Qinghai. Because of his advancing years, Weng was brought back to Zhejiang in 1988 to continue his sentence at a prison in the south of the province. He Xianchun committed suicide in prison in 1977.[82] It is debatable whether the province will see the likes of the rebel trio again. The vast majority of its citizens would probably hope not. Yet it is uncertain that the social grievances and political dissatisfaction that the rebels in their own way reflected and gave vent to will not one day burst forth and produce spokesmen who will again act in ways that unsettle the status quo.

Several more general concluding remarks deserve mention. This study has attempted to show that the factionalism of the period 1973–1976 in Zhejiang possessed structural features and behavioral patterns that set it apart from manifestations of the Cultural Revolution proper. One striking phenomenon was the dual tactics employed by the three rebel cadres. They fastened onto the phrase "going against the tide" the 1960s slogan "It is right to rebel" to express this feeling of rebellion against authority. Additionally these ex–Red Guards and worker rebels had accumulated a certain amount of valuable experience in the political ring, where the ability to parry, feint, and deliver knockouts was continually tested. They had displayed an unusual aptitude for building up their organizational strength even if it was achieved by unorthodox means. They had paralyzed the local administration and effectively neutralized its leadership for months on end.[83] Finally, they had demonstrated a talent for mobilizing mass support from among certain sections of the urban population to threaten action if the local authorities did not cave in to their ultimatums.

Zhejiang was not alone in the appearance of virulent factionalism. The comments and speeches from various provinces in 1975 cited earlier attest to the prevalence of "bourgeois factionalism" at that time. Deng Xiaoping likewise took up the issue as a major theme in speeches he delivered during the year.[84] Alan Liu has claimed that the central radicals established clientelist relations with first Party secretaries in such provinces as Henan, who in turn cultivated a series of such ties down through various levels of administration.[85] Although Wang Hongwen was apparently unable to recruit Zhejiang First Secretary Tan Qilong to the radicals' camp, it was not for want of trying. Tan's disappearance from Hangzhou after September 1975 perhaps indicates his determination to escape the pressure that both Wang Hongwen and Deng Xiaoping were applying to force him to choose sides.

In contrast to Yunnan Province, where local officials were evidently able to exercise a certain degree of autonomy from central affairs,[86] Zhejiang is located in the geographic heartland of Chinese polity and economy. Despite examples of local recalcitrance toward central directives, especially by the less politically socialized rebel leaders, Beijing could not afford prolonged disruption and lack of discipline in the province. Leaders of all central factions apparently concurred on this score. The dispatch of over 10,000 troops into the factories of Hangzhou in July–August 1975 served to convey the message in stark simplicity.

Although there were suggestions in 1974 that a "second Cultural Revolution" was about to erupt, and certain aspects of the campaign of that year conjured up images of 1966–1968, the elements of idealism that characterized the earlier period seemed almost entirely absent. Whereas in 1966 students rebelled against powerholders partly at least for class-based socioeconomic reasons, the revolt of 1973 in Hangzhou was a blatant grab for power. Radical slogans of dissent had turned into ritualistic clichés. Loyalty to the Chairman and his vision of continuous revolution provided a veneer to disguise promotion of self-interest. Responsibility for this tragic perversion lies chiefly with those who ensured that the mass organizations of the 1960s, denied their legitimate role in the political structure after 1968, were transformed into clientelist factional groups better able to fasten onto and become enmeshed in the political system of the 1970s. Weng and his colleagues proved capable performers in this endeavor, but at the cost of most of the values that had initially impelled them into the political arena.

PART TWO

Economics

Neither Plan nor Market: Mao's Political Economy

CARL RISKIN

China's economic performance during the Cultural Revolution decade is often attributed, for better or worse, to the policies advanced by Mao Zedong. The main features of this performance, summarized in Table 1, are by now well known: rapid growth of industry (after a faltering beginning) and of population, mediocre growth of agriculture, and stagnant consumption and productivity.[1]

This performance, however, was largely the product of the political stalemate that characterized the Chinese leadership for much of this period. Neither its details nor even its contours can be explained by appealing to China's growth strategy, whether Maoist or other, because one could hardly have been said to exist, aside from the very special Third Front strategy discussed by Barry Naughton in this volume (Chapter 7). The policies and practices of the era were an uneasy and even accidental compromise between the preferences of sharply contending factions. Al-

TABLE 1 Indicators of Economic Growth, 1965–1975

Indicator	1965	1975	Averge Annual Growth Rate (%)
Population (millions)	725.4	919.7	2.4
GNP (index)	100	191	6.5
GNP per capita (index)	100	151	4.1
Gross value of industrial output (index)	100	269	10.4
Gross value of agricultural output (index)	100	148	4.0
Consumption per capita			
Current yuan	125	158	2.4
Index	100	124	2.2
—of agricultural population			
Current yuan	100	124	2.2
Index	100	123	2.1
—of nonagricultural population			
Current yuan	237	324	3.2
Index	100	133	2.9
Grain output (millions of metric tons)	194	284	3.7
Grain output per capita (kilograms)	267	309	1.1

Source: Carl Riskin, China's Political Economy: The Quest for Development since 1949 (New York, Oxford University Press, 1987), p. 185.

Notes: Indexes are calculated in constant prices. Growth rates for GNP, GNP per capita, grain output, and grain output per capita are estimated by regression; others from endpoints.

though this became crystal clear in 1976, many nevertheless persist in treating the economics of the pre-1976 period as if it had emerged from a homogeneous set of policies and a unified politics. In reality the leadership of the first half of the 1970s can be likened to an imaginary U.S. coalition of Milton Friedman and Michael Harrington, from which no coherent policy could emerge.

Nevertheless, one of the players in this stalemated contest was a radical political economy developed out of Mao's thought and promoted by his supporters. It made itself felt in certain concrete policies and just as much in its effective opposition to alternative ones. As China's development path converges on more conventional roads, it is of interest to reexamine this approach. It was a kind of shoehorn for getting a precapitalist foot into a socialist shoe. The Soviet way was manifestly unsuited to China, and "market socialism" was a heretical idea still confined to Yugoslavia. If one tries to imagine a socialist road that avoids both Soviet-type centralization and market society, then something like Maoism logically comes to mind. This chapter expands upon reflections on the etiology and fate of this approach in my economic history of the PRC.[2]

The common foundation of Maoist policies was the conviction that the social and political relations among people were the arena in which the rate of progress toward the goals of economic development and the advance of socialism would be determined. Unlike most observers in the West and many in China, Mao thought that "socialist transformation" of the relations of production would stimulate rapid economic development by mobilizing the population and promoting what Western economic theory calls "x-efficiency." He saw human initiative as the key to success in all great endeavors; therefore the conditions arousing greatest initiative were those that promised greatest success.

Both his critique of Soviet experience and his observation of events in China since 1949 convinced Mao that inertial forces threatened to halt progress toward a more equitable society, to abort the revolution, and to lead to "capitalist restoration." Beginning in the mid-1950s he began resisting in various ways the concentration of political and economic authority at the center; the growth of an urban privileged elite of officials and technocrats; the concomitant stifling of mass participation and initiative, especially of the rural population; and the spread of bureaucratism, reinforced by long cultural tradition and complementary Leninist principles of Party organization.

Mao's response aimed to reduce the Three Great Differences (between city and countryside, worker and peasant, and mental and manual labor) by reducing the size and role of functional bureaucracies, decentralizing economic initiative, and promoting mass campaigns under central ideological guidance. His principal contributions to the policies of the Cultural Revolution decade are understandable in these terms.

For some part of this period rural industries were built, farmland terraced and irrigated, cooperative medical insurance plans established, and other endeavors accomplished by the human initiative Mao's policies sought to arouse. Interpersonal income gaps were also reduced, and health and education resources redistributed to the countryside. Workers briefly participated in management of industrial plants and for a longer time cadres had to perform manual labor; the shield of automatic authority wielded by officials was pierced, and ordinary people could put up *dazibao* (wall posters) criticizing local cadres or national leaders.

On the whole, however, the condition in which China emerged from two decades of struggle strayed far from these principles. Savage factional conflict had generated a fear antithetical to popular intiative, while the power of arbitrary intervention by leading Party-state officials was greater than ever, not being subject to restraint by law (always a weak reed in China), by custom (now discredited as part of the reactionary past), or by mass movements (now either suppressed or carefully controlled by one faction or another).

In addition, living standards stagnated while capital accumulation rates knew no limits. Workers, made cynical by years of contradiction between rhetoric and practice and by the failure of wages to rise, emerged more money-conscious than ever. The coloring of virtually all policy questions with heavy political meaning led to a ubiquitous fear of making decisions, with the result that all the classic manifestations of bureaucratism—buck-passing, delay, and avoidance of responsibility—became the norm. At the same time, the central planning system increasingly malfunctioned: useless goods were produced and piled up in warehouses, while things that were acutely needed were not produced at all or produced in inadequate quantities. Economic sectors advanced or not under their own momentum, in accordance with their administrative command over resources and with little relation to their links with other sectors. The quality of planning progressively deteriorated under the ideological assault of the antibureaucratic agenda and the political attacks on many of the planners. Allocative decisions became arbitrary, unpredictable, and subjective, forcing individual enterprises and localities to take various defensive measures (such as hoarding) that were irrational from the larger, social perspective.

To understand these perverse results requires understanding both the Maoist objectives themselves and the circumstances in which they were pursued, which together produced the crippled hybrid that was the political economy of the Cultural Revolution period.

This chapter discusses the development of a key element in Mao's economic approach—administrative decentralization—in the events leading up to the Cultural Revolution. It also deals with self-reliance, the core of the Maoist principle of resource allocation; egalitarianism, the distinctive Maoist distributive principle; and, briefly in conclusion, the distorted and malfunctioning political economy that emerged from Maoism's relations with central planning.

ADMINISTRATIVE DECENTRALIZATION

Central command planning revealed its weakness in China from the mid-1950s, when the government essentially took over what remained of the private sector in industry and commerce and then faced increasing difficulty in exercising effective control from the center over a widely dispersed and ever larger and more complex economy. In agriculture, retarded growth after the recovery of the early 1950s and the unanticipated complexities of gradual cooperativization threatened the success of the First Five-Year Plan and called into question its strategy of rapid heavy industrialization.

Mao analyzed these problems in terms of a series of contradictions, the core of which was the Party's use of its monopoly of political power to *administer* the economy by means of a central bureaucracy. Two broad options existed for reducing centralized political power over the economy. The first was to expand the authority of individual enterprises at the expense of government administrative organs, whether central or local. This choice would entail an enhanced role for the market. At the beginning of the period in question, only renegade Yugoslavia was pursuing such a "market-socialist" path.

The second option, which Mao favored, was to pass much control of economic matters down to lower administrative levels. These would run relatively comprehensive and self-sufficient local economies with a minimum of supraregional linkages requiring a central coordinative bureaucracy. Such an approach called for the establishment of trustworthy local public institutions that could exercise effective leadership. The original agricultural collectives, which Mao prodded into existence in July 1955, and the rural communes that followed them three years later in the Great Leap Forward, were to be such institutions.

Consistent with the administrative decentralization approach, the Great Leap rejected the model of central planning in two basic ways. First, it substituted locally initiated mass economic activity for the detailed blueprints worked out by professional planners. Second, it gave great economic and political authority to local and regional units—the communes and the provinces, respectively.

Mao's idea was to centralize control only of major macroeconomic variables and of the large-scale modern "backbone" industries. Other activities would be the responsibility of the regions and localities, using technologies appropriate to their sizes and resource bases and adopting the policy of "self-reliance." A principal theme of the 1960s and early 1970s, self-reliance was supposed to relieve the center of investment responsibilities outside the modern, large-scale sector; stimulate the full exploitation of locally available resources; and provide a clear link between a region's development and its own efforts as a kind of collective incentive to spur local development.

With respect to the lagging agricultural sector, Mao advocated local self-reliance to provide farmers with both incentives and means to raise yields and output rapidly. He saw it as an alternative to either centralized extraction of farm surplus ("draining the pond to catch the fish") or the use of pecuniary incentives. Under the auspices of the communes, rural industries were to spread rapidly over the country and take on the mission of upgrading and modernizing farm technology. Initial surpluses for supporting this diversification were to be produced by herculean efforts by the farmers in intensive cultivation and in the construction of dams, reservoirs, and irrigation and drainage canals.

The characteristic features of the Great Leap are consistent with the logic of Mao's solution to the problems of bureaucratism and administrative overcentralization: the establishment of quasi-autonomous localities with power to allocate resources and distribute income according to broad criteria enunciated from the center and worked out in consultation with lower levels (the "mass line"). Thus the strategy of "walking on two legs" reserved for the control center of large-scale modern industries, especially those with substantial forward linkage, while ceding other industries to provincial or local control. The communes were to be institutions of local governance with sufficient size and resource-mobilizing power to make local efforts productive, but also large (and few) enough to be effective channels of communication from the center to the peasants. In its extraordinary labor-intensive efforts, the Great Leap sought to capitalize on the one resource in abundant local supply.

One particularly noticeable feature of economic decision making during the Cultural Revolution was introduced in the Great Leap: its extreme politicization. By this I mean three things specifically: first, the extensive use of general criteria of choice (for example, that industry should support agriculture, that each locality should strive to build up a comprehensive and relatively independent industrial system, and that rural incomes should be distributed basically according to work done and secondarily on a per capita "supply" basis), passed down from the central Party and government organs as general directives; second, that these and other guidelines for choice were expressed in slogan form ("Walk on two legs," "Both red and expert," "Get going with local methods"); and third, that ideological polarities (self-reliance versus slavish compradore philosophy, socialist road versus capitalist road, and the like) came to be substituted for objective technical or economic standards of choice.[3]

These characteristics of "politicization" follow directly from Mao's response to the problem of bureaucratization. Rejecting both centralized commands and the apolitical market, Mao needed a means of aligning the quasi-autonomous decisions of provinces, municipalities, counties, and communes with the broad directions mapped by the center. This essentially coordinative role was to be played by ideology, stripped to a bare and functional form characterized by the broadcast of simple directions that could be grasped in their essence by everyone, yet were general enough to be adapted to local circumstances.

But ideology is a blunt instrument. Inevitably its use in this way caused disagreements about economics to be translated into ideological differences, and matters of degree to be seen as matters of kind. The need to use ideology to obtain compliance gave the Maoist program a quality of messianic irrationality that not only produced major disasters but also finally compromised its own credibility. The *political* weaknesses and failures of this program, in retrospect, like its economic ones, can be traced to its own logic as much as to the intractability of the social conditions in which it was tried.

During the years between the collapse of the Great Leap and the beginning of the Cultural Revolution, another approach, already discussed in intellectual circles in the mid-1950s, was resurrected to challenge the central command economy: a limited market-socialism option. Propounded most eloquently by the economist Sun Yefang (1908–1983), it made its bid for recognition in the vacuum left by the post-Leap erosion of rural collectivism. Mao opposed this path as much as he did the one it sought to reform, but for different reasons: market socialism exalted bourgeois values—individualism, inequality, competition, and profit orientation—over their socialist (and nationalist) opposites—cooperation, egalitarianism, solidarity, and patriotism.

SELF-RELIANCE

Self-reliance was the default response to a lacuna in Mao's economic thought, namely, the lack of a solution to the problem of macroeconomic coordination. He wanted to simplify and deprofessionalize administrative macroplanning, but unless China was to become a confederation of self-sufficient communities, this would require a corresponding strengthening of market institutions to take over the myriad allocative decisions no longer to be handled by plan. To strengthen the market, however, seemed to contradict the goal of socialist transformation. Indeed many, if not most, policies associated with late Maoism were conscious rejections of the allocative and distributional trends that a relatively unfettered market would have produced with Chinese relative factor endowments and political institutions. (The 1975 campaign to "limit bourgeois right," for instance, is a particularly clear example.) But this left virtually no coordinative principle at all.

With neither market nor central planners to coordinate the economy, there was no choice but to try to minimize the need for coordination. This is the structural basis of self-reliance, the sine qua non of Cultural Revolution economic policy. To the question of how to allocate resources nonbureaucratically and without a market, self-reliance posed the negative answer: Let each locality, region, or enterprise rely as much as possible on its own resources. This was the theory, if not always the practice.

Self-reliance as an economic-development posture stressed the following: (1) utilization of all available resources, including labor and skills; (2) reliance on local experience in preference to imitating outsiders' methods; (3) exclusive use of local saving to finance capital accumulation; and (4) establishment of a comprehensive industrial system. These principles were to apply to all levels of society; thus individual provinces and even counties were at times urged to establish "independent and comprehensive industrial systems" as well as to rely on their own resources, capital, and experience—the latter an injunction that appears often to have been honored in the breach (see Christine Wong's contribution to this volume).

Regions and Localities

As a principle of local initiative and independence, self-reliance is unobjectionable. It is as a principle of resource allocation, where it amounted to a commitment to import substitution, that the term is ambiguous and problematic. There are two broad rationales for a strategy of import substitution to stimulate the development of a comprehensive industrial system. One is military-strategic: to build an industrial capacity in order to enhance military power. Ordinarily this applies to a nation as a whole, not to regions and localities.[4] The second rationale, which refers as well to "regions, communes, and enterprises," has to do with learning and motivation. However large a region's static comparative advantage in agriculture or extractive industries may be, its prospects for harnessing science and technology and achieving long-term economic development depend on mastering "the tricks of manufacture." From this perspective, as Thomas G. Rawski points out, the rationale for self-reliance

lies in the widely shared conviction that excessive division of labor masks hidden technical potentials. The obvious short-term costs of trade restriction may be smaller than the long-run gains obtainable from exploiting these unsuspected capabilities. The resulting strategy is one of planned and partial truncation of commodity exchange designed to force regions, communes, and enterprises to muster latent skills in planning and administration and to foster the growth of problem-solving capabilities that come only from sustained grappling with technical difficulties.[5]

Examined more closely, however, this rationale is satisfied by the promotion of *some* local activities with relatively advanced and demanding technologies. It does not require extensive vertical integration or "comprehensive and independent" local economies. Post-Mao Chinese discussions have concluded that attempts to implement the latter policies resulted in great inefficiency from duplication, inadequate division of labor and specialization, and sacrificed economies of scale.

Why then did Mao push "comprehensive and independent" economies for regions, localities, and even enterprises? As already suggested, the resource-allocative dimension of self-reliance was the Maoist answer to the problem of allocation *sans* market or planning bureaucracy. Its purpose was to simplify coordinative requirements in the economy by localizing allocation decisions and minimizing external links, so that residual planning functions could be carried out by a smaller, less articulated, and more politically controllable bureaucracy. If self-reliance at the national level was a way of opting out of dependence on the world market, at the subnational level it was a *substitute* for either a domestic market or administrative planning. With bureaucracies reduced in role and size and the external links of localities and enterprises simplified, changes in management, incentives, distribution, and other aspects of "production relations" could proceed within each production unit or local area with few external constraints.[6]

This interpretation of Mao's objective in promoting independent and comprehensive development at various subnational levels is buttressed by Mao's explicit comments about the Soviet textbook *Political Economy*. Rejecting the text's advocacy of division of labor among socialist countries, Mao comments:

> This is not a good idea. We do not suggest this even with respect to our own provinces. We advocate all-round development and do not think that each province need not produce goods which other provinces could supply. We want the various provinces to develop a variety of production to the fullest extent. . . . The correct method is each doing the utmost for itself as a means toward self-reliance for new growth, working independently to the greatest possible extent, making a principle of not relying on others.[7]

Mao goes on to explain this seemingly irrational view by arguing that the maintenance of centuries of political unity exacted a price in the form of bureaucratism, "under the stifling control of which local regions could not develop independently, and with everyone temporizing, economic development was very slow." It was thus China's long bureaucratic tradition, which had not vanished with the Communist victory, that provided a basic rationale for Mao's views on decentralized self-reliance.

Some notable success stories were produced by self-reliance at the county level and below, where vigorous and innovative local leaderships seized the opportunity to carry out development projects that raised local productivity and income. In such cases Mao's conviction was borne out that development depends more on the effective release of human energies ("x-efficiency") than on the efficient allocation of fixed supplies of resources.

In general, however, appropriate institutions and political conditions proved difficult to identify and establish, and self-reliance raised as many problems as it solved. At what level should it be achieved? How much self-sufficiency did it imply? How should it be combined with "socialist cooperation" between enterprises and localities, so as to capture economies of comparative advantage and specialization? How to avoid conflicts between local investment and national priorities, the duplication of existing facilities with excess capacity, or competition for raw materials with more efficient, large-scale plants?

Perhaps most fundamentally, self-reliance did nothing to correct the inherent weaknesses of administrative planning—especially its lack of mechanisms for motivating efficient and innovative performance. Only at the lowest levels—perhaps that of the village (brigade)—might the link between self-reliant production and community income be direct enough to provide such motivation. At higher levels it was apt to be a case of arbitrary decisions made not by central bureaucrats but rather by local and provincial ones, who possessed even less planning skill. The rigidity of administrative planning was thus compounded by various geographic and sectoral imbalances, and the resulting disarray, to which the campaigns and disruptions of the Cultural Revolution and subsequent years contributed, called for the corrective of renewed centralization. At such times the national leadership, including Mao, always opted for stronger *adminstrative* centralization. In this way the famous "recurring cycle" was generated, in which "centralization leads to rigidity, rigidity leads to complaints, complaints lead to decentralization, decentralization leads to disorder, and disorder leads back to centralization."[8]

By the 1970s, however, centralization had lost much of its restorative capacity. The quality of central planning, never high in China, declined perceptibly and was marked by numerous errors. While the full story of the sharp technical regress in planning remains to be told, the main factor must have been the mutual incompatibility of central administrative planning and Maoist ideology. The former requires complete and detailed reporting of data from the basic level to the center; a stratified chain of command to ensure local compliance with central decisions; and a large corps of technicians at the center. It assigns most important decisions to the center and gives an essentially passive and subservient role to the direct producers and the localities.

Cultural Revolution ideology, on the other hand, called for a much reduced and simplified planning bureaucracy; decision-making power vested in localities; and participative reforms in management that eliminated or reduced special staff departments for collecting, processing, and transmitting data. The locality and enterprise were to be dynamic, innovative, socially experimental bodies. Mao referred to the factory as a "university." These values, repeatedly promoted by Mao until his death, survived the Cultural Revolution proper and ruled out effective central administrative planning. At the same time, the periodic interventions by the center to impose order prevented genuine implementation of the ideology and subverted its intent; the heavy hand of the Party, the army, or the bureaucracy came in fact to run the enterprise revolutionary committees, dictate sowing plans to the nominally independent and self-reliant production teams, and thrust "socialist cooperation" ahead of "self-reliance" in rural counties. With radical principles undermined by ad hoc interference from above but still strong enough to deter a true central-planning regime, China by the mid-1970s had arrived at the worst of both worlds.

Enterprises

In factories, self-reliance gave rise to the "comprehensive" production unit that made for itself a large part of the materials and intermediate goods needed to turn out its main product line. Each enterprise would be located at the appropriate administrative level, under the leadership of the relevant Party and government organ, and thus be responsive to the demands of its locality or region. Interenterprise links that would compromise self-reliance and remove decision-making authority from the enterprise's local political patron would be reduced in number and importance by making each enterprise "comprehensive," that is, capable of "diversified undertakings and multiple utilization" and able to produce its own materials and intermediate goods. This of course would also give the factory greater flexibility in adapting to unforeseen contingencies and is quite in keeping with common practice in rigid and unresponsive central-planning systems that in other respects diverge sharply from the Maoist ideal.

In sum, an industrial system in which (1) a maximum amount of activity is subsumed within individual production units, (2) interenterprise relations are simplified as much as possible, and (3) productive units are geared to local needs and subject to local political leadership had the best conditions for propagating "revolution" within the enterprise. In such a system the innovations needed to break down management-worker dichotomies, reduce administrative hierarchy, create worker technicians, and involve workers directly in management would be least hampered by external constraints and distant bureaucracies.

Now, it is possible for an optimal division of labor to be organized among the specialized production units constituting large, integrated enterprises. To some degree larger Chinese enterprises functioned this way, and it is unclear the degree to which efficiencies of specialization were realized or sacrificed in them. However, "completeness" often meant that factories maintained general machine shops that turned out the odd pieces of equipment needed for expansion or technical renovation. This kind of completeness was apt to be quite expensive.

With respect to small plants that made entire products (such as farm-machine factories), the case for greater specialization and division of labor among them would depend on the extent of the market. It is arguable that, when rural *xian* (counties) were first setting up factories, demand and supply conditions did not permit extensive specialization among factories, but that greater division of labor was called for when industry developed and factories spread throughout the countryside. Whatever economic conditions in the abstract may have dictated, however, institutional and administrative conditions intervened.

The fact that the best-known Maoist models of enterprise management were large, nationally important enterprises, such as Daqing and Anshan, indicates that the local political orientation of the approach was not meant only for small, local enterprises, although they seemed the natural environment for it.

Daqing was touted mainly for two characteristics: its integration of leadership and work force ("Democracy in politics, production, and economics") and its combination of industry with agriculture, town with countryside.[9] Managerial democracy was promoted by means of a charter that gave workers the right to criticize cadres, elect basic-level cadres, refuse improper orders, and decline to work in unsafe conditions or with inadequate work rules, as well as the right to participate in the economic accounting of the enterprise and in the management of its dining halls.

Daqing also came to epitomize the ideal of narrowing the gap between city and countryside. It established a number of small towns and several dozen residential points with but a few hundred households each, instead of constructing a large urban center. These clusters were organized into "livelihood bases" containing such facilities as tractor and agricultural extension stations, primary schools, book stores, and health clinics. Dependents of oil-field workers engaged in farm work (making the complex self-sufficient in cereals), service and auxiliary industrial trades, road maintenance, and management of the residential points.

The Daqing ideal thus combined a nonbureaucratic management system with a close integration with local conditions. There is no doubt that Daqing's management system also included detailed regulations guiding its interaction with higher-level planning authorities, since the oil field came to produce over half of China's crude oil. However, this aspect of Daqing, important as it was to the country, was not part of what was to be "learned from Daqing."

The Anshan Iron and Steel Complex, of course, was the origin of Mao's core document on enterprise management, the 1960 Anshan Constitution. This, it will be recalled, consisted of five principles: (1) stress putting politics in command, (2) strengthen Party leadership, (3) promote mass movements, (4) institute the two-one-three (participatory) system of management,[10] and (5) vigorously carry out technical revolution.[11] In reports from Anshan it was the "face-to-face" leadership style, like that of Daqing, that was celebrated. The five points essentially concern the proper structuring of the relations of production within the enterprise, not the articulation of Anshan's crucial place in the national economy. The Anshan Constitution is quite silent on this subject, on its responsibility to users of iron and steel, and on the importance of fulfilling various quotas and norms, whereas its first and (especially) third points referred to practices that during the Great Leap had proved antithetical to strengthening the external links that must integrate an enterprise with the economy around it. Thus here too the lesson was a *social* one: that the orientation of plant leadership and technical personnel was *downward* toward the rank-and-file and the locality, rather than upward toward a national technocratic elite and planning bureaucracy.

The comprehensive factory would seem to call for a less articulated division of labor among individual workers. Mao's writings did indeed favor the idea of the generalist—for example, the peasant who was also worker, intellectual, and soldier—as an aspect of the drive to reduce the Three Great Differences. This idea undoubtedly contributed to the ideological background for rural industrialization from the late 1950s to the mis-1970s as well as for various experiments in participatory management carried out over the same period. With respect to the work process itself, however, there was little or no deviation from Western practice (other than that dictated by the relative backwardness of technology) and little interest on the part of managers and other authorities in the issue of work alienation, which was commonly dismissed as a problem of a more advanced stage of development.

Comprehensive enterprises were not so much desirable in and of themselves, but because they were the *only* possible way to organize production with no market and only skeletal planning. During the Cultural Revolution years, the main planning institutions—State Planning Commission, State Economic Commission, Capital Construction Commission, State Statistical Bureau, and State Price Bureau—"were merged and reduced to a skeleton staff." [12] Goods still had to be allocated administratively, but neither the resources nor the will existed to do so competently. "[A]llocation decisions became more and more arbitrary and subjective as central management became increasingly ineffective." [13] Enterprises then reacted defensively and rationally (from their viewpoint) to insulate themselves from undependable suppliers by making themselves self-sufficient, that is, comprehensive. Conversely, when central planning was periodically resurrected to rescue the economy from chaos, it was confronted with institutions and attitudes adapted to its absence. Not only had the planners themselves been sent down to the countryside or dispersed to other jobs, but planning could not function well against hositility to its organizational requirements.

In the late 1970s and early 1980s, Chinese economists identified these defects and the disrepute into which they had brought planning itself. Ma Hong, then director of the Institute of Industrial Economics of the Chinese Academy of Social Sciences, wrote:

There were some mistakes and faults in planning for some time in the past. . . . Thus, a plan could not be drawn up scientifically and ended in failure *in most cases*. *Some people doubted and even negated the system of planned economy* when they saw some defects and mistakes in planning. . . . The authoritativeness of planning depends on the scientific nature of planning. [14]

Other economists observed that the phenomenon of comprehensive enterprises, both large and small, had become ubiquitous in Chinese industry. Indeed, besides attempting to meet all of their own productive needs, such enterprises became the main locus of social provisioning—housing, schooling, medical care, and so on—for their work forces and thus came to constitute entire "communities":

Of course, the emergence of such a scene was not entirely due to the internal causes of an enterprise; imbalance among production, supply and marketing, failure . . . to fulfill contractual obligations (such as failing in supplying materials . . .) and many other causes also forced an enterprise to go for completeness. [15]

Thus, in the course of the 1960s and 1970s, self-reliance of industrial enterprises appears to have been transformed from its original conception as a bold, antibureaucratic stance emphasizing resourcefulness and problem solving at the factory level to a defensive posture of survival and growth in an undependable macroeconomic environment.

EGALITARIANISM

If self-reliance was Mao's antibureaucratic principle of social organization, a chief positive social goal was to narrow the Three Great Differences. This goal was expressed in certain policies of a highly egalitarian character that after Mao's death came to be denigrated as "everyone eating from the same big pot."

China emerged from the era of "late Maoism" with an unusually even distribution of urban and rural personal income, taken separately. The World Bank puts the Gini coefficient of China's *urban* distribution in 1981 at 0.16, less than half the value of every one of the eight other Asian countries with which it was compared.[16] The Gini coefficient for *rural* personal income in 1979 was put at 0.26,[17] also significantly below that of other Asian countries with which China was compared (whose coefficients were in the range 0.30–0.35). The estimate applies to rural incomes after taxes but before relief subsidies; if the latter were included China's performance would probably look even better, despite an apparent weakening in interprovincial food redistribution between the 1950s and 1970s.[18] This is because, however weak it was, China's "safety net" was probably stronger than elsewhere at an equivalent level of development. The official, self-deprecating revelations of widespread poverty that were made in the mid-1970s referred to the unfortunate reliance of poor areas on "resold grain for their food supply, loans for production and subsidies for day-to-day living,"[19] yet these were all instruments of state relief less available to the desperately poor in, for instance, much of south Asia. The World Bank's conclusion that China's poorest, despite the new publicity given them, were "far better off than their counterparts in most other developing countries"[20] is almost surely right.

Because of the still wide urban-rural gap, China's relative advantage in distributive equality at the end of the Maoist era diminishes somewhat when rural and urban incomes are combined. Indeed, official figures, shown in Table 2, indicate that all of Maoism's emphasis on closing the gap between city and countryside had not prevented the urban-rural differential in per capita consumption from widening continuously from the 1950s onward, and even during the Cultural Revolution decade itself.

TABLE 2   Consumption per Capita of Agricultural and
Nonagricultural Populations, 1952–1979

Year	*Index of per Capita Consumption (1952 = 100)*			*Growth in Relative Advantage of Nonagricultural Population (1952 = 100)*
	National Average	*Agricultural*	*Nonagricultural*	
1952	100	100	100	100
1957	123	117	126	108
1965	126	116	137	118
1975	157	143	181	127
197͘	185	165	215	130

Source: State Statistical Bureau, *Zhongguo jingji nianjian* (Economic yearbook of China; Beijing, 1981), sec. 6, p. 25.

The relative advantage of the nonagricultural population was 10 percent higher in 1979 than it had been in 1965. Moreover, by 1978 the ratio of urban to rural disposable income was 2.35 to 1, excluding the effects of extensive state subsidies, most of which further raised urban incomes relative to rural incomes. The chief political factor behind this failure was the continued urban bias of government policies, especially price policies. Highly selective official price indexes showed the "scissors gap," or price differential between farm and industrial prices, to be narrowing throughout the period from the early 1950s on. Yet it was evidently as wide as ever in the mid-1970s, when such common consumer goods as portable radios, sewing machines, and alarm clocks exchanged for two to ten times as much rice in Guangzhou or Shanghai as in Hong Kong.[21] Such a price differential served as a de facto tax by which the state extracted resources from the countryside to support very high investment rates and to shore up urban consumption.

The fundamental economic factor behind the growing urban-rural gap was the enormous disparity in labor productivity that had grown up between the two sectors. The bottom row of Table 3 shows that the already-great relative productivity advantage of industrial workers in 1952 more than doubled by 1965 and was not reduced during the Cultural Revolution decade. Indeed, given the continuation of antimigration policies and generally slow growth in farm output, it is remarkable that industry's relative advantage did not continue to increase during that

TABLE 3   Relative Sectoral Labor Productivity, Industry and Agriculture, 1952, 1965, and 1978

Sector	1952	1965	1978
Employment shares of industry and agriculture			
Agriculture	.92	.91	.83
Industry	.08	.09	.17
Gross output shares of industry and agriculture (1970 prices)			
Agriculture	.64	.42	.26[a]
Industry	.36	.58	.74[a]
Relative gross output per worker in industry (agriculture = 1)	6.50	14.00	14.00[a]

Sources: Hongqi (Red flag) 16:24–25 (August 1987); Beijing Review, 14 December 1987, pp. 29–30; Carl Riskin, China's Political Economy: The Quest for Development since 1949 (New York, Oxford University Press, 1987), p. 270; State Statistical Bureau, Zhongguo tongji nianjian (Statistical yearbook of China; Beijing, 1986), pp. 167, 274, and Zhongguo tongji zhaiyao (Statistical abstract of China; Beijing, 1987), pp. 4–5.

a. 1979 data.

decade.[22] The state suppressed the growth of urban personal incomes by keeping wages virtually unchanged for twenty years, but it could not (or did not) suppress the growth in the urban labor-force participation rate, which permitted the average urban income to continue growing away from its rural counterpart.

Yet, despite the perverse result with regard to urban-rural differences, the degree of overall inequality at the end of the Cultural Revolution decade was still low in an international comparative context, indeed, "clearly one of the lowest in the world."[23] The policies that achieved such a relatively even income distribution directly embodied a rejection of the influence of the market, as well as of the unequal distribution of political power, on the allocation of resources, the distribution of income, work incentives, and general social values. Indirectly, however, they tended to subvert that effect: policies that divorced income from output or redistributed income among units stood in direct contradiction to self-reliance. They required political intervention from above the "self-reliant" unit and tended to conflict with the interests of the unit itself and even with the interests of the intervening authorities, who were beneficiaries of the existing system. Not only did this generate conflict, but it also furnished a further rationale for strengthening the authority of the state. The sweeping away of legal, traditional, and bureaucratic sources of authority concentrated more power at the political center where privilege was endemic.

THE ODD COUPLE, MAOISM AND CENTRAL PLANNING

To some of the reform-minded, the fundamental problem of China's economic system was the inherent inadequacy of central planning itself. This view asserts that central command planning is inevitably distorted by the lack of adequate information or incentives and the particularistic missions of its players. Other observers, however, have focused on the incompetence with which the system was operated, a position that spotlights the specific damage done to planning by two decades of "late Maoism."[24]

We have seen that, however serious the intrinsic problems of a central administrative planning regime, it had probably nowhere else been as poorly implemented as in China during this period. During the Great Leap Forward, as Mao himself acknowledged, the drawing up of material balances had for a while simply ceased. The different sectors of the economy steamed ahead on their own without regard to markets and suppliers. A similar thing happened during at least parts of the 1966–1976 period: "Those who were in charge of planning and production or construction no longer devoted themselves to the study of comprehensive balancing," which predictably led to "chaos in the economy."[25]

Central command planning without "comprehensive balancing" is a virtual contradiction, like markets without buying and selling. There was no conscious intent to abandon planning per se; rather, the prevailing conditions made it impossible. First, the atmosphere of mass campaigns clashed with the requirements of central planning. Second, a large part of the staff that prepared, implemented, and supported planning was attacked and purged: "The statistics work of the whole country was literally suspended for almost three years [1966–1969]," according to Sun Yefang, who was a former deputy director of the State Statistical Bureau.[26] During these years statistical offices were disbanded, personnel were transferred, and "large quantities of materials were burned." Even in 1981 the bureau had at its disposal only 193 statistical workers at the national level.[27] Evidently planners operated largely in the dark.

Third, Mao and the left promoted a particularly imprecise and voluntaristic approach to planning in order to overcome the generally acknowledged problem of passivity imposed by the central-planning regime on everyone subordinate to the top decision makers. "Active" (or "positive" or "long-line") balance meant setting targets up to the capacity of the more advanced sectors and units, as opposed to "passive" balancing, which trimmed plans to the constraints of the economy's weak links. The point of "active" balancing was to put pressure on the weaker units to catch up. Behind this idea lay Mao's dictum that balance is always "relative and temporary," whereas imbalance is "absolute and constant." During periods when "left" ideology was in the ascendancy, however, this idea was easily interpreted to mean that imbalance was intrinsically preferable to balance.

In light of these various factors, both objective and subjective, one better understands how and why planning came to be virtually abandoned at times and the economy left without direction. Looking back at these experiences and the conditions they were reacting to, it seems that the encouragement of local enterprise always led to general anarchy, while macroeconomic order required that all initiative be stripped from the hands of economic agents below the very top. China under Mao, in pursuing certain populist goals ("revolutionizing the relations of production"), exhibited a tolerance of overall disorder that was unique to the centrally planned countries. Ironically, that very disorder inevitably compelled the restoration of central control, the redeployment of the accouterments of command planning. But at each turn of the wheel, the material and psychological conditions for central planning were weaker, its conflict with the prevailing ideology more disabling. The gap between ideology and reality effectively discredited the former and in doing so finally eroded whatever tenuous restraining influence the more idealistic aspects of the ideology still had on the arbitrary use of power.

Industrial Policy during the Cultural Revolution: Military Preparation, Decentralization, and Leaps Forward

BARRY NAUGHTON

In the mid-1960s China's industrial development policies were dramatically reshaped in a way that came to characterize the entire Cultural Revolution decade (1966–1976). While maintaining the general characteristics of a "big-push" industrialization strategy, in which high rates of investment were used to further the priority development of heavy industry, Chinese planners recast their investment policy in two ways.[1] First, central government investment was focused to an unprecedented extent on the development of an industrial base in remote inland China with a predominantly military rationale. This construction program, called the Third Front, dominated central government resource allocation, especially between between 1964 and 1971. Second, while central government efforts were concentrated on the Third Front, a gradual program of decentralization put local governments in control of a substantial portion of total investment resources. By 1976, when the death of Mao brought the Cultural Revolution decade to a close, these two processes had fundamentally reshaped Chinese industry, altering its geographic distribution, its operating efficiency, and the distribution of decision-making authority among different governmental levels.

This chapter has two basic objectives. The first is simply to describe Chinese investment policy during the years from 1964 through 1976, since it is interesting, occasionally bizarre, and almost totally unknown. Little reliable economic data of any kind were available from China during those years, and because of the military and strategic motivation of much industrial investment, an especially impenetrable curtain of secrecy was erected around central investment policy decisions, particularly those involving the Third Front. Even when the urgency of military considerations began to fade, intense political conflict around questions of investment allocation meant that there was little possibility that the Chinese would publish a balanced appraisal of past investment policy. In fact, no description of Chinese investment policy during these years has previously appeared either in Chinese or in English. The second objective of the chapter is to argue that the actual investment policies that China carried out were extremely costly and inefficient and had a major adverse effect on China's industrial development. Although it is widely recognized that Chinese industrial growth decelerated during the 1970s, there has been little serious discussion of the causes of this deceleration. Slower growth has been attributed to the inherent shortcomings of a centrally planned economy; to the absence of material incentives, and to pervasive "leftism" in the political realm; or to the disruption and factional conflict of the Cultural Revolution era. While a rigorous test of alternative explanations for retardation of growth is not yet possible, I argue that the most obvious, most immediate, and probably most important cause of industrial retardation was the inappropriate and costly investment policy carried out over a period of more than ten years.

Considered from the standpoint of industrial development policy, the larger period considered here breaks down into two distinct subperiods. Between 1964 and 1971, investment policy overall was dominated by the centrally directed Third Front policy, carried out at maximum speed and with all the mechanisms of a "command economy." This first subperiod also witnessed the beginning of a program of decentralization, designed and carried out by the central leadership as part of a program of restructuring the economic system. Although this program was ultimately to have a major impact on the economy, its early stages had only a limited effect. Thus, although the first subperiod was characterized by the beginnings of a movement toward decentralization, and in spite of the fact that it included the peak period of disruption of the narrowly defined Cultural Revolution (1966–1968), intentional decisions taken at the central level overwhelmingly dominated actual investment policy. The second subperiod began at the end of 1971 as central planners abruptly shifted away from the top priority accorded to Third Front construction. From 1972 through 1976 investment policy was predominantly characterized by the dispersion of investment resources among competing priorities. Earlier decisions permitting decentralization now took effect with the dispersion of investment authority among different governmental levels, and the center found itself unable to impose a coherent overall investment policy. The result was a prolonged period of deadlock as the central government was frustrated in its effort to reestablish control over the economy. Thus the ultimate outcome of these processes was a loss of control over the economy, ironically not because of the social disruption of the era, but because an increasingly unwieldly planning apparatus, combined with the absence of a coherent investment policy, created an accumulation of problems with which the bureaucratic economic system was not adequate to cope. Ultimately this failure created the conditions in which China's leadership accepted the necessity for a major reorientation of economic policy and, subsequently, for major economic reforms.

THE EMERGENCE OF A NEW POLICY

In the early 1960s China was struggling to recover from the enormous economic catastrophe it had suffered in the wake of the Great Leap Forward. Even as the immediate crisis passed, China faced a substantial deterioration in both its domestic economic and its international strategic positions. In the domestic economy, agriculture had been set back to well below the 1957 level, requiring import of grain for the foreseeable future; workers' real incomes had been eroded by inflation; serious industrial imbalances had emerged, including shortages of steel, coal, and transportation capacity; management and control structures throughout the economy were in chaos; and Soviet aid had been terminated, depriving China of its primary source of modern technology and leaving significant debt. Moreover, the break with the Soviet Union had left China strategically isolated just as it was threatened by increasing American involvement in Vietnam. Even after the immediate problems of the post-Leap catastrophe had been contained, China's basic position was much less favorable than it had been during the 1950s.

During the worst years of the post-Leap crisis, China had been forced to suspend the big-push industrialization strategy, cutting investment and sending workers back to the countryside. Now, as the economy began to recover, the question arose of how to modify long-run objectives in the face of substantially less favorable circumstances. The initial Chinese response was to set more moderate goals. A central work conference in September 1963 assessed the unfavorable situation and proposed a three-stage long-range plan: (1) three more years of "readjustment," 1963–1965; (2) approximately fifteen years of basically self-sufficient industralization permitting China to "approach advanced world levels"; and (3) beginning around 1980, the comprehensive "Four Modernizations," permitting China to emerge as a world industrial power through assimilation of advanced world technology. This program, subsequently outlined in Zhou Enlai's 1964 speech to the National People's Congress, was based on the realistic judgment that China would be forced to be self-sufficient: its access to world technology would be severely restricted in the medium run, because of the urgent need to import food grain, limited export capacity, and the absence of any likely source of foreign aid.[2] Work went forward on the Third Five-Year Plan (for 1966–1970) in order to give specific form to this general set of goals. The initial draft was oriented toward restoring consumption levels. Although provisions were made for nuclear weapons development, the "central task" was to ensure a level of modest sufficiency of food and clothing for the entire population. Realistic growth rates were projected, moderate investment levels were called for, and attention was given to the possibility of a shift in industrial investment away from the steel-machinery complex and toward the chemical industry, which could provide fertilizer and synthetic fibers for consumption purposes. Moreover, the bulk of investment was to go to coastal areas, where the return to investment was highest.[3]

In May 1964 a draft of this plan was presented to Mao Zedong, who rejected it and advanced several alternative principles. He urged greater attention to basic industries, such as coal and steel, and the adoption of a long-run perspective, implying less attention to improvements in current consumption; he advocated the importation of less grain, in order to purchase more advanced technology; and he called for a greater effort in the construction of inland industries and local armaments industries. Clearly Mao was advocating a fundamentally different response to China's weakened position: instead of reducing aspirations, he was calling for belt-tightening and arduous struggle. Since 1962 Mao had been defining his vision of socialism in the ideological realm; beginning in May 1964 he sought to bring that vision to bear on industrial development and the planning process.[4] Mao's vision—which we might call austerity socialism—was inextricably linked with external events over which China had little control. On 4 August 1964 the United States claimed that North Vietnamese torpedo boats had attacked two American destroyers in the Gulf of Tonkin, and the next day American bombers attacked North Vietnam in reprisal. The Chinese denounced the Tonkin incident as a fabrication and condemned the United States action. Two weeks later Mao addressed a special work conference and called for drastic acceleration of the pace of inland construction, based on the imminent danger of war and the vulnerability of China's coastal industrial regions. Mao called for movement of existing plants inland and for maximum-speed construction of railroads in inland areas, even if that meant tearing up existing lines to obtain rails. This dramatic appeal converted the existing plans for inland development into an emergency response to external threat. From this time, plans for the development of a "third front" of Chinese industry became the top priority of central planners, and these plans dominated investment decision making for the next seven years.[5]

For a brief period planners had contemplated the modification of the big-push industrialization strategy in order to place more emphasis on improving living standards, but during 1964, following Mao's direct intervention in the planning process, China's development strategy reverted to the traditional emphasis on heavy-industrial development. From the outset, though, the perceived urgency of the international situation gave the renewed big push its own special characteristics: China engaged in a militarized leap forward in which rapidly increasing investment was channeled into the interior of China. This massive commitment of resources was to leave an indelible imprint on the Chinese industrial structure.

THE THIRD FRONT

The name "Third Front" *(san xian)* is a military metaphor with economic resonance. The "first front" refers to the industrialized coastal regions vulnerable to attack, and the "second front" refers to inland regions that would become vulnerable to bombing raids and other hostile action in a protracted conflict. The Third Front was the secure base area, nestled in the mountainous regions of inland China. Third Front areas included all of Sichuan, Guizhou, Yunnan, Gansu, Ningxia, and Qinghai, as well as parts of Shaanxi, Henan, Hubei, and Hunan (see Figure 1). The inland plains around Wuhan, Baotou, and Taiyuan, which had received large investments during the 1950s—and thereby corresponded to the second phase of Chinese industrialization—were not included. The policy was thus intended both to provide a strategic third line of defense and to bring modern industry to a third major section of China.[6]

The Third Front policy as a whole was carried out on a massive scale. Moreover, most individual projects were large, and many of them involved large-scale interprovincial cooperation. Construction was carried out at high speed on a top-priority basis, with massed construction teams and army engineering corps carrying out much of the work, aided by large groups of temporary construction workers. Plants were purposely dispersed away from population centers, generally placed in mountainous terrain, and even dug into mountainsides. In some cases the workshops of a single factory were separated and scattered across several square miles of rugged country. The intention was to create an entire industrial base—not just an armaments industry—that could survive a prolonged war. The program was so huge that it can fairly be said that, with the exception of petroleum development, the central government's industrialization policy from 1965 through 1971 *was* the Third Front.

The first phase of Third Front construction was focused on the southwestern provinces of Sichuan, Guizhou, and Yunnan. National investment grew rapidly in 1965 and 1966, and this investment was concentrated on two massive industrial complexes in the Southwest. The first complex consisted of machine-building and armaments factories built in northern Guizhou and linked by a new rail line to the steel facilities of Chongqing. The second complex centered on a new comprehensive steel mill at Panzhihua in extreme southwestern Sichuan. This facility was linked to several sophisticated heavy-machinery plants north of Chengdu and to the Liupanshui coal-mining district in western Guizhou. Simultaneous, high-priority construction of three different railroad lines linked the various parts of these complexes and integrated the Southwest into a rail network for the first time. These projects were very expensive: The Panzhihua mill cost 3.74 billion yuan, and the most difficult railroad line—the Chengdu-Kunming link—cost 3.3 billion.[7]

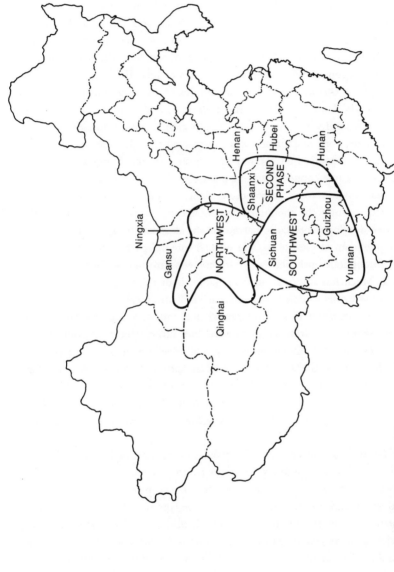

Figure 1 Third Front Regions

Investment was reduced during the peak years of Cultural Revolution disruption (1967 and 1968), but beginning in 1969 investment again soared, and China was engaged in another "leap forward." Between 1969 and 1971 a second phase of Third Front construction unfolded: while construction in the Southwest continued, the focus shifted to the mountainous area on the border of western Hubei and Henan and southern Shaanxi. In this phase priority was given to machinery construction, and the largest single project was the No. 2 Automobile Factory in Shiyan, Hubei, begun in September 1969. Scores of related factories were built throughout the area, including a complex of machine-tool factories further up the Han River in southern Shaanxi, and eighteen factories were built specifically to supply No. 2 Automobile with components. Once again a network of railroads was constructed to link these areas, including a north-south line connecting Luoyang to the Yangtze River near Yichang, a line connecting Hunan and Guizhou, and a third line linking Wuhan to the No. 2 Automobile plant, a line that was eventually extended through the mountains to Chongqing. Finally, extensive hydropower development, culminating in the decision in 1970 to build the Yangtze dam at Gezhouba, was also an integral part of this phase.[8]

Throughout both phases investment was directed to the Northwest as well. Much less information is available about this region, since it is the center of China's nuclear and aerospace industries. We do know that top-priority construction of an integrated steel mill at Juiquan in Gansu (begun during the Great Leap Forward but subsequently abandoned) was resumed in 1965. Extensive hydropower development near Lanzhou was combined with energy-intensive nuclear and nonferrous-metals development, and large numbers of machinery enterprises were moved to the Northwest beginning in 1970. As in other Third Front regions, enterprises were dispersed in the countryside away from major population centers.

Third Front development involved construction of large, new enterprises, but many factories were moved from coastal locations as well. This practice was especially important in the machinery and chemical industries and was the main source of the complex developed rapidly in northern Guizhou. From 1964 through mid-1971, 380 large-scale factories were moved to Third Front regions (about one-fifth of the total number of large plants in the Third Front). In some cases only a portion of the existing plant was moved *(yi fen wei er)*, and additional investments were made to allow production to continue at both locations.[9] Even in cases of new plant construction, existing coastal enterprises were drawn on heavily for technical assistance, manpower, and machinery. Most of the workers at Panzhihua came from Anshan, and most of the workers at No. 2 Automobile came from the Changchun (No. 1) Automobile Factory. Moreover, existing plants were called on to "guarantee" various phases of construction of Third Front plants. More than 140 factories and design institutes "guaranteed" various parts of No. 2 Automobile. As such a program implies, most Third Front construction was done on the basis of domestic technology, with a few selected imports.[10]

How big was the Third Front? Table 1 gives the proportions of national capital construction that went to the Third Front.[11] Between 1965 and 1971 exactly half of capital construction went to the ten provinces of the Third Front. To put this into perspective, these ten provinces produced only 19 percent of national industrial output in 1965.[12] The shift in priority is most evident in the Southwest provinces, where investment shot up from 10 percent to 23 percent of the national total during the Third Front period. The Northwest and Second Phase regions display moderate shifts, each increasing their share of total investment by two percentage points. In general, only a provincial breakdown of investment figures is available, and in these regions the provincial figures obscure the dramatic change in investment allocation. Large cities such as Wuhan, Xi'an, and Zhengzhou are in these regions and received substantial investment during the 1950s. During the Third Front, investment shifted sharply away from these urban centers and toward isolated rural areas in the same provinces. Similarly, in the later 1970s large investments were initiated in Wuhan, which kept high the share of na-

TABLE 1 Third Front Investment as a Proportion of National Investment

Region	1953–1964	1965–1971	1972–1980	1981–1987
Southwest[a]	10%	23%	11%	8%
Northwest[b]	10	12	9	7
Second Phase[c]	13	15	15	11
Third Front Total	32	50	35	26

a. *Southwest:* Sichuan, Guizhou, Yunnan.
b. *Northwest:* Shaanxi, Gansu, Ningxia, Qinghai
c. *Second Phase:* Hubei, Hunan, Henan.

tional investment going to the Second Phase region. By the 1980s Third Front regions were getting slightly more than a quarter of national investment, a level much closer to their near-term relative economic potential (see Figure 2).

This region received over half of national investment between 1964 and 1971, and a substantially larger proportion of state budgetary industrial investment. Nonindustrial investment is much more evenly distributed over the population (since it consists largely of agriculture and service investments), and control over much of this investment was decentralized to the provinces before the Third Front began, while extra-budgetary investment was primarily concentrated in existing industrial centers. It is possible to estimate that about two-thirds of budgetary

Figure 2 National Capital Construction in Third Front Areas, 1953–1987

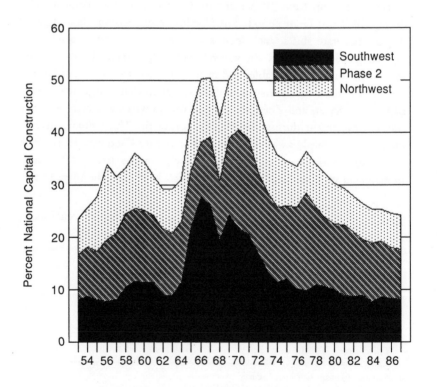

industrial investment went to the Third Front during its peak construction period, although those regions had previously been producing only one-sixth of industrial output.[13] Given that during this same period the state was also investing substantial sums in oil-field development and refining (nearly all of which was in coastal regions and the Northeast), virtually all large state projects in sectors other than petroleum and petrochemicals were located in the Third Front during this period.

Two points remain to be made about the Third Front. First, it was a massive centrally directed investment program, and it was carried out in a highly centralized manner. On 26 February 1965 a Southwest Construction Commission was created with comprehensive powers over Third Front construction. Li Jingquan was the head, and Peng Dehuai became the deputy head. At the same time, separate "command posts" were created to oversee construction of the largest complexes of production facilities. A general command headquarters was created for the huge Panzhihua steel mill, under the leadership of the Ministry of Metallurgy; another headquarters was created for Chongqing under the Machinery Ministry; and another was placed in charge of the construction of several major coal-mining districts in Guizhou (designed to provide fuel for Panzhihua) under the Coal Ministry in coordination with the Panzhihua command.[14] These command posts had overall responsibility for every aspect of these high-priority construction programs. The systems of material supply and financial control were altered to conform to the system of centralized direction. Both money and materials were delivered directly to the command posts by special branches of the national Bank of Construction and the Material Supply Bureau, respectively.[15] The Third Front was a classic manifestatioin of the power of a centrally planned system to dispose of resources according to priorities determined by the political authorities. Decentralization and local initiative played no role in the Third Front.[16]

Finally, the Third Front was the specific form in which China engaged in militarized leaps forward in the late 1960s and early 1970s. Each phase of the Third Front corresponded with a massive surge of investment and with a specific external threat. The first surge, focused on the Southwest, enhanced China's ability to aid Vietnam against the threat from the United States and increased the credibility of China's threats to intervene if its security were threatened. This phase was brought to an end by the eruption of open social conflict in 1967, but in 1969 an even greater Leap Forward erupted, and a nationwide period of mobilization begun. This time Third Front investment was focused in more northerly areas and designed to provide protection against the Soviet Union. Production grew at extremely rapid rates during 1969 and 1970, but this output growth was being obtained at the cost of an accumulation of serious economic problems. Ultimately the need to cope with those problems would bring an end to the near-total devotion to Third Front construction.

RESTRUCTURING THE ECONOMIC SYSTEM

During the same series of extraordinary meetings of central planning organs in 1964 that produced the Third Front policy, a series of new regulations governing authority over industry were drafted. Not all of these regulations were implemented immediately, but in succeeding years nearly all were eventually adopted. These new regulations had an important cumulative impact and resulted, by the end of the period, in an economic system that was substantially more decentralized than a traditional Soviet-style system. Thus the period from mid-1964 through the end of 1971 was marked by an incremental decentralization of the industrial management system.

It seems paradoxical that a single period can both be dominated by a centrally directed redistributive investment policy and also see the institution of a major decentralization program, but this apparent paradox can be resolved in practice. First, the goal of war preparation served as the justification for both programs. Third Front construction moved resources inland, but true "survivability" required that the various regions of the country, including the Third Front, be able to operate "basically self-sufficient industrial systems" in the event of war. This obviously required that a decentralized management system be in place as well. Second, precisely because the central government was redistributing such a large proportion of the investment resources it controlled directly, it could tolerate local control over a portion of resources and still be confident that its priority objectives would be reached. The decentralization of the management system envisioned a central government role that was limited to redistribution, with regional systems able to manage the bulk of ordinary decisions related to industrial production. Third, both programs were designed and carried out by the central leadership. The center did not "lose control" over investment allocation during this period, nor did it seriously intend to relinquish control over its principal investment priorities. Rather, central leaders felt confident that their priority objectives—above all, defense preparation—could be obtained in the framework of a decentralized economic system. Thus Third Front construction and decentralization were originally seen as complementary programs. [17]

One of the most important characteristics of the decentralization measures adopted between 1964 and 1971 is that their effects were cumulative. No individual measure had a determinative influence on the functioning of the economic system, but together they fundamentally altered the character of the Chinese planning system. Two parallel, but conceptually distinct, decentralization processes took place during these years. The first process gradually created the conditions for substantial rural small-scale industry networks to develop completely outside the control of the regular state planning system. Local governments were given the right to run independent industrial systems, with autonomous control over output, pricing, investment, and (to a lesser extent) hiring. This process began in September 1964, when a central work meeting sketched the general outlines of a major decentralization program. Following this meeting, local governments were granted the legal right to control output from the small-scale factories they had built. Moreover, local governments were also given the right to hire "temporary workers" outside the state plan and given control over finances, including depreciation funds in industry and nearly all nonindustrial investment. [18] With these complementary powers, local governments were in a position to run truly autonomous industrial systems. Nevertheless, the importance of this sector was initially slight. It took time for even the wealthiest localities to accumulate the resources to develop local industry, and only then could local control over resources "snowball" into something of significant magnitude. The central government, however, proved itself generous in assisting these manifestations of local enthusiasm: in July 1970 the central government committed 8 billion yuan to the development of local industry over the following five years, and also permitted new rural factories to retain 60 percent of 'the profits, while granting unprofitable factories access to subsidies and bank credits. [19] These cumulative processes gave the rural sector significant stature by the early 1970s: in 1972 rural enterprises accounted for 60 percent of chemical-fertilizer production and 40 percent of cement. [20] Thus, while the vast majority of large-scale construction projects were under way in the Third Front, myriad small-scale projects elsewhere were gradually acquiring cumulative significance.

A parallel process of decentralization went on simultaneously within the centrally planned economy. Beginning at the same September 1964 meeting, steps were taken to reduce the level of detailed control that the Central Planning Commission exerted over the economy and to expand the powers of provinces and multiprovince "big economic regions."[21] But the climactic event in this process was the decentralization of large enterprises decided on in 1969. During the course of 1970 nearly all nonmilitary enterprises—with the exception of a few Third Front enterprises such as Panzhihua—were placed under provincial control. In 1965, 10,533 enterprises, accounting for 47 percent of state-run industrial output, had been under central ministerial control. By 1971 only 142 factories, accounting for 8 percent of state industrial output, remained under central control. Moreover, in 1970 the entire planning apparatus—including the former Planning and Economic commissions, Material Supply Bureau, and Statistical Bureau—was amalgamated into a single "revolutionary committee" with only 610 employees, 12 percent of the former personnel.[22] One of the most important results of the enterprise decentralization was that the depreciation funds of large enterprises (amounting to about 5 billion yuan annually) were remanded to local governments, giving them a reliable, large-scale funding source for the first time. With this important financial decentralization and the contemporaneous growth of local industrial systems, local governments had control over money, materials, and manpower, which they could use to carry out their own investment policies.

The impact of these major decentralization measures on the industrial economy was scarcely evident through 1971. There were delays in implementation and lags before changes in regulations were translated into changes in the actual control of resources. More important, the center continued to insist that the overall goal of military preparation was to be the primary focus of local investment policies. Indeed, the whole economy was still engaged in a feverish leap forward in pursuit of these goals. Thus industrial investment, regardless of the level at which it was controlled, was directed toward a relatively narrow range of heavy industries, and duplication of projects was seen as desirable on strategic grounds. As had been the case in the first Great Leap Forward, the forced draft of resources into industrialization produced rapid results and obscured the waste and inefficiencies caused by a near-total lack of coordination. The decentralizing measures were simply part of a general process by which each locality prepared for war by creating a self-sufficient local industrial system as quickly as possible.

THE SEARCH FOR SOLID ECONOMIC GROUND

At the end of 1971 a series of intersecting changes brought the Third Front period to an abrupt end. The fall of Lin Biao and the beginnings of rapprochement with the United States diminished China's strategic isolation and led rapidly to the curtailment of the Third Front investment policy. At approximately the same time, the series of decentralization measures introduced between 1964 and 1971 began to take effect, and with the reduced priority according to military preparation, local governments began to pursue their own development agendas. As a result, central leaders had to struggle to coordinate the economy under drastically new conditions. These fundamental policy and system changes were brought to the surface by the urgent need to restore macroeconomic balance to the economy. China had been "leaping forward" again, and the specter of a major economic crisis similar to that which had followed the Great Leap Forward loomed. The rapid growth in investment in preceding years had led to an extremely rapid growth in numbers of both permanent and temporary state workers, placing great strains on China's supplies of food and other consumption goods. The immediate task was to reduce the strain on consumption-goods supplies by reducing the flow of resources into investment.

Zhou Enlai resumed direct control over the government after the fall of Lin Biao, and one of his first actions was to reduce budgetary investment by 2 billion yuan, the first cutback after three years of extremely rapid growth. Nonbudgetary forms of investment increased by 1.5 billion, so this resulted in only a modest decrease in total investment. Control over labor recruitment was also recentralized: temporary workers were to be either included in the state plan or dismissed, and a substantial number of temporary construction workers were returned to their villages.[23] This was not a fundamental shift in development strategy, but a simple attempt to ameliorate the worst effects of a clearly excessive investment effort. These measures were sufficient to avoid economic crisis, although an exceptionally poor harvest in 1972 prevented conditions from improving dramatically either. But far deeper problems in the economy emerged as the flow of investment was controlled. Most important, the problem of how to deal with the immense volume of resources already committed to a stock of unfinished investment projects became even more difficult to solve as the flow of investment was curtailed. This problem raises that of the legacy of the Third Front.

Investment in the Third Front was extremely costly. Projects executed in remote locations are inevitably more expensive than similar projects located near the transportation, production, and supply facilities of existing economic centers. Third Front projects were doubly remote, being located not only away from the advanced economic centers of the coastal cities, but also away from inland urban centers that had achieved moderate levels of development. Moreover, since Third Front projects were intentionally located in difficult terrain, additional higher costs were necessarily created by the simple reality of plant locations. Obviously, placing workshops in mountainside caves is an extreme case of this general truth. Similarly, the difficult terrain meant that costs of railroad construction were more than twice as high as construction costs in more accessible areas. The higher costs unavoidably given by the remoteness of Third Front projects were only part of the story. The great haste with which Third Front projects were initiated meant that in most cases design and preparatory work were inadequate or nonexistent. Nearly every project about which we have information ran into substantial additional costs and delays because of inadequate preparatory work. Big dams at Gongzui in Sichuan and Gezhouba in Hubei developed dangerous structural flaws that required suspension of work and extensive remedial construction. Large steel mills under construction at Jiuquan in Gansu and Wuyang in Henan ran into repeated problems with ore availability and site selection, problems that in these two cases were so serious that they have remained intractable up to the present day, so that neither plant is a significant steel producer. Railroads were plagued by cave-ins that prevented normal operation.[24] Even the Panzhihua steel mill, which was begun after extensive preparatory work carried out in the early 1960s, ran into significant delays. While the first blast furnace there was blown in during 1970, it was not until 1975, a full ten years after the project was initiated, that regular production of finished steel began. Even then, problems with the separation and exploitation of titanium in the iron ore were not solved until the early 1980s.[25]

These delays and cost overruns meant that the volume of uncompleted investment projects in the Third Front grew steadily. Nevertheless, new projects had been continuously initiated. The Fourth Five-Year Plan, drawn up during a 1970 planning conference, called for an extremely ambitious investment program (so-called large scale construction *{daguimo jianshe}*) and projected very high output levels for 1975. Following this planning conference a series of sectoral work conferences occurred that engaged in competitive "leaping," setting high targets and ambitious investment projects in each sector. One of the outstanding characteristics of this period was the very large number of individual projects begun simultaneously. The Ministry of Metallurgy began work on a total of 227 sets of steel-rolling equipment in one year; the Chemical Ministry decided to make *nine* copies of an imported Japanese vinylon factory in Beijing; and other ministries followed suit in drawing up grandiose plans. Altogether, 2,963 large and medium-sized projects were initiated during the Fourth Five-Year Plan, and virtually all of these would have been started in 1970–71.[26]

It was simply impossible that China could mobilize sufficient resources to complete a substantial proportion of these projects in a reasonable time period of perhaps five years. As a result, huge volumes of material, money, and manpower were tied up in uncompleted construction. The Chinese data on uncompleted construction projects are not detailed enough to permit an accurate tracing of their volume. But we can gain some insight through simple arithmetic. Of budgetary capital construction, about 50 percent was devoted to "large and medium-sized projects." If we take, therefore, 50 percent of budgetary capital construction and divide by the number of large and medium projects under construction, we derive a figure for the average annual expenditure possible on each project. That figure dropped to about 8 million yuan in 1971 and was still only 12 million in 1978. But the *average* total cost of large and medium projects in the late 1970s was 180 million yuan.[27] If we assume that the size and cost of large projects did not increase too much between the early and late 1970s, it would take fifteen to twenty years to finish the average investment project. And in fact there are many examples of plants in China that have been under construction for that long and even longer. Throughout these prolonged construction periods, such investments simply tie up resources and make no contribution to the national economy.

Thus, in their initial phase, the moderate economic policies adopted by Zhou Enlai succeeded in coping with the most immediate macroeconomic problems but could not resolve the long-term problems created by

Third Front construction. Indeed, the reduction of investment made it even more difficult to complete projects already under way in the Third Front. It was essential that central planners move on to devise an overall policy that would redirect investment resources to a set of feasible objectives. In attempting to formulate that policy, however, central planners had increasingly to cope with a new reality in which power had been decentralized to a significant degree. Moreover, with the reduction in the priority accorded to military preparation, central planners could no longer take it for granted that local agendas would automatically correspond with central government priorities.

OPERATING A DECENTRALIZED ECONOMY

As we have seen, by the early 1970s the small-scale local industrial sector was becoming increasingly significant. By contrast, the decentralization of planning authority over the largest enterprises had been much less smooth. It quickly became apparent that provinces lacked the experience and information necessary to plan the output and supply relations of large-scale enterprises. Although planners had been interested in creating basically self-sufficient regional economies, the actual reality of the economy was that large-scale enterprises still had substantial interregional linkages. As a result, despite the nominal decentralization of enterprises, the crucial material-supply planning for most large enterprises continued to be performed by the central ministries, who used the "direct-supply" method to provide materials directly to "their" factories. Of the 2,400 large enterprises decentralized immediately after October 1969, almost 2,000 remained in this ministry-dominated supply mode. Another 400 enterprises were transferred to provincial supply plans in 1972; and another 166 in 1976, which still left 1,400 enterprises nominally decentralized but incorporated into central government supply plans.[28] The attempt to put current operations of large enterprises on a decentralized basis had failed. In the meantime, the large-scale sector was enmeshed in an increasingly unwieldly planning system. The ambiguity of enterprise decentralization left enterprises subject to the authority of many different levels of government (so-called *duotou lingdao*), while the weakening of the planning system caused by the Cultural Revolution crippled the ability of central planners to impose a reasonable direction on the industrial economy.

As already described, however, the decentralization of enterprises did mean that their depreciation funds were no longer remitted to the budgetary authorities but instead came under the effective control of the provinces and the enterprises themselves. Since the large enterprises possessed the bulk of fixed capital and depreciation funds, this decentralization caused a large block of financial resources to escape the control of central planners.[29] Thus the decentralization of enterprises was never particularly successful in terms of the planning and management of current output and supply decisions. Its main importance was through the decentralization of control over a portion of fixed investment. The single clearest summary indicator of decentralization of investment is the division of financial resources between budgetary and nonbudgetary finances. (The bulk of nonbudgetary resources go into fixed investment.) In Figure 3 the total amount of nonbudgetary finance is plotted against the total amount of budgetary funds in each year. It can be seen that the relationship between the two remained stable through 1972, with increased finances dividing about 80–20 between budgetary and nonbudgetary funds. After 1972, however, increased revenues split 40–60, with the bulk of marginal revenues flowing into nonbudgetary funds. The importance of the 1971/72 dividing line emerges clearly from this figure.

From 1972 onward, the Chinese industrial system can be characterized as a partially decentralized one. This decentralization, however, was of a very particular kind. Control over investment funding and over a few standardized investment goods was decentralized to a substantial degree, so that the central government surrendered its ability to directly control national investment policy in a detailed and specific fashion. But it was inconceivable that central planners would simply abandon overall control over the economy. The catastrophe of the Great Leap Forward had shown the disastrous consequences of losing control over crucial consumption goods, given that China remained close to subsistence levels. Therefore central planners retained direct control over the crucial determinants of demand and supply of consumption goods. Comprehensive hiring quotas were reimposed by central planners in 1972, and the banking system was used to tighten control over wage outlays. At the same time, central planners retained tight control over the two crucial raw materials for consumption goods: grain and cotton. As Christine Wong has described:

State control over light industry was maintained through tight agricultural procurement policies which left very little of the raw materials needed for local light industrial production. In addition, ideological restraints against "going after high profits"

Figure 3 Budgetary and Nonbudgetary Income

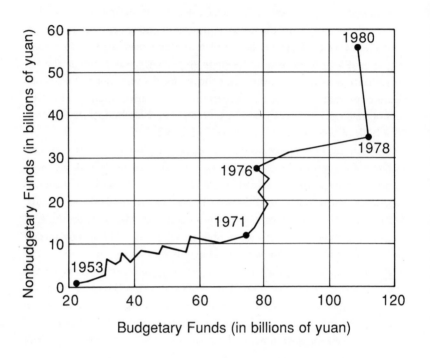

played a role in limiting local entry. It was this tight grip on light industry that allowed the central government to maintain control over the orientation of local investment—long after it had lost control over the pace—ensuring that the pattern of heavy-industry dominated investment was replicated in every province.[30]

Such a system ensured that the central government could maintain the broad outlines of a given development strategy, but it left the center few tools to shape specific investment policies.

Socialist economists since Oskar Lange have proposed models of market-oriented decentralization within the socialist economy. A crucial feature of such models generally is that central planners retain control over new investment, whereas decisions on current output and sales are determined by enterprises on the basis of price and profitability considerations. Indeed, in the early 1960s the Chinese economist Sun Yefang proposed a related model for China, in which he advocated extensive use of the market to regulate current enterprise operations, but took it for granted that socialism required continued central control over investment decisions.[31] Actual Chinese practice as it evolved in the early 1970s was the inverse of this model. While current production and supply decisions remained within an administrative, and often fairly centralized, framework, much of the control over investment was decentralized to local governments and even to the enterprise level. "Indirect centralization" combined with direct controls over consumption goods could ensure the maintenance of the general "big-push" strategy without economic catastrophe, but it could not ensure that specific investment policies would be well coordinated or efficiently carried out. Such a decentralization pattern suggests that the most serious economic difficulties are likely to emerge precisely in the sphere of investment control. In the absence of any kind of reasonable economic signals either generated by prices or flowing administratively through the planned economy, there is little reason to expect local investment to follow desirable patterns, and the problem of coordination between central and local investment is bound to be difficult. Moreover, China has always had difficulty controlling the pace of investment growth, with serious problems having emerged as early as 1956. Thus the difficulties of managing a decentralized industrial system in China were likely to be especially severe in the course of developing intelligent investment policies. Yet, as we have seen, it was precisely at this period that central government investment policy was thrown into disorder by the necessity of dealing with the uncompleted Third Front policy.

Even after changes in the international environment had led to a substantial downgrading of the priority given to the Third Front, the problem of dealing with the enormous volume of resources already committed to Third Front projects remained. About 150 large projects (out of 1,600) were suspended in 1972, but "due to the difficulty of obtaining unanimous agreement," only 81 projects were actually canceled in 1972 and 1973. Again in 1975 and 1976, efforts were made to reduce the scale of investment efforts, but during those years not a single project was canceled.[32] Yet while central planners could not reduce existing investment projects signficantly, their new post–Third Front priorities led them to initiate a large batch of new projects. In January 1973 planners approved the "4.3" plan, so-called because it called for the expenditure of 4.3 billion U.S. dollars for complete plant imports. Although this plan incorporated a positive recognition of the potential benefits to China of access to advanced world technology, it also represented an additional massive commitment of resources on the part of central authorities (eventually amounting to 24 billion yuan) at a time when they were still saddled with unresolved commitments from the previous era.[33] Moreover, as part of this general shift in investment priorities, planners had to give increased attention to a series of related infrastructural investments in the eastern part of the country. High priority was given to port expansion, in order to facilitate both the import of complete plants and the export of commodities needed to pay for them. Ultimately planners succeeded in pushing through this import program, in part by according the same kind of centralized priority direction to the imported projects that they had accorded to the major Third Front projects.[34] However, the cost was substantial, in the continuing inability to complete existing projects and in the political opposition that this program ultimately generated.

In essence, by the mid-1970s China's investment resources were dispersed among three separate investment policies. The first was the Third Front policy, relegated to the background and partially discredited, but still making a claim on investment resources because individual projects had not been dropped from the investment plan. Second was the program of technology imports and associated infrastructure construction. Central government resources were divided between these two largely incompatible programs. Simultaneously, a de facto third investment policy emerged from the bulk of decentralized resources now controlled by local governments. Local authorities seeking self-sufficiency channeled those resources into numerous small-scale heavy-industrial facilities, creating factories that were often extremely energy inefficient and that competed for raw materials with more efficient large-scale factories.[35] By the middle 1970s planners faced an impossible task. The resources at their disposal were simply inadequate to allow them to carry out their priority investment program and simultaneously satisfy the other demands (political and otherwise) made on them. Unable to direct a development program, planners were reduced to keeping current flows in the economy in some kind of rough balance. Whenever imbalances in the economy emerged, central planners were forced to reduce central investment in order to reduce excess demand. This can be seen by examining the growth rate and variation of budgetary and nonbudgetary investment. Before 1972, nonbudgetary investment grew twice as fast as budgetary investment (from a very low base) and also displayed twice as much fluctuation, so that the coefficients of variation for the two types of investment were almost identical. After 1972, budgetary investment displayed greater variability than nonbudgetary investment, even though its growth rate was much lower, and its coefficient of variation was much higher (see Table 2). The similarity in this respect between the mid-1970s and the "reform" period of the late 1970s and 1980s is very striking.

Planners experimented through the 1970s with a variety of planning systems designed to cope with this new reality. "Local balancing" of materials, supplemented by centrally designated interregional transfers, was attempted for a number of years. Regulations giving localities responsibility for all but the largest capital construction projects were promulgated. A succession of different budgetary systems for dividing control between the center and the provinces followed one another. It is impossible to go into these experiments in detail here, but it is fair to say that none was particularly successful. By 1975 Deng Xiaoping had taken over direction of central government work from an ailing Zhou Enlai, and he was prepared to attempt a recentralization of the economy. The government promulgated a document recentralizing control of transportation, communications, and large investment projects; drew into the central budget 20–30 percent of depreciation funds, the largest single source of decentralized investment financing; and drew up further plans for centralization and improved management of industry.[36]

This recentralization program was never implemented. The failure of

TABLE 2 Growth and Variability of Investment

Investment	Mean	Deviation	C.V.[a]
Budgetary, 1954–1972	.14	.37	2.64
Nonbudgetary, 1954–1972	.29	.70	2.41
Budgetary, 1972–1977	.02	.09	4.50
Nonbudgetary, 1972–1977	.10	.07	0.70
Budgetary, 1977–1983	.04	.21	5.25
Nonbudgetary, 1977–1983	.17	.19	1.12

a. C.V. is the coefficient of variation, or the standard deviation of the growth rate divided by its mean. A larger C.V. indicates greater instability.

this recentralization and the inability to decide on a single investment policy may have been as much political as economic. The conflict between the Gang of Four and the group around Deng Xiaoping in ideological matters is well known. But the most violent points of contention between the two groups were specifically related to the choice of industrialization policies. The Gang of Four criticized both the program of plant imports and the moves to recentralize control over investment. According to a 1977 New China News Agency dispatch, the Gang of Four "knew of" the import program and participated in the highly politicized process of project-site selection. Zhang Chunqiao claimed that "too many items have been imported; they have been clustered together."[37] From an economic standpoint, this is an entirely reasonable statement; from a political standpoint, it may have represented an attempt to organize a coalition of provincial leaders (especially those from inland provinces) who would oppose a reorientation of investment policy. A reduced import program would have been more likely to allow continued decentralized control over investment and renewed central government investment in finishing uncompleted inland projects. Whatever the specific politics of the day, it is unquestionable that investment policy was central to the bitter succession struggle taking place, and that coalitions based on interest—as well as ideology—formed against the recentralizing technology-import program of the Deng Xiaoping group. While the Gang of Four were unable to assume control over investment policy, they were able to block the proposed reorientation of the Deng group. In late 1975 political power shifted in Beijing: Deng Xiaoping was deposed and the Gang of Four dominated daily policymaking. Recentralization measures, including renewed central control of depreciation funds, were immediately rescinded. Thus at no time between 1972 and 1976 was the central government able to mediate between competing investment programs and impose a coherent direction on development. The deadlock continued until after the death of Mao.

Chinese industrial growth was not slow during the Cultural Revolution era. The regional differentials in industrial growth, however, were astonishingly small considering the magnitude of redistribution in investment policy. Taking the group of provinces that included Third Front areas, we find that they increased their share of national industrial output from 19.4 percent in 1965 to only 23.3 percent in 1980, notwithstanding the massive investments made there in the intervening period. As for the three Southwest provinces (Sichuan, Guizhou, and Yunnan), in 1984 they had 12 percent of industrial fixed capital but produced only 8.1 percent of industrial output (8.8 percent of state industrial output).[38] Full interpretation of these figures requires more information about the sectoral structure of output in different provinces; yet the figures are sufficiently strong to allow us to conclude that, although investment policy was redistributive, lower efficiency of inland projects greatly diminished the extent to which actual output was redistributed. Lower efficiency in inland areas also implies that China's overall growth rate was reduced. By the late 1970s the greater part of China's industrial fixed-capital stock was in inland areas, but this industrial capacity was operating at a substantially lower efficiency than that in coastal areas.

The two strands of Chinese investment policy during the Cultural Revolution decade—Third Front construction and decentralization—can be traced in the evolution of specific industrial sectors. The steel and machine-building industries are the center of the traditional big-push strategy: in a sense, the entire purpose of that strategy has been to create a powerful machine-building industry along with a strong ferrous-metals industry to feed the prodigious appetite for steel thereby created. Indeed, the steel industry was the focus of China's planning and development procedures during the Cultural Revolution era, with the slogan of "Taking steel as the key link" (*yi gang wei gang*). Yet by the mid-1970s China's steel industry not only had completely failed to fulfill the overly ambitious Fourth Five-Year Plan targets, but had also failed to fulfill the substantially lower targets set in 1972. To this day steel remains a crucial bottleneck constraining China's industrial development; thus China's investment policy has failed to fulfill the objectives dictated by the big-push strategy itself.

Some of the responsibility for the shortcomings of the Chinese steel industry lies with that industry's strategy of "focusing on the central process [basic steelmaking] and bringing along the two ends [iron mining and steel finishing]," which was unsuited to China's resource endowment of poor-quality, though abundant, iron ore. But the combination of Third Front and decentralized investment policies bears an even greater responsibility. Central government investment was concentrated on the most difficult and inaccessible regions, thus making completion of any given project more costly and time-consuming. But simultaneously that investment was dispersed across several very large-scale projects, making it even more difficult to complete any of those projects. As if that were not enough in itself, at least two of those projects (Jiuquan in Gansu and Wuyang in Henan) were initiated in areas where there were serious problems with the quality and composition of iron ore, thus compounding all the problems inherent in the overall development strategy for the steel industry. The large-scale mills at Jiuquan, Wuyang, and Shuicheng in Guizhou all produced trivial quantities of steel well into the 1980s, in spite of the investment of billions of yuan, and only Panzhihua in Sichuan has emerged as a major producer. Thus central government dedication to the Third Front policy meant that the enormous sums it had spent on the steel industry did not produce increased steel output that was anywhere near commensurate with the resources invested.

While the central government was thus mired in an unproductive policy, local governments enthusiastically pushed the development of small-scale steel mills. Of course, central government policy during this time encouraged the proliferation of local steel mills, but local governments were also forced to develop local steel industries because they were unable to obtain from the central government the steel they needed for local development policies. Unable to procure steel and possessed of significant investment resources, they naturally used those resources to develop local steel industries. With a few exceptions, these local steel industries were of uneconomically small scale and extremely energy inefficient. Their proliferation pushed up the cost and energy consumption of steel production while producing a relatively small increment to total national output, and subsequently, during 1979 and 1980, a very large proportion of these mills were permanently shut down.[39] Thus steel industry development during the 1960s and 1970s followed a two-pronged strategy, both sides of which must be judged to have failed. The legacy of that failure was not only a relatively slow growth in output but also a geographic distribution of iron, steel, and steel-finishing capacity that was so unbalanced that semifinished products were sometimes shipped *thousands* of miles for the next step of processing. It is not surprising that by the late 1970s the Chinese were tempted to recast entirely their steel development strategy and to begin importing complete modern steel facilities.

The industrial base under construction during the 1960s and 1970s was designed to culminate in machine building, both military and civilian, but especially heavy-machine building. Regardless of the specific industrialization strategy adopted, this sector is critical to the development process, because it equips all the other industrial sectors with modern productive facilities. Just as an individual facility in this sector draws on a complex web of skills and supporting facilities in its own production, so the sector as a whole feeds crucially into the expansion and technological improvement of other sectors. But in its development of this sector, China placed its own most advanced technology, and crucial items of imported technology, in the most inaccessible locations in the country, maximizing the difficulty involved in spreading advanced technology to other sectors. If the Third Front strategy—which is in its essence a strategy drawing on a highly centralized resource allocation system—had been matched by a highly centralized and detailed planning system, some of these problems might have been alleviated. But in fact China, having placed its machine-building capacity in the mountains, was unable then to bring its output in sufficient volume out of the mountains to the plains, where the bulk of ordinary industrial output naturally remained concentrated. One of the most striking phenomena we observe in China as of the mid-1970s is that the growing local industrial systems were equipped largely with relatively low-technology machinery. China has a huge stock of simple, low-quality machine tools but only modest supplies of precision, high-quality machine tools. Similarly, although production facilities for highly sophisticated (and large-scale) industrial boilers were built in the Third Front, local industrial systems unable to obtain such equipment have been forced to equip themselves with low-quality, low-pressure, fuel-inefficient small boilers, often produced by collective enterprises.[40] While some of these problems with the diffusion of technology are endemic to planned economies, China seems to have encountered these problems to a much greater extent than other planned economies.

The Third Front policy had similar effects on national transportation development. The creation of the transportation network in the Third Front was in itself an impressive accomplishment. By the end of 1983 the Southwest had 16.6 percent of the national modern transportation network, proportionately about the same as other populated areas of the country, and it was intensively utilized.[41] However, the country paid a large price for this concentration of investment, with the persistent railroad and harbor bottlenecks in the eastern half of the country a direct result of their neglect for almost ten years. During 1966–1975 only 10 percent of railroad investment went to the upgrading of existing lines (compared with 25 percent during the 1950s and 30 percent after 1976).[42] Thus we can measure part of the cost of the Third Front strategy by the low incremental output/capital ratios in the Third Front region itself; but an additional cost was created by the resultant distortion in the investment structure in the remainder of the country, which tended to worsen the impact of energy and transportation constraints on industrial development across the board.

Thus during the 1970s the Third Front became a tremendous drain on central government resources. The immense volume of resources already committed to the region's development but still tied up in uncompleted projects continuously exerted a pull on current investment resources. It is in this context that the decentralization of investment authority needs to be understood. A maximum of some 40 percent of investment finances were controlled by local governments, so that the central government always controlled an absolute majority of investment decisions. Moreover, in some places with favorable initial conditions— such as Jiangsu Province, described by Penelope B. Prime in Chapter 9 of this volume—local investment was effectively used to fuel industrial growth rates that were quite respectable by any standard. Thus while the decentralization of investment authority created problems of duplication, uneconomically small-scale production, and low-capacity utilization, these problems by themselves were not enough to account for the poor performance of the industrial economy.[43] Indeed, an intelligent and vigorously executed program of central government investment could easily have been combined with partial decentralization of investment to produce sustained high-speed industrial growth. Although coordination difficulties would still have been significant, effective central government planning would have ensured higher growth rates of the centrally controlled part of the economy, which would have allowed local governments to concentrate investment in sectors where small-scale production was economical, relying on the central government to provide transportation networks and the inputs produced by large-scale heavy industries. Instead, central investment projects produced relatively meager results in terms of expanded output, and, as shown in Figure 3, central government revenues stagnated. Instead of compensating for local investment by developing complementary large-scale industrial and infrastructure projects, central planners were forced to compensate for local investment in the sphere of macrocontrol, repeatedly cutting back their own investment program in order to keep the economy in balance. The instability and slow growth of central investment resources further hampered central development efforts, and China's administered economy became mired in a vicious circle of uncompleted development initiatives and inadequate development resources.

Perhaps a unified leadership, aided by a planning apparatus with adequate technical backup, could have liquidated the worst Third Front mistakes quickly after 1972. In fact, that leadership was weakened by political divisions and lacked the material or informational resources needed to reorient development policy. As a result, during the second subperiod the leaders lost control over the economy and were reduced to a passive attempt to steer the economy away from disastrous imbalances. Eventually planners seeking to move away from this role of "putting out fires" became receptive to new ideas about economic-system reform that they hoped would free them to devote more time to a coherent strategy of economic development. After the dramatic change in China's political environment at the end of 1978, the central government moved to implement a policy of "readjustment." This involved reducing current investment, but more crucially canceling projects under construction that could not hope to be completed, thereby concentrating resources on promising projects and reducing the continuing drain on central government resources. As that effort unfolded and the attempt to define a new development strategy got under way, a new leadership was installed in Beijing. The new head of the government, Premier Zhao Ziyang, had shown his merit by successfully coordinating the reorientation of development policy in Sichuan Province during the difficult period when massive Third Front investments there had been drastically curtailed. He was a logical choice to preside over a similar reorientation on the national level.

The Maoist "Model" Reconsidered: Local Self-Reliance
and the Financing of Rural Industrialization

CHRISTINE P. W. WONG

Rural industrialization was a central pillar of Mao's development strategy.[1] During the Cultural Revolution period, substantial resources were devoted to promoting rural industrialization, a program that offered radical approaches to key issues of development, including choice of technology, industrial location, urbanization, participation, and income distribution. By 1979, at the end of the Cultural Revolution, there were nearly 800,000 rural industrial enterprises, plus almost 90,000 small hydroelectric stations, scattered in villages and small towns, employing some 24 million workers and producing an estimated 15 percent of the gross value of industrial output. They dominated in the agriculture-related industries, producing all the farm tools and nearly all the small and medium-sized farm machinery, more than half of the chemical fertilizers, two-thirds of the cement, and 45 percent of the coal output.[2]

In many respects rural industrialization seemed the perfect embodiment of the Maoist principle of local self-reliance at the grass-roots level. Built under the strategy of "walking on two legs," rural small enterprises were supposed to augment industrial growth by using local resources with low opportunity costs to produce goods for local needs. In this way they would supplement and progressively replace output from the modern sector, alleviating demands on urban state industry while spurring local agricultural growth. Contemporary reports of model collectives during the CR emphasized the ability of rural industry to develop without competing with the urban, modern sector for scarce resources: because of their small scales and lower technical requirements, these enterprises could be financed from local savings, using local material and labor to produce for a local market. Although they were often set up with some "seed money" and technical aid from the state, once in operation these enterprises were locally managed and self-sustaining, requiring little supervision or coordination from above.

Self-finance was a frequently claimed advantage. One report told the story of how the Changshou County Chemical Fertilizer Plant (in Jiangsu) was financed: Peasants were overjoyed when they heard in 1966 that plans were under way in the county to build a small fertilizer plant. To contribute toward investment, production teams vied with one another in withdrawing their collective accumulation funds from the bank. Because total investment costs for the plant (with an annual capacity of 5,000 tons of ammonia) worked out to only a little more than 2 yuan per *mou* for the county's farmland, the burden was well within local financial capability. Even so, the county revolutionary committee gave careful consideration to the needs of agricultural production and decided to borrow 3.09 million yuan from one-third of the county's communes and production teams. The rest of the investment, another 1.25 million yuan, was raised by the county financial departments. In return, since going onstream in May 1970, the plant supplied 40 kilograms of fertilizer per year to each *mou* of farmland, which was instrumental in pushing forward agricultural modernization and allowing the county to shift from double- to triple-cropping. When the plant turned a profit, loans from production teams were repaid with interest.[3]

New information now available on the CR period paints a vastly different picture of how rural industrialization was carried out. Although some of the investment funding for rural industry was raised locally, outside of the state sector, available aggregate statistics show the share of total investment financed by state funds to have been surprisingly large. Specifically, survey data from the Ministry of Chemical Industries indicate that the combination of budgetary allocations and "replacement and renovation" *(gengxin gaizao)* funds had financed over 8 billion yuan of the investment in small nitrogenous fertilizer plants during 1958–1979, accounting for up to two-thirds of the estimated total investment during the period.[4] For the farm-machinery industry, which was one of the main recipients of budgetary allocations, state grants alone provided some 8–9 billion yuan during 1966–1978, accounting for more than half of total investment in the industry.[5] Even for industries not specifically targeted for state grants, recent information reveals that state funds were made available through a variety of "informal" channels.

With information pieced together from fieldwork, interviews, and published and unpublished reports, this chapter reexamines the financing of rural industrialization to investigate the true extent of contribution from local resources. Aside from determining whether local self-reliance was myth or reality, the source of funds is important for several reasons. First, it sheds light on the extent and nature of state participation in rural industrialization. Second, efficiency arguments for the walking-on-two-legs strategy depend critically on the local sector's ability to mobilize resources that are unavailable or unsuitable for use in the modern sector: only in this way can development in the local sector be unambiguously growth-enhancing. If the local sector is competing with the modern sector for state funds, then growth in the local sector may simply be displacing that in the modern sector, and the net effect of local development is uncertain. Finally, the source of funds has important incentive implications. Under decentralized management, local funds are more likely to be carefully husbanded because of their higher opportunity costs to the localities. By contrast, from the local perspective, funds earmarked to be remitted upward bear essentially zero costs.

This investigation of the financing of rural industrialization provides some crucial answers to explaining the program's extremely poor performance.[6] By showing that state funds were readily available for use in investment, I argue that this "easy money" fed excessive growth in the program so that, by the mid-1970s, rural industries had expanded beyond optimal scales and local supply capabilities, creating enormous technical, supply, and financial problems. The braking and corrective effect that local management should have imposed was nonexistent because decentralization policies had created a lopsided incentive structure that was entirely in favor of local expansion. With policies allowing enterprise losses easily to be passed along to the state budget while leaving virtually all output of rural industry for local allocation, localities bore few financial costs but reaped all the benefits of production.

At the same time, I argue that the extent of state financing in rural industrialization was probably unintended and resulted partly from the difficulty of monitoring the use of informal mechanisms that allowed local governments to divert state funds to finance investment. However, rather than attributing this to the breakdown of financial discipline during the Maoist period, I argue that the causal link ran in the opposite direction: the origins of many of these practices to divert state funds can be traced to specific policies of the 1960s and early 1970s, and it was the use of these methods that led eventually to a complete breakdown in financial discipline. In this chapter *state* refers to the central government and its agencies, and *local* refers mostly to provinces and counties, which were the key levels of administration for rural industry.

THE FINANCING OF RURAL INDUSTRIALIZATION

Sorting out the financing of rural industrialization is unfortunately not a straightforward exercise. First of all, few aggregate statistics were published during the CR period, and financial data were especially scarce. Second, under the push for local self-reliance, reports tended to emphasize the extent of local finance, often understating or neglecting to mention state contributions. Third, under the decentralization policies that were implemented (see Chapter 7), many state resources were transferred to local management, and funds that ostensibly came from county or prefectural allocations might have originated from central revenues. Finally, as we shall see, the use of unconventional accounting methods was widespread during this period, and the very nature of these practices makes it difficult to know the true valuation of investment, far less the source of finance. Although we can show that much of what was called local self-finance *(difang zichou zijin)* actually consisted of state funds diverted from other categories, it is not possible to determine the total amounts so used. Nevertheless, the picture that emerges contains some crucial pieces of the puzzle of rural industrialization.

Designated Funds

We begin by enumerating the major sources of state funding. Among the *designated* sources of funds for investment in rural industry were state grants under the categories of "special funds for the five small industries" and "aid to people's communes." Because of their critical assigned role in providing inputs for agricultural mechanization, which was itself a key priority during the CR,[7] a special allocation of 8 billion yuan was made during the Fourth Five-Year Plan (1970–1975) for use in building key projects in the "five small industries."[8] It is not known whether additional allocations were made during the Fifth Five-Year Plan. In addition, it was decided in 1970 (partially retroactively) that funding under the budgetary item of "aid to people's communes" should be used for farm mechanization. During 1966–1978 much of the over 7 billion yuan allocated under this category went to setting up farm machinery repair and manufacturing stations at the commune and brigade levels.[9] Together these two budgetary items provided as much as 15 billion yuan, the lion's share of which went to the farm machinery industry, which received some 8–9 billion yuan during 1966–1978 from these allocations. A third source of state funds was bank loans, which provided the bulk of working capital for rural state-owned enterprises, as well as investment in selected collective enterprises, such as special low-interest loans for building hydroelectric stations. Although the total of bank lending to rural industry is not known, we can estimate that working capital for the five small industries alone totaled nearly 20 billion yuan.[10]

Aside from funds specifically designated for investment in the five small industries, a variety of other funding sources were employed. To distinguish between funds that were specifically designated for rural industrialization and those that were diverted from other uses, I will call the latter *informal* sources of funds.[11] The three major sources of informal funds for local investment were depreciation allowances retained by enterprises under the category of "replacement and renovation" funds, enterprise profits, and tax revenues.

Informal Funds

Replacement and renovation (*gengxin gaizao*) funds constituted a major source of informal investment funding for local enterprises during the CR. These funds are set aside by enterprises annually to replace worn-out machinery and equipment; the amount is usually 4–5 percent of the value of capital equipment and entered as current operating cost. Until 1967 these amounts were remitted by the enterprises to their supervisory agencies (whether a ministry or a local industrial department) and pooled for centralized allocation. As part of the fiscal decentralization policy that sought to place more resources under local management, beginning in 1967 enterprises under local jurisdiction were allowed to retain their depreciation and major-repairs allowances. The original intent of this change was to allow for more timely maintenance and replacement of equipment, needs that were often neglected by the state bureaucracy. Throughout the CR period, however, these funds were commonly pooled by local governments and industrial bureaus and diverted to investment in new enterprises. With the 1968–1970 decentralization of virtually all non-military enterprises to local management, local governments gained control over most of these depreciation funds (see Chapter 7), which became the largest and most stable source of local investment funds. Nationwide, these funds had grown to over 10 billion yuan per year by 1975, "the greatest part" of which was used for new construction and expansion projects.[12] In 1977 these locally controlled replacement and renovation funds financed nearly 14 billion yuan of investment in fixed assets.[13]

Another important source of informal funds was the diversion of enterprise profits, which took place in several ways: by including investment expenditures in current production costs; by allocating "assignments" to state enterprises to provide equipment, funds, and technical aid to new enterprises; and by "borrowing" funds, equipment, and personnel across enterprises. All of these methods involved transferring investment costs to the state budget through depleting profits or creating losses, which showed up as shortfalls in revenues that were more or less routinely absorbed.

Throughout the CR period the practice of including investment expenditures under current production costs was ubiquitous. The origin of these practices could be traced to the State Council "Draft Regulations on the Financial Management of State Industrial and Transport Enterprises" issued in December 1965. To facilitate technical renovation, the regulations allowed enterprises to include under current production costs selected investment expenditures for small projects. These comprised technical renovation projects costing less than 1,000 yuan for large and medium enterprises and 500 yuan for small enterprises. For the purchase of some equipment and materials, the limits for inclusion in production costs were 800 yuan for large enterprises, 500 yuan for medium enterprises, and 200 yuan for small enterprises. In addition, these regulations opened the way for the "temporary" use of working capital to supplement technical renovation funds, which may have allowed some diversion of bank loans to investment in capital construction as well.[14] Even though the decentralization of depreciation funds in 1967 and 1971 should have eliminated the need for bypassing regular procedures in financing projects of this type, this practice apparently continued and was extended to investment in new productive capacity.

Through the mid-1970s these provisions were liberally interpreted by some local officials as a carte blanche for investment in capacity expansion. This was reflected in the typical development path followed by small fertilizer plants, almost all of which began with design capacities of 3,000 or 5,000 tons of ammonia per year. Once their initial technical problems were solved, many plants embarked on expanding capacity by adding a second or even a third set of equipment. For example, the Xinhui County Plant (Guangdong) went onstream in 1972 with a capacity of 5,000 tons. By 1974 it had begun the second phase of construction, when a second set of equipment was added to double the plant's capacity. In a visit to the plant in 1982, I was told that most of the 7-million-yuan investment for the second phase was "raised" by the plant itself, with only a minor portion coming from state allocations. The manager explained that "most of the cost of construction and new equipment was included under production costs *(tanru chengben),* which accounted for our huge losses during the mid-1970s." The neighboring Kaiping Plant similarly attributed its high costs during the early 1970s to an expansion project, saying that "we had large basic capital construction expenses during those years."[15] Under the aegis of "self-reliance," these practices were extolled in slogans such as "Snowballing," "Raising hens to lay eggs, laying eggs to hatch chickens," and so on. When enterprises were expected to make the bulk of their own machinery and equipment, it was routine to assign workers to tasks associated with expansion projects and simply include the wages and material costs in current production accounts.

Another way in which profits were diverted to investment was the practice of assigning to older enterprises responsibilities for helping to set up new enterprises, including training technicians and managers and providing technical know-how as well as start-up equipment and materials. This was first proposed in 1966 as a way to accelerate the construction of iron and steel bases in inland areas.[16] Later this practice spread to other industries. In the fertilizer industry older, key-point plants were responsible for training workers for new plants. In addition, they were often obligated to send technicians to solve problems or to conduct in-house training at other plants. In the farm machinery industry, repair and manufacturing plants at the county level were largely responsible for setting up and maintaining operations at the commune and brigade plants. Sometimes they were even obliged to provide subcontracting work to sustain profitability at these plants.[17] Even in the cement industry, which was not targeted for special state aid, Heilongjiang Province reported that nearly 100 small plants were set up during 1974–75 with help from the big cement plants.[18] In this way profits in one enterprise were diverted to defray investment and start-up costs in other enterprises. For provinces hard-pressed to promote local development, these practices provided a way to "milk" the large-scale enterprises decentralized to nominal local management, whose output and finances often remained under tight central control.

The diversion of tax revenues was a natural outgrowth of and closely related to the various methods of profit diversion. In 1970 provinces were authorized to approve temporary tax relief for enterprises in the five small industries that were facing financial difficulties.[19] In March 1972 localities were officially given the authority to set taxes and grant exemptions to new enterprises, including those at the commune and brigade levels.[20] This tax-exemption authority often included turnover (industrial-commercial) taxes, which applied to state-owned as well as collective enterprises. Because these turnover taxes are, as in standard Soviet practice, paid by production enterprises and embedded in the structure of prices, exemption from such taxes lowers the total costs and thereby raises profits for the beneficiary enterprise. During the CR period this provided another mechanism for diverting funds destined to be state revenues: by exempting enterprises from turnover taxes, local officials routinely shifted funds from the state treasury to the local pool. In fact, the ability of local governments to reduce or exempt taxes provided an added incentive for enterprises and local governments to transfer profits to other uses, since only money-losing enterprises were eligible for preferential tax treatment.

These informal financing methods had a mutually reinforcing effect. For example, when older enterprises were obligated to help build new ones, this obligation extended naturally from providing technical help and discarded equipment to giving up their depreciation allowances and technical renovation reserves for use in new construction. Indeed, under the slogan "Raising hens to lay eggs, laying eggs to hatch chickens," funds, equipment, and even personnel were freely "borrowed" from older enterprises for use in setting up new ones. Over time, the pooling of enterprise profits (and losses) was so accepted that opportunities to set up enterprises in profitable industries came to be *allocated* to localities as ways of offsetting losses in agriculture-related industries.[21]

By shifting funds across categories and across enterprises, these mechanisms made a mockery of enterprise accounting during the CR period. Given the extremely convoluted bookkeeping this entailed, the amount of investment financed through such diversion of state funds will never be known, although anecdotal evidence indicates that it was substantial. Referring to Shandong, the leading province in developing small cement plants, Song Yangchu, minister in charge of the building materials industry, said that "in recent years, over 85 percent of the total investment in small cement plants had come from funds raised by prefectures, counties, and enterprises themselves, of which the majority came from including [investment] under current production costs and incurring [artificial] losses." As an example, Song cited the Jiaonan County Cement Plant, which had received only 70,000 yuan from county budgetary allocations. All the rest of the plant's 2.1 million yuan in fixed assets was financed by the plant itself, through shifting state subsidies from other lines of production and incurring "losses" that were automatically covered by the state budget.[22]

These practices of diverting profits from within and across enterprises were condoned and even encouraged by the various levels of local government since, under the system of remitting most or all industrial profits and losses to the state budget, neither local governments nor enterprises had any interest in profitability per se. This remained true even after decentralization measures partially reassigned enterprise profits to local governments. As long as retained profits went into "in-budget" revenues, their net retention ratios were subject to budgetary negotiations with higher levels, and their use was constrainted by budgetary stipulations. In any case, an asymmetry existed between profits and losses: whereas county governments were allowed to retain only 60 percent of the profits of the five small industries in the first two years of operation, losses were absorbed at 100 percent by budgetary subsidization in perpetuity (or until the rules changed).

ASSESSING THE SOURCES OF FINANCE

From this accounting of financial sources for rural industry, it is clear that very generous funding was provided from budgetary allocations, which included state grants and bank loans for the priority industries such as chemical fertilizer and farm machinery. Even for lower-priority industries it was possible to "raise" substantial funds *from state resources* through the various informal mechanisms allowed by regulatory changes. Even though all the data and examples cited in this chapter are drawn from the five small industries, these findings can be generalized to the whole rural industrialization program during the CR.

Because of their key role in the agricultural mechanization program, the five small industries were probably the main recipients of state funds, both designated and informal. However, since they comprised the vast majority of rural enterprises and nearly two-thirds of total rural industrial output, they were hardly atypical.[23] (In 1978 they accounted for approximately 9,000 state-owned enterprises at the county [mostly] and prefecture levels, along with nearly 500,000 farm machinery workshops at the commune and brigade levels and nearly 90,000 hyroelectric stations scattered at all levels of rural administration.) Moreover, since they were designated as the "backbone" of the rural industrialization program, it seems fair to focus on them as the standard for gauging the efficacy of the Maoist strategy. Finally, even though this picture of majority state financing probably did not apply across the board to all rural industry, state funds were more or less available to all. Even the lowliest collective enterprises at the commune and brigade levels enjoyed tax holidays throughout the 1970s, which constituted substantial state-funded incentives to help finance their development.

As noted earlier, the growth-augmenting advantages of rural industry depended significantly on its ability to mobilize *additional/marginal* resources. In this light its case is considerably weakened by the finding that state funds financed a major and sometimes overwhelming share of investment. For the purpose of evaluating rural industrialization as a development strategy, I will divide all financial resources into two pots: state resources, which can be mobilized for state projects, and local resources, which cannot be easily mobilized by the state. For this purpose the informal funds used for financing rural industrialization belong in the same pot as designated funds, since they were all monies that either originated from or were destined for the state treasury. With rural industrial growth being financed mostly from the same pot of state funds as that used for modern industry, the program could have been growth enhancing only when rural industry used resources more efficiently than modern industry. This condition was clearly not met in most of the five small industries.[24]

Having ruled out the capital-augmentation argument for rural industry, we can turn to evaluating the efficiency implications of the different sources of finance. That is, accepting that rural industry was largely financed from state funds, we need to ask whether these financing methods were efficient in achieving the objective of growth maximization.[25] Two key issues of allocative control and incentives are treated in turn.

State control was obviously greatest over the designated sources of funds, whose amounts and methods of disbursement were set by state authorities. Among the informal sources, important distinctions can be noted between the replacement and renovation (R&R) funds and the diversion of profits and taxes. R&R funds are more akin to designated funds in that their amounts are determined by state policy through the setting of depreciation rates, and their disbursement is assigned to the local (county/provincial) government by state authorities. At the same time, state control was weaker over R&R funds than over designated funds, since their allocation among competing uses was left to the local authorities. In contrast, state control over funds diverted from profits and taxes was extremely weak: Once the regulatory changes were instituted, the amount of diversion became extremely difficult to control.

Efficiency arguments for decentralized control rest on the assumption that lower-level units are better able to make investment and production decisions than higher-level ones both because they possess superior information about local conditions and because they have better implementation capability. (For the rural industrialization program, decentralized control was in part necessitated by the inability of the state to manage and supervise the several hundred thousand far-flung enterprises.) For decentralization to produce the desired result, however, local agents must be given appropriate incentives that induce them to manage the resources efficiently. These incentives differed significantly among the four sources of funds. R&R funds had the best incentives. Indeed, aside from the problem of the continuing neglect of repair and maintenance needs, local management of R&R funds comes close to the ideal of decentralized control by making block transfers of funds to lower-level units and giving them a free hand to allocate these funds according to local needs. As the main source of local investment funds whose use was relatively unrestricted, R&R funds had opportunity costs that were determined by local economic conditions. Local allocative decisions would be guided by these opportunity costs, at least in principle. In contrast, designated funds that had no alternative use bore zero opportunity costs to the locality, which had no obvious incentive to husband its use of the funds.[26]

In combination with problems of allocative control, the incentive effects of diverting funds from profits and taxes were extremely harmful. Because of the difficulty of monitoring and controlling the diversion of these funds, the use of informal funding mechanisms had the effect of removing, or at least greatly "softening," financial restraints to local investment. This completely undermined the spirit of local participation that had been intended by decentralization policies and the call for self-reliance. In my view, the Maoist strategy was designed to turn over resources to local management, to provide financial and technical aid in setting up turnkey plants in selected industries, and to strengthen local machine-building capabilities, so that localities could gradually acquire the technical and productive capabilities for building, managing, and supplying local industries to meet local needs. In this way a nested hierarchy of responsibility and authority would evolve, whereby local planning and coordination would gradually supplant central planning and reduce the need for coordination across administrative units. However, the use of informal financing methods inadvertently opened a back door to the state treasury. Rather than using state resources only for "pump-priming" and redistributive purposes, local governments took advantage of the informal channels to finance the bulk of investment in rural industry with state funds, saving local resources for other uses. On the face of it, it is not surprising that Maoist China was characterized by lax financial control, except that it ran counter to the logic of self-reliance and severely eroded what Carl Riskin has called the "collective incentive" for efficient management of resources.

At the same time, it led to runaway investment, since decentralization policies had created incentives that were entirely in favor of local expansion. With investment costs easily shifted to the state budget, local governments could finance expansion largely at state expense while extending their control over material resources (with new enterprises creating more claims for state supplies while producing output that was mostly subject only to local allocation). The overexpansion of rural industry beyond technical and supply capabilities had become a major source of inefficiency by the mid-1970s, when rural enterprises were operating at very low rates of capacity utilization, contributing to high costs and huge losses.[27]

The official largesse that was created, albeit inadvertently, ultimately doomed the rural industrialization program. In the process, the central government also lost control over total investment, a crucial macroeconomic lever: the combination of local allocation of growing portions of industrial output, "deep pockets" for financing investment, and the development of local machine-building capabilities had by the early to mid-1970s freed local development from the pace set by central policies.

This examination of the financing of rural industrialization has provided the basis for revising the conventional view of resource allocation during the Maoist period. The conventional view, based on Chinese policy statements emphasizing local self-reliance and supporting evidence from model units, holds that resources were heavily concentrated in the urban, modern sector and that the rural sector was left to develop largely on the basis of its own resources.[28] This view must now be revised to take into consideration the substantial resources provided to the rural industrialization program. In addition, this examination has provided some crucial answers to the puzzle of why local management failed to realize the supposed advantages of flexibility, why it failed to prevent the construction of inappropriate projects, and why mistakes were replicated everywhere, with outcomes that look like a uniform implementation of national policy. The problem was created by the uneven pace of decentralization of control over resources, which left financial control separated from control over investment and materials. Throughout the CR the financial system remained highly centralized under the unified budgetary system, with all profits and losses of state-owned enterprises remitted upward through the hierarchy. Yet investment decisions had been substantially decentralized, along with the allocation of materials. The availability of designated and informal funds for rural industrialization meant that local governments could obtain state funds for investment and pass along all losses to the state budget, while retaining virtually all output of the enterprises for local use. With incentives that allowed localities to socialize (financial) losses while privatizing the (material) gains, local governments had little incentive to prevent inappropriate projects or to run the enterprises efficiently.

The problems of the rural industrialization program clearly illustrate the contradictory impulses that motivated Maoist economic policies. Rural industrialization was implemented under the principle of local self-reliance, where development was to be based largely on local resources and local initiative. Yet it was a program initiated from the top, which determined the scope and objectives of rural industrialization. The conflicting aims of local participation and central control interacted to produce a situation in which control often became divorced from responsibility, with unforeseen and extremely undesirable outcomes.

In earlier papers I have argued that problems of technology choice accounted for only part of the difficulties in the Maoist rural industrialization program, while the main culprits were the excessive pace of development and an irrational regional distribution pattern.[29] This study has concentrated on the policy environment and shown that the seeds for overinvestment and locational and supply problems are to be found in the incentive structure for rural industrialization, particularly in the financial sphere. Furthermore, it has shown that Mao's propensity to use ad hoc and informal methods to fight bureaucratization severely undermined the government's ability to guide development. In the presence of contradictory policies and conflicting incentives, even sensible programs inevitably strayed off course, leading to their ultimate demise. In spite of the numerous technological improvements made since the Great Leap Forward, and in spite of substantial ministerial supervision in the program's reintroduction, rural industrialization fell prey to a variety of Maoist excesses during the Cultural Revolution, like so many other promising programs.

Central-Provincial Investment and Finance: The Cultural Revolution and Its Legacy in Jiangsu Province

PENELOPE B. PRIME

Mention of the Cultural Revolution elicits tales of making "revolution." Struggle sessions, political study, and Red Guard battles left schools and factories barely functioning. After the worst of the turmoil in 1966 and 1967, however, promoting production became part of making revolution. Existing enterprises were revived and new ones were built. Responding to the slogan "Grasp revolution, promote production," even Red Guard students planted gardens and ran small factory workshops at their schools. As a result, production recovered after 1968 and growth rates, particularly industrial growth rates, were high for the rest of the CR period (1966–1976).

China's growth during the Cultural Revolution was shaped by Mao's development policies. Three key policies were the decentralization of enterprises between 1968 and 1970; the promotion of small-scale industry;

and central, Third Front investment in inland provinces to ensure China's survival in case of a coastal attack. These policies are analyzed in Chapters 6–8. In this chapter I examine the economic results of these policies in one particular case, Jiangsu Province.

One issue raised by the nature of these CR policies is what effect they had on central-local relations.[1] For example, Christine Wong has argued, in this volume and elsewhere, that decentralization and the small-scale industry program increased economic production initiated at the county level with concurrent increases in local control over funds and output. At the same time there is evidence that the central government increased spending on its projects and maintained the ability to shift resources between regions and sectors. For example, between 1971 and 1975 the center's budgetary expenditures were 212.5 billion yuan, compared with 153.8 billion yuan during the previous five years.[2] The number of local enterprises and the importance of their output also increased substantially, and yet the type of investment that occurred continued to reflect the center's priority of emphasizing heavy industry.

In the case of Jiangsu I show evidence that decentralization and county-commune industrialization indeed occurred. But these developments did not result in any significant change in central-provincial revenue flows: the provincial budget did not gain at the expense of the center. This suggests the hypothesis that the 1970 decentralization was basically administrative, and that the province's industrial growth was financed primarily by shifting resources horizontally from other sectors rather than vertically from the center to the provinces.

This is not to say that the Maoist policies did not affect China's economy during the CR period. For example, local officials clearly cared about the funds and output they gained with the small-scale industry program, leading them to overinvest in industry whether profitable or not. This is one of the unintended consequences of Maoist policies described in Chapter 8. A second consequence was the weakening of central planning, but without replacing planning with markets, as described in Chapters 6 and 7. But the case of Jiangsu suggests that these phenomena were not significant enough to alter fundamentally the central-provincial balance of power as reflected in budgetary flows. This result is underscored by events in the reform period that began a different type of decentralization characterized by major increases in economic activity outside the state budgetary system altogether.

To develop this hypothesis this chapter first looks at growth in Jiangsu to show that substantial increases in industry occurred, with a growing share of industrial output produced at local levels. The second section analyzes the investment patterns behind Jiangsu's industrial growth during the Cultural Revolution. It shows that provincial investment increased compared with central investment in the province, but that the decentralization of enterprises and shifts in budgetary expenditure toward industry explain much of the rise in provincial investment. The third section analyzes the province's collection and remittance of budgetary revenue to the center. The data imply that the provincial budget did not gain at the expense of the central budget during the CR. Rather, once decentralization and economic growth are accounted for, revenue flows appear normal compared with historical trends, with the province continuing to maintain its financial contribution to the center. Finally, the chapter concludes with some comments on the representativeness of Jiangsu and the implications of these results for understanding China's economy during the culmination of Maoist economics.

GROWTH WITH LOCAL CHARACTERISTICS

Except for 1967 and 1968, both the national and Jiangsu's provincial economies were characterized by substantial industrial growth during the CR period, as shown by Table 1. In 1967 and 1968 output fell an average of 8.2 percent in Jiangsu and 9.5 percent nationally. If we exclude the first two years, industrial growth averaged 16.3 percent per year in Jiangsu and 13.5 percent nationally between 1969 and 1976. Even including the poor-performance years, however, Jiangsu's average annual growth was 11.9 percent between 1966 and 1976, and the national average was 9.5 percent for the same years. So, despite the political turmoil, industrial growth in Jiangsu during the Cultural Revolution exceeded average annual growth rates during the First Five-Year Plan and the Great Leap Forward, and was slightly higher than the average for the thirty years between 1953 and 1982.

In addition to overall industrial growth rates, there is evidence that industry was growing faster at local levels. Unfortunately a complete breakdown of industrial growth of state-owned enterprises managed at different administrative levels, and by collective and commune (township) industry, is not currently available by province.[3] Selected figures for collective and commune industry, however, provide a partial indica-

TABLE 1 Comparative Annual Average
Growth Rates of Gross Value of
Industrial Output in China and
Jiangsu, 1953–1982

Year	China	Jiangsu
1953–1957	18.0	10.7
1958–1962	3.8	4.7
(1959–1962)	(−6.0)	(−5.7)
1963–1965	17.9	19.2
1966–1976	9.5	11.9
(1966–1968)	(−0.3)	(1.1)
(1967–1968)	(−9.5)	(−8.2)
(1969–1976)	(13.5)	(16.3)
1977–1982	9.4	13.2
1953–1982	10.7	11.4

Sources: *Zhongguo tongji nianjian, 1983* (China's statistical yearbook, 1983; Beijing, Zhongguo tongji chubanshe, 1983),
p. 17; *Jiangsu jingji nianjian, 1984* (Jiangsu's economic
yearbook, 1984; Nanjing, Jiangsu tongji ju, 1984), pp.
93–94.

Note: These compounded growth rates are calculated from in-
dices and data on the gross value of industrial output based
on comparable prices. The rates are sensitive to the years
included in each subperiod. When the continuous rates
are particularly sensitive to the endpoints, figures for alternative subperiods are also given, in parentheses.

tion of the increased importance of enterprises that were primarily under
the jurisdiction of municipal, county, or commune administrations.

Table 2 presents both collective (including commune) and commune
industry as proportions of total gross value of industrial output for China
and for Guangdong, Liaoning, and Jiangsu, for selected years. Guangdong and Liaoning have been included as a comparison to the trends
observed in Jiangsu. These figures show that increases in local industry
during the Cultural Revolution varied in magnitude by province, but in
each case increases occurred that were consistent with the national trend.

Looking first at total collective industry, we see that in China nationally the share of industrial output produced by collectively owned enterprises increased from .099 in 1965 to .192 in 1978. In Guangdong the
proportion of collectives increased from .191 in 1965 to .254 in 1975

TABLE 2 Collective and Commune Industry as Proportions of
Total Gross Value of Industrial Output in China,
Jiangsu, Guangdong, and Liaoning, 1962–1985

	China		Jiangsu		Guangdong		Liaoning	
Year	Collective	Commune[a]	Collective	Commune[a]	Collective	Commune[a]	Collective	Commune[a]
1962	n.a.	n.a.	.268	.016	.243	.028	.083	n.a.
1965	.099	n.a.	.114	.011	.191	.017	.066	.003
1970	.110	n.a.	.088	.031	.213	.006	.084	.005
1975	n.a.	n.a.	.280	.065	.254	.036	.154	.023
1978	.192	(.102)	.340	.120	.274	.067	.164	.034
1980	.207	(.119)	.368	.154	.295	.072	.179	.034
1983	.220	(.151)	.394	.177	.313	.079	.185[b]	.037[b]
1985	.249	.104 (.119)	.407	.166	.301	.110	.217	.075

Sources: For China—*Zhongguo tongji nianjian, 1986* (China's statistical yearbook, 1986; Beijing, Zhongguo tongji chubanshe, 1986), p. 273, for total and collective gross value of industrial output. These output figures are given in 1952 prices for output up to 1957, 1957 prices up to 1970, 1970 prices up to 1980, and 1980 prices up to 1985. Figures for commune industrial output are not currently available from Chinese published sources except for 1985. Figures in parentheses are Christine P. W. Wong's estimates, which take changes in reporting methods into account ("Interpreting Rural Industrial Growth in the Post-Mao Period," *Modern China* 14:3–30[1988]). Note that China's 1986 statistical yearbook gives two figures for commune industry in 1985, one on p. 273, which results in a proportion of .277, and one on p. 282, which results in a proportion of .104 (included in this table). This difference probably reflects an attempt to account for changes in how commune-level output is counted, especially after 1984, as described by Wong.

For Jiangsu—Commune industry: *Guanghui de sanshiwu nian: Jiangsu sheng guomin jingji he shehui fazhan tongji ziliao, 1949–1983* (The glorious thirty-five years: Statistics on Jiangsu's national economy and social development, 1949–1983; Nianjing; Jiangsu tongji ju, 1984), pp. 21–22, for total gross value of industrial output, and p. 44, for commune and brigade industrial output. The brigade output is also listed under agricultural output on p. 29. I have included only commune industrial output in the calculations in this table. This source does not state what prices were used, but if one compares these data with others, the prices appear to be in constant 1980 prices. Collective industry for 1962–1983 was derived by subtracting reported gross value of industrial output for state enterprises from total gross value of industrial output. State industrial output was estimated from figures on the province's industrial labor force provided by the Jiangsu statistical bureau (Penelope B. Prime, "The Impact of Self-Sufficiency on Regional Industrial Growth and Productivity in Post-1949 China: The Case of Jiangsu Province," PhD dissertation, University of Michigan, 1987, table 4.16, p. 109), and from figures for state industrial output per worker (*Guanghui de sanshiwu nian,* p. 46).

For Guangdong—*Guangdong sheng tongji nianjian* (Guangdong's statistical yearbook; Hong Kong, Xianggang jingji daobao she, 1984), p. 146, given in 1957 prices for 1952–1971, in 1970 prices for 1971–1981, and in 1980 prices for 1981–1983.

For Liaoning—*Liaoning jingji tongji Nianjian, 1983* (Liaoning's economic yearbook, 1983; Shenyang, Liaoning renmin chubanshe, 1983), p. 361. The Liaoning data are based on 1952 prices for 1949–1957, 1957 prices for 1957–1971, 1970 prices for 1971–1981, and 1980 prices for 1981 and 1982.

All 1985 figures were calculated from *Zhongguo tongji nianjian, 1986,* p. 282.

a. Proportions of commune industry are subsets of collective proportions; total gross value of industrial output used in denominator includes commune industrial output.

b. 1982 figure.

and then to .274 in 1978. In Liaoning it increased from .066 in 1965 to .154 in 1975 and to .164 in 1978. In Jiangsu the proportion of collective industry rose from .114 in 1965 to .280 in 1975. By 1978 this proportion had increased to .340—a full third of the province's total gross value of industrial output.

The proportion of commune industry also increased substantially for these three provinces. In Guangdong the proportion of commune industry in total gross value of industrial output in 1965 was .017. It had increased to .036 by 1976 and to .067 by 1978. In Liaoning in 1965 the same proportion was .003, increasing to .023 in 1975 and to .034 in 1978. In Jiangsu the proportion of commune industry was .011 in 1965, .065 in 1975, and .120 in 1978.

In Jiangsu, then, the growth of both collective industry and commune industry was faster than the national average. These higher-than-average local contributions to industrial output help to explain Jiangsu's relatively faster growth seen in Table 1. If state-owned enterprises in the "five small industries" could be added to collective and commune figures, the increase in industrial output produced locally primarily for local consumption would be even higher.

Evidence from particular areas of Jiangsu also indicates a growing importance of local industry within this province. Wuxi County and Changzhou are two of the better-known cases. A third example is Rudong County near Nantong. Between 1966 and 1976 the total number of industrial enterprises in this county increased from 107 to 396.[4] The components of this increase were as follows: state-owned enterprises from 23 to 42, cooperative factories from 14 to 58, rural town enterprises from 7 to 20, and commune and brigade enterprises from 5 to 222. The only decrease was in handicraft shops, which declined from 58 to 54.

Some of these changes in Rudong and elsewhere were no doubt reclassifications, and perhaps some enterprises were divided into several "new" ones. Nevertheless, the substantial increases in the number and share of collective enterprises, as well as the increases in total industrial output, indicate that provinces, and especially Jiangsu, responded to calls from the center to "promote production" at all levels of the economy.

PATTERNS OF INVESTMENT

One important aspect to consider in trying to understand how the growth of local industry might have affected central-provincial relations is how this growth was financed. Although separate data on investment in collective industry before 1978 are not available, information on the shares of investment supplied through the provincial and central budgets and on the share of investment going to industry is adequate to explain at least part of Jiangsu's industrial growth.

The largest category of budgetary fixed investment is state capital construction investment, or "basic construction" (*jiben jianshe*). Table 3 gives total state capital construction investment as well as separate figures for this investment in Jiangsu contributed by the central budget and Jiangsu's own capital construction expenditure (at the provincial level and all levels below the province).

Figures supplied elsewhere on budgetary investment for the whole of China indicate that the CR period was characterized by high investment levels. Table 3 shows that investment in Jiangsu mirrored these national trends. Total (provincial and central) budgetary capital construction investment in the province increased from .416 billion yuan in 1966 to 1.244 billion in 1976. This represents an average increase of 18 percent per year. Investment in 1976 alone was greater than the total for the entire First Five-Year Plan.

Separating provincial (and lower-level) investment from central investment shows that investment from the provincial budget increased from .214 billion to .878 billion yuan over the same period. Between 1970 and 1978 provincial funds represented an average of 75 percent of total capital construction investment in the province; the remaining 25 percent was contributed by the center. This compares with a provincial contribution of between 40 and 50 percent in the 1950s, 1960s (excluding the Great Leap Forward), and 1980s.

This growth in provincial investment also represents an increase relative to the size of the provincial economy measured by provincial income. Provincial income (Table 4) refers to the provincial equivalent of national income (*quomin shouru*), a measure similar to gross national product.[5] Adjusting changes in investment for growth in the economy provides an indicator of the importance of these levels of investment.

Table 5 and Figure 1 show provincial, central, and total investment in Jiangsu as proportions of provincial income. The second column in Table 5 gives Jiangsu's provincial budgetary capital construction investment as a proportion of provincial income. In 1966 this proportion was .024, increasing to .057 by 1976. The average for the period was .042. This compares with an average of .019 during the First Five-Year Plan

TABLE 3 Provincial, Central, and Total Budgetary
State Capital Construction Investment in
Jiangsu, 1953–1987
(in billions of yuan, current prices)

Year	Provincial	Central	Total
1953–1957	0.413	0.666	1.079
1957	0.128	0.237	0.365
1958	0.842	0.074	0.916
1959	0.942	0.270	1.212
1960	1.080	0.284	1.364
1961	0.293	0.119	0.412
1962	0.131	0.083	0.214
1963	0.149	0.164	0.313
1964	0.190	0.266	0.456
1965	0.210	0.237	0.447
1966	0.214	0.202	0.416
1967	0.157	0.152	0.309
1968	0.137	0.131	0.268
1969	0.259	0.087	0.346
1970	0.501	0.100	0.601
1971	0.595	0.161	0.756
1972	0.731	0.184	0.915
1973	0.810	0.190	1.000
1974	0.704	0.157	0.861
1975	0.761	0.314	1.075
1976	0.878	0.366	1.244
1977	0.815	0.460	1.275
1978	1.143	0.635	1.778
1979	1.429	0.775	2.204
1980	1.820	0.795	2.615
1981	0.913	0.863	1.776
1982	1.048	0.995	2.043
1983	0.982	1.516	2.498
1984	1.182	2.030	3.212
1985	2.055	2.680	4.735
1986	2.569	3.473	6.042
1987	3.242	4.647	7.889

Sources: *Guanghui de sanshiwu nian*, pp. 57–58; *Jiangsu jingji nianjian 1988* (Jiangsu's economic yearbook, 1988; Nanjing, Nanjing daxue chubanshe, 1988), p. III–59; *Jiangsu tongji nianjian 1988* (Jiangsu's statistical yearbook 1988; Nanjing, Zhongguo tongji chubanshe, 1988), pp. 243–244.

TABLE 4 Annual Provincial Income for Jiangsu, 1952–
1987 (in billions of yuan, current prices)

Year	Provincial Income	Year	Provincial Income
1952	3.563	1970	10.372
1953	4.028	1971	12.107
1954	4.017	1972	12.929
1955	4.476	1973	14.232
1956	4.636	1974	14.157
1957	4.869	1975	15.146
1958	5.812	1976	15.387
1959	6.075	1977	16.583
1960	6.630	1978	20.828
1961	5.232	1979	25.792
1962	4.986	1980	27.289
1963	5.650	1981	29.857
1964	7.032	1982	33.500
1965	7.489	1983	38.240
1966	8.843	1984	46.631
1967	7.861	1985	57.846
1968	8.123	1986	66.390
1969	8.857	1987	77.453

Sources: Jiangsu jingji nianjian, 1986 (Jiangsu economic yearbook, 1986; Nanjing, Jiangsu
renmin chubanshe, 1986), p. III–11; *Jiangsu jingji nianjian, 1988*, p. III–21.

and .027 between 1962 and 1965. Only the Great Leap had higher provincial investment/income ratios.

But to what extent was the increase in provincial investment due to
the 1970 decentralization? If accounting substitution was occurring as a
result of decentralization, we would expect central capital construction
funds to fall as provincial funds rose. In absolute terms the center's capital construction contribution to Jiangsu did not fall during or after 1970;
in fact it began to increase (Table 3). But if we look again at central
capital construction investment in Jiangsu as a proportion of provincial
income (Table 5 and Figure 1), we see that the center's investment did
fall between 1969 and 1974 in relation to provincial growth.[6] So part of
the jump in Jiangsu's investment from the provincial budget was no
doubt due to accounting changes from the 1970 decentralization, and
not just to additional resources supplied by the province.

TABLE 5 Provincial and Central Budgetary State
Capital Construction Investment as
Proportions of Provincial Income in
Jiangsu, 1953–1987

Year	Provincial	Central	Total
1953–1957	.019	.030	.049
1957	.026	.049	.075
1958	.145	.013	.158
1959	.155	.045	.200
1960	.163	.043	.206
1961	.056	.023	.079
1962	.026	.017	.043
1963	.026	.029	.055
1964	.027	.038	.065
1965	.028	.032	.060
1966	.024	.023	.047
1967	.020	.019	.039
1968	.017	.016	.033
1969	.029	.010	.039
1970	.048	.010	.058
1971	.049	.013	.062
1972	.057	.014	.071
1973	.057	.013	.070
1974	.050	.011	.061
1975	.050	.021	.071
1976	.057	.024	.081
1977	.049	.028	.077
1978	.055	.030	.085
1979	.055	.030	.085
1980	.067	.029	.096
1981	.031	.028	.059
1982	.031	.030	.061
1983	.026	.040	.066
1984	.025	.044	.069
1985	.036	.046	.082
1986	.039	.052	.091
1987	.042	.060	.102

Sources: Tables 3 and 4 in this chapter.

Figure 1 Provincial and Central Budgetary Capital Construction Investment

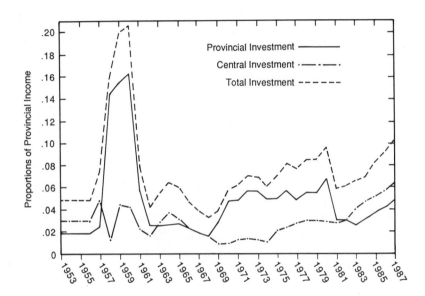

Nevertheless, beginning in 1969 total budgetary investment in the province clearly increased, in both absolute and relative terms. The initial decrease in the center's share was more than compensated for by increases in investment through the provincial budget. By 1976 the proportion of total state capital construction investment relative to provincial income was higher than in any previous period except for the Great Leap Forward, and it continued to increase until 1980.

Where did these additional funds for investment come from? One major source was a shift in expenditures first toward "accumulation" (*jilei*) and away from consumption, and second, within expenditures for accumulation, toward "productive accumulation" (for example, machinery) and away from "nonproductive accumulation" (for example, housing).

Table 6 summarizes these shifts for Jiangsu. The share of accumulation in provincial income was 19.5 percent during the First Five-Year Plan, with a corresponding share of consumption of 80.5 percent. The accumulation share rose to 24.1 percent during the Great Leap Forward and then fell to 21.2 percent in the recovery period. Then, since the beginning of the Cultural Revolution, the accumulation share rose steadily to 22.8 percent between 1966 and 1970 and to 30.5 percent between 1971 and 1975. This rise continued into the reform period to reach 33.1 percent between 1981 and 1985. Within accumulation, expenditures for productive investment followed a similar pattern until it peaked at 91.9 percent during the 1971–1975 period. This extremely high level was not sustained after 1975.

Concurrently with a shift in expenditure toward investment, there was a shift within investment toward industry. Table 7 shows that industry's share of total investment in Jiangsu averaged 60 percent between 1966 and 1975, a level comparable to the Great Leap period. In the 1950s industry's share had been less than 40 percent, and between 1963 and 1965 it was less than 50 percent. Also, within industry, heavy industrial investment represented a full 90 percent of all industrial budgetary investment in the province between 1966 and 1975.[7]

Clearly horizontal shifts in expenditure priorities contributed significantly to the industrial growth that occurred in Jiangsu during the CR

TABLE 6 Proportions of Provincial Income used for
Accumulation and Consumption in Jiangsu,
1953–1985

Year	Consumption	Accumulation	Productive Investment within Accumulation
1953–1957	.805	.195	.780
1958–1962	.759	.241	.899
1963–1965	.788	.212	.858
1966–1970	.772	.228	.859
1971–1975	.695	.305	.919
1976–1980	.679	.321	.793
1981–1985	.669	.331	.648

Source: Calculated from figures given in *Jiangsu jingji nianjian, 1988*, pp. III–24 and III–25.

TABLE 7 Proportions of Total State Budgetary Capital
Construction Investment by Sector in Jiangsu,
1953–1987

Year	Indus-try	Agri-culture	Trans-port	Com-merce	Culture, Educa-tion, and Health	Urban Infra-struc-ture	Other
1953–1957	.386	.348	.043	.054	.137	.029	.003
1958–1962	.575	.181	.155	.018	.043	.017	.009
1963–1965	.482	.277	.129	.021	.049	.035	.007
1966–1970	.568	.217	.120	.040	.020	.023	.013
1971–1975	.614	.176	.124	.037	.024	.011	.013
1976–1980	.606	.118	.108	.045	.039	.039	.044
1981–1985	.544	.039	.133	.056	.057	.062	.107
1987	.605	.023	.143	.032	.057	.058	.082

Source: Calculated from figures given in *Jiangsu jingji nianjian, 1988,* p. III–64.

period. These horizontal shifts in expenditure between sectors have also been shown to have occurred within the central budget as well.[8] Some vertical shift in budgetary expenditure from the center to the province occurred because of decentralization, but the evidence is inconclusive on whether this was more than just an accounting change.

A final consideration with respect to investment is that state capital construction investment is only part of total investment. Sources of "extrabudgetary" funds became more important from the late 1960s onward, and local officials often used these funds for investment in new enterprises (see Chapters 7 and 8). For example, enterprises were allowed to retain their depreciation funds after 1967, ostensibly for "replacement and renovation" *(genxin gaizao)* investment, and collective enterprises could retain a proportion of their profits. To the extent that these funds were available and used for new investment, provincial and therefore total investment in the province would be even higher than Tables 3 and 5 show. The importance of these funds in Jiangsu during the period is not known, because figures for Jiangsu on replacement and renovation investment, and extrabudgetary funds generally, are not available before 1978. However, the next section looks at budgetary data for additional clues to the central-provincial equation during the CR period and suggests that the role of extrabudgetary funds was relatively minor until the reform period.

CENTRAL-PROVINCIAL FINANCE IN JIANGSU
DURING THE CULTURAL REVOLUTION

A key factor in central-provincial relations is the budget. In China's "unified" budgetary system, the majority of revenues are collected at the provincial level and below, and then are remitted to the center. Collected revenues, then, refer to the sum of profits and taxes paid to the finance offices at all provincial administrative levels, excluding profits and taxes of centrally run enterprises, which go directly into the central budget.[9] Remitted revenues are the portion of the province's collected revenues that is turned over to the central budget by the provincial finance bureau. The remaining portion of the province's collected revenues is allocated through the provincial budget.

Table 8 presents Jiangsu's collected revenues, remitted revenues, and revenues retained by the province for expenditures.[10] In absolute terms both the revenues collected by the province and the amount the province remitted to the center increased after 1969, with the exception of 1974.

It is again more revealing to look at these revenue categories as compared with growth in the provincial economy. These proportions are given

TABLE 8   Revenues Collected, Revenues Remitted,
and Revenues Retained in Jiangsu,
1952–1987 (in billions of yuan)

Year	Revenue Collected by Province	Revenue Remitted to Center	Revenue Retained as Expenditure
1952	0.680	0.470	0.210
1953	0.778	0.528	0.250
1954	0.867	0.579	0.288
1955	0.847	0.558	0.289
1956	0.966	0.558	0.408
1957	1.010	0.530	0.480
1958	1.782	0.655	1.127
1959	2.494	1.058	1.436
1960	2.619	0.867	1.752
1961	1.745	0.879	0.866
1962	1.331	0.744	0.587
1963	1.370	0.707	0.663
1964	1.724	0.974	0.750

Year	Revenue Collected by Province	Revenue Remitted to Center	Revenue Retained as Expenditure
1965	1.940	1.142	0.798
1966	2.289	1.384	0.905
1967	1.702	0.908	0.794
1968	1.620	1.006	0.614
1969	2.174	1.316	0.858
1970	2.866	1.733	1.133
1971	3.412	2.161	1.251
1972	3.784	2.287	1.497
1973	4.222	2.591	1.631
1974	3.951	2.162	1.789
1975	4.341	2.571	1.770
1976	4.402	2.531	1.871
1977	5.165	3.169	1.996
1978	6.109	3.271	2.838
1979	5.928	2.722	3.206
1980	6.245	3.350	2.895
1981	6.304	3.925	2.379
1982	6.661	4.198	2.463
1983	7.307	4.078	3.229
1984	7.628	3.713	3.915
1985	8.899	3.846	5.053
1986	9.872	3.256	6.616
1987	10.717	3.917	6.800

Sources: *Jiangsu jingji nianjian, 1986*, p. III–50; *Jiangsu jingji nianjian, 1988*, p. III–87.

Note: Figures for remittances are calculated as the difference between revenues collected and expenditures. Note that revenue and expenditure data for Jiangsu published in 1988 had been adjusted for 1984 and 1985 compared with figures for these years published in 1986. Also, in 1986 data for 1952–1966 had been adjusted from figures released earlier.

in Table 9 and Figure 2. With decentralization in 1970, the proportions of both revenue collected by the provincial government and revenue remitted to the central government increased. Between 1970 and 1978 the proportion of collected revenue averaged 29 percent, compared with only 20 percent during the First Five-Year Plan and 24 percent between 1963 and 1969. This increase would be expected as a result of decentralization, since more enterprises turned over their profits and taxes to the provincial budget instead of directly to the central budget. This proportion reached a high of 34 percent during the Great Leap Forward for the same reason. But Jiangsu's remittances to the central budget as a proportion of total provincial income also increased during the CR period. This proportion averaged .17 between 1970 and 1978, compared with an average of .15 during the First Five-Year Plan and Great Leap Forward and .13 during the 1960s. If decentralization had meant a weakening of central control, we might expect provincial remittances to have decreased, since more government revenue was now incorporated into the provincial budget. The fact that remittances to the center increased suggests that decentralization did not result in smaller revenue transfers from the province to the center.

Further strengthening this result is the fact that the proportion of retained revenues that made up the province's budget remained stable during the CR period. This proportion fluctuated between 10 and 12

TABLE 9 Revenues Collected, Revenues Remitted, and Revenues Retained in Jiangsu, 1952–1987

Year	Revenue Collected by Province	Revenue Remitted to Center	Revenue Retained as Expenditure
1952	.191	.132	.059
1953	.193	.131	.062
1954	.216	.144	.072
1955	.189	.124	.065
1956	.208	.120	.088
1957	.207	.108	.099
1958	.307	.113	.194
1959	.411	.175	.236
1960	.395	.131	.264
1861	.334	.168	.166
1962	.267	.149	.118
1963	.242	.125	.117
1964	.245	.138	.107
1965	.259	.152	.107
1966	.259	.157	.102
1967	.217	.116	.101
1968	.199	.123	.076

Year	Revenue Collected by Province	Revenue Remitted to Center	Revenue Retained as Expenditure
1969	.245	.148	.097
1970	.276	.167	.109
1971	.282	.179	.103
1972	.293	.177	.116
1973	.297	.182	.115
1974	.279	.153	.126
1975	.287	.170	.117
1976	.286	.164	.122
1977	.311	.191	.120
1978	.293	.157	.136
1979	.230	.106	.124
1980	.229	.123	.106
1981	.211	.131	.080
1982	.199	.125	.074
1983	.191	.107	.084
1984	.164	.080	.084
1985	.154	.067	.087
1986	.149	.049	.100
1987	.138	.050	.088

Sources: Annual revenue and expenditure figures are from *Jiangsu jingji nianjian, 1986,* p. III–50, and *Jiangsu jingji nianjian, 1988,* p. III–87; provincial income is from Table 4 in this chapter.

percent between 1969 and 1973, and then between 12 and 14 percent until 1979. Again it does not seem that the provincial budget gained at the expense of the central budget as a result of either the 1970 decentralization or the growing importance of local industry in the province. These results also suggest that extrabudgetary revenue probably did not increase significantly in proportion to growth in the provincial economy.

These trends during the Cultural Revolution stand in sharp contrast to what occurred during the reform period. Compared with 17 percent in the 1970s, remittances as a proportion of provincial income averaged only 10 percent between 1978 and 1987, falling to 5 percent in 1986 and 1987. This change, however, did not mean the provincial budget therefore rose. Revenue collected as a proportion of provincial income also began to fall after 1977, when it had reached it highest level since the Great Leap Forward. The net effect has decreased the province's re-

Figure 2 Revenues Collected, Revenues Remitted, and Revenues Retained

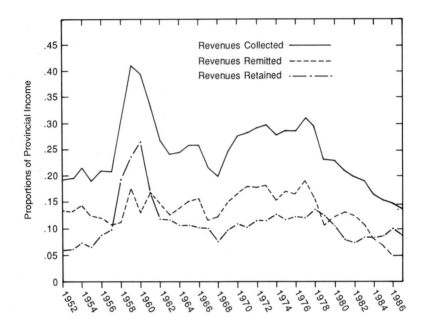

tained revenue, and therefore the size of the provincial budget relative to growth in the provincial economy, to an average of 9.6 percent since 1977, hitting a low of 7.4 percent in 1982.

The overall effect on decentralization of the reform policies has been very different from that of the Cultural Revolution and earlier periods. As the provincial economy has grown, the role of the state budget at both the provincial and the central levels has shrunk significantly. If access to funds outside the state budgetary system has any relation to local control, as we might expect, then the change in the central-provincial balance of power during the 1980s and later has surely been much greater than during the 1970s or earlier.

Looking at a specific example of the combined effects of Maoist economic policies during the Cultural Revolution adds perspective to our understanding of this period. For example, in provinces that did not receive Third Front, central investment, we might expect industrial growth to have been modest; or where industrial growth was concentrated at local levels, we might expect to see that local financing grew as the center's role fell. In Jiangsu neither of these was the actual outcome. Instead, all levels of the economic system responded to directives and incentives to increase investment in industry, with little apparent effect on the central-provincial budgetary system.

As a result of the response to industry, a key characteristic of this period was a major horizontal shift in resources to industry from other sectors. As during the Great Leap, even agriculture was to be promoted by increasing industrial inputs, with the result that industrial development was put first. This priority can be clearly seen in both investment and output trends.

The problem was, however, that the industrial strategy was neither coordinated nor based on economic criteria. Some enterprises were profitable, but many were not. Problems of duplication, input shortages, and poor technology led to inefficiency and waste, paid for by the increasing share of resources going to industry. This investment bias within the system was reinforced by the increasing local role, but there was little to ensure proper use of investment funds. The resulting imbalances and inefficiencies eventually worsened enough to cause a crisis at the center. The maintenance of the flow of funds from localities to the center throughout the Cultural Revolution is perhaps one reason the crisis did not occur sooner.

Whether all the trends observed in Jiangsu were also occurring elsewhere in China remains to be explored. Figures for the national level suggest that the growth of local industry and the industrial investment bias were occurring in many places. With respect to the budget, if the growth of local industry was affecting revenue flows, we would expect to see evidence of this influence in Jiangsu, where local industry grew substantially faster than the national average. That it did not suggests that provinces and municipalities that historically contributed major shares of their revenues to the center, like Jiangsu, probably continued to do so.[11] If this is the case, Jiangsu's story suggests a hypothesis that would explain the coexistence of ambitious central projects with local industrialization.

PART THREE

Culture

Arts Policies of the Cultural Revolution: The Rise and Fall of Culture Minister Yu Huiyong

RICHARD KRAUS

Yu Huiyong was minister of culture in 1975 and 1976, at the end of the Cultural Revolution, and China's de facto chief arts administrator after 1971. Although Yu has been forgotten by most Chinese, he was once famous by his pen name, Chu Lan, over which appeared the left's major proclamations about the arts. Moreover, Yu was the theorist behind the CR's model stage works and was their chief creator after 1969.[1] A musician, Yu participated in radical arts reforms even before 1966, and his importance grew as China's arts institutions became increasingly disabled, then were reorganized. In some ways his is a familiar story of a young man from the country who goes to the big city, joins a fast crowd, and rises high, only to fall hard in the end.

Whereas we now know much about the roles of Mao Zedong, Zhou Enlai, Jiang Qing, and other top Party figures during the CR, we know much less about the next rank of leaders. Yu Huiyong's career helps illustrate this still poorly understood second tier of radical leadership. More important, an examination of Yu also compels a reexamination of the arts policies of the CR: a policy area of great noise but little sustained success. At the simplest level CR arts policy was to replace old culture with new. In practice the CR was far better at destruction than at construction. Although Yu helped create dramatic and popular new works of art, they were few in number and concentrated in the theater, at the expense of other genres. Even radical leaders admitted the shortage of art products and tried unsuccessfully to cope with it, unwilling or unable to give up their close control for a decentralized, more spontaneous culture. The arts shortage became a bitter political issue in the last years of the CR and contributed significantly to the fall of Chinese radicalism. The rapid pace of change in arts institutions encouraged cultural bureaucrats to rely on the easily regulated model stage works as the approved technique for reform. Moreover, the arts shortage was compounded by the radicals' faulty sociological understanding, which denied not only the legitimacy but even the existence of an urban middle-class audience for culture; the most sophisticated of China's arts consumers were denied any art not designed for workers and peasants. Yu Huiyong helped shape these policies. By examining his career, we can better understand the political constraints that turned art from the strongest weapon of the Chinese left into an instrument of its demise.

THE MAKING OF A CULTURAL REVOLUTIONARY

Yu Huiyong was fifteen when he joined the revolution as a musician in Shandong's Jiaotong Cultural Association in 1947.[2] The earliest story about Yu is unflattering. As a naïve youth, unsophisticated in the ways of revolutionary war, Yu hid his bundled belongings when his troupe came under Guomindang attack, attaching a note addressed to the "Brethren Officers and Men of the Chiang Army," imploring them to pass his things on to his aging mother, should he perish in the battle.[3] After the Communists repelled their attackers, Yu's letter was discovered, and he was temporarily assigned to another unit.

Yu evidently proved himself in other ways, as he continued with his music after Liberation, joined the Communist Party, and was selected to attend the Shanghai Conservatory. The Shanghai Conservatory is China's oldest music school, and arguably its most bourgeois unit of higher education. Its students were overwhelmingly urban and middle class, and its cultural ambience was self-consciously European. The piano department was its most popular course of study, where after 1949 visiting Soviet Russians replaced expatriate White Russians and Italians in teaching young Chinese to play Chopin, Schubert, and Beethoven. Yu stood out sharply in this environment, where he was a kind of affirmative-action student, selected because his musical ability matched a politically reliable family background and activist credentials, at a time when China's leaders pressed educators to change the social composition of higher education.

Unsurprisingly, many at the conservatory looked down on Yu because of his background. Most students had been raised in Western-oriented, intellectual families and had practiced European instruments from childhood. Yu and other students transferred from cultural work teams tended to be shunted into the Department of National Music, where instruction was offered in traditional Chinese instruments and folk songs. Cosmopolitan music professors looked down on this department as artistically backward, a politically necessary haven for the dying music of Chinese feudalism. They regarded the department and its music as easy and used it as a dumping ground for countrified students whom they had not wanted to admit in the first place.

The conservatory's president, composer He Luting, was condescending. He regarded China's traditional musical instruments as unmodernized and unscientific, incapable of producing accurate sounds.[4] He also resisted the politicization of his conservatory students: when central officials called for students to take part in labor, he limited their participation.[5]

After graduation, Yu was retained as a composition teacher in the National Music Department. Other conservatory faculty presumed that he was there because of his political credentials and mocked him as the "melody composer" for his poor understanding of the European arts of harmony and accompaniment. Yu's cosmopolitan critics presumed that his interest in native music reflected his lack of ability to learn "real" music.

Yu grew quite resentful as a second-class member of the conservatory faculty. In 1955 he vented some of his feeling in an angry article in *People's Music,* the journal of the Chinese Association of Musicians.[6] Ostensibly Yu criticized Peng Boshan, a Shanghai cultural official who was under fire as a "Hu Feng element." In fact, Yu used his article to strike back against the contempt toward Chinese music that he encountered in the conservatory. Yu complained that the Eurocentric vocal music department would not perform Chinese folk music, which had been struck from the conservatory's concert programs. "What was especially painful was for some teachers to say openly to their classes: 'Let's not sing these things any more!' " Yu said that they also held the performers of native music in contempt. "Who wouldn't understand? Artists—professional singers and instrumentalists who come from the midsts of the laboring people—who have already endured past suffering from social contempt, how can they put up with the continuation of this kind of scorn today?"

Here, in the heart of Westernized culture in China, Yu struck out at the interrelated bias against native music and prejudice against artists with working backgrounds. Such an outburst did little to increase Yu's popularity with his more bourgeois colleagues, but it may have ensured that they would treat him with greater caution.[7] At the same time, Yu was an active scholar, editing several collections of folk songs and writing on tonality in Chinese music.[8]

YU HUIYONG ON THE EVE OF THE CULTURAL REVOLUTION

The source of Cultural Revolution arts policies was the early 1960s battle to reform Beijing opera. Yu Huiyong's resentments helped make him receptive to this movement, where his compositional skills were welcomed rather than mocked. He contributed music for *Taking Tiger Mountain by Strategy* and was the principal composer of the music for *On the Docks* in early 1965. *On the Docks (Haigang)* was a project of Shanghai's Beijing Opera Troupe; the first of the model operas to be set after Liberation, it featured the struggle of militant stevedores to load a ship for Africa despite counterrevolutionary sabotage. It was much loved by Jiang Qing, and it was on this project that Yu came to her attention.[9]

Yu came late to *On the Docks*. This opera began in 1963 as *Morning on the Docks,* a *Huaiju* (northern Jiangsu opera) under the patronage of Shanghai's Mayor, Ke Qingshi. Jiang Qing was taken by its modern, industrial theme, which placed former coolies on stage, and urged that it be made into her favorite form, Beijing opera. The revised version was less revolutionary and stressed the cultivation of revolutionary successors. The opera came to focus on the young worker Han Xiaoqiang, who was portrayed as "ideologically backward and with a confused state of mind." This was suggestive of "middle characters," whose representation in art was under fire for suggesting lack of commitment to revolution.[10] Jiang Qing criticized the revision, scolding the *On the Docks* troupe: "I oppose putting middle characters on stage. You have to be truly possessed to let an excellent performer portray a middle character!" Jiang complained that the actors did not look like dock workers but like university students or school teachers, showing smiles instead of strength.[11]

Jiang Qing had not met Yu Huiyong but had liked two of his articles on opera reform. She invited Yu to help restore *On the Docks* to political rectitude, stressing the heroes of the proletariat.[12] The controversy over middle characters raged through the early 1960s over the question of for whom artists were to create their works. Zhou Yang suggested a relatively broad audience that reflected most of the groups in Chinese society: "Workers, peasants, soldiers, intellectuals, students, staff members and commercial workers, etc., are people we serve. The present situation is different from that in the days when the Yan'an forum on literature and art was held, because the scope of service is much wider today."[13]

In contrast, radicals stressed the continuing relevance of the formula in Mao's Yan'an talks: literature and art for workers, peasants, and soldiers. As the celebration of guerrilla ways intensified, the Maoists demonstrated their power by purging Zhou Yang's depty, Shao Quanlin. At the 1962 Dairen conference on writing short stories for peasants, Shao had urged writers to describe middle characters, who had recognizable mixtures of virtues and faults, and who would be more plausible to peasant readers than the wooden and unrealistically perfect figures of an earlier era in Yan'an.[14]

Yu recognized that the middle-character controversy was a metaphor for China's class system. Middle characters were the middle class, and a cultural reform that sought to replace "emperors, kings, generals, and ministers" on the stage by images of laboring people could not be sidetracked by effete clerks, indecisive office workers, and self-anguished intellectuals. No matter that these urban, middle-class groups existed in China and in fact were increasing along with industrialization. The sacred text of Mao's Yan'an talks demanded art for workers, peasants, and soldiers, and this is what Yu produced. The sociology of China inherent in *On the Docks* suggested that the radicals were prepared to ignore the existence of urban, middle-class Chinese and thereby to be freed of any need to acknowledge this class through united-front policies in art.[15]

The collaboration of Yu and Jiang Qing worked well. Yu later insisted that *On the Docks'* "every word and sentence, every tune and beat, is permeated with" Jiang Qing's "heart blood." [16] *On the Docks* was not yet a "model" opera; that designation would await the outbreak of the Cultural Revolution. When Jiang Qing, Ke Qingshi, and other radicals determined to make their stand in the battle over culture on the stage, they created a need for personnel like Yu Huiyong, who was professionally trained and politically radical.

Literature has traditionally been the art closest to the center of China's politics. The radicals chose the opera for their innovations precisely because literature was more firmly in the control of their adversaries. Not only was it easier to seize power in the theater, but Jiang Qing's own background gave her a kind of self-confidence about the stage that she lacked in other art forms. Opera is also a more popular genre than literature, making it more suitable for populist reforms. Finally, the operas did lend themselves to presentation as models in a way that novels or poems did not. This choice gave the arts of the Cultural Revolution immediate vitality and political direction, but we shall see that it also diminished the role of spontaneity and amateur inspiration, two important elements for a revolutionary program for culture.

UPWARD MOBILITY AND INSTITUTIONAL DISARRAY

Yu Huiyong was caught up in the turbulence that opened the Cultural Revolution. Before it was over, he had become a prime example of the new leaders raised up to replace those brought down by the movement. As an activist in Jiang Qing's opera reform, Yu was enthusiastic about toppling the existing cultural establishment. Although colleagues and students from Yu's Department of National Music were prominent in the campaign against the conservatory president, He Luting, in the summer of 1966, Yu was not publicly among them. [17] As a professor at the Shanghai Conservatory, Yu was himself a member of that establishment (even if a disgruntled one) and was attacked in the summer of 1966 for propagating feudalism through traditional Chinese music. His enemies denounced him to Zhang Chunqiao, but with little impact. Yu was transferred to Beijing in September 1966; the central cultural apparatus was increasingly paralyzed, and Jiang Qing wanted her own man on the scene.

But telegrams of protest followed Yu from Shanghai, and before a house could be arranged for him, Zhang decided in November that Yu should "return to Shanghai and undergo a test!" [18] Yu was needed more in Shanghai than in Beijing. Zhang commissioned Yu to restore order to the conservatory, scene of extremely bitter and violent Red Guard struggles. Yu did not have an easy time of it; in July 1967 Zhang had to silence continuing Red Guard objections by declaring that Yu's critics were "setting up a rival stage in opposition to the proletarian headquarters." After this, Yu became head of the conservatory's revolutionary committee; in April 1968 Yu presided over the televised criticism of He Luting, his predecessor as head of the conservatory. Eventually Yu managed to quiet its conflicts until the institution was effectively closed.[19]

Yu, then thirty-five, had begun a political ascent relying on the patronage of two of the most powerful radical leaders, a fact he admitted in 1977.[20] Yu never hesitated to express his loyalty: "Without Jiang Qing, there would be no Yu Huiyong." Nor were his patrons bashful about indicating their relationship; Jiang Qing called Yu "my minister of culture."[21] But Yu's patrons were also becoming dependent on him. For Zhang Chunqiao, Yu was a valuable assistant in his successful effort to restore order to Shanghai.[22] Yu's tough persistence and loyalty were rewarded when Zhang promoted him to head Shanghai's Municipal Cultural Bureau (and to be secretary of its Party committee). Because of Shanghai's trend-setting role in China's arts, this was a post of national importance.

Jiang Qing also had further need for Yu. Despite her zeal for reforming opera and music, Jiang had no formal musical training beyond youthful piano lessons. Yu Huiyong became her most important musical adviser. Cultural Revolution arts projects continued to demand attention, while Jiang herself was increasingly busy with more overtly political issues.[23] Yu Huiyong, a politically seasoned and trusted professional, became her viceroy for musical revolution.[24]

In this capacity Yu worked on such projects as *The Red Lantern with Piano Accompaniment,* an adaptation of the model opera that signaled to China's musicians that European instruments and techniques could play a role in the Cultural Revolution. Reflecting on his experiences as an object of scorn at the conservatory, Yu must have enjoyed denouncing middle-class music in *People's Daily,* where he said the piano had formerly spread the backward ideology of the bourgeoisie, prettified its exploitation, pushed individualism, and encouraged musicians to seek a false "peaceful coexistence" through international competitions.[25]

The personalism that helped make Yu indispensable to his superiors was intensified by the uncertainty that accompanied rapid change in arts institutions. Old centers of power in culture died (such as the Writers' Association) or were reconstructed (such as several opera troupes). Personal bonds, such as the shared hometown of Jiang Qing and Kang Sheng, offered reassurance and the semblance of security in an atmosphere of intrigue. Yu also turned to personal ties as he sought loyal subordinates, hiring the leader of his 1947 cultural work team to work with him in Beijing.[26]

As Yu rose to higher positions—he was a delegate to the Ninth Party Congress in 1969—he had to cope with the problem of how to build an institutional base for the arts programs of the Cultural Revolution. He had learned to be suspicious of the extensive ad hoc organization that characterized the opening of the movement. Revolutionary committees, rebel alliances, and even the Central Cultural Revolution Group were necessary for overthrowing the arts establishment. But after the radicals already controlled culture, the uncertainty and constant flux of guerrilla-style organizations exacerbated factionalism and intrigue, tendencies of the arts even in the most stable of times.

Stability and control, however, were achieved only at the expense of artistic spontaneity. When the Cultural Revolution did inspire unrehearsed artistic impulses early in the movement, they received little central support and often were suppressed. Perhaps the most famous spontaneous art of the movement was the play *Madman of the Modern Age.* When everyone associated with this production was jailed as a May 16 element, it did little to encourage further spontaneous artistic activity.[27]

Yu Huiyong discouraged freewheeling and impetuous art and instead channeled popular participation through bureaucratically predetermined forms. The concept of the model was central to the radicals' vision. It permitted maximum bureaucratic control with minimum decentralization of resources. Members of arts units were free to emulate official models but not to offer their own creations. Jiang Qing early rejected suggestions to "organize small detachments and send them down to produce fragments and minor items for the viewing of workers, peasants, and soldiers." Of course it could be done, she said, but then "it would be impossible to produce things really serving socialism and really suitable for the needs of workers, peasants and soldiers. To combat self-interest and repudiate revisionism is a hard and difficult matter. It would be wrong indeed if some people should attempt to escape from it by exploiting the activities of going to the countryside and the factories."[28] Instead, Jiang wanted to retain central control over the models, then to disseminate them throughout the country through movies, which would set standard versions for local live performances and adaptations.[29]

Control was more important than rapid production. Jiang Qing rebuked a film company for too speedily making a documentary on some revolutionary operas:

After I saw the movie last evening, I felt uneasy. Is it possible for you to make some supplementary filming? If it is shown in the whole country as it is now, those workers, peasants, and soldiers who have not seen these operas before would not be able to understand them; for they, unlike us, are not familiar with these operas. You should not be impatient to show it, but should see how to reform it well. . . .

Comrade Tan Yuan-shou of Peking First Troupe of Peking Opera is one of the impatient ones.[30] He complained that no new operas have been produced (of late). This sentiment is understandable; but, if new ones are produced crudely as was done in the past, people would still strike us down. It would be preferable that our eight model operas occupy the stage for the time being.[31]

The demand for control undermined another part of the radical cultural program, the cultivation of amateur artists. The highly polished model works demanded skilled professional performers. In addition to films, amateurs who staged local productions of the models studied manuals that specified minor details (including measurements of props and fabric for costumes).[32] Amateur activity remained an important and relatively successful part of the radical arts program, but it was always carefully guided.[33]

New centers of power emerged in the world of culture, such as the People's Liberation Army, and new rural models of cultural activism, such as Dazhai's Xiyang County, Hu County (home of the amateur painters), and Tianjin's Xiaojinzhuang (Jiang Qing's favorite). Beijing and Shanghai remained important centers of cultural power but were chastened and had to share power with such upstart areas as Shenyang, home of Mao Yuanxin. Power also shifted among genres in ways that aided Yu's rise.

The long reign of literature as the central art form was broken as music was raised to new heights through the model operas and the revival of mass singing of revolutionary songs. The new cultural stars were the singer Qian Haoliang and the dancer Liu Qingtang (later made deputies to Yu in the Ministry of Culture), as well as the pianist Yin Chengzong (composer of the *Yellow River Concerto,* who became deputy head of the Central Philharmonic).

Yu and his patrons chose discipline over spontaneity, leading easily to a new prominence for the People's Liberation Army. The army had long been a major cultural center through its massive General Political Department. Radicalized before 1966, the army looked like a steady hand for the arts. Jiang Qing held a Shanghai Forum on Literature and Art with PLA cultural officials in February 1966, followed by a series of national, regional, and local conferences throughout the army.[34]

This was the background for the curious phenomenon of the transfer of control over the Beijing First Opera Company from the capital's municipal committee to the army in November 1966, a pattern that was soon followed by other major ensembles, such as the Central Philharmonic. "It was as if the Pentagon suddenly took over the Metropolitan Opera Company and all other performing arts groups in New York City, and stipulated that their subsequent work be directed personally by a close female relative of the President."[35] The army looked good, not only because of its radical politics, but also because it was a safe haven in a turbulent time and provided good housing, food, and facilities. Lesser artists then also pressed to be absorbed into the army's revolutionary and protective embrace. But the process was protracted, and the issue frequently arose when leftist leaders addressed rebel groups in the arts. In April 1967 Jiang Qing and Yao Wenyuan announced to a group of enthusiastic ballet students that the problem of joining the army had been resolved for them but not for their presumptuous classmates whose work she had not seen.[36] But in November Jiang still had to urge patience about joining the army: Lin Biao had issued an order to Yang Chengwu and the Military Commission "to select several cadres of the army or division level to take charge of this matter. . . . If you clamor for joining the army all day long, you would forget about everything else."[37]

YU HUIYONG AS CHU LAN

The promised stability of army influence was broken by the Lin Biao affair in 1971, which led to a rapid decline in military influence over culture. As China began to regularize its administration in 1971, the State Council established a "culture group," directed by Wu De.[38] Yu Huiyong was appointed Wu's deputy and quickly became the effective head of the new body, as Wu was kept busy as mayor of Beijing and head of its Communist Party. When the culture group was elevated into a proper ministry in 1975, Yu was appointed to be its head. From this position Yu served as Jiang Qing's "top-grade watchdog," taking a prominent role in the growing feud between the left and Zhou Enlai.[39] Yu was charged with keeping the Cultural Revolution alive in the arts and resisting efforts to tone down its more militant aspects.

The death of Lin Biao also meant the downfall of Yu's rival in music administration, the radical head of the Shenyang Conservatory, the composer Li Jiefu. The popular "Jie Fu," whose musical settings of Mao quotations were an alternative to Yu's operas, allegedly had prepared a new national anthem for a China under Lin's leadership. The demise of Qi Benyu in 1968, charged with leadership of an allegedly counterrevolutionary "May 16 Corps," had similarly removed a rival leftist leader with influence in the musical community.[40]

Yu received little publicity for his role, at least under his own name. As Chu Lan, however, he became famous throughout China. Yu was the head of the "writing group" of the Ministry of Culture. Chu Lan (First Wave) was the name under which most of the 165 articles directed by Yu appeared.[41] Just as Liang Xiao (the writing group of Beijing and Qinghua universities) maintained steady pressure for the leftist line in education, so Chu Lan was the voice of radical arts policies.[42]

The articles are full of bombastic rhetoric and are too platitudinous for anyone ever to have regarded them as monumental contributions to Marxism-Leninism. Yu kept drumming for worker-peasant-soldier culture and against the more elitist arts policies of Zhou Yang, which he would link to whatever campaign was then current, such as the study of the dictatorship of the proletariat.[43] He praised the novels of Hao Ran, and railed against the apparently restorationist Shanxi opera *Going Up to Peach Peak Three Times*.[44] And he continued to praise Jiang Qing, especially in his commemoration of the tenth anniversary of her 1964 speech on opera reform and, implicitly, of his own work on this project.[45]

The Chu Lan articles that seemed closest to Yu Huiyong's heart were about his own art of music. Yu organized the 1974 campaign against "music without titles," which gave him another opportunity to avenge himself against the Eurocentric snobs of the conservatory world. By "music without titles," Yu meant the great tradition of nineteenth-century European classical music, much of which is abstract, or "absolute" (for example, a Symphony no. 4, or a Sonata in D), in contrast to titled, or program, music (for example, *Pictures at an Exhibition*). Yu's position, which was echoed throughout China, was that abstract music is bourgeois and thus should be avoided.

This campaign was rooted in China's growing diplomatic activities, which increasingly featured cultural exchanges. In 1973 both the London Philharmonic and the Philadelphia Orchestra visited China, performing standard European classical repertory that had not been played by Chinese artists for a decade.[46] The campaign against music without titles was the left's reaction against these visits, but the controversy was in fact raised by the concert of a violinist and a pianist from Turkey in the autumn of 1973. In the bureaucratic discussions to approve their proposed program of mostly abstract music, one report identified the composers and explained the music, cautiously stating that "from a class viewpoint . . . most of the musical works were composed under the influence of the bourgeois movement of enlightenment and . . . reflected the mental outlook of a newly emerging bourgeoisie in varying degrees." The report further noted that most of the works had no profound social content. This shows that most of the musical works to be performed were relatively progressive historically speaking, but that they did not fully reflect the nature of society. Yao Wenyuan added a comment to the report: the "theoretical question of 'no social content' and absolute music should be studied."[47]

The campaign that Yao requested began in Beijing and Shanghai and spread across the nation through three Chu Lan articles and dozens of critiques by others. Yu's opening shot appeared in *People's Daily* in January 1974, where he argued the unexceptional position that European classics are products of bourgeois society. Yu's view on the social content of music was only slightly more controversial. He rejected the idea that a piece of music without a title had no social content: "Can the 'feelings' expressed in a musical work have nothing to do with its composer's era, class and experiences of social life, political attitude, ideological tendency, world view, artistic stance, etc.?" But Yu went beyond this position to conclude that the performance of untitled music would lead to a relaxation of hard-won standards, and foreign culture would spread through China once again.[48]

Yu's first article reflected an understandable cultural nationalism. His second crossed from nationalism into xenophobia. Perhaps some readers had misunderstood him to be saying that European program music was acceptable: "All bourgeois music, programme and absolute, are weapons to shape opinion to serve the bourgeoisie for seizing and consolidating political power." Untitled music is "merely a means by which bourgeois composers conceal the class content of their works." But even when they claim inspiration from such things as pines, fountains, and moonlight, it masks "the decadent, chaotic life and depraved sentiments of the bourgeoisie the weird cacophony represents."[49]

In his final article in April Yu reminded everyone that a 1963 campaign against Debussy (instigated by Yao Wenyuan and resisted by He Luting) had already revealed the problems of titled music. Europe's classical music encompasses a theory of human nature which maintains that art can transcend class. To relax standards now would take China back to before the Cultural Revolution, when "revisionists" said, " 'Let the people all enjoy' Western capitalist music's 'healthy and forthright compositions,' even to the point of nonsensically saying that classical music can 'inspire us today to struggle even more fiercely for peace, progress, and for the glory of all humanity.' " Yu rejected Beethoven as especially humanistic and advised Chinese listeners to turn to the "Internationale" for good European music. It is no accident that it appeared in 1888, contemporary with Debussy. The "Internationale" is "the emblem of the rise of proletarian music," but Debussy, even with titles, is "the emblem of capitalist music already on the road to decline and decadence."[50]

What was this campaign about? After Yu's purge, his critics said that he wanted to subvert cultural exchange and to criticize Zhou Enlai.[51] There is some truth to this. Yu was certainly not trying to stimulate cultural exchange, at least with the West (he viewed Third World exchanges much more positively). The logic of the campaign resembles the 1974 "Black Art Exhibition," which was more clearly directed against Zhou.[52] But the campaign against music without titles may not be so obscure as many others of the late Cultural Revolution. As Yu claimed, it was a drive to keep up class consciousness in culture. This problem had been intensified by the artistic expectations of the urban middle class, which heard foreign artists perform music that Chinese had not played since 1964. Yu wanted to make it clear that these concerts were not a signal for eroding the policies of the CR; this led directly to conflict with Zhou.

Moreover, the revival of European classical music was an implicit threat to Yu's program for model theatrical works. Yu and his co-workers had introduced European musical techniques in unprecedented ways, however much they rejected Western compositions. It was important to keep China's violinists busy on works such as *The Red Detachment of Women*, rather than having them show their resistance by playing Mozart. The campaign was motivated by a considerable amount of fear. Yu's resentment toward his former persecutors in the conservatory was sincere. He was now persecuting them in turn and had a very realistic appreciation of the power of elitist, foreign culture to overwhelm his shallow-rooted efforts to fashion a new and revolutionary culture for China.[53]

It is also important to recognize that Chinese instrumental music does in fact always bear titles, as it is much more closely bound to literary texts and conventions than is European music. It may evoke a mood, such as the sorrow of "River Waters" or the tranquillity of "Pinghu Autumn Moon." It may be narrative, such as the famous *pipa* music "Surrounded on All Sides," which describes a 202 B.C. battle between the states of Chu and Han. It may be imitative of nature's sounds, such as the *erhu* piece "Racing Horses on the Grassland" or the Cantonese piece "Night Rain on the Banana Leaves."[54] Thus Yu Huiyong's personal pride is striking against European music was joined to national pride in China's own cultural traditions; and thus the stance that Yu adopted is more easily comprehended by Chinese than by Western readers.

The campaign against music without titles underscored China's international isolation. Cultural Revolutionaries berated their predecessors for seeking recognition from capitalists and revisionists in the arts. Yet Yu and his comrades made grandiose and pathetic claims for the international success of their own cultural products. Yao Wenyuan, for instance, proudly pointed out that the Albanians stopped their own ballet *Women Guerrillas* after seeing the glories of China's revolutionary dance.[55]

Yu Huiyong took his art abroad in 1974, in his only foreign trip, leading the *Azalea Mountain (Dujuan Shan)* troupe to North Africa to celebrate the twentieth anniversary of Algerian armed resistance to French colonialism. Yu had led the revision of *Azalea Mountain;* Jiang Qing was closely involved with the journey, arranging photographers for the star performers, approving posters and the program booklet, and the like. As this was the first export of a model theatrical work, the entire Political Bureau (except the ailing Zhou Enlai) came to the Beijing airport to send off Yu and his delegation of 162. A diplomat reporting on this trip found Yu to be naïve and troublesome, although much of his report may reflect organizational conflict between leftist cultural leaders and Zhou Enlai's diplomatic corps.[56] But the art of the Cultural Revolution was ill-suited to win the admiration of foreigners, even in Algeria and Albania. This art was built around the most national of forms—Chinese opera—and celebrated patriotic incidents in China's own revolution.

THE POLITICS OF CULTURAL FAMINE

Yu was elected to the Central Committee at the Tenth Party Congress in 1973. His title was changed to reflect his responsibilities in 1975, when he became China's first minister of culture since 1966. Radical cultural policies were firmly in place. Old art had been swept from the stages and screens of the nation and was being replaced by new model stage works. But the new art was insufficient in quantity and too unvaried in style. When this became a political issue in 1975, Yu faced an impossible situation. Recognizing the need to produce more art, he also was keenly aware that increased production would lessen his control and offer opportunities to his enemies to gain influence in the cultural arena. As minister, Yu fought and lost his final political battle over the issue of a chronic arts shortage.

It is of course false that art consisted only of the eight model stage works: five operas *(On the Docks, Shajiabang, Red Lantern, Raid on White Tiger Regiment, Taking Tiger Mountain by Strategy),* two ballets *(White-Haired Girl, The Red Detachment of Women),* and the symphonic music *Shajiabang.* Models are meant to be imitated, and by 1976 Bonnie McDougall counted eighteen model theatrical works, as well as new local operas (and old ones revised according to models). In 1974 and 1975 forty-eight regional forms were revived through model transplants.[57]

Without attempting a systematic survey, one can add five more operas, a piano concerto, a symphony, three sets of sculptures, a couple of ballets, some plays and films, the novels of Hao Ran, and local *quyi* (ballad singing) and puppet theater that Yu was said to have forced on Shanghai.[58] In addition, China's arts included Mao's poetry, *Water Margin,* legalist literature reprinted during the campaign against Lin Biao and Confucius, and large quantities of amateur writings, songs, and paintings. For the politically privileged, foreign movies and novels were available through internal distribution. What is striking is to be able to jot down most of the art available to the citizens of such a populous and cultivated nation. Despite the cultural loosening that began when Yu became the chief cultural administrator after the fall of Lin Biao in 1971, this is a ghastly record.[59]

Why was there so little art? Cynics might speculate that the availability of more art distributed only within the elite made Yu and his patrons insensitive to the cultural shortage; Jiang was fond of watching foreign movies, and Mao had a series of twenty classic operas filmed for his private viewing.[60] But Yu was well aware of popular criticism. As early as April 1972 he referred to "persons who use 'eight flowers blooming' to criticize us for not having enough creative works" and attempted to justify the arts shortage dialectically.[61]

Some might be tempted to explain the arts shortage as the inevitable consequence of leftist cultural policies, but the CR arts famine stands in sharp contrast to the Great Leap Forward's vigorous profusion of amateur poems, songs, paintings, and dances. A major difference between the Great Leap and the Cultural Revolution was that the latter movement was much more obsessed with class struggle; the Leap, while leftist, never sought to homogenize China's culture according to a model of what workers, peasants, and soldiers ought to like.

There are several reasons why the CR left produced artistic famine instead of plenty. The victorious Cultural Revolutionaries sincerely wanted a thriving, enthusiastic, and revolutionary culture to supplant all that had gone before. But the leaders of the CR were ultimately *fearful of what mass participation in the creation of a new culture might unleash.* In 1971 Zhang Chunqiao urged a modest decentralization in the supervision of the arts, instructing that new songs need not be approved by central authorities. But five years later the Ministry of Culture still had an office for evaluating new songs, including six hundred tunes attacking Deng Xiaoping and "right deviationism."[62] The refusal to utilize a more decentralized cultural program ensured eventual shortages of output.

The *selection of opera as the primary vehicle for revolutionary art* raised other problems. There had been other efforts to reform opera in this century, and all had encountered problems in transforming "its complex, unwritten rules of composition" into scores and scripts for imitation by others.[63] Writing as Chu Lan, Yu Huiyong emphasized the difficulties of opera reform, such as resistance from many artists and political figures and the lack of precedents to follow in putting workers, peasants, and soldiers on the stage. "We must realize that the landlord and capitalist classes fostered the Peking opera for some two hundred years, developing it from among a great variety of Chinese operas into a theatrical form demanding exceptional skill." Thus it was not easy to take it over and remake it in short time. Yu denied that things were going too slowly: "If we review the history of the literature and art of mankind, we see how many years the exploiting classes took to create a literature and art of their own!" Feudalism had thousands of years, and capitalism had hundreds, yet the revolution is impatient.[64] But Jiang Qing estimated that it took two or three years to put together a model opera, which meant that the artworks most central to the movement's cultural program could be only slowly produced.[65]

The radicals, like all Chinese politicians, also had *difficulty reorganizing the film industry,* even though Jiang Qing had imagined that films would be a key medium for propagating model stage works among the peasantry. In desperation even Yu was put to work at writing film scripts, but had no success at this unfamiliar art form.[66] The rehabilitation of some older directors offered some hope for increasing movie output, but soon led to conflict with the Ministry of Culture.[67]

Rivalries over control of the arts encouraged Yu to view with hostility arts projects outside his own institutions. For instance, after 1973 there was a growing conflict with the army's cultural organs. Li Desheng, then a member of the Political Bureau, tried to consolidate his control over the units directly under the General Political Department, which he headed, such as the August 1 Film Company, the PLA press, the Military Museum, and a large number of performing ensembles. He failed in his effort to replace revolutionary committees with a system of political commissars, and by 1975 Zhang Chunqiao had become head of the General Political Department. In the course of this feud, however, Yu and his patrons slowed the cultural output and innovation of the army.[68]

The *thoroughness of the purge of old culture* kept the radicals from reviving older works of good political color, such as the much-cited *Driven up Liangshan,* the Yan'an opera praised by Mao. Before the Cultural Revolution, it had not been restaged because it was "immature."[69] It is not clear what kept if from the stage after 1966, but it may well have been tainted by too close an association with some fallen cultural figure. This is how China lost its national anthem, whose words had been written by Tian Han. The amount of purged art was enormous, as the CR had rejected all that was tainted by either feudalism, capitalism, or revisionism. It proved much more difficult than the radicals imagined even to begin to replenish the storehouse of Chinese culture.

Furthermore, *political harassment of professional artists* did little to stimulate greater output. Cautious artists found that it was easier to remain idle than to risk conflict with the Ministry of Culture. Efforts to replace professionals in the arts with new amateurs from the ranks of workers, peasants, and soldiers were not successful.[70] The rejection of artistic spontaneity no doubt contributed to this failure, as China's artists retreated to the safety of pseudonyms and collective writing groups.

Despite such obstacles, Yu Huiyong's cultural army was not paralyzed and in fact was speeding up its work after the Lin Biao crisis. But it could not do so quickly enough to keep up with political changes.[71]

After Lin Biao's death made it possible to rehabilitate old cadres, Yu began to face new competition for cultural leadership. The rehabilitees were a complex group. Some enthusiastically joined the radicals, such as Feng Youlan or Wu Lengxi, to name two of the more craven. Others, however, such as Deng Xiaoping, Hu Qiaomu, and Hua Guofeng's cultural adviser, Zhang Pinghua, were quick to seize the shortcomings of the radical leaders. The cultural shortage was an easy pigtail to grab.

Because the radicals denied the existence of an urban middle class, art that appealed to such a class could not legitimately be produced. However truncated, battered, and physically dispersed this class might have been, it was the inheritor of the May Fourth generation, the traditional consumer of China's most elaborate arts as well as of those imported from abroad. Its sophisticated tastes could not be satisfied indefinitely on a diet of simplified class-struggle art. Much of the art shepherded by Yu Huiyong was initially very popular, both for its novelty and for its professional polish. Young Chinese, coming of age during the Cultural Revolution, often report that they had no sense of missing greater cultural variety. But older Chinese did, and their discontent was to have political consequences.

The strategy of the veteran cadres was to divide Mao from Yu, Zhang, and Yao. Hu Qiaomu gathered reports based on interviews with frustrated artists in 1974. These were forwarded to Deng Xiaoping, who used them to argue with Mao for changes in arts policies.[72] It is difficult to write with assurance about Mao in his last years. He was clearly ill and was manipulated by many around him, with mixed political results for each side. He did have misgivings about the arts policies, which could be trapped effectively by Deng's supporters. As the arts shortage was called to Mao's attention, he expressed his unhappiness. It is unclear whether this indicates that Mao turned against the policies of the early Cultural Revolution or, instead, whether he believed more strongly than did Yu Huiyong that policies already implemented had successfully cleansed Chinese culture of its greatest defects.

Yu must have been aware of these investigations even before they resulted in reports to the Chairman. He responded by intensifying his criticism of new artworks that were created by personnel and units beyond his control, suspicious that they would rival his model productions.

He attacked *Song of the Gardeners,* a Hunan opera-movie about two teachers that was patronized by Hua Guofeng. Claiming the film turned back educational policy and pushed idealism, Yu antagonized Hua and the Hunan propaganda chief Zhang Pinghua.[73] When Mao visited Hunan in November 1974, he saw the film. Told that it was being criticized, Mao said, "I think it's a good movie."[74]

Yu was thought to be an upstart by the old Party veterans; they did not regard his appointment to be minister of culture as legitimate and had no qualms about circumventing him to seek Mao's intercession. In July 1975 Deng succeeded in eliciting from Mao a rebuke for the policies of the Ministry of Culture: "There are too few model plays; moreover, even the slightest mistakes are dealt with by criticism. There is no more blooming of a hundred flowers. The others cannot bring up their opinions; that's no good. There is a fear of writing articles, writing plays, novels, poems, and songs."[75]

Later in July, under conditions that have not been explained, Mao wrote some rambling comments that, amid nonliterary remarks about Lin Biao, elaborated on his statements to Deng Xiaoping:

The Party's policies toward literature and art should be readjusted to gradually enlarge the repertoires of literature and art during the following year, two years, or three years. There is a lack of novels, a lack of prose, and a lack of literary criticism.

The Dream of the Red Chamber and *The Water Margin* are now reprinted for publication. Don't be impatient; get things into action in one or two years, even in three, four, or five years is also all right.

Mao also felt that help should be given writers who had not committed "serious counterrevolutionary crimes" and that people like Zhou Yang should not be locked up, thus "allowing them to become divorced from the masses."[76]

In the same month, Deng forwarded a letter from Zhang Tianmin, scriptwriter of the film *Pioneers,* an oil-drilling saga that Yu had criticized extensively. Mao annotated this petition on 25 July 1975: "This film contains no great mistakes. Recommended it be accepted for publication. Don't demand perfection. Moreover, there are ten charges against it; that's too much. It will be harmful to the adjustment of the literature and art policy in the Party."[77] These words were written on Deng's copy of the letter, not Mao's, suggesting that Deng took the letter in person to the Chairman. However Deng coaxed these words from Mao, they were powerful ammunition against the Ministry of Culture.[78]

Yu Huiyong had made ten charges against *Pioneers,* including a sane suggestion to cut forty minutes from this three-and-a-quarter-hour epic. Yu also protested insufficient references to Mao and the quoting of the living leaders Yu Qouli and Kang Shi'en (then military representative to the Yumen Oil Field).[79] Yu thus antagonized the leaders of the powerful petroleum faction, as he had earlier offended Li Desheng and Hua Guofeng. Yu no doubt regarded his stance as loyalty toward Jiang Qing and Zhang Chunqiao, but his dogged protection of their control over cultural policy contributed to the political isolation of his patrons and to Yu's own political demise.

Even before Mao made his comments, Yu and Jiang Qing conferred frequently about how to defend themselves. Jiang told Yu in one phone conversation that he must report all of his ministry's work to Zhang Chunqiao (who had become more directly involved in cultural matters as the new head of the army's General Political Department).[80]

After Mao's comments on *Pioneers,* Yu Huiyong could only make a self-criticism: "My consciousness was not high enough in previous implementation of the 'two-hundred' policy."[81] Jiang tried to distance herself from the *Pioneers* affair, claiming she and Zhang had not favored publishing Yu's criticisms. She publicly rebuked Yu at a meeting in Dazhai in September 1975: "Yu Hui-yung, you speak up. You know all about what happened. Why don't you speak up? The ten charges were consolidated by the Department of Culture from the opinions of the masses. (Yu: There are letters from Henan.) The Department of Culture does have its shortcomings; and the ten charges are indeed excessive in nature."[82]

In order to defend his ministry against growing charges of responsibility for cultural famine, Yu commissioned a series of at least eight reports in 1975 to show the allegedly healthy state of the arts. The report on novels claimed that the People's Press "published only two long novels last year, while eight had been published by August of this year with a total of 15 to be completed for this year. There are now more than 100 new works of literature being planned and in writing, which is the highest figure since the establishment of the state." The report on publications discussed a similar increase since 1972, with more than fifty-one literature and art periodicals appearing by 1975.[83]

In March 1976, just before the second purge of Deng Xiaoping, Yu wrote once more as Chu Lan about the tactics being used by "that unrepentant capitalist roader." Yu seemed rather desperate, but he still identified Deng's tactic correctly—old intellectuals in literary and art circles were encouraged to "submit memorials" to reverse verdicts in the arts, with "a salient characteristic: to focus the attack on the model revolutionary theatrical works in a vain attempt to make a breakthrough here." Yu charged Deng with holding the view that "model theatrical works cannot blossom as the only flower" and that they "hinder the development of literature and art." After citing quantitative measures of success, Yu complained that Deng never mentioned classical opera's lack of audiences before the Cultural Revolution, when it represented the "blooming of only one flower." In any event, argued Yu, it is a fine thing to hinder art that is reactionary.[84]

Yu and his patrons pushed even harder to create greater numbers of acceptable works as they came under fire for undue harshness toward art produced by their enemies. In February 1976 Jiang Qing complained to Yu that "the plays staged by these model troupes are too shopworn, with very little content of the socialist period. In particular, there is not a single play dealing with the struggle against the capitalist roaders." Despite the lack of lead time, Yu was immediately to direct two Beijing opera troupes to adapt three films into new revolutionary operas in time for performances on National Day, if not sooner.[85]

Yu summoned eighteen writers to a week-long meeting in March to plan more works on the theme of capitalist roaders. Yu, who had worked on the first of the revolutionary operas to be set in socialist China, urged them to put aside fears of using art to criticize high-ranking officials. In the end, Yu mapped out a program for new works: five dealing with industry, five with agriculture, five with railways, one with sea transport, four with education, and two with scientific research. There would be five novels, three novellas, three short stories, three screenplays, and two dramas. Eight would deal with capitalist roaders at the central or provincial level and twelve at the local level. Thus did Yu Huiyong assign battle orders to his troops for the final conflict.[86]

THE PURGE OF YU HUIYONG

Yu was increasingly desperate toward the end; he sought to honor both Mao's insistence on more artworks and his own need to defend the left by encouraging new works attacking recently rehabilitated officials. Unlike the slights directed specifically against Hua Guofeng or Yu Qiuli, this project more ambitiously took on an entire class of officials. Criticism of high officials is certainly an appropriate topic for revolutionary art, but it is also potentially a suicidal one.

Yu did not survive the fall of his patrons in the autumn of 1976. According to Zhang Pinghua, who was raised to be national propaganda chief by Hua Guofeng after the overthrow of the Gang of Four, the recapture of the Ministry of Culture had higher priority than the city of Tianjin.[87] Yu was arrested and classified as a "first-category Gang of Four element." He provided testimony that was used against Jiang, Zhang, and Yao, although it was not particularly damaging. The last public mention of Yu was made on 1 March 1977. Sometime after this date he killed himself by drinking DDT.[88]

There was a brief and intense campaign against Yu Huiyong, but it paled in comparison to the blows dealt his patrons. The verdict in 1977 was still that Yu was in fact a secret rightist and counterrevolutionary, so the articles have an surreal air about them, as they seek to prove his "bourgeois" ways. They make much of his youthful letter to Chiang Kai-shek's army and insist that he favored rightists in the political movements of 1955 and 1957. Yu was accused of plagiarism, even to the point of stealing the tunes of a blind musician. Shanghai Conservatory critics made token efforts to lay blame for their school's violence during the Cultural Revolution on Yu's shoulders, but the effort was half-hearted. The greatest violence at the conservatory was committed by Red Guards while Yu was still under criticism himself.[89]

How does one assess Yu Huiyong's career? Was he just another opportunistic Chinese politician who ended up getting what he dealt to others? There is a certain similarity to Wu Han, first victim of the Cultural Revolution, who had opened the antirightist campaign in 1957.[90]

Yu was Jiang Qing's hireling, but he rose also because his organizational and musical abilities were needed by his radical patrons. Still, he never built a separate political identity, and he was no match for the returning veteran cadres in the mid-1970s, who swept him aside with ease. The political issue of the cultural famine proved intractable largely because of Yu's social analysis and the artistic techniques he favored.

Some of Yu's successes are simply irrelevant by the standards of his successors. In 1963 Mao said, "If nothing else is done, the Ministry of Culture should be changed into the Ministry of Emperors, Kings, Generals, Ministers, Scholars, and Beauties, or the Ministry of Foreign Things and the Dead."[91] Yu took him seriously and changed the face of the ministry to reflect, however coarsely, the proletarian, the Chinese, and the living. Similarly, Yu's flawed effort to cultivate amateur artists of laboring-class origin is a not a meaningful goal for the professionals in charge of the arts today. But one should bear in mind that the arts of the "seventeen years" before the Cultural Revolution are unlikely to live longer in Chinese memory than the arts sponsored by Yu Huiyong and his radical patrons. There was greater variety in the 1950s and early 1960s, but the arts were still of a consistently low quality.[92]

Yu's control over the cultural sector, even after years of purges and reorganization, was minimal. The speed of the movement to rehabilitate disgraced cultural figures surprised Yu, driving him to seek greater control at all costs and never to show his enemies the weakness of compromise. And even at the height of his power there were underground, manuscript novels and private music lessons that were never within the sphere of the Ministry of Culture.

Art is ultimately a treacherous political base.[93] Although it can stir consciousness and mobilize popular support, as at Yan'an or in the early stages of the Cultural Revolution, art is deceptive in its power. Art presents its message as universal, even when it represents only a partial reality. This is not a disabling liability for politicians who can supplement culture with other bases of support. But toward the end of the Cultural Revolution, arts and propaganda institutions were the radicals' only remaining power base, which made Yu Huiyong's position ever more important and ever more fragile. The reality of Yu's power proved so much less than the outward impression of control that he was to maintain to the very end.

Yu Huiyong rose to power because of his youth, his resentment toward foreign art, and his outsider status, all of which corresponded to the radical trend of the times. But his inability to manage the deep tensions within modern Chinese culture finally destroyed him, along with the whole Cultural Revolution enterprise. Perhaps only Mao Zedong possessed the resources and skills to straddle the fissures of modern China's cultural politics, and even he seemed barely able to hold the pieces together in the last years of his life.

Models and Misfits: Rusticated Youth
in Three Novels of the 1970s

RICHARD KING

The rustication of several million urban adolescents who were sent "up to the mountains and down to the villages" *(shangshan xiaxiang)* was one of the most unpopular and divisive policies of the Cultural Revolution. Launched in late 1968 with the immediate tactical objective of dispersing the increasingly troublesome Red Guards, this massive relocation also had a strategic goal with its antecedents in the Communist Party's halcyon Yan'an days: the reform of urban intellectuals by immersing them in the practical values, hard work, and plain language of the peasantry. For the cadres and artists of the 1940s, the "sending-down" had been short term; for the urban youths of the 1960s and 1970s, the immersion was, in theory at least, for life. Perhaps it was this specter of permanent exile that made the activists' tasks of filling quotas for volunteers so arduous.[1] It must certainly have become all the more difficult once urban youths began to flee the countryside, returning to the cities with tales of hardship, starvation, abuse, and suicide.

Strenuous efforts were made by the Party media to counteract unfavorable popular perceptions of the rustication policy. Letters were published from relocated youth to family members in Shanghai that detailed hardships welcomed and reservations overcome, and portrayed a life of fulfilling endeavor among a supportive peasantry.[2] In the mid-1970s poems, stories, and novels combined in an uplifting chorus to the glory of the rustication movement, a chorus that persisted in the official media until it was jarred by dissonant voices in the national soul-searching that followed the Cultural Revolution.

The lives of the displaced urbanites as reflected, or distorted, in Chinese literature will be examined here through analysis of three major works of fiction dating from the 1970s. Guo Xianhong's *The Journey* (1973),[3] written by an urban author as a Party assignment, is a tale of adventure that follows the first group of high-school graduates from Shanghai to the Soviet border in Heilongjiang. Zhang Kangkang's *The Dividing Line* (1975)[4] looks at that same generation five years later in the climate of the political and ideological struggles that followed the downfall of Lin Biao. The final work to be considered is *The Path of Life* (1979)[5] by Zhu Lin, who is, like Zhang Kangkang, a former rusticated youth; the novel views with post-Mao disillusion (or "critical realism")[6] the plight of urban youths still in the countryside some eight years after their initial rustication.

The three works share many features of characterization and plot standard in 1970s novels about rural life: a young hero and a village bad element, the sabotage of irrigation projects and exposure of the saboteur, and the conflict between profitability and political activism in rural policymaking. What sets them apart from other rural novels is their concern with a major dilemma for the urban youths relocated in the countryside: whether to leave *(zou)* or to stay *(liu)*.[7] In each of the three novels this dilemma is personified by presenting a model youth determined to stay and a misfit (or in the case of *The Dividing Line,* two misfits) equally determined to return to the city. In the pages that follow, the three novels will be introduced, then the model and misfit character types will be discussed; a final brief postscript will carry rusticated-youth fiction into the early 1980s.

THE JOURNEY: VILLAGE AS BATTLEFIELD

Letters and stories documenting the experiences of exemplary urban youths had stressed the value of the village as a place for testing and maturing. Guo Xianhong's thriller, the first rustication novel and one of the first on any subject to have the Cultural Revolution as its background, presents the rural setting as a battleground, the military theme capitalizing on the Red Guards' image of themselves as warriors and harking back to the civil war heroics of the Yan'an period. Narrator and hero indulge in a flurry of militaristic language, which the less sympathetic characters eschew.

The Journey is as much a military romance as a peacetime novel can be. As they leave for Manchuria, "the young generals' [Red Guards'] resolve is as unerring in its heroic advance as an armor-piercing shell fired from a canon."[8] The given name of the Red Guards' leader, the novel's hero, Zhong Weihua, has military connotations ("protect China"), and every challenge that he and his young colleagues face is described in military terms. As they arrive in Heilongjiang, Zhong Weihua spurns the transport provided by their hosts and proposes a "route-march" from the railway station to Pine-Tree Brigade through the bitter cold of a Manchurian winter:

Route-march duty officer Lu Hao spiritedly barked out the order "Number off!" . . . "One, two, three, four, five. . . ." The numbers rattled out like machine-gun fire.[9]

Once at the brigade, agricultural production is no less a battle; witness the terms in which the hero volunteers the new arrivals to harvest a crop of beans buried under an unexpected snowfall:

Zhong Weihua sprang to his feet and spoke in ringing terms: "I declare on behalf of the entire youth platoon that we will respond to the call of the brigade Party branch, and that in this battle to reap crops we will temper hands of steel, as we put Mao Zedong Thought in command, venerate the poor and lower-middle peasants as our teachers, and take the poor and lower-middle peasants as our models! We resolve to overcome all difficulties and win a magnificent victory!"[10]

In a succession of battles that runs throughout the novel's 737 pages, Zhong Weihua does indeed win a series of magnificent victories, in conflicts with natural forces and human foes alike. The urban youths bring no class enemies among their number: the requirement of Cultural Revolution literature for the portrayal of class struggle is met from within the village, in the unprepossessing person of Zhang Shan, a former officer-interpreter with the Japanese army of occupation and current Soviet agent now posing as a poor peasant. Zhang Shan may have lain low for twenty years among the villagers, but he is immediately suspect to the hero because he does not live up to this young urbanite's idealized notion of a poor peasant, a notion derived from the wholesome, selfless, and militant figures of official myth. In a classic Cultural Revolution conflict between a young hero and a class enemy, Zhang Shan is exposed and humiliated in as action-packed a finale as a reader of pulp fiction anywhere could demand: there is a cache of money, arms, and radio equipment; an abduction; poisoned liquor; a time bomb under the hero's pillow; a sled/horse/jeep/motorcycle chase; and a dramatic ambush and arrest.

A further conflict is endemic in the brigade before the young urbanites arrive. This is what we might call the management-versus-ideology conflict, and it pervades Cultural Revolution village fiction. The managers stress profitability, efficiency, and appropriate material reward for work done; they are damned by their association with the ideas of the purged state chairman, Liu Shaoqi. The ideologues emphasize mass mobilization and class struggle as a means to accelerated development, and their close identification with Mao Zedong and his works guarantees (in Cultural Revolution rhetoric) that they will be more productive as well as more correct politically. At Pine-Tree Brigade, the brigade leader, Yu Chunbao, is the befuddled manager and Party secretary Li Dejiang the prescient ideologue. When Yu hears that the authorities are sending "thirty," he assumes tons of fertilizer and is aghast to learn that he is getting Shanghainese high-school graduates instead:

"What? What's that you're saying?" Yu Chunbao stood up abruptly, his fingernails rasping against his crewcut pate as it flushed purple, his brow furrowed deeply: "If the county's not going to give us fertilizer, what are they doing sending us thirty kids from Shanghai? For a start they're not worth as much as fertilizer, and anyway they can't do farm work. It's . . ."

"It's a political duty [said Party secretary Li]. It's the noble task of grooming successors, a plan for the next thousand, the next ten thousand years of the proletarian revolutionary cause!" [11]

The battles with the elements and a concealed enemy, and the management-versus-ideology debate that we see in *The Journey,* are the staples of Chinese village fiction. They can be found in, and may well have been lifted from, *Ode to Dragon River,* the only one of the model works[12] of the 1960s to be set in the countryside. In one specific struggle, however, *The Journey* breaks new ground. This is the conflict for and within the hearts and minds of those urban youths less perfectly suited than the hero Zhong Weihua to their new life. Placed between Zhong Weihua, Party secretary Li Dejiang, and the idealized poor peasant family of Grandpa Guan on the one hand and the odious class enemy Zhang Shan on the other are three of the new arrivals: two young men, Zhang Dawei ("Big-deeds") and Tao Abao ("Precious"), and one young woman, Wan Lili. Each has some trait that Zhang Shan can exploit in an attempt to sow dissension among the new arrivals and discredit the rustication policy. Zhang Dawei's failing is his longing to act the *haohan* (tough guy); Tao Abao's is his sense of mischief. Zhang Shan is able to gull the youngsters into misdemeaors that would cause disaster but for the intervention of the hero. When Zhang is exposed, they can denounce his deception, purge themselves of their undersirable traits, and thus fit into the roles assigned to them. Their dilemma is one of how to transform themselves in order to stay. The case of Lili (which will be discussed at greater length below) resembles theirs both in that Zhang is able to take advantage of failings (in her case loneliness and alienation from her peers) and in that she is saved from herself and the villain by the final intervention of the hero; but hers is the more fundamental (and, one suspects, more universal) dilemma of whether to stay in the countryside or return to the city.

The conflicts of *The Journey* are characterized by an absolutely clear choice of right and wrong. There is no doubt, for example, that the tasks for which Zhong Weihua volunteers will be gloriously completed, that the course of events in the novel will shame the managers and vindicate the ideologues, and that the arguments for staying in the village are stronger than those for leaving it. The Cultural Revolution, in literature and polemic (if not in fact), appears before the reader as an age of moral absolutes, when simple (or simplistic) adherence to a Maoist tenet ensures victory and villains are easily identifiable, theatrically gross, and reassuringly incompetent. Voices of authority within the novel—the narrator, the hero, the Party secretary, and the peasant sage—combine to show the correct course of action and thought at every stage. Problems that might dampen the ardor of the intended youthful audience are raised by unsympathetic characters and given a normative solution by reliable ones.

Such conflict between clearly defined good and evil is a characteristic of melodrama, which *The Journey* clearly is; the novel is an exercise in revolutionary-romantic fantasy rather than an attempt to address in any thoroughgoing way the issues that faced urban youths in the countryside.

THE DIVIDING LINE: THE SPECTER
OF THE CAPITALIST ROAD

The fervor of *The Journey*, feasible for 1968, the year in which the novel is set, was at best implausible by 1973, the year of its publication, and would have been unconscionable by 1975, when *The Dividing Line* was released. By that year the harsh realities of rustication were generally known and defied glamorization; to present these realities in a favorable light (as any author wishing to be published had to do) was an ever more daunting task.

By the mid-1970s the first group of urban youths had been in the countryside six years and had reached marriageable age. They realized, however, that to marry, especially to marry peasants, would greatly diminish their chances of returning to the city. Thus many remained single despite the official encouragement to settle down exemplified by this 1974 report from a young Shanghainese in Jiangxi:

Most of our group had graduated from high school in 1966 or 1967 and are now 27 or 28. With advancing years, another question appears on the agenda—what should be our attitude to getting married? Young Yang and Young Zhang answered this question very well. They reasoned that the question of love and marriage cannot be avoided by a young person as he gets older, and . . . since we are resolved to strike roots in the village, why shouldn't we set up home here too? They backed their resolve with action, and made their homes in Jinggangshan. Fourteen of our group of fifty-two students have already married, of whom three . . . have married the offspring of poor and lower-middle peasants. Their actions have won the praise of the peasants and the support of their peers.[13]

That the marriage of a quarter of a group of adult urban youths (one in seventeen into peasant families) should be cause for celebration among advocates of rustication is some indication of the majority's resistance to anything that might prolong their stay in the countryside. Given Zhang Kangkang's experience, including romantic experience, in the countryside, it is surprising that none of those characters in *The Dividing Line* dedicated to staying in the countryside (jocularly named *yongjiupai* [eternals] after a brand of bicycle manufactured in Shanghai) considers love and marriage. They are all too occupied with irrigation projects and political activism to have time for affairs of the heart. The only one of the urban youths to contemplate marriage is the misfit Yang Landi, who sees a city husband as a passport back to Shanghai.[14]

New realities of the mid-1970s permeate the novel; not those of the countryside, but rather those of the internecine fighting within the Communist Party elite during the months following the Tenth Party Congress in the summer of 1973. Confirmation of the downfall of Lin Biao allowed him to be used as a scapegoat for disaffection among the relocated youths; attribution to him of the notion that rustication to state farms was "prison camp in disguise" turned a commonly held view into a vile slander.

The principal threat to the apparently ascendant Maoist faction in the mid-1970s was the reinstatement of officials condemned in 1966 and 1967, Deng Xiaoping among them. This group, stigmatized as "capitalist roaders," furnished most of the villains of late Cultural Revolution fiction. Thus, although there is in *The Dividing Line* a class enemy corresponding to *The Journey*'s Zhang Shan (this one called You Fa) to mislead the impressionable, attempt sabotage, and be apprehended by the hero *in flagrante delicto,* he poses only a limited threat and is even used as the butt for some comic business as he imagines himself the object of a children's game of "hunt the bad egg." The real danger lies within the Party itself, with Huo Li, one of very few unsympathetic female characters in Cultural Revolution fiction. The leader of a Party "work-team" overseeing Manchurian state farms, Huo Li bears a strong resemblance to deposed state chairman Liu Shaoqi's widow, Wang Guangmei, herself a work-team leader in the "Four Cleans" campaign of the mid-1960s; Huo's pet Sunrise Peak Farm corresponds to Wang's Peach Peak Brigade of a decade earlier.[15] Huo Li and her local ally Song Wang are prototype capitalist roaders with their disdain for Maoist mass mobilization, their concern for the bottom line, and their vaunting of long service to the Party.[16] The management-versus-ideology conflict of *The Journey* becomes more explicitly a struggle between capitalism and socialism in *The Dividing Line,* Huo Li and her kind being implicitly accused of attempting to restore capitalism while the hero and his supporters fight to keep alive the faith that brought them to Manchuria. Since both sides profess absolute loyalty to the Communist Party, this effectively means that there is a schizophrenic Party with a good (Maoist) side and a bad (capitalist roader) side.

In *The Dividing Line* the hero is the matured urban youth Geng Changjiong (lit., "light constantly burning."). He is supported at the local level by the local Party secretary and an elderly model peasant (Zhou Pu and Li Qingshan, respectively). The ground on which their battles are fought is a patch of newly cultivated land called the Great Eastern Swamp. Geng plans to drain the land by means of an irrigation canal dug with a massive burst of collective energy and to grow grain in accordance with the Cultural Revolution totem of "grain as the key"; Huo Li advocates abandoning the swamp and making up deficits by growing cash crops on land now planted with staples. Her unsuccessful attempts to frustrate Geng Changjiong include trying to transfer him away from the farm and even placing him under house arrest as floods threaten the farm. Although Huo Li, as a Party cadre of long service, cannot be treated as a class enemy, she and Geng Changjiong are diametrically opposed, their differences symbolized by the dividing line of the title, between (as Zhou Pu expresses it) the "meadowland" of socialism and the "wilderness" of capitalism.[17]

Such metaphor is common in *The Dividing Line*, which is a more consciously literary novel than *The Journey*. Geng Changjiong's younger brother, newly arrived and finding the going tough, is advised by the old peasant Li Qingtian that "it takes two years to break a shovel in properly,"[18] and, lest the point be lost, "blades are honed on stone, men are tempered in adversity."[19] When the boy plays with a kite in a rare break from work, he is urged by his brother not to be flighty like the kite, but sturdy and rooted like a tree; the younger Geng himself draws the moral, that "there are some prepared to work a lifetime in the village and others that are ill at ease and want to fly away. Right?"[20] Description of the hero often involves figurative language that is, in keeping with his name, associated with light and fire:

Geng Changjiong's words, like a spark on dry tinder, instantly lit an ardent flame in the hearts of his comrades.[21]

Much of the most elegant writing in the novel is in anthropomorphic passages celebrating the victory of mobilized masses over nature. For example:

The [spring] gale blew for days . . . but the people paid no heed to its assault; they delivered fertilizer in the gale, they leveled land in the gale, they ate in its sand-storms and sang to its howling . . . Obediently the gale withdrew, stretching out its hand to push the waters of the Great Eastern Channel, [so that] the water gushed away toward Reclining Dragon River.[22]

In dealing with the question of whether or not to remain in the village, Zhang Kangkang shows herself more sympathetic to those who do not immediately and absolutely conform than was Guo Xianhong; among the unambiguously positive characters are a practical joker (whose pranks are predictably directed at the local capitalist roader) and a lad whose father had arranged his return to the city before he decided himself to settle in the countryside. The question of how youth should conform in order to fit in is less important in *The Dividing Line* than it was in *The Journey*. Rather the urban youths are shown picking the jobs to which they are best suited. So Shidai Hong ("Age of red," a Cultural Revolution sobriquet) pursues her dream of herding cattle despite official opposition and the villain's interference. All these youths, plus the Party secretary, the old peasant Li Qingshan, the Youth League secretary, and the narrator, are absolutely reliable sources of opinion. So hard is it to find a youth prepared to adopt a dissenting position that, when Geng Changjiong tries to debate publicly the issues confronting youth (staying versus going, ideology/socialism versus management/capitalism), a stool pigeon must be found. The volunteer is an obvious choice as a wearer of glasses (myopia being habitually associated with bourgeois intellectuals), but he capitulates rapidly in the face of Geng's arguments. It is left to the novel's two misfits, Young Landi and Xue Chuan, to present through their actions (as forcefully as the times would allow) the reasons for trying to get away.

THE PATH OF LIFE: PERCEPTIONS REVERSED

The final urban-youth novel to be considered was a beneficiary of the "ideological liberation" of 1979, the year of its publication. It was written between 1975 and 1978, but in no previous year of Communist rule could a novel so bleak and critical have got by the Party censors. The telling of shocking truth that lies at the heart of the "exposure literature"[23] of 1979 represents the anguish of lost innocence, or perhaps the admission that the moral certainty of the Cultural Revolution was a cruel illusion. Accordingly the moral absolutes and clear-cut decisions of the previous novels are absent from *The Path of Life;* the reasons the misfit protagonist Tan Juanjuan advances for leaving the countryside are as valid in their way as those that make her model boyfriend, Liangzi, want to stay. Optimism concerning the ascendancy of humanity over nature is replaced by despair at a hostile environment and an inauspicious fate; natural disasters present challenges to be overcome in Cultural Revolution fiction, but in *The Path of Life* they cause destitution and anguish.

As the novel begins, heavy rains in the spring of 1976 have destroyed a recently built dam and caused extensive flooding in Hushan Brigade in Anhui Province. An unscrupulous local official, Cui Haiying, whose sabotage caused the dam's collapse, blames the resultant disaster on the former Party secretary and thereby seizes power in the brigade. Essays unjustly condemning the Old Party Secretary as a "capitalist roader" are composed on Cui's orders by Tan Juanjuan, a young woman desperate to return to Shanghai after seven years of rustication; she is dependant on Cui for the recommendation to university that she hopes will provide her means of escape. When Juanjuan's boyfriend, Liangzi, returns to the brigade after four years in agricultural college, he sides instinctively with the Old Party Secretary. He and Juanjuan thus find themselves on opposing sides, their relationship destroyed by leftist politics.

The dramatic reversal between the fiction of the mid- and late 1970s in the presentation of the relationship of people to the elements is paralleled by equally dramatic reversals in human relations. Zhu Lin's novel shares with its two predecessors the Cultural Revolution setting and the struggle within the village between ideologists/Maoists and managers/ capitalist roaders; but here the peasants are less susceptible to motivational rhetoric—one young peasant observes sarcastically that "these days you have to have the correct political line on eating dinner and having babies." [24] Such scorn is justifiable, since the ideologues, led by the Party secretary Cui Haiying, are hypocrites and opportunists, whereas the managers, most notably the deposed Old Party Secretary, are the ones who care for the people's welfare. The perfidious ideologue Cui Haiying reflects on the revolutionary polemic that he has used to seize power and still employs to subjugate the villagers:

There may well be perils in political struggle—if you don't rely on trickery and intrigue, how can you acquire the power of which you dream daily? Aren't relations between people simply men bullying men, men oppressing men, everyone for himself? This class struggle is, to put it bluntly, doing people in. [25]

Cui is as good (or bad) as his word: the upright Old Party Secretary is harassed and humiliated by Cui and his henchmen, and a letter appealing to Chairman Mao written by the old man's grandson (a sure panacea in Cultural Revolution writing)[26] only leads to more trouble.

The peasantry of *The Path of Life* are a downtrodden and dispirited group. If there is a typical peasant family to correspond with those of Grandpa Guan and Li Qingtian in the earlier works, it is that of the destitute Louwa, whose daughter is drowned gleaning submerged crops, whose wife attempts suicide, and who is last seen trudging away to a life of beggary, a combination of disasters that in a pre-1979 novel could only have been set in the "old society" before Communist rule.[27] What makes peasant life worse (at least in the eyes of the female protagonist) is the inevitable continuity of peasant suffering:

Of course, peasants are human too, they seek a happy life and deserve to achieve it. But when will they ever change the poor and primitive face of the countryside . . . ? Year after year they are doomed to shoulder huge burdens, to plod barefoot through mud and rain, and their only reward will be less sweet potato and sorghum than they need for subsistence.[28]

To say that the life of Chinese peasants was poor and primitive and likely to remain so would have been unthinkable before 1979, even from the mouth of a villian. Facts and beliefs regarding the relocated youth that could not have been openly voiced before the publication of *The Path of Life* also find their expression in Juanjuan: the fact that young urban women were raped by the officials who were put in charge of them (documented in Bernstein's study and returned to by Zhu Lin in subsequent fiction)[29] and the opinion, which contradicts that of all the urban youths in the two previous novels, that the urbanites are incompatible with the peasants and would do better to get out. Fond of each other as they may be, Juanjuan is quite simply different from her devoted peasant friend and roommate Lizi:

Juanjuan liked Lizi for her warm and honest simplicity. But she felt that her own mind was more complex and mature than Lizi's, her perspective broader, and her burden greater.[30]

And, contemplating the miseries of the peasants after the collapse of the dam and the flooding of their fields, Juanjuan concludes:

We aren't saviors of the world, we can't save anyone else, we'd do better to save ourselves.[31]

That such an outright refutation of a continuing Party and state policy could be tolerated, even in an interlude of ideological liberation, is perhaps explained by the ambiguity of Juanjuan's position. She is the central character (earlier titles proposed by the author but rejected by her editors underline this point),[32] but she is not the dispenser of absolute truth that Zhong Weihua and Geng Changjiong are. She has, after all, knowingly confected lies designed to oust the Old Party Secretary. What Juanjuan offers is only psychological and emotional truth, as distinct from Liangzi's political truth; he is, by contrast, insensitive to emotional needs that are not subjugated to political and material ones.

The perceptions of narrator and heroine toward the countryside and the place in it of the urban youths allow a very different reading of a situation that is similar in many respects to those of the first two novels: A heroic rusticated youth (Liangzi) supports an irrigation project promoted by an enlightened cadre and sabotaged by the villain. There is a good side and a bad side to the Party (though good and evil occupy reversed positions across the dividing line of the previous work); there are peasants who side with the hero and a conflict to persuade a waverer (this time Juanjuan) to stay in the countryside. The hero Liangzi, though outranked and arrested by the representative of the Party's sinister side, is still vindicated in the eyes of the peasantry. Where the plot takes an unprecedented turn is in the treatment of Juanjuan, whose inability to reconcile herself with the village condemns her, alone among the misfits, to destruction. Estranged from Liangzi, raped and impregnated by Cui Haiying, and rejected by the authorities handling university applications, Juanjuan returns distraught to the village, writes her confession as a suicide note to Liangzi, and throws herself in the river.

THE "ETERNALS": MODELS FOR RUSTICATED YOUTH

In the novels introduced above, the argument for remaining in the countryside is made most strongly in the words and actions of a single male heroic figure, whereas one young woman in each novel, plus an additional male figure in *The Dividing Line,* presents the case for departure. That the misfits are predominantly female is more an acknowledgment of the vulnerability of the rusticated women than misogyny on the part of the authors, two of whom are women themselves.

The models—Zhong Weihua of *The Journey,* Geng Changjiong of *The Dividing Line,* and Liangzi of *The Path of Life*—are rusticated youths as the authorities would have them be, and thus they are extremely similar.

First, in common with one another, though with very few of their historical counterparts, they do not have to be there: Zhong Weihua renounces the realization of his boyhood dream of military service to lead his group to Manchuria; Geng Changjiong could be in Shanghai ministering to his sick mother, and also turns down the offer of a place at Qinghua University (for which he had not even applied) in order to remain; and Liangzi, alone among his contemporaries, chooses to return to Anhui after college graduation.

Second, their choice of role models places them firmly in the Chinese Communist heroic tradition. Zhong Weihua's primary heroes are, in keeping with his militaristic proclivities, martyred boy soldiers, drawn from war- and peacetime mythologies. They include the civil war heroes Qiu Shaoyun and Huang Xuguang, who sacrificed themselves for their comrades;[33] Luo Shengjiao, hero of the Korean War who froze to death saving a local child; and the official peacetime cult heroes Wang Jie, Ouyang Hai, and the perennial Lei Feng.[34]

The collective qualities of these role models, as represented in the hagiographies, are courage, self-sacrifice, and absolute loyalty to their Party superiors. Analytical thinking is, for them, a matter of consulting supreme authority on any given subject. Thus:

Zhong Weihua, a young fellow skilled at considering problems . . . came to the realization that every time you follow Chairman Mao's teaching and take a step forward along Chairman Mao's revolutionary line, you invariably prove the greatness and correctness of Mao Zedong Thought.[35]

Lei Feng, a role model to Geng Changjiong as well as to Zhong Weihua, is the boy soldier whose deeds are most copiously documented, apocryphal as many of them may be. A contributing factor in securing Lei Feng his place in posterity was the diary in which he recorded his acts of charity and his devotion to the Party, a private document designed for public consumption. Zhong Weihua and Geng Changjiong keep similar journals. Lei Feng was also the most self-effacing of heroes, whose highest ambition was to be an "unrusting screw," a minute but tireless component in the great revolutionary machine. Geng Chang-jiong's ambition is, if anything, humbler still:

"What a lofty spirit there is in a piece of road-gravel!" Geng Changjiong couldn't help but think. "Though it's too small for anyone to notice, still it has great practical application. It makes people's lives easier, but remains silent; isn't this a quality worth emulating?"

Geng Changjiong had long had a particular affection for road-surfacing gravel.[36]

Liangzi, whose good deeds are as manifest as those of any Cultural Revolution model, is as unwilling as Lei Feng to claim credit. Thanked for contributing his life savings to the Old Party Secretary's impromptu disaster fund, he offers the disclaimer: "Don't thank me, this is a token of the Party's concern."[37] As the only one of our three heroes to be romantically involved, Liangzi is able to demonstrate a further facet of Chinese heroism shared with the sage emperor Yu the Great, the collectivist peasant Wang Guofu, and the preeminent creation of Cultural Revolution fiction Gao Daquan:[38] the propensity for sacrificing those he loves in the public interest. Liangzi is more interested in investigating the collapse of the dam and organizing the villagers than in understanding the complexities of Juanjuan's situation and character, and his neglect of her contributes to her destruction. The romantic alternative that Liangzi (and all such heroes) must inevitably accept is the woman who demands nothing of him—the adoring peasant girl Lizi, for whom washing his clothes is a sensual delight and who vows that she will "stick with him to the end."[39]

Third, the three heroes perform prodigious feats and win the adulation of the peasants among whom they have chosen to live. Among Zhong Weihua's achievements are rooting out the concealed villain, preventing a bridge from being swept away by a flood, and single-handedly capturing the region's former tyrant. Small wonder then that the mother-figure in the model Guan family warms his frostbitten feet on her bared breast, or that Zhong is, within a year of leaving Shanghai, militia chief and virtual leader of the entire brigade. Geng Changjiong is similarly adored and seems at times superhuman: on his first appearance a bogged-down cart is lifted "as though moved by a giant hand,"[40] and as he returns haggard after seven days' continus work, his "hot hands" soothe an injured colleague.[41] Liangzi is even more a mythical figure, being associated in the popular imagination with a magic phoenix of local legend whose return will free the village from the malign influence of a tiger and a dragon.

Our three model heroes are essentially a composite of ideal qualities commended by the Communist Party for urban youth wishing to make a success of their rustication. This is as might be expected in the case of the two pre-1976 novels, but surprising in the case of *The Path of Life,* a work that otherwise rejects the constraints of Cultural Revolution composition. However, while the narrators and reliable informants of *The Journey* and *The Dividing Line* are unanimous in their approval of the heroes, Zhu Lin uses the criticisms of sympathetic characters to tarnish Liangzi's aura. When he complains to his mother that Juanjuan does not share his ideals, she berates him:

"Idiot! Dogmatist! . . . Ai, we spoiled you, we let you have it too easy, we were too old-fashioned, and we finish up with a little dogmatist like you!"[42]

And Juanjuan, realizing at last that Liangzi's love for her is outweighed by his sense of duty to the villagers and his vendetta with Cui Haiying, soliloquizes:

Enough, I can fool myself no longer. Life has taught me that all those who sing the fine strains of politics are actually stamping on the heads of others as they scramble to the top. They are the most selfish! selfish! selfish! To use my love to keep me here as a sacrificial object in your struggle for power is the most selfish of all![43]

Certainly the lofty altruism he shares with the other heroes—"it is [he says] the responsibility of every rank-and-file Party member to save mankind"[44]—seems less laudable in Liangzi, given his neglect of Juanjuan.

THE MISFITS: FROM A SPOILED BRAT TO A TRAGIC HEROINE

A recent Chinese commentator has perceptively characterized the experience of the rusticated youths as one of lovelessness, suggesting that the city teenagers

bade farewell to the loving atmosphere of the traditional Chinese family and were catapulted into an environment where even to declare love was a crime. There they were nursed with wolf's milk and schooled in the philosophy of struggle, and they lost the right to love.[45]

For our three heroes, as for the young letter writers of the early 1970s, the class love of the peasantry was more than adequate compensation for the lost warmth of family. It cannot have been so for all the rusticated youths. In the two Cultural Revolution novels under consideration, an attempt is made to undermine the validity of the desire to leave the countryside by portraying those who seek to return to the city as inadequate misfits who must be rescued by the hero from their delusion. In the terminology of Cultural Revolution literary analysis (derived from the disposition of characters in the model works), these misfits are "turnabout characters" *(zhuanbian renwu)*, initially doubting but later won over to the position of the hero.[46] Of our three novels, the post–Cultural Revolution work *The Path of Life* is the only one in which the hero fails to persuade the misfit, and in which the misfit is regarded with sympathy.

The Journey's single misfit, Wan Lili, is the antithesis of the hero and represents everything that a rusticated youth should not be. Her ancestry is, from a Cultural Revolution perspective, highly suspect: she is the daughter of the factory manager who had exploited Zhong Weihua's mother when the latter was indentured as a child textile worker, and her name may (by a homophone on the given name) mean "big profits."[47] True to her class (as the characters of Cultural Revolution fiction are), she is vain, materialistic, and less committed than her peers to the rustication policy; she takes three pedicab loads of luggage and the return train fare with her to Manchuria. On her first day in the Northeast, the hapless girl disgraces herself when she cannot eat her coarse cornmeal bun and tries to throw it away, when she prefers woolen socks to the dried grass the Party secretary gives her to insulate her shoes for the march, and when she attempts to keep warm by carrying a hot-water bottle that freezes solid in the cold temperatures. She ends up frostbitten and exhausted in mid-march, where she is roundly criticized for "bringing her bourgeois lifestyle to Heilongjiang."[48]

Lili's inept attempts at physical labor also incur the derision of her peers. Her soft hands stick to a frozen well handle; her technique with a sickle is more theatrical than agricultural; she cannot get the hang of a machine that strips soybean pods from their stems. Zhong Weihua uncomplainingly lacerates his hands digging holes for power-line poles in the frozen earth, whereas Lili wears gloves, shirks, and still complains. What earns her the greatest sarcasm of her peers and the narrator alike, however, is her artistic and romantic disposition, which is scorned as idle frippery out of place in the austerity of the new environment. When she practices her violin in the piggery, where she is consigned to work with the former landlord's daughter (the only indigenous youth of similarly suspect origins), her playing of the proscribed *Butterfly Lovers* Concerto[49] is described by one urban youth as sounding like a piglet;[50] the narrator later says her playing is "like a sick pig."[51] A similar revolutionary philistinism greets Wan Lili's adolescent romanticism as she weaves garlands of flowers, one of which becomes tangled in her hair:

Yu Yingtian had a ready tongue; she ran her fingers down her cheek and giggled: "Quick, take a look, we've got a bride here!"

"Ha, ha, ha!" Everyone on the cart, male and female, except Zhong Weihua [Lili's cousin], Fang Ming, and Zhang Dawei, burst out laughing. Zhang Dawei looked back at Wan Lili with a sneer: "New bride, old bride, looks more to me like the white-bone demon's nanny."

"Ha, ha, ha!" Another gale of laughter, which made the laughing stomachs ache, caused the usually composed Lili to blush purple, and even her neck turned red.

Before the laughter had died down, Wan Lili had torn the garland from her head.[52]

Ostracized by her peers, Lili's desire to return to the city, attend college, and pursue a musical career intensifies. Unloved, she becomes easy prey for the villain Zhang Shan as the only person apparently sympathetic to her artistic temperament and her only link to the outside world. Zhang bears (and reads) her letter to her mother expressing her longing to flee to "Swan Lake," and reminds her of it as he attempts to abduct her to Tchaikovsky's Russian homeland.

Lili is narrowly saved by Zhong Weihua, and rescue brings about her transformation. Seeing what has happened, she "hated Zhang Shan for tricking her, hated herself for letting the side down, for failing Zhong Weihua."[53] Catharsis engenders engagement. which in turn brings acceptance. Lili's last appearance is as she sings to entertain her colleagues a song dedicating them all to their life in the countryside.

Before her transformation, Wan Lili's waywardness, need for affection, and failure to conform make her, in the terms of the novel, a spoiled bourgeois brat, whose selfish desire for intellectual, professional, and emotional fulfillment must be jettisoned before she can take the place assigned to her in society.

Yang Landi of *The Dividing Line* is a character similar to Wan Lili, though her case unfolds in a less dramatic manner and without the narratorial sarcasm of the previous work. Initially contented with the new life and accepted by peers and peasants, she becomes disaffected after falling under the spell of villain You Fa and his wife. Thereafter city affectations reassert themselves, as she finds herself resenting the darker complexion and robust physique that her years on the farm have brought her. Her disaffection is not, as Wan Lili's was, the inevitable result of a nonproletarian background; in fact, her worker parents and sister reject her pleas to find her a job or a marriage partner in the city and urge her to stay put. Even permission to visit Shanghai, originally granted by farm management, is rescinded by Geng Changjiong, who insists she stay to work on his irrigation project. With the aid of You Fa she sneaks away, the unwitting carrier of messages between him and a shadowy black-market network in Shanghai. When his treachery is exposed, she, like Wan Lili before her, can blame him for her irresolution and renew her commitment, a change of heart rather more plausible in a sturdy proletarian than the dainty bourgeoise of *The Journey*.

The more interesting case in the same novel, both psychologically and for its reflection of the peculiarities of life in China in the early 1970s, is that of Xue Chuan, a longtime friend of Geng Changjiong and a leader among the urban youths. With the universities reopened and setting quotas for students from state farms, Xue applies and sets about preparing himself for the entrance examinations. There is a catch in the selection procedure, however: since political activism is a requisite for acceptance to university, and since activists must (as we have seen) commit themselves to a lifetime in the countryside, manifest ambition to succeed in the entrance examination is liable to lead to failure. Surreptitious as Xue may be, his enthusiasm for leaving the village does not elude the attention of Geng Changjiong or the villain You Fa, who steals and hides a letter from Xue's professor father advising him on his application. It does Xue no good either to align himself with Huo Li and her materialist policies: Geng Changjiong displaces Xue as leader of his own group and as speaker at a meeting on agricultural policy, and Huo Li selects Geng, rather than Xue, for university in an attempt to get the troublesome hero out of the village. Geng obliquely informs Xue of the hopelessness of his quest by giving him a straw hat (such as fieldworkers wear and students shun); he then gives Xue the opportunity to join in an act of valor that reunites the two men and confirms Xue as an "eternal" in the village. This comes in a euphuistic passage in what is otherwise (for its times) a rather restrained work, the difference in tone being due in part to the fact that the scene seems to have been lifted from the man-versus-nature climax of the model opera *Ode to Dragon River.* The sluice gate between the channel and the fields is cracking in a heavy storm, and time is needed to shore it up:

"A panel on the sluice gate is cracked!" said Geng Changjiong anxiously. "If we don't shore it up, the whole of the Great Eastern Swamp could be affected."

"You direct things here, I'll go down!" Xue Chuan took off his rainboots.

"No, I'm stronger than you are, I should go down."

"Changjiong . . ." Xue's eyes sparkled with tears.

"No more delay!" shouted Geng Changjiong, and pushing Xue Chuan aside with his mighty hands, he slid resolutely down the dike.

Xue Chuan was speechless. Could he abandon a comrade-in-arms at such a crucial time? . . . he slid down after Geng Changjiong toward the sluice gate. . . . Xue Chuan and Geng Changjiong stood shoulder to shoulder, arms entwined, battling together in the rushing torrent. Each could feel the other's breathing, the other's heartbeat, each giving the other inestimable strength.[54]

With the bonds between the two men reestablished by this gallant act of commitment, it is no longer conceivable that Xue would contemplate leaving the farm.

Tan Juanjuan of *The Path of Life,* like Xue Chuan, sees university entrance as the way to get back to the city; Juanjuan realizes the hazards of declared ambition and protests instead her determination to remain in the village. She is more successful than was Wan Lili at concealing her artistic sensitivities from the villagers, taking care to dress as rustically as possible. Zhu Lin's narrator is kinder toward pride in appearance than was Guo Xianhong's—what is bourgeois vanity in Wan Lili is a city girl's love of beauty in Juanjuan (none of the three authors, urbanites all, credits peasants with any aesthetic sense).

The need to suppress her real feelings from public view drives Juanjuan, like Wan Lili and Yang Landi before her, into the clutches of an apparently sympathetic villain. For Juanjuan there is an additional sexual threat, expressed in the symbolism of the nocturnal predator as she tries to leave Cui Haiying's house after soliciting his support for her university application:

"Look at you, where are you off to now?" Cui Haiying had moved up behind Juanjuan; he patted her shoulder tenderly and murmured: "I just said that since we were alone we could have a good chat. Why did you rush away like that before I'd finished what I was saying?"

At these words, Juanjuan turned slowly, her eyes wide as they stared through the darkness at Cui Haiying. The sad and chilling screech of a distant owl filled the darkness. Cui Haiying smirked in the shadows and questioned her further: "Would I be that kind of man? eh?"[55]

He is, of course, precisely that kind of man, raping her after making her drink drugged wine, ostensibly in a toast to her future success. Were *The Path of Life* a Cultural Revolution novel, there would have been, up to the point of her rape, a clearly correct path for Juanjuan to follow: reveal publicly her involvement in Cui's misdeeds, abandon her desire to leave the village, and dedicate herself to Liangzi's utopian vision. But the physical violation of the protagonist takes the plot beyond the somewhat puritanical parameters of Cultural Revolution fiction;[56] in any case, such a course of action would be psychologically impossible in Zhu Lin's post–Cultural Revolution world for a woman so completely misplaced in the countryside.

Juanjuan is, by contrast with the other misfits, a tragic heroine, a pure woman[57] hopelessly compromised by her attempts to escape from a situation beyond her control, a plaything of malign forces. Thus she is a far cry from Wan Lili, the spoiled brat of *The Journey*. In the character of Juanjuan, the full force of post-Mao discontent is directed against the Cultural Revolution exhortations to, and eulogy of, conformity with Party-sponsored models. That the misfit is as noble as the model is a sign of the end of the moral certainty of Cultural Revolution literature and the beginning of the anxiety and ambivalence that characterize the post-Mao period of ideological liberation.

POSTSCRIPT: RUSTICATED URBANITES IN 1980s FICTION

The three novels discussed above reflect the profound changes in the relocated urbanites' perception of rural China and their place in it. In *The Journey* the countryside is a place for thrills and military-style heroics; though this adolescent romanticism may be absent from *The Dividing Line,* there is nonetheless the promise of peer-group support and the reward of recognition for those who stay. In the post–Cultural Revolution novel *The Path of Life,* the village is a cruel and alien environment where the urban youths can never belong. From being a place for the hero to display his prowess, the countryside has become a hell from which to escape,[58] and both the model youth's decision to stay and the misfit's attempt to leave must be judged from this new perspective.

In the literature of the early 1980s, perhaps in response to the intractable problems posed to the authorities by the millions of rusticated youths demanding to return to the cities, there are indications of a renewed romanticism about the countryside, coupled with a rustic's unease with the big city. Perhaps the most influential work in this vein was Zhang Xianliang's *Body and Soul* (1980),[59] whose protagonist, Xue Lingjun, refuses his expatriate father's offer of a luxurious life overseas and returns instead to his life as a teacher in a community of herdsmen. Throughout the story, the city (represented by the Beijing Hotel and its environs) is portrayed as decadent in contrast to the "simplicity, purity, and appropriateness"[60] of life in the village; the "effeminate-looking men and masculine-looking women"[61] on the hotel dance floor compare unfavorably with Xue's salt-of-the-earth neighbors; and his father's fashionable secretary is found wanting in comparison with Xue's simple and devoted peasant wife. The lure of the village is no longer the thrill of battle; rather it is sensual delight in open space and the feelings of a man in harmony with nature that induce "a sense of well-being so rustic as to border on the primitive."[62] Presented with the choice of staying or going, Xue Lingjun makes the same model choice as the heroes of the 1970s novels, whom he greatly resembles.

In another story, Wang Anyi's *The Destination* (1981),[63] the protagonist is a misfit who after ten years manages to return to Shanghai to take the job vacated by his mother's retirement. It is not the romantic charm of the village that punctures his delight at return, but the harsh realities of the city: noise, crowded buses, factory work, and, most important, a shortage of living space that results in severe family tensions. Wang Anyi says little about the village her protagonist left behind but clearly suggests in the words of one of her characters that "the sacrifices I made to return to Shanghai aren't worth it."[64]

By the 1980s the choice of whether to stay or to go, which had provided a central tension in rusticated-youth fiction, was no longer an issue for most of those in the countryside—those who could have returned to the city, and those who remained were likely there for life. Such is the background to a retrospective story by Zhang Kangkang, the author of *The Dividing Line* and herself long since returned to the city. In *The Pagoda* (1983)[65] four rusticated youths now returned to Hangzhou meet with a fifth, Song Weiliang, who has remained in the Northeast and is visiting the city with his peasant wife. His return allows all of them to reflect on their shared experiences and their different lives since parting.

One thing is clear: Song Weiliang, who had always been the leader of the group (and who may therefore be seen as an older version of *The Dividing Line*'s Geng Changjiong), is now the outsider, instantly recognizable to city dwellers as a "hick" *(xiangbalao)* and a "black devil" *(heiguir,* after the province of Heilongjiang, "Black Dragon River," where he has remained). Although resigned to his fate, Song still has regrets: had he been offered the alternatives facing Xue Lingjun of *Body and Soul,* he knows that he would not have gone home to his peasant wife.[66]

Song Weiliang's friends pity him his life in Heilongjiang; all of them further share a sense of self-pity for their entire generation. Those who have remained among the peasants are still regarded with suspicion, assigned like Song to jobs below their capabilities, while those who have returned similarly find their qualifications belittled and their experience in the countryside a source of shame rather than pride. The euphoric sense of mission celebrated at the start of *The Journey,* if it ever really existed, has long since evaporated, leaving a generation that feels itself slightly out of step with the rest of the nation, no longer youths, most of them no longer rusticated, moving uneasily into middle age.[67]

Dramas of Passion: Heroism in the Cultural Revolution's Model Operas

ELLEN R. JUDD

One may easily forget, after all the intervening years, that the Cultural Revolution was not only a power struggle and an experiment in socioeconomic reform but also an intensely felt human drama full of hope and of pain. Its occurrence and unfolding involved the active participation of millions of people in pursuit of a vision able to touch their souls. As Mao Zedong said in conversation with André Malraux years before the Cultural Revolution began and in reference to the earlier revolutionary process, "Revolution is a drama of passion; we did not win the people over by appealing to reason, but by developing hope, trust and fraternity."[1] An adequate perspective on the CR requires attention to this vision of hope and its subsequent history.

This chapter explores one central aspect of this vision as it was expressed in the symbolism of heroism in the CR's model operas. I would ask readers who remember the era to summon before their eyes an image of the dramatic pose, *liangxiang,* in the model operas. Imagine Yang Zirong in *Taking Tiger Mountain by Strategy* posed before a detachment of PLA soldiers and officers against the background of an unfurled red flag, or imagine Li Yuhe in *The Red Lantern* standing upright in blood-stained shirt, striking fear into the hearts of his torturers. Or Ke Xiang in *Azalea Mountain* in chains and in prison but defiantly holding her right fist high.

These scenes, which seem melodramatic today, were the central dramatic images of the Cultural Revolution as it moved from critique of revisionist drama to an affirmation of its particular vision of proletarian culture. In 1966 eight works were declared models: five Beijing operas, two dance dramas, and one symphony. The number of models was gradually expanded during the following decade, and they acted as a major influence on the entire literary and artistic world throughout the CR. From 1970 the model operas formed the core of efforts to create a new popular culture, in the movement to popularize the revolutionary model operas. They also were called on to legitimize an emerging body of prescriptive literary and dramatic theory centered on the concept of the "three prominences."[2] In short, the model operas were the artistic centerpiece of the Cultural Revolution. In the words of Jiang Qing, "Since as long ago as the Paris Commune, the proletariat had not resolved the problem of its own direction in literature and art. Only since our work with revolutionary model operas from 1964 has this problem been resolved."[3]

This chapter analyzes what it was in the model operas that made them the subject of such a grand claim. My study focuses on the highly innovative symbolism of heroism in these works. The discussion is limited to the designated model Beijing operas in their definitive versions: *Taking Tiger Mountain by Strategy (Zhiqu weihushan), Shajiabang (Shajiabang), On the Docks (Haigang), Raid on the White Tiger Regiment (Qixi baihutuan), The Red Lantern (Hongdengji), Ode to Dragon River (Longjiang song), Azalea Mountain (Dujuanshan), Fighting on the Plains (Pingyuan zuo zhan),* and *The Red Detachment of Women (Hongse niangzijun).*[4]

Other major restrictions on the scope of this study merit explicit mention. Undoubtedly the creation and presentation of the model operas were components of a complex power struggle.[5] Except insofar as that issue is intrinsic to the symbolism of heroism, I shall leave it to one side. The dramatic theory associated with the "three prominences" may seem more pertinent to this discussion, but I shall for the most part, leave that aside as well, in part because I have addressed it elsewhere,[6] and in part because it does not actually fit the model operas as closely as it claims. My objective here is to examine both the construction of heroism in the designated operatic texts and its reference to the world beyond the texts, that is, the social context.

Heroism is the pivot of the dramatic construction and emotive force of model opera symbolism. While there is no way of directly entering the felt experience of the Cultural Revolution at this distance, symbolic analysis is available as a method of approaching that experience and attempting to comprehend it. I shall discuss heroism as a key symbol in the model operas and, by extension, in the Cultural Revolution. Indeed, while it is possible for more than one key symbol to exist in a given cultural field, heroism is the dominant one here and could even be termed the "main key symbol." As Sherry Ortner has pointed out, there are two methodological approaches to identifying key symbols. One may select those symbols to which the culture itself gives explicit prominence, or one may analyze the cultural system for its underlying elements and then seek symbols that most clearly embody those.[7] The approach I take will be to show that heroism is such an explicit key symbol and then to analyze its underlying implicit symbolism. In this latter respect I shall give particular attention to the role of a (multivocal) key symbol in articulating pervasive and powerful tensions vertically present in a cultural field.

Heroism immediately attracts one's attention on viewing or reading texts of the model operas. It is clearly central to the meaning and the action of every one of the model operas and is also marked in terms of performance by such features as the dramatic pose mentioned earlier. Commentary of the time declared that the basic task *(genben renwu)* of literature and art was to create proletarian heroic models, and that this was the core of the model operas.[8] The "three prominences" underlined heroism still more heavily.

But it is essential to consider what is meant by heroism in the context of the model operas. It is all too easy to see the central characters in the model operas as heroes in one of the more simplified senses available to us from our own culture—a very good person who overcomes formidable difficulties to vanquish very bad persons in (usually) action-packed adventure. Clearly there are some similarities here that enable us to recognize and label the heroism of these exotic opera characters, but the quality and meaning of their heroism require closer attention and an effort to place this attribute in its appropriate symbolic and social context.

The Red Lantern, one of the best known of the original five model Beijing operas and one that is still heard and spoken of with approval in China at the present time,[9] exemplifies some of the general features of heroism common to the model operas and also shows some revealing peculiarities (see the summary scenario in the Appendix to this chapter). *The Red Lantern* might be read as a forthright war drama celebrating the subsequent victory and commemorating those whose sacrifice made it possible. But there are hints of a wider, allegorical significance in this as well as the other model operas. They share or provide variations on a set of themes that invite another level of interpretation.

The similarities between the model operas and the pattern of heroic myth classically summarized by Joseph Campbell are striking.[10] A hero ventures out of the everyday world into exceptional circumstances, confronts fabulous forces against which he or she is victorious, and returns with the power to benefit others. The hero is good but not only good—the heroic character also possesses and shares some transcendent power. As Campbell noted, the old myths have lost much of their force in our secular society, but similar themes can be found in contexts we categorize differently—indeed, to be effective they must be called something other than myths. Campbell would not have missed the mythic element of the model operas, as in his view "The problem is nothing if not that of rendering the modern world spiritually significant"[11] and achieving a transcendence of individual human limitations. It is worthwhile to look more closely at the particular variant of heroism conveyed in the secular political myths of the model operas.

The best starting place is the knotty question of the social structural categorization of the main heroic character of each model opera. The traditional opera had been severely criticized for allowing the elite to dominate the stage; the model operas were presented as a showcase for inverting this dominance. The critics referred to Mao Zedong's letter of encouragement after seeing the Yan'an drama circles' first effort to reform Beijing opera.[12] Mao declared that *Driven up Liangshan (Bi shang Liangshan)* was a watershed in the portrayal of history because it returned to the people *(renmin)* their proper place as its creators. In the later era and political rhetoric of the Cultural Revolution, this was rephrased as requiring that the proletariat take center stage. Whether this was actually done in the model operas has been raised as a serious question within the framework of the CR's own claims, and the charge that they did not adequately accomplish this has been leveled against them in China in recent years as well. Unlike Li Yuhe, the main heroic characters of all the other operas under discussion can be described as basic-level cadres: scout platoon leader *(Taking Tiger Mountain by Strategy, Raid on the White Tiger Regiment,* and *Fighting on the Plains);* company political instructor *(Shajiabang* and *The Red Detachment of Women);* local Party secretary *(On the Docks* and *Ode to Dragon River);* and Party representative *(Azalea Mountain).* Whether this pattern is problematic or not is a matter of interpretation. When I discussed this with authoritative informants toward the end of the Cultural Revolution, they agreed that this pattern existed, but did not view it as a problem on two explicit grounds: (1) Cadres are not separate from or opposed to the laboring people. They are not a class, and therefore there is no problem. (2) Drama requires the playing out and resolution of conflict *(maodun chongtu).* The heroes must accomplish this and so must be placed in a structural position in the drama that enables them to do so.

In fact, the structural position of these heroes is complex and ambiguous, and it is precisely this ambiguity that is central to their roles as key symbols. Although all the main heroes except Li Yuhe have a leadership position in a formal organization, this organizational status is very much deemphasized. Even those with military leadership roles who could well be portrayed more extensively in those roles are not so portrayed. Yang Zirong in *Taking Tiger Mountain by Strategy* is perhaps the clearest illustration: although described as a scout platoon leader, he acts as an individual hero on a solo underground mission. Further, he eclipses the role of his commanding officer, who, exceptionally, also appears in the opera. (The usual pattern is that the low-ranking hero holds the highest formal status in the opera, with the exception of enemy characters.) This represents a consistent pattern in the model operas wherein the hero does not depend on his or her formal organizational status in heroic actions but is simply enabled to take those actions as a consequence of the legitimate opportunities for leadership provided by that status. What is actually essential and emphasized in the heroes is reconcilable with formal leadership status but qualitatively distinct. Each hero acts autonomously and efficaciously by virtue of access to a transcendent source of power, sometimes materially represented, as in the case of the red lantern. This source of power is the Communist Party (and perhaps also the hero's devotion to it), but it is a Party conceptualized as distant, disembodied, and ideological and not as immediate, concrete, and organizational. The hero has implicitly direct and unmediated access to this source of power by virtue of superior moral qualities and dedication. The consequences of this access to power are demonstrated in the hero's ability to defeat enemies and to lead other heroes and "positive" characters.

The heroes have other honorable attributes as well. They are demonstrably good people linked in ties of solidarity with other good (if less heroic) people. In every opera the hero is portrayed generously giving to others despite consequent hardship or personal risk. In *The Red Lantern,* for example, Li Yuhe gives the gift of safety to the liaison man at the risk of his own safety and that of his family. Indeed, most of Li Yuhe's actions in the opera are open to interpretation as being gifts on some level. Another common form of giving is the offering of food. In this opera it is the other heroes, Li Yuhe's mother and daughter, who present this gift, but it fits the same pattern. In all these cases the gifts of the heroes are reciprocated by other heroic or positive characters. Close ties are formed and demonstrated with some dramatic emphasis. This recurrent pattern undermines one of the common criticisms of the main heroic characters as being overly individual. On the contrary, their heroism largely consists of their ties with others, as in the extreme case of Li Yuhe's martyrdom and succession by his daughter. It is worth noting as well that it is not simple goodness and giving that are being portrayed— the main heroic characters never give anything to the enemy, and there are no episodes of their generosity being taken advantage of by others. Li Yuhe is not shown trusting Wang Lianju, for example. The function of the gift giving in the operas is better viewed as establishing ties of solidarity between heroes and other positive characters than as demonstrating simple goodness.

Another quality of heroes is intellectual, although this is somewhat underplayed. The anti-intellectual and vocally egalitarian strains of the Cultural Revolution could not easily accommodate displays of intellectual superiority. Nevertheless, the heroes never mistake their friends or enemies, make no strategic or tactical errors, resourcefully outwit their enemies, and in some cases show an exceptional grasp of policy.

The heroes are also invariably courageous. They show their heroic qualities under severe testing and never doubt their cause. Their courage helps them either to triumph in adversity or, in what could perhaps be seen as an indirect triumph, to pass on a legacy to others who will triumph in the future. But courage is not the distinguishing feature of these heroes, for others have it as well, and indeed none of the positive characters lack courage.

The heroes are almost always portrayed as suffering hardship or even death, the exceptions being those in operas with post-1949 settings *(Ode to Dragon River* and *On the Docks)*. This is typically also the case for lesser heroes and for positive characters in general, as suffering symbolically validates moral worth. It is an important attribute of heroism but not an essentially defining characteristic.

The outstanding distinguishing feature of the main heroic characters is slightly different and quite specific. It is not some intrinsic moral quality, such as goodness, generosity, or courage, even though those are present. It is also not action on the nonhuman world, such as taming nature or confronting spirits, neither of which is portrayed. Rather it is action on the human world in the form of powerful moral-political leadership. The heroes are portrayed as extremely efficacious, and the medium through which they exert this efficacy is influence over others. This is portrayed in the dual form of vanquishing enemies and leading their own people.

The Red Lantern shows these qualities at their irreducible minimum. Li Yuhe's formal status is that of a worker who is an underground Communist Party member. This is the "lowest" status of any of the main heroic characters viewed from the perspective of an organizational hierarchy, but it is possible and reasonable to view any Party member in that context as occupying a leadership status. Being underground poses a larger dramatic problem: How can he be portrayed acting as a leader? While he does appear engaged in courier duties, this is primarily and most effectively accomplished through his leadership within his household. This is, indeed, a striking feature of *The Red Lantern* compared with other model operas in which the main heroic character is a woman *(Shajiabang, Ode to Dragon River, On the Docks,* and *Azalea Mountain)*. In those cases the woman's family is not even referred to, with the sole exception (in *Azalea Mountain*) of the revelation of Ke Xiang's recent widowhood. In *The Red Lantern* Li Yuhe is able to demonstrate his moral-political leadership in his family without either contravening conventional values or directly reinforcing them—the family, after all, is his moral-political creation by an act of will, and his leadership in influencing his mother and daughter to follow in his footsteps can be and is strongly portrayed. Although he and his mother are martyred, he accomplishes his immediate goals and bequeaths the source of his heroism to his daughter. Criticisms recently voiced in China about the model operas' failure to portray the families of female main heroes are misplaced when viewed from this perspective. The importance of portraying the heroes as leaders and of making that dramatic image compelling precluded inclusion of the families of main heroes who were women.

Neither Li Yuhe nor any other main heroic characters of the model operas have been spared questions about their validity as proletarian heroes. Such questions arise about two aspects of these heroes: their larger-than-life unidimensional perfection and their difference as leaders (and highly efficacious ones) from ordinary people. The first of these aspects can be viewed as an irony. The main heroic characters are a role type in a popular dramatic tradition that is well established in China and only disconcerting here because it appears in an otherwise noticeably iconoclastic context, that of an art form fusing elements of traditional popular drama (characterization) with elite art (didactic, moralistic content) and imported staging conventions (modern dress and scenery). Despite the Cultural Revolution's repudiation of prior folk culture, as Robert Hegel has argued, the characters of the model operas owe much to a tradition of type characters oriented toward action rather than toward moral introspection.[13] The apparent perfection of these characters can in part be interpreted as adherence to this dramatic tradition.

The characterization of the heroes can also be viewed from another angle, one that requires us to put our own perspectives into question as much as the objects we are perceiving. There has been a prevalent conflation of two conceptually distinct issues: whether the characters are acceptably proletarian (or plebeian, more generally) and whether their portrayal must necessarily conform to the conventions of realism or, put more extremely, of naturalism. It is arguable that the move toward realism in Chinese drama—which has never been thorough and has for decades been explicitly described as a fusion of realism and romanticism—together with our own expectations of modern-dress drama, has led us to misinterpret the heroes of the model operas as inadequate by a standard of realism (or naturalism) that had never been appropriate. It might be argued in rebuttal that Chinese commentators are also critical of the model opera heroes in similar terms, but I would doubt that their rejection has been quite so automatic or profound. If one removes the criterion of realism, one may then ask whether these heroes speak in some other way of or to the Chinese worker, peasant, or soldier, as claimed.

It is helpful to view the symbolism of heroism in the model operas in the same light as one might view other instances of political symbolism, including those in which some or all of the political import is hidden or implicit, thereby enabling or magnifying its efficacy. Political symbols, in common with all other symbols, are ambiguous and multivocal—the plurality of their meanings is one of the qualities that makes them effective as symbols. As Abner Cohen has argued, the most powerful political symbols link general existential aspects of selfhood, on the one hand, with relations of power, on the other.[14] Following this line of analysis, one may see the main heroic characters of the model operas as a displaced mythical embodiment of deep human aspirations for autonomy and efficacy in the social world. There is no self-evident reason why ordinary people need be debarred from this aspiration or its expression, although its realization may well be problematic. A tightly drawn tension between this aspiration, heightened in the CR, and its limited potential for realization, underlined by the course of the CR, was a central conflict of the era and one whose expression in the heroes of the model operas made their heroism a key symbol.

In examining the more narrowly political aspect of the symbolism, the relations of power, the major relevant observations regarding the texts have been made above, but it is useful to turn to context as well. There are, of course, numerous resonances of the heroism of the model operas, not only with mythic heroism as a genre but with longstanding themes in Chinese culture and with the immediate context of the Cultural Revolution. The most pertinent resonance is in the status of the operas and their heroes as models; that is, the internal portrayal of proletarian efficacy within the operas is repeated in the public presentation of the operas and their exemplary heroes as efficacious in the world beyond the operas.

Although the term for "model opera" *(yangbanxi)* is not derived from the Confucian heritage of cultivating and emulating superior men,[15] the conception of models and model emulation is connected with that prior cultural theme and with other contemporary Chinese practices regarding models. The core of this conception consisted of a set of assumptions about human nature: that it is malleable and perfectible, that people differ in their degrees of moral attainment, and that people are naturally attracted toward the good. The tension between what people perceive in themselves and their perceptions of models of goodness spurs emulation. Since such models are human and concrete, emulation of them can be highly effective. They can also be intentionally cultivated to serve this purpose. Donald Munro has gone so far as to argue that such models are a Sinicized version of the classical Marxist-Leninist apparatus of "transmission belts,"[16] but although the effect may be similar, the mechanism is distinctively moral rather than organizational.

Models have been widely used in educational contexts in contemporary China and in political movements such as the campaigns to learn from Dazhai and Daqing. Closer to the model operas and their individual heroic models, there have been recurrent campaigns to emulate historically existing individuals. Mary Sheridan traced the development of this trend in promoting individual models from what she identified as the first case in a type of hero emulation, that of Lei Feng in 1963.[17] An analysis of that and subsequent campaigns leading up to and continuing into the early years of the Cultural Revolution showed variations that she related to conflicting political tendencies. In simplified form these models could be characterized as a youthful PLA hero deeply devoted to Mao Zedong, on the one hand, and as an older hero whose outstanding feature was his hard and valuable work, on the other. By 1967 there were signs of crossovers between the two types, and Sheridan predicted further shifts after 1967 as the political status of revolutionary youth declined.

The heroes of the model operas should be seen in this context as well as in that of the operatic traditions. If the plebeian heroes of the model operas and other operas on contemporary themes were a departure from operatic tradition, they were so in a cultural context that had already seen extensive nonoperatic popularization of such "ordinary" heroes as Zhang Side, the soldier commemorated in Mao's essay "To Serve the People." The model opera heroes also had a vital existence beyond the bounds of their operas. In campaigns to teach the heroic arias of the operas on radio and in recurrent waves of the campaign to popularize the model revolutionary operas from 1970 to 1976, the population at large was called on to sing the heroes' words as well as to learn from their actions and thereby internalize their qualities and become more like them. Their quality as operatic characters contributed through music and visual performative images to make them more vivid and attractive models and to give an added artistic dimension to this campaign.

Certain of the commonalities and shifts in features between the model types analyzed by Sheridan and those of the model operas are instructive. The young "red" PLA hero, such as Lei Feng, was thoroughly ordinary except in his goodness and ideological correctness, up to the level of willing self-sacrifice for the public good. He (they seem all to have been men) did not fully symbolize the tension of proletarian leadership to be found in later model heroes. He was not himself a leader, and he might readily break regulations and laugh about it. To the extent that such behavior persists in the model operas, it is in the contemptuous disregard of enemy authority in pre-1949 settings—indeed, higher organizational authority in the model operas is usually in the hands of the enemy. The older "expert" model type, in contrast, could occupy leadership positions, as in the case of Daqing's Wang Jinxi, but was defined more in terms of exceptional accomplishments in work than in terms of political relations. The third type, which emerged with the Red Guard movement at the beginning of the Cultural Revolution, displayed several significant features. Prominent individual models, such as Lei Feng or Wang Jinxi, gave way to numerous fleeting models more embeded in their society. They could be of any age but all showed the "red" characteristics of ideological correctness typical of the earlier youth-model type. And they moved from heroism in the matters of everyday life, such as production, to heroism in crises and did so without recourse to higher authority or mediators but as effective, autonomous actors. Here it is possible to see precursors to the heroes of the model operas as they became codified from 1970.

It would be simplistic to look on the heroes of the model operas as mere reflections of the Red Guard movement, however. These heroes are much more complex and ambiguous. As argued above on textual grounds, they tap underlying existential contradictions, and they do so in a manner that grounds those contradictions in the reality of the contemporary political relations of their society. Further, the operas themselves, as is well known, were not new creations but were adaptations of work dating from as early as the 1940s. Processes of revision during the 1960s provided a channel for the entry of Cultural Revolution themes in the form of changes in characterization, plot, and explicit content.[18] It is important to note that, although one can identify themes of early CR aspirations and conflicts in the model operas, the peak and codification of the model operas came in a distinctly later phase when the CR was in retreat. The stridency of the model operas can be at least partly attributed to a rear-guard effort to generate support for a faltering and profoundly compromised revolution. The definitive texts adopted for each of the models, beginning in 1970, represent a tight, multivocal fusion of general existential, persistent cultural, and specifically mid–Cultural Revolution elements. Further, they do so not only as a textual reflection of wider cultural and social processes but as willed intervention in those processes.

Indeed, human will and corresponding action are persistent cultural themes in Chinese culture and not uniquely or exceptionally features of the Cultural Revolution. As Frederic Wakeman, Jr., has argued, these elements found their way into a major position in Mao Zedong's reinterpretation of the orthodox Marxism of his times.[19] This is perhaps most clearly expressed in Mao Zedong's own words: "It is man's social being that determines his thinking. Once the correct ideas characteristic of the advanced class are grasped by the masses, these ideas turn into a material force which changes society and changes the world."[20] The emphasis on will, combined with the concept of ideas being materialized (and thereby privileged in Marxist terms) in their realization in people, imparts even more force to the role of heroic characters than did the traditional dramatic conventions in themselves, powerful and congruent as those were as cultural patterns. Additionally, if ideas gain their material force through human embodiment in the masses, then the role of imparting those ideas and winning the masses over to them assumes special importance. Leadership of a moral-political nature is central, and the recurrent emphasis in the characterization of the heroes of the model operas on precisely that dimension of heroism can be seen in a context wider than that of the Cultural Revolution. At the same time, much of the most intense struggle in the CR, as well as its rationale, concerned winning the hearts and minds of the people. In this respect one can discern a pattern of relations showing this influence at ascending levels. The moral-political leadership of the main heroic character in relation to other heroic and positive characters in the operas is homologous to the relation of the Party to the masses in the social context beyond the operas, and again homologous to the relation between transcendent power and human beings on a mythic level.

Conflict appears in the dramatic working out of this multifaceted process of human transformation, and this can, on one level, be interpreted as more characteristic of the Cultural Revolution than of an earlier Chinese culture that stressed harmony.[21] But it should also be kept in mind that all the conflicts are successfully resolved in ultimate harmony by the concluding scene, and, if the world has not been wholly harmonized, all the lines of conflict in the opera have been happily concluded. Despite explicit emphasis on conflict, the underlying dramatic structure powerfully conveys a presentation of reality as ultimately harmonious beneath its apparent turmoil and struggle. Still, this is not to say that conflict has given way to harmony. The ultimate picture of harmony at each opera's end is one clearly achieved through deep conflict, and the image of harmony itself implies conflict beyond the opera in any effort to emulate it. An image of future harmony acts as a spur to present conflict, and the result is best described as artfully heightened tension between the two values.

This tension between conflict and harmony can be related not only to general existential and Chinese cultural dimensions of symbolism but also to the specific contemporary context of the later Cultural Revolution years. The heroes of the model operas can, in part, be interpreted as a representation of Red Guards or CR activists more generally—in their activism in conflict, in their autonomy from mediating levels and direct association with higher levels of power, and in their intense devotion to the revolutionary cause. But it would be simplistic and misleading to view these heroes so simply. Their final form in the definitive versions of the model operas shows other elements as well. Some of the lack of individuality of the heroes can be viewed as a corollary of their status in exceptionally (in the Chinese context) fixed texts. These were no longer subject to revision and so required sufficient generality and ambiguity to be appropriate as models in future years as well.

The ambiguity of the heroes' organizational status then becomes essential. Each acts autonomously, in accordance with the populist vision of the early Cultural Revolution, but each holds formal status in the Party or army that legitimizes this activity and conversely also legitimizes Party and army. The heroes never act against their own authorities, and their rebellion against enemy authority need not be interpreted (although it could be) as an allegory of rebellion against "capitalist roaders."[22] The actions of the heroes are even open to interpretation as exceptional successes in implementing their own authorities' policies, although in the texts themselves their own authoritiees and the heroes' relations to them are treated consistently, and very significantly, by almost total silence. The resulting ambiguity both allows the model operas to be open to changing interpretations and political uses based on those in the future and also creates a current and continuing internal tension between autonomy and hierarchy. As in the movement to popularize the revolutionary model operas, this tension (or contradiction) pervaded the practice of the model operas as well as the larger culture of later Cultural Revolution years.[23]

The capacity of the heroic images of the model operas to embody so clearly the central tensions of their time that they could act as a key symbol of CR culture was connected with the sponsorship of these operas as models by the dominant political force in the CR. Ideas, as people as diverse as Marx, Weber, and Geertz have pointed out, are at their most powerful when held by powerful social groups and materially institutionalized by them.[24] The propagation of the model operas represents just such an institutionalization and one that was carried out intentionally. That is both a feature of much officially promoted culture in modernizing societies[25] and a characteristic of the conscious use of culture long established in elite Chinese culture.

The particular quality of the operas with their key symbol of mythic heroism requires some attention in this context of an intentionally engineered cultural revolution. Our own culture inclines us to look at cultural phenomena in narrowly rational terms ("Rationality is our rationalization"),[26] and this tendency is reinforced in the study of China by Marxism's explicit claim to be scientific socialism. But the symbolic practice of the Cultural Revolution may draw our attention beyond rationality. As Antonio Gramsci wrote, "Only antiquated intellectuals believe that a conception of the world can be destroyed by rational criticism."[27]

The symbolic practice of the Cultural Revolution draws on a sensitivity to the diverse dimensions of symbolism that can be found within the Marixist-Leninist tradition but that has not been fully recognized there. It is perhaps closer to the views of an early twentieth-century revolutionary who is not part of the Marxist-Leninist genealogy, Georges Sorel. In his own words: "Men who are participating in a great social movement always picture their coming action as a battle in which their cause is certain to triumph. These constructions, knowledge of which is so important for historians, I propose to call myths; the syndicalist 'general strike' and Marx's catastrophic revolution are such myths."[28]

I have no evidence that CR leaders knew of Sorel and his views, although this may represent a case of unidentified borrowing; I am more inclined to see parallel invention here, on the basis of some prior or shared cultural elements. The replication was certainly not exact, in several respects. Sorel was explicit about his use of "myths," although defining them as valid on another level: "These myths are not descriptions of things, but expressions of a determination to act."[29] The Chinese image of mythic heroism was intentionally created, as was Sorel's idea of a general strike, but, artistic conventions aside, was less explicitly artificial. Chinese dramatic theorists did hold to the value of "revolutionary romanticism" but only in combination with "revolutionary realism"; dramatic representations in this scheme were to be both descriptions of things and expressions of will. While the specific cases of operatic heroism were carefully and consciously created, and these processes of creation and revision at least partly opened to the public, the concept of creating mythic heroism as such was more deeply embedded in a culture receptive to it—in terms of symbolic artistic conventions and the habitual political use of art—and may have drawn more deeply on shared cultural presuppositions than the myth of a general strike was ever able to do.

The Cultural Revolution's mythic heroism was also more complex in its expression, perhaps in part because it affected a larger portion and more facets of its society. The connection between the myth of a general strike as an idea and as a practice was close, and the practice more defined than the idea. In contrast, the Cultural Revolution's heroism was elusive and diffuse in practice, however mixed with various events of the decade, but more clearly defined in a specialized ideological representation, that of the main heroic characters in the model operas. There was a noticeably higher degree of popular spontaneity embedded in and advocated for the general strike than was the case for these models, which took their definitive form after the high tide of spontaneity had ebbed in the CR and newly consolidating authorities were engaging themselves in promoting these models. The heroes of the model operas are an ideologically concentrated expression of complex tensions in their process of creation as well as of complexities on a symbolic level.

As Raymond Williams has noted in a different context (the analogy is imperfect), drama has a capacity to break new ground in a shifting cultural field and to speak with a newly authoritative voice when older cultural vehicles are in question. It can be exceptionally open to new experiences and symbolic expressions and give concentrated voice to them: "The drama of any period, including our own, is an intricate set of practices of which some are incorporated—the known rhythms and movements of a residual but still active system—and some are exploratory—the difficult rhythms and movements of an emergent representation, rearrangement, new identification. Under real pressures these distinct kinds are often intricately and powerfully fused; it is rarely a simple case of the old drama and the new."[30]

The model operas and their images of mythic heroism can be viewed as an exceptionally clear and concentrated expression of a cultural theme of mythic heroism, made visible and in part made effective through its embodiment in secular dramatic form. But what one sees in the heroes of the model operas, vivid and grand as they are, is only a small portion of a wider and deeper key symbol. To summarize, the multivocal myth of transcendent human potential for transformative action on the human world appears in the form of embodied heroes in the model operas, replete with tensions of possibility and constraint. A broader version of the same theme of transcendent human efficacy applies to the cultural role claimed by the model operas within the Cultural Revolution and is again centrally defined by the tension of possibility and limitation. And the Cultural Revolution itself can be viewed as the same heroic enterprise of transformation and transcendence. The symbol of the mythic hero is unusual in its deep vertical articulation of the culture and exceptional in its political power.

The revolutionary potential of changes in consciousness is unquestionably one of the prime concerns of interpreters of twentieth-century China, as it has also been of those who have led its path in this century. There is no one who any longer denies at least relative autonomy to consciousness, but how this autonomy functions is still at issue. At present we have not an answer but another set of questions. If consciousness operates with symbols that have their own material existence in mutliple dimensions—in texts and artifacts, in human acts and actors, in movements and revolutions—the questions to be asked are those of how this consciousness in materiality operates.

The heroism of the model operas is a revealing social experiment in the ideational and material engineering of symbolism through the creation of myth.

APPENDIX

Summary Scenario: The Red Lantern[31]

(THE SETTING IS A RAILWAY TOWN DURING THE WAR WITH JAPAN.) The opera opens with the appearance of its main character, Li Yuhe, a railway switchman and underground Communist Party activist, entering with a red signal lantern on his way to meet a comrade arriving by train with a secret code. Another comrade distracts the Japanese gendarmes and is captured, while Li Yuhe helps the liaison man to the safety of Li Yuhe's home. The secret code is entrusted to Li Yuhe together with instructions to deliver it via a local knife-grinder to nearby guerrillas, and the liaison man departs. Li Yuhe meets the knife-grinder, but before he can deliver the code, the Japanese gendarmes arrive; only with courage and resourcefulness do both men escape with the code intact but still in Li Yuhe's possession. Meanwhile the captured comrade of the opening scene, Wang Lianju, breaks under torture and reveals that Li Yuhe is a Party member.

The center of action then shifts to Li Yuhe's home. He tells his "mother" that the code is safely hidden and departs, leaving her alone with his teenage "daughter," Tiemei. As the older woman polishes the red lantern and decides to tell the younger their family secrets and current situation, they are interrupted by the cries of a hungry child next door. They give some cornmeal to the child's mother, despite their own short supplies, and assert that they and their neighbors are like a single family. The neighbor has just left when an enemy agent arrives to try to get the code, but the older woman detects his falsity and Tiemei throws him out. Li Yuhe returns and, expecting to be arrested, tells his "mother" where the code is hidden and how to send it to the guerrillas. He has just finished when he is summoned to a feast with the Japanese commandant. He drinks a farewell bowl of wine offered by the two women and takes his leave heroically. Agents then search the house for the code and leave without success. When the two women are alone again, the older woman tells Tiemei the family history. Her husband had been a master worker on the railway who was killed in a railway strike in 1923 together with one of his apprentices, Tiemei's father. His other apprentice, Li Yuhe, was wounded but survived to reach his master's home with the red lantern in one hand and the infant Tiemei in his other arm. He adopted the older woman as his mother and the younger as his daughter and continued to work tirelessly for the proletarian cause and later against the Japanese occupation. His mother urges Tiemei to follow in his footsteps, and she vows to do so. The scene ends with the two women posing together dramatically in the light of the red lantern they are holding aloft.

The Japanese commandant, Hatoyama, tries to win Li Yuhe over with recollections of former care when he was a physician. Li Yuhe rejects these and other overtures. He refuses to provide the secret code even when confronted with Wang Lianju. Li Yuhe is threatened with torture, scoffs at it, and strides off to the torture chamber in a manner that shakes his foes. He does not give in under torture and reappears on stage to intimidate his enemies again with his courage.

The Japanese put Li Yuhe's house under surveillance, but Tiemei goes out by way of the neighbor's house to search for the knife-grinder. She fails to find him and returns. Hatoyama arrives and arrests both women when they refuse to provide the secret code. Each women has the opportunity to see Li Yuhe in the hidden presence of a microphone, and they take courageous farewells of each other. Li Yuhe tells Tiemei that he is bequeathing the red lantern to her, and she accepts the gift and vows to care for it. Hatoyama sends all three to the execution ground, and they exit arm-in-arm to the strains of the "Internationale." They call out revolutionary slogans as shots are fired. Then Tiemei is dragged on stage alive—the others have been killed but she has been kept as a possible key to the location of the secret code. She returns home and is helped to escape by her neighbors, at considerable risk to themselves.

Tiemei retrieves the code and delivers it to the knife-grinder together with a plea to help her endangered neighbors. Some guerrillas depart for that purpose while others engage Hatoyama, Wang Lianju, and the Japanese soldiers who are in pursuit. The guerrillas are victorious and kill all the enemies.

In a brief final scene, the knife-grinder takes Tiemei to the guerrilla leader, to whom she delivers the secret code. The curtain falls on Tiemei holding the red lantern aloft before the assembled guerrilla forces.

NOTES

The following abbreviations are used:

CQ	*China Quarterly*
FBIS	*Foreign Broadcast Information Service*
GMRB	*Guangming ribao* (Guangming daily)
HZRB	*Hangzhou ribao* (Hangzhou daily)
RMRB	*Renmin ribao* (People's daily)
SSRC-ACLS	Social Science Research Council—American Council of Learned Societies
SWB	*Summary of World Broadcasts*
ZGTJNJ	*Zhongguo tongji nianjian* (Statistical yearbook of China)

Introduction: New Perspectives on the Cultural Revolution by William A. Joseph, Christine P. W. Wong, and David Zweig

1. See, for example, the annual editions of ZGTJNJ (Beijing, State Statistical Bureau) or *Zhongguo jingji nianjian* (Chinese economic yearbook; Beijing; Economic Management Publishing House), beginning in 1980. See also sectoral yearbooks such as *Zhongguo nongye nianjian* (Chinese agricultural Yearbook), *Zhongguo qing gongye nianjian* (Chinese light industry yearbook), and *Zhongguo yejin gongye nianjian* (Chinese metallurgical industry yearbook).

2. See, for example, *Zhongguo renmin gongheguo jingji dashiji* (Major economic events in the People's Republic of China; Beijing; Social Sciences Publishing House, 1984) and *Zhongguo nongye dashiji, 1949–1980* (Major economic events in Chinese agriculture, 1949–1980; Beijing, Agricultural Publishing House, 1982) or Wang Haibo, *Xin zhongguo gongye jingji shi* (History of the industrial economy of new China; Beijing, Jingji Guanli, 1986).

3. For example, *Nie Rongzhen huiyi lu* (The recollections of Nie Rongzhen; Beijing; Jiefangjun chubanshe, 1984); Suo Guoxin, "78 Days in 1967: The True Story of the 'February Countercurrent,' " *Chinese Law and Government* (Spring 1989); Tie Zhuwei, *Chen Yi yuanshuai zai 'wenhua da geming' zhong: Shuang zhong se yu nong* (Marshal Chen Yi during the Cultural Revolution: When frost is thick, the colors become richer; Chengdu; Jiefang jun chubanshe, 1986); or Zhang Yunsheng, *Mao jiawan jishi: Lin Biao mishu huiyi lu* (Factual record from Mao Jiawan: The memoirs of Lin Biao's secretary; Beijing; Chunqiu chubanshe, 1988). For a discussion of several studies, see Michael Schoenhals, "Unofficial and Official Histories of the Cultural Revolution—A Review Article," *Journal of Asian Studies* 48:563–572 (August 1989).

4. The Maoism of the Third Front and the CR revolved around exaggerated notions of the threat posed to China by both internal and external enemies; but the geopolitical realities of the early 1960s, such as U.S. military escalation in Indochina and the exacerbation of Sino-Soviet tensions, lent credence to Beijing's siege mentality and its responses like the Third Front.

5. Other important second-rank national leaders who have been little studied include Zhuang Zedong, the table-tennis star who became minister of sports; Qiao Guanhua, the diplomat who was often said to be "foreign minister" of the Gang of Four's "shadow cabinet"; Mao Yuanxin, Mao's nephew who ruled Liaoning Province and exerted great influence at the center as Mao's health failed; and Zhang Tiesheng, the rebel worker-student who as a national model became a member of the National People's Congress Standing Committee.

6. The best studies of this kind already completed include Lowell Dittmer's study of the power base of the Gang of Four and Anne Fenwick's study of the Gang of Four as a political opposition. See Lowell Dittmer, "Bases of Power in Chinese Politics: A Theory and an Analysis of the Fall of the 'Gang of Four,' " *World Politics* 31:26–60 (October 1978), and Anne E. Fenwick, "The Gang of Four and the Politics of Opposition: China, 1971–1976," PhD dissertation, Stanford University, 1984. For a preliminary effort toward explaining why Mao could resist the efforts of men of significant political and personal strength to restrain the CR in the spring of 1967, see Thomas P. Bernstein, "Chinese Communism in the Era of Mao Zedong, 1949–1976," paper prepared for the Four Anniversaries China Conference, Annapolis, 10–15 September 1989.

7. The proliferation of semiofficial research institutes in the past few years in China affords Western scholars opportunities to see new data and discuss with Chinese colleagues their perspectives on the Red Guards. One effort by a Chinese scholar studying in the United States to apply Western concepts to the study of the Red Guards is Wang Shaoguang, "Understanding the Role of the Masses in the Cultural Revolution," paper presented at the Conference on New Perspectives on the Cultural Revolution, Harvard University, 15–17 May 1987. For a sum-

mary of recent work on the Red Guards and suggestions for future research, see Anita Chan, "Looking Back at the Chinese Cultural Revolution," *Problems of Communism,* March–April 1988, pp. 68–75. Some of the best work on the CR concerns the Red Guards; see, for example, Hong Yong Lee, *The Politics of the Chinese Cultural Revolution* (Berkeley, University of California Press, 1978); Stanley Rosen, *Red Guard Factionalism and the Cultural Revolution in Guangzhou* (Boulder, Westview Press, 1982); Jonathan Unger, *Education under Mao: Class and Competition in Canton Schools, 1960–1980* (Seattle, University of Washington Press, 1982); and Anita Chan, *Children of Mao: Personality Development and Political Activism in the Red Guard Generation* (Seattle, University of Washington Press, 1985).

8. A preliminary effort to address these issues is Edward Friedman, "Total War on Revisionism: Mao's Cultural Revolution Foreign Policy," paper presented at the Conference on New Perspectives on the Cultural Revolution, Harvard University, 15–17 May 1987.

9. For recent works by scholars not in this volume that shed light on certain aspects of the CR, see John King Fairbank and Roderick L. MacFarquhar, eds, *Revolutions within the Chinese Revolution,* Vol. XV of *The Cambridge History of China,* (Cambridge, Cambridge University Press, forthcoming); Julia Kwong, *Cultural Revolution in China's School, May 1966–April 1969* (Stanford, Hoover Institution 1988); and Thomas P. Lyons, *Economic Integration and Planning in Maoist China* (New York, Columbia University Press, 1987). See also the reasessments of the CR by Lucian Pye, Stuart Schram, Robert Michael Field, and Bill Brugger in *CQ* 108 (December 1986). Significant scholarly work on the CR is also being done in the PRC. See Schoenhals, "Histories of the Cultural Revolution."

10. "On Questions of Party History—Resolution on Certain Questions in the History of Our Party since the Founding of the People's Republic of China," *Beijing Review,* 6 July 1981, pp. 20–26.

11. Decision of the Central Committee of the Chinese Communist Party Concerning the Great Proletarian Cultural Revolution," 8 August 1966, in *Important Documents on the Great Proletarian Cultural Revolution in China* (Beijing, Foreign Language Press, 1970), p. 153.

12. See Dwight Perkins, "China's Economic Policy and Performance during the Cultural Revolution and Its Aftermath," in Fairbank and MacFarquhar, *Revolutions within the Chinese Revolution.*

13. *RMRB,* 10 November 1966.

14. David Zweig, *Agrarian Radicalism in China, 1963–1981* (Cambridge, Harvard University Press, 1989).

15. See Gao Yuan, *Born Red* (Stanford, Stanford University Press, 1988). Interviews by David Zweig and Marc Blecher corroborate the important role ascribed to the military in *Born Red* for Jiangsu and Guangdong provinces, respectively.

16. Nicholas P. Lardy, *Agriculture in China's Modern Economic Development* (New York, Cambridge University Press, 1983).

17. Niu Ruofang, "Does 'taking grain as the key link' suit measures to local conditions?" *GMRB,* 8 December 1979. This assessment contrasts with one by Dwight Perkins, who argues that the CR did not disrupt the rural economy to any major extent. However, Perkins relies primarily on the growth in grain

output and a few key crops. By excluding the decline in many subsidiary food products and nonfarm income-generating activities, Perkins underestimates the corrosive impact of radical policies on rural incomes and diet. See Perkins, "China's Economic Policy and Performance."

18. *ZGTJNJ 1986*, p. 274.

19. Li Chengrui, "An Analysis of China's Economic Situation in the Ten-Year Period of Internal Disaster—and a Look at the Reliability of Statistics from This Period," *Jingji yanjiu* (Economic research) 1:23–31 (January 1984), in *FBIS*, 7 March 1984, pp. K2–K15.

20. Field estimates that economywide, the capital/output ratio rose 18.5 percent between 1966 and 1975, in the absence of significant structural change, indicating declining efficiency in the use of capital. See Michael Field, "The Performance of Industry during the Cultural Revolution: Second Thoughts, *CQ* 108:633–635 (December 1986).

21. Ma Hong and Sun Shanqiang, eds., *Zhongguo jingji jiegou wenti yanjiu* (Research on the problems of China's economic structure; Beijing, People's Publishing House, 1981), p. 3.

22. Among the recent additions to memoirs by participants in and victims of the CR are Fulang Lo, *Morning Breeze: A True Story of China's Cultural Revolution* (San Francisco, China Books and Periodicals, 1989); Gao Yuan, *Born Red;* Nien Cheng, *Life and Death in Shanghai* (New York, Grove Press, 1986); and Yue Daiyun and Carolyn Wakeman, *To the Storm: The Odyssey of a Revolutionary Chinese Woman* (Berkeley, University of California Press, 1985). For a scholarly analysis of the psychological impact of the CR on individual Chinese, see Anne F. Thurston, *Enemies of the People: The Ordeal of the Intellectuals in China's Great Cultural Revolution* (New York, Knopf, 1987).

23. "Circular of the Central Committee of the Chinese Communist Party," 16 May 1966, in *Important Documents*, pp. 118–119.

24. Fenwick, "Gang of Four."

25. Zweig, *Agrarian Radicalism in China*, pp. 91–97.

26. See "Dialogue with Responsible Persons of Capital Red Guards Congress," 28 July 1966, in *Miscellany of Mao Tsetung Thought, Joint Publications Research Service* 61269-2, 20 February 1974, pp. 469–497.

27. For earlier prespectives on this point, see Parris H. Chang, "Provincial Party Leader's Strategies for Survival during the Cultural Revolution," and Richard Baum, "Elite Behavior under Conditions of Stress: The Lessons of the 'Tangch'uan Pai' in the Cultural Revolution," in Robert A. Scalapino, ed., *Elites in the People's Republic of China* (Seattle, University of Washington Press, 1972), pp. 501–539 and 540–574, respectively.

28. See E. L. Wheelright and Bruce MacFarlane, *The Chinese Road to Socialism* (New York, Monthly Review Press, 1970).

29. William A. Joseph, *The Critique of Ultra-Leftism in China, 1958–1981* (Stanford, Stanford University Press, 1984).

30. For an insightful and complex study of agricultural policy during the CR decade, see Edwin A. Winckler, "Dimensions of Agricultural Policy: Hebei, Jiangsu and Guangdong in the 1970s," paper prepared for the Conference on Bureau-

cracy and Rural Development, Joint Committee on Contemporary China, SSRC, 26–30 August 1981.

31. For a discussion of recent Chinese evaluations of the Great Leap Forward and comparisons between the GLF and the CR, see William A. Joseph, "A Tragedy of Good Intentions: Post-Mao Views of the Great Leap Forward," *Modern China* 12:419–457 (October 1986).

32. "Introduction: The Political Economy of Reform in Post-Mao China: Causes, Content, and Consequences," in Elizabeth J. Perry and Christine Wong, eds., *The Political Economy of Reform in Post-Mao China,* Harvard Contemporary China Series, no. 2. (Cambridge, Council on East Asian Studies, Harvard University, 1985), p. 2.

33. See Christine Wong, "Between Plan and Market: The Role of the Local Sector in Post-Mao China," *Journal of Comparative Economics* 11:385–398 (1987).

34. Roderick MacFarquhar, "The End of the Chinese Revolution," *The New York Review of Books,* 20 July 1989, pp. 8–10.

35. See *Jiushi niandai* (The nineties; Hong Kong), October 1989.

36. "Speech at the Meeting in Celebration of the Fortieth Anniversary of the Founding of the People's Republic of China," *Beijing Review,* 9–15 October 1989, p. 18.

Chapter 1. Learning from Trauma: The Cultural Revolution in Post-Mao Politics by Lowell Dittmer

I wish to thank Julia Strauss for research assistance and the Wilson Center of the Smithsonian Institution, as well as the Center for Chinese Studies at the University of California at Berkeley, for facilities and research support. I am grateful to the anonymous reviewer and to William Joseph, Christine Wong, and David Zweig for their perceptive criticisms of an earlier draft.

1. "Many people in West Germany in the 1960s once asked their parents: 'What were you doing during the Nazi years?' We, who experienced the 'Cultural Revolution,' may well ask ourselves, 'What were we doing then?' " " 'Chinese' Has Lessons for All," *China Daily* (Beijing), 29 August 1986, in *FBIS,* 29 August 1986, p. K5.

2. For a more detailed periodization of the Hua Guofeng period, see William A. Joseph's perceptive analysis *The Critique of Ultra-Leftism in China, 1958–1981* (Stanford, Stanford University Press, 1984), pp. 151–182. See also Joseph's methodologically similar approach to the Great Leap Forward (with comparison to the CR) in "A Tragedy of Good Intentions: Post-Mao Views of the Great Leap Forward," *Modern China* 12:419–458 (October 1986).

3. "Long Live the People; On the Revolutionary Mass Movement in Tiananmen Square," *RMRB,* 21 December 1978, in *FBIS,* 22 December 1978, pp. E1–E13.

4. To wit: (1) Discontinuation of the CR was made explicit in the statement that "large-scale, turbulent class struggles of mass character have, in the main, come to an end." The attempt through abstraction to avoid directly impugning the CR gave rise to the impression that mass movements were being disavowed,

which has proved incorrect. (2) The depiction of the CR in terms of anarchic factionalism was officially adopted, implying that the appropriate remedy was institutionalization, the "rule of law," and so forth. (3) The ideological dogmatism associated with the CR was repudiated in favor of pragmatism ("seeking truth through facts, proceeding from reality, and linking theory with practice"). (4) A shift was made from continuing revolution to economic modernization as the highest political priority. (5) The fallibility of Mao was for the first time conceded, albeit by implication: "It would not be Marxist to demand that a revolutionary leader be free of all shortcomings and errors." Collective leadership was also endorsed, in implicit contrast to Mao's leadership style: "No personal view by a Party member in a position of responsibility . . . is to be called an 'instruction.' " "The Whole Party Shifts to Socialist Modernization," communiqué of the Third Plenum of the Eleventh Central Committee, 18–22 December 1978.

5. Ibid., p. E11.

6. "Formation of the CCP Central Committee's Commission for Inspecting Discipline: First Plenary Session," 4–22 January 1979, in *FBIS*, 25 January 1979, pp. E4–E7; see also "Notice Released by the First Plenary Session of the CCP Discipline Inspection Commission," issued 26 January 1979; released and published 26 March 1979, in *FBIS*, 26 March 1979, pp. L1–L10; and "The Whole Party Strives to Rectify Party Style and Insure the Strict Observation of Discipline," *RMRB*, 25 January 1979, in *FBIS*, 25 January 1979, p. E9.

7. Xi Chen, "A Great Struggle to Defend Party Principles—Revealing the True Nature of a Major Political Incident: The 'February Adverse Current' Concocted by Lin Biao and the 'Gang of Four,' " *RMRB*, 26 February 1979, in *FBIS*, 28 February 1979, p. E19.

8. See, for example, an article published just before the Third Plenum, "On reversing the verdict of Tiananmen: The 'Gang' is seen as 'counterrevolutionaries who could never hide their rightist features by disguising themselves as 'Leftists,' " *Hongqi* (Red flag) 12:77 (December 1978).

9. Jin Wen, "Thoroughly Criticize the 'Left' Deviationist Line Viciously Pursued by Lin Biao and the Gang of Four," *GMRB* 23 January 1979, in *FBIS*, 2 February 1979, p. E11.

10. Zhang Decheng, "Stop Saying 'Grasp Revolution, Promote Production,' " *RMRB*, 9 March 1979, in *FBIS*, 19 March 1979, pp. L5–L7.

11. Lu Dingyi, "Cherish the memory of comrade Zhou Enlai—Good Premier of the People," *RMRB*, 8 March 1979, p. 2.

12. "We should also see that it is generally understood abroad that our Party is not 'deMaoifying.' In fact, our Party is restoring Mao Zedong Thought to its original form by refuting the distortions of Lin Biao and the 'Gang of Four.' " Dong Ta, "The Experience and Lessons of Dealing with 'Foreign Comment,' " *RMRB*, 9 March 1979, in *FBIS*, 22 March 1979, p. L3.

13. For example, "We are opposed to exaggeration of class struggle and to the fallacy spread by Lin Biao and the 'Gang of Four' that class struggle is becoming more and more acute, but we do not mean that class struggle no longer exists. Not only must we realize that a handful of counterrevolutionaries and criminals

who hate and undermine the socialist system still exist in the present society, but we must also realize the existence of class struggle in the realm of ideology and the struggle between two kinds of ideology to win over the young people. We must also realize that, in the wake of expansion of contacts with other countries, the influence of bourgeois ideology and way of life will also increase." "Modernization Demands Powerful Ideological and Political Work," *RMRB*, 16 April 1979.

14. See David Zweig, "Context and Content in Policy Implementation: Household Contracts and Decollectivization, 1977–1983," in David M. Lampton, ed., *Policy Implementation in Post-Mao China* (Berkeley, University of California Press, 1987), pp. 255–284.

15. *Xinhua* (n English), 12 May 1979, from that day's *RMRB*, in *FBIS*, 14 May 1979, p. L4.

16. Guo Luoji, "We Must Emancipate Our Minds and Be Thorough in Doing Political Work," *Hongqi* 3 (March 1979), in *FBIS*, 13 April 1979, pp. L4–L8.

17. "Strengthen the Legal System, Develop Democracy, Accelerate the Four Modernizations," *RMRB*, 5 July 1979, in *FBIS*, 10 July 1979, p. L6. See also Song Zhenting, "Wang Ming and the 'Gang of Four,'" *GMRB*, 1 September 1979, in *FBIS*, 6 September 1979, p. L4.

18. "Distinguish Between the Two Ideological Lines: Uphold the Four Basic Principles," *GMRB, RMRB,* and *Jiefang junbao* (Liberation Army news), 11 May 1979.

19. Ibid.

20. "Further Promote an Atmosphere for Theoretical Research," *RMRB*, 24 May 1979, in *FBIS*, 14 May 1979, p. L4.

21. Hua Guofeng, "Report to the Fifth NPC on the Work of the Government," in *FBIS*, CHI–79–128, supplement 015.

22. "Strengthen the Legal System, Develop Democracy, Accelerate the Four Modernizations," *RMRB*, 5 July 1979, in *FBIS*, 10 July 1979, p. L6.

23. Li Chun and Liu Qingsen, "Counterrevolutionary Crimes Must Be Out and Out and Unmistakable Ones," *RMRB*, 24 July 1979, in *FBIS*, 31 July 1979, p. L8.

24. "Ye Jianying Speech at Rally in Celebration of the Thirtieth Anniversary of the Founding of the PRC," *Xinhua* (Beijing), 28 September 1979, in *FBIS*, 1 October 1979, p. L16.

25. Ibid., pp. L16–L21.

26. See Gu Zhaoji, "On Anarchism," *Jiefang junbao*, 23 November 1979, in *FBIS*, 26 November 1979, p. L7; Li Ping, "Counterrevolutionary Elements Must Not Be Allowed to Sabotage Stability and Unity," *Beijing ribao* (Beijing daily), 18 November 1979, in *FBIS*, 3 December 1979, p. L4; Yong Qian, "Anarchism Is Bourgeois Liberalism in Another Form," *Gongren ribao* (Workers' daily), 22 November 1979, in *FBIS*, 11 December 1979, p. L1; Li Xiaolin and Zhao Guoliang, "Communists Should Set an Example in Observing Discipline," *RMRB*, 26 December 1979, in *FBIS*, 28 December 1979, p. L4; and "Oppose Extreme Individualism," *Beijing ribao*, 5 January 1980, in *FBIS*, 14 January 1980, pp. L12–L13.

27. Lu Zhizhao, "Stability, Unity, and Socialist Democracy," *RMRB*, 28 January 1980, in *FBIS*, 5 February 1980, p. L15; see also Guo Luoji, "Commenting on

the So-called 'Confidence Crisis,' " *Wen hui bao* (Cultural report), 13 January 1980, in *FBIS*, 30 January 1980, pp. L9–L11.

28. "Develop Political Stability and Unity," *RMRB*, 21 February 1980, in *FBIS*, 22 February 1980, p. L7; see also "Stability and Unity Are the Basic Prerequisites for the Realization of the Four Modernizations," *GMRB*, 25 January 1980, in *FBIS*, 8 February 1980, p. L16.

29. "Communiqué of the Fifth Plenary Session of the Eleventh Central Committee," 29 February 1980, in *FBIS*, 29 February 1980, p. L4; *Xinhua*, 14 April 1980, in *FBIS*, 16 April 1980, p. L1.

30. *Xinhua* (Beijing), 12 March 1980, in *FBIS*, 22 March 1980, p. L1.

31. "The Distinction Between Marxism and Revisionism Should Not Be Blurred," *RMRB*, 3 April 1980, in *FBIS*, 4 April 1980, pp. L1–L5; see also Huang Nanshen et al., "The Relations of Revisionism, Dogmatism, and Empiricism to the Political Line," *Hongqi* 6 (March 1980), in *FBIS*, 15 April 1980, pp. L13–L14.

32. See "Restore the True Qualities of Mao Zedong Thought," *RMRB*, 16 May 1980, in *FBIS*, 15 May 1980, pp. L3–L6; also "Correctly Understand the Role of the Individual in History," *RMRB*, 4 July 1980, in *FBIS*, 7 July 1980, pp. L4–L7.

33. Elizabeth Chang reporting on Salisbury's interview, 28 July 1980, in *FBIS*, 28 July 1980, p. L1.

34. Reprinted in *Gongren ribao*, 29 October 1980, in *FBIS*, 18 November 1980, pp. L6–L8.

35. Liu's widow, of all people, wrote in a memorial article to an old friend: "We are oversimplifying the problem if we attribute the cause to the mistakes made by someone or the evils done by Lin Biao and the 'Gang of Four.' Our Party made mistakes in the past . . . what were the conditions which gave Lin Biao and the 'Gang of Four' and Kang Sheng the chance to do evil? What was the root cause?" Wang Guangmei, "He Showed His Integrity in a Difficult Time, the Spirit of Justice Will Be Preserved Eternally in Memory of Comrade An Ziwen," *Gongren ribao*, 14 July 1980, in *FBIS*, 5 August 1980, p. L13.

36. Liu Maoying, "A New Interpretation of the Story of the 'Foolish Old Man Who Moved the Mountains,' " *Wenhui bao*, 13 August 1980, in *FBIS*, 28 August 1980, p. L2; Li Honglin, "The Leader and the People," *RMRB*, 18 September 1980, in *FBIS*, 22 September 1980, pp. L1–L9; see also Wang Zikai, "Commenting on Kang Sheng's Theory of 'The Supreme and Ultimate Criterion,' " *Beijing ribao*, 8 August 1980, in *FBIS*, 22 August 1980, pp. L9–L14; Ruan Ming, "An Important Task on the Ideological Front," *RMRB*, 28 August 1980, excerpted from *Lilu yu shiyan* (Theory and practice; Liaoning), no. 9; "Power Must Not Be Overconcentrated in the Hands of Individuals," *Hongqi* 17 (September 1980), in *FBIS*, 17 September 1980, pp. L24–L26.

37. "Solemn Decision," *RMRB*, 30 September 1980, in *FBIS*, 30 September 1980, p. L1.

38. Text of the Indictment Against the Gang of Four, *Xinhua* (Beijing), in *FBIS*, 20 November 1980.

39. See "Monument to Socialist Democracy—Commenting on the Trial of the Lin

Biao—Jiang Qing Counterrevolutionary Cliques," *RMRB,* 22 December 1980, in *FBIS,* 24 December 1980, p. L5; "Questions and Answers on the Trial of the Lin-Jiang Counterrevolutionary Cliques," *Banyuetan* (Fortnightly talk) 16 (December 1980), in *FBIS,* 22 December 1980, pp. L11–L12.

40. Deng Xiaoping, "On the Reform of the System of Party and State Leadership," 18 August 1980), in *Selected Works of Deng Xiaoping, 1975–1982* (Beijing, Foreign Languages Press, 1984), pp. 302–326.
41. See Lowell Dittmer, "China in 1981: Reform, Readjustment, Rectification," *Asian Survey* 22:33–47 (January 1982).
42. "Literature and Art Must Contribute to Building the Spiritual Civilization," *RMRB,* 4 February 1981, in *FBIS,* 19 February 1981, p. L5; also see *GMRB,* 18 February 1981.
43. "Calling on All PLA Units and the Broad Masses of PLA Commanders and Fighters to Further Conduct Extensive Activities in Learning from Lei Feng and Other Heroes and Models," *Xinhua,* 23 February 1981, in *FBIS,* 24 February 1981, p. L5; "Unite and Work Together to Build a Socialist Spiritual Civilization," *GMRB,* 22 February 1981, in *FBIS,* 3 March, p. L15; "The Value of Socialist Spiritual Civilization," *GMRB,* 22 February 1981, in *FBIS* (10 March 1981), p. L21; "Correctly Understand the Situation and Uphold the Four Basic Principles," *Hongqi* 5 (March 1981), in *FBIS,* 25 March 1981, pp. L7–L17.
44. *Resolution on Party History* (Beijing, Foreign Languages Press, 1981).
45. Text of Hu Yaobang's Report to the Twelfth CCP Congress, *Xinhua,* 7 September 1982, in *FBIS,* 8 September 1982, pp. K2–K3.
46. Deng Liqun, in answering questions raised at a meeting with Associated Press reporters, discussed the meaning of spiritual pollution: "There are worries among friends abroad that the Party consolidation might be superficial or that it might take the form of the 'Cultural Revolution,' " he said. But most of those leading the campaign had themselves been subjected to such methods during the CR and had suffered enough: "We will not do unto others what they did unto us." *Xinhua,* 1 November 1983, in *FBIS,* 2 November 1983, p. K2.
47. For example, one writer argues: "It is one-sided and wrong just to link the movement for emancipation of the mind with opposition to 'leftism' and to hold that opposition to rightism is binding the mind. . . . Are not people's minds also bound up by bourgeois liberalization, extreme individualism, trends of commercializing spiritual products, and so forth?" "Eliminating Spiritual Pollution Is Also a Kind of Emancipation of the Mind," *RMRB,* 14 November 1983, in *FBIS,* 14 November 1983.
48. Hu Qiaomu, "On Humanism and Alienation," speech delivered at the Party Central School, 3 January 1984, *RMRB,* 27 January 1984, in *FBIS,* 7 February 1984, pp. K27–K29.
49. Decision on Party Rectification, 11 October 1983, cited in *FBIS,* 13 October 1983, pp. K7–K8.
50. For example, "Although what we have today is only the lingering effect of factionalism, it is corroding our body organism." "Enhance Party Spirit, Eliminate Factionalism," *JFJB,* 8 May 1984, in *FBIS,* 9 May 1984, p. K14; see also "An Important Task in Unifying Thinking in the Course of Party Rectification,"

Yunnan ribao, (Yunnan daily), 9 May 1984, in *FBIS,* 11 May 1984, p. Q2; and Wang Fang, "Do Away with the 'Theory of One Faction Being Correct,' Completely Wipe Out Factionalism," *RMRB,* 23 October 1984, in *FBIS,* 29 October 1984, p. K23–K24.

51. "We Must Precisely Totally Negate the Cultural Revolution," *RMRB,* 23 April 1984, in *FBIS,* 23 April 1984, p. K1.

52. "Questions and Answers about Thoroughly Negating the 'Cultural Revolution,' Eliminating Factionalism, and Strengthening Party Spirit," *Jiefang junbao,* as reprinted in *GMRB,* 28 July 1984, pp. 1–2, in *FBIS,* 3 August 1984, p. K1. According to another report, "Some people say: Was there really nothing good in the Cultural Revolution?" "It Is Good to Raise the Proposition of Thoroughly Negating the 'Cultural Revolution,' *Nanfang ribao* (Southern daily), 10 May 1984, in *FBIS,* 15 May 1984, p. P1.

53. Beyond those articles already cited, see Tian Ming, "The Guangzhou PLA Units Totally Negate the 'Cultural Revolution,' " *Dagong bao* (Workers' daily; Hong Kong), 10 May 1984; "We Must Thoroughly Eliminate the Influence of Leftist Mistakes," *Guangxi ribao,* (Guangxi daily), 29 May 1984, in *FBIS,* 31 May 1984, pp. P2–P3; "Circular No. 9," *Xinhua* (Domestic Service), 30 June 1984, in *FBIS,* 2 July 1984; "It Is Essential to Conduct Profound Education in Totally Negating the 'Great Cultural Revolution' for the Broad Party Members and Cadres," *Hongqi* 14 (July 1984), in *Joint Publication Research Service,* 19 September 1984; "Completely Negate 'Extensive Democracy,' " *RMRB,* 15 August 1984, in *FBIS,* 16 August 1984; Wang Qianghua et al., "Why We Must Thoroughly Negate 'Extensive Democracy,' " *GMRB,* 13 September 1984, in *FBIS,* 20 September 1984; Zhai Sishi, "Dividing One into Two and Thoroughly Negating the 'Great Cultural Revolution,' " *Hongqi* 17 (September 1984), in *FBIS,* 28 September 1984; "First Phase Party Rectification Units in PLA Uphold Principle of Self-Education, Score Fine Results in Totally Negating the 'Cultural Revolution' from Theory to Practice," *RMRB,* 5 December 1984, in *FBIS,* 10 December 1984, pp. K1–K3; Ke Ling, "Concentrate Efforts on Rooting Out the Stubborn 'Leftist' Disease," *RMRB,* 31 December 1984, in *FBIS,* 9 January 1985, pp. K8–K9; and others. To my knowledge, the only previous notice taken in Western China scholarship of this major campaign is Keith Forster, "Repudiation of the Cultural Revolution in China: The Case of Zhejiang" *Pacific Affairs* 59:5–27 (January 1986).

54. *Xinhua ribao* (New China daily; Nanjing), 14 August 1984, in *FBIS,* 31 August 1984, p. O5–O6.

55. " 'Cultural Revolution' Must Be Thoroughly Eradicated," *Zhejiang ribao* (Zhejiang daily), 11 July 1984, in *FBIS,* 25 July 1984, p. O4.

56. Xiu Yun, " 'We.' So What?!" *RMRB,* 2 June 1986, in *FBIS,* 5 June 1986, p. K10; see also Yu Haoching, "The Double Hundred Policy and Its Guarantee by the Legal System," *RMRB,* 30 May 1986, in *FBIS,* 20 June 1986, p. K9; and Du Feijin, "Talking about the 'Double Hundred' Policy and its Guarantee by the Legal System," *RMRB,* 15 June 1986, in *FBIS,* 25 June 1986, p. K16.

57. Hu Sheng, "Several Questions Concerning the Strengthening of the Study of Social Sciences" (edited from parts of two speeches delivered by the author at

the Chinese Academy of Social Sciences in August and December 1985), *Hongqi* 9 (May 1986), in *FBIS,* 28 May 1986, pp. K11–K17.

58. Gong Yuzhi, "Study Theory and Combine the Study of Current Conditions with the Study of History—Starting with a Discussion of the Second Volume of 'The Selected Works of Liu Shaoqi,' " *RMRB,* 23 December 1985, in *FBIS,* 2 January 1986, p. K17.

59. Gao Wenqian, "Arduous but Brilliant Last Years—On Zhou Enlai in the 'Great Cultural Revolution' Period," *Wenxian he ganjiu* (Documents and studies) 1 (1986), as reprinted in *RMRB,* 5 January 1986, in *FBIS,* 24 January 1986, pp. K12–K18.

60. "An Unavoidable Reflection," *Wenzhai bao* (Digest daily), 15 May 1986, in *FBIS,* 27 May 1986, p. K13.

61. Liu Zaifu, "Breaking Through and Deepening Literature in the New Period" (excerpts of the speech given by the writer at the symposium on China's Literature in the New Period), *RMRB,* 8 September 1986, in *FBIS,* 18 September 1986, p. K19; Wang Shibai (professor at Xiamen University), "Inheriting Chinese Traditions and Culturally Opening Up to the Outside World," *RMRB,* 27 June 1986, in *FBIS,* 30 July 1986, p. K12.

62. See *Zhongguo xinwenshe* (China news), 19 August 1986, as cited in *FBIS,* 21 August 1986, p. K18.

63. "Reunderstanding the 'Great Cultural Revolution,' " *RMRB,* 13 October 1986, in *FBIS,* 15 October 1986, pp. K18–K19.

64. On the one hand, in favor of staging the *yangbanxi:* "Now these writers do not mind young people singing pop songs and dancing at discos, but they kick up a fuss when we sing the songs of the model dramas. They turn a blind eye to the return of capitalist culture, but they cannot tolerate our great and perfect revolutionary heroes." Shu Zhan, "There Is Still a Need for Singing 'Thank You, Mom' during the Spring Festival," *Yangcheng wanbao* (Yangcheng evening news; Guizhou), 2 December 1986, in *FBIS,* 12 December 1986, p. K8. On the other hand: "Ten years have passed since the 'Gang of Four' completely collapsed and everything is going ahead by leaps and bounds in our time, but we are still discussing the question of model dramas. It seems that what we suffered in the ten-year catastrophe is nothing. . . . I think the best thing we can do is to conclude a 'gentlemen's agreement.' You are free to sing model dramas and I am free not to listen to them." Zhang Ming, "Impressions on the Twentieth Birthday of the 'Wolf Child,' " *Yangcheng wanbao,* 6 December 1986, as cited in *FBIS,* 12 December 1986, K11. It seems the *yangbanxi* were revived, at least on a limited scale.

65. Wang Ruoshui, "The Double Hundred Policy and Civil Rights," *Huasheng bao,* 8 August 1986, as reprinted in *Zhengming* (Hong Kong) 107 (September 1986).

66. This refers to the tendency to turn blame inward rather than seeking scapegoats. See B. Christiansen, *Attitudes Towards Foreign Affairs as a Function of Personality* (Oslo, Oslo University Press, 1959).

67. Typical examples include "Defend the Current Good Situation," *Zhongguo qingnian bao* (China youth), 23 December 1986, in *FBIS,* 24 December 1986, p. K2; "The 'Four Bigs' Are Not Democracy in Any Sense of the Word," *Gongren*

ribao, 27 December 1986, in *FBIS,* 31 December 1986, p. K14; Zhang Ming-shui, "Improve the Political Quality of the Citizens," *GMRB,* 21 December 1986, in *FBIS,* 6 January 1987, p. K12.

Chapter 2. Cultural Revolution Radicalism: Variations on a Stalinist Theme by Andrew G. Walder

Critiques by Jean Oi, Lucian Pye, Jonathan Unger, and David Zweig significantly aided the preparation of this chapter.

1. Two important contributions in this genre are Maurice Meisner, *Marxism, Maoism, and Utopianism: Eight Essays* (Madison, University of Wisconsin Press, 1982), and John Bryan Starr, *Continuing the Revolution: The Political Thought of Mao* (Princeton, Princeton University Press, 1979).

2. See Stuart R. Schram, "Introduction: The Cultural Revolution in Historical Perspective," in Schram, ed., *Authority, Participation and Cultural Change in China* (Cambridge, Cambridge University Press, 1973), pp. 1–108.

3. This genre is vast. Representative titles in English include Gao Yuan, *Born Red* (Stanford, Stanford University Press, 1986); Yue Daiyun and Carolyn Wakeman, *To the Storm* (Berkeley, University of California Press, 1986); Ruth Earnshaw Lo and Katherine Kinderman, *In the Eye of the Typhoon* (New York, Harcourt, Brace, Jovanovich, 1983); and Anne B. Thurston, *Enemies of the People* (New York, Knopf, 1987). A widely ignored precursor was Ken Ling and Miriam London, *The Revenge of Heaven* (New York, Putnam, 1972).

4. Independent Chinese observers have not missed this connection. For example, Wang Xizhe's 1980 essay, "Mao Zedong and the Cultural Revolution," in Anita Chan, Stanley Rosen, and Jonathan Unger, eds., *On Socialist Democracy and the Chinese Legal System* (Armonk, M. E. Sharpe, 1985), pp 177–260.

5. See the Stalinist codification of party history, *History of the Communist Party of the Soviet Union (Bolsheviks)* (Moscow, Foreign Languages Publishing House, 1938), chaps. 10–12, esp. pp. 368–369, 396, 400–407, 427–429; and Robert C. Tucker, "Stalin, Bukharin, and History as Conspiracy," in Robert C. Tucker, *The Soviet Political Mind,* rev. ed. (New York, Norton, 1971), pp. 49–86. Tucker argues (p. 56) that Stalin's distinctive contribution to Leninism was that class struggle would intensify under socialism and that it would henceforth take the form of a hidden conspiracy.

6. *History of the Communist Party,* pp. 429–430. Stalin promoted this "greater democracy" because history taught him that the Party must have "wide connections to the masses," that it must always "hearken to the voice of the masses," and that it must "not only teach the masses, but learn from the masses" (p. 446). If one did not maintain this organic link with the masses and maintain vigilance against class enemies and traitors, the revolution would be subverted and socialism overthrown.

7. Some Chinese analysts argue that Stalin's 1936 declaration that classes and class struggle no longer exist made it impossible to understand contradictions in society and led him to treat all who disagreed with him as imperialist spies and traitors. They contrast this with Mao's "correct," albeit temporary, understand-

ing of 1956 and early 1957: while remnants of old exploiting classes still exist, they are a minor contradiction. See Jin Chunming et al., *Chedi fouding 'wenhua da geming' shi jiang* (Thoroughly repudiate the 'Cultural Revolution': Ten lectures; Beijing, Jiefang jun chubanshe, 1985), pp. 23–39.

8. According to one Chinese postmortem, the 1956 uprisings in Poland and Hungary, coming on the heels of Khrushchev's repudiation of Stalin, created a sense of crisis in world socialism and "gave our party a great shock." The harsh criticisms of the Party unleashed during the Hundred Flowers of 1957 led some in the Party to conclude that harsher repression of class enemies was necessary, a mistaken mentality that would lead directly to the Cultural Revolution. Ibid., pp. 26–27.

9. The Chinese were among the most vigorous immediate defenders of Stalin from what they termed Khrushchev's "complete repudiation" of him in his 1956 speech to the Soviet Communist Party's Twentieth Congress, and from Yugoslav interpretations that identified Stalinism's excesses with the statist and bureaucratic Soviet system. See the famous *People's Daily* editorials of April and December 1956, which responded to Khrushchev and Tito, translated in *The Historical Experience of the Dictatorship of the Proletariat* (Beijing, Foreign Languages Press, 1959). The defense of Stalin became more strident in the Sino-Soviet polemics in the early 1960s: see *On the Question of Stalin* (Beijing, Foreign Languages Press, 1963).

10. This practice is not peculiar to our own specialty. Bernard Bailyn has made an identical critique of interpretations of the American Revolution: *The Origins of American Politics* (New York, Vintage, 1970), pp. 10–11.

11. For example, Jack Gray, "The Two Roads: Alternative Strategies of Social Change and Economic Growth in China," in Schram, ed., *Authority, Participation, and Cultural Change,* pp. 109–157; Lowell Dittmer, *Liu Shao-ch'i and the Chinese Cultural Revolution* (Berkeley, University of California Press, 1974), chaps. 6 and 7.

12. For example, Stephen Andors, *China's Industrial Revolution* (New York, Pantheon, 1977), chaps. 6 and 7; Richard M. Pfeffer, "Serving the People and Continuing the Revolution," *CQ* 52:620–653 (October–December 1972); and the various essays in Victor Nee and James Peck, eds., *China's Uninterrupted Revolution* (New York, Pantheon, 1976).

13. This is a clear but unstated implication of the superb work on the political sociology of the Red Guard movement: for example, Hong Yung Lee, *The Politics of the Chinese Cultural Revolution* (Berkeley, University of California Press, 1978); Stanley Rosen, *Red Guard Factionalism and the Cultural Revolution in Guangzhou* (Boulder, Westview Press, 1982); and Anita Chan, Stanley Rosen, and Jonathan Unger, "Students and Class Warfare: The Social Roots of the Red Guard Conflict in Guangzhou," *CQ* 83:397–446 (September 1980).

14. The case that fascist movements are "revolutionary," not "reactionary," is made by Eugen Weber, *Varieties of Fascism: Doctrines of Revolution in the Twentieth Century* (Malabar, Fla., Krieger, 1982); David Schoenbaum, *Hitler's Social Revolution: Class and Status in Nazi Germany, 1933–1939* (New York, Norton, 1966); and A. James Gregor, *Italian Fascism and Developmental Dictatorship* (Princeton, Princeton

University Press, 1979). The last traces the descent of fascist ideas from Marxist syndicalism in Italy before World War I.

15. See Mannheim's presentation of the "conservative idea" and the "liberal humanitarian idea" in *Ideology and Utopia* (New York, Harcourt, Brace, Jovanovich, 1936), pp. 219–239.

16. See Stephen F. Cohen, "The Friends and Foes of Change: Reformism and Conservatism in the Soviet Union," in Stephen F. Cohen, Alexander Rabinowitch, and Robert Sharlet, eds., *The Soviet Union since Stalin* (Bloomington, Indiana University Press, 1980), pp. 11–31, and Moshe Lewin, *Political Undercurrents in Soviet Economic Debates: From Bukharin to the Modern Reformers.* (Princeton, Princeton University Press, 1974).

17. The political legacies of Stalinism are analyzed by Stephen F. Cohen in the course of his outline of suppressed alternatives in *Rethinking the Soviet System* (New York, Knopf, 1985); the economic legacies, in Lewin, *Political Undercurrents,* chap. 5.

18. Lewin, *Political Undercurrents,* chap. 8.

19. Two leaders in Europe, Ochab in Poland and Rakosi in Hungary, were removed with Soviet blessing in 1956 for precisely these errors. See Paul Kecskemeti, *The Unexpected Revolution: Social Forces in the Hungarian Uprising* (Stanford, Stanford University Press, 1961), and Imre Nagy, *On Communism: In Defense of the New Course* (New York, Praeger, 1957). Soviet reformers criticized the same tendencies in Maoism as a way to criticize Stalinism indirectly after Khrushchev's fall. See Gilbert Rozman, *A Mirror for Socialism: Soviet Criticisms of China.* (Princeton, Princeton University Press, 1985).

20. See Cohen, "Friends and Foes of Change."

21. See Kecskemeti, *Unexpected Revolution,* p. 72.

22. Whether there were in fact enough real "reformers" in China at that time to justify such an extreme reaction is debatable, but this does not affect the thrust of my argument here. Whether justified or not, the fears were real.

23. *On Khrushchov's Phoney Communism and Its Historical Lessons for the World* (Beijing, Foreign Languages Press, 1964), pp. 6–7.

24. Ibid., pp. 7, 9.

25. Ibid., p. 9.

26. Milovan Djilas, *The New Class: An Analysis of the Communist System of Power* (New York, Prager, 1957).

27. *Historical Experience,* pp. 35, 39–41.

28. China's leadership even objected to the use of the term *de-Stalinization,* on the grounds that it served only to weaken proletarian dictatorship and aid the plots of imperialism. Stalin had many great achievements, and to talk of "de-Stalinization" threatened all the gains of the revolution. Ibid., pp. 39–41.

29. *On Khrushchov's Phony Communism,* pp. 27–28.

30. Ibid., p. 41. This mentality was already apparent in the 1956 response to Tito, in which Maoists argued that de-Stalinization could only lead to revisionism, since it pitted "socialist democracy" against the dictatorship of the proletariat, the latter already *defining* the highest possible degree of socialist democracy. *Historical Experience,* pp. 48–49.

31. Many Hundred Flowers critics raised this issue, and paid for their impertinence

with stints in labor camps. For example, Lin Xiling explicitly enumerated the Stalinist tendencies of Mao and other leaders in her speeches at Beijing University in May 1957, drawing on the criticisms of Stalinism made by Khrushchev and Tito and showing how well they fit China. Calling attention to the role of public security organs in falsifying records during the many suppression campaigns of the 1950s, she openly rebutted Mao's verdict on Hu Feng and stated that Khrushchev and Tito were right in saying that the *system* was flawed, and Mao wrong in his contention that a superficial rectification would suffice. See Dennis Doolin, ed., *Communist China: The Politics of Student Opposition* (Stanford, Hoover Institution, 1964), pp. 23–42.

32. Wang Xizhe, "Mao Zedong and the Cultural Revolution," makes this point at greater length.

33. Maoist doctrine and political strategy bore definite resemblances to Mussolini's, which, according to Gregor (*Italian Fascism*, p. 28), was "an opportunistic activism inspired by dissatisfaction with the existing order, but unwilling or unable to proclaim a precise doctrine of its own and emphasizing rather the idea of change, as such, and the seizure of power."

34. For example, Mao used three distinct definitions of class and never resolved the inconsistencies. See Stuart Schram, "Classes, Old and New, in Mao Zedong's Thought, 1949–1976," in J. L. Watson, ed., *Class and Social Stratification in Post-Revolution China* (Cambridge, Cambridge University Press, 1984), pp. 29–55.

35. Gao Yuan, *Born Red,* pp. 200–252, 270–295, illustrates perfectly the way that factional struggles spurred alliances that had little to do with a group's proclaimed political orientation.

36. The first and second are what many past writers have referred to as "conservative" and "radical" rebels; the third earned the epithet "ultraleftism" from Maoist leaders. Another variety, "interest-group radicalism," was composed of marginal groups, notably sent-down youths, contract and temporary workers, and demobilized soldiers, who transparently used the conspiracy theory as an a means to express their grievances. They claimed that revisionist officials established policies that harmed their interests and that these policies should be reversed.

37. In the literature on the Cultural Revolution, these groups are identified variously as the "original" Red Guards, "good class" Red Guards, or "conservative" Red Guards. See Lee, *Politics of the Cultural Revolution,* and Rosen, *Red Guard Factionalism and the Cultural Revolution in Guangzhou,* chap. 3. Their activities are described in personal memoirs of the Cultural Revolution published in China and abroad, and in such recent historical works as Yan Jiaqi and Gao Gao, *Zhongguo "wenge" shinian shi* (A history of the "Cultural Revolution" decade; Taibei, Zhongguo wenti yanjiu chubanshe, 1987; reprint of 1986 Tianjin publication), chap. 4.

38. Anita Chan, *Children of Mao* (Seattle, University of Washington Press, 1984), traces the origins of this mentality and its consequences.

39. See, for example, Liu Guokai, *A Brief Analysis of the Cultural Revolution,* ed. Anita Chan (Armonk, M. E. Sharpe, 1987; translation of the unofficial publication, *Renmin zhi sheng,* December 1980), pp. 58–59.

40. Andrew Walder, "Communist Social Structure and Workers' Politics in China,"

in Victor Falkenheim, ed., *Citizens and Groups in Contemporary China,* Michigan Monographs in Chinese Studies, no. 56 (Ann Arbor, Center for Chinese Studies, University of Michigan, 1987), p. 82.

41. One cannot read Paul Boyer and Stephen Nissenbaum's *Salem Possessed: The Social Origins of Witchcraft* (Cambridge, Harvard University Press, 1974), without noting striking similarities with personal memoirs of the early stages of the Red Guard movement in China. See, for example, Gao Yuan, *Born Red,* pp. 39–84.

42. Rosen, *Red Guard Factionalism,* chap. 4.

43. Walder, "Workers' Politics," pp. 82–83.

44. See Rosen, *Red Guard Factionalism,* chap. 6, and Liu Guokai, *Brief Analysis of the Cultural Revolution,* pp. 106–114.

45. See, for example, the analysis by former Canton radicals in a famous 1974 wall poster; Li Yizhe, "On Socialist Democracy and the Legal System," in Chan, Rosen, and Unger, *On Socialist Democracy,* pp. 40–45; and Liu Guokai, *Brief Analysis of the Cultural Revolution,* pp. 114–129.

46. See "Whither China?" in Klaus Mehnert, *Peking and the New Left: At Home and Abroad,* China Research Monographs, no. 4 (Berkeley, Center for Chinese Studies, University of California, 1969), pp. 82–100.

47. One may trace the same evolution in the thinking of Liu Guokai and Chen Erjin, the latter's 1977 manifesto translated as *Crossroads Socialism,* trans. Robin Munro (London, Verso, 1984).

48. Andrew Walder, "Some Ironies of the Maoist Legacy in Industry," in Mark Selden and Victor Lippit, eds., *The Transition to Socialism in China* (Armonk, M. E. Sharpe, 1982).

49. Ibid., and Chapter 6 in this volume.

50. See Chapter 7 in this volume and Andrew Walder, *Communist Neo-Traditionalism: Work and Authority in Chinese Industry* (Berkeley, University of California Press, 1986), chap. 6.

Chapter 3. Agrarian Radicalism as a Rural Development Strategy; 1968–1978 by David Zweig

Thanks to Dwight Perkins for comments on an earlier draft and to William Joseph for his editorial comments on this chapter.

1. Richard Baum, "The Cultural Revolution in the Countryside: Anatomy of a Limited Rebellion," in Thomas W. Robinson, ed., *The Cultural Revolution in China* (Berkeley, University of California Press, 1971), pp. 367–476.

2. I date these events from 1968 and not from 1966 because initially central policy sought to protect agriculture from the politics of the CR. Following the defeat of the conservative 1968 "February Counter Current," Chen Boda and Lin Biao began efforts to radicalize rural policy and the rural areas. See *Zhejiang ribao* (Zhejiang daily), 29 November 1978.

3. For a more complete discussion of these strategies, see David Zweig, *Agrarian Radicalism in China, 1968–1981* (Cambridge, Harvard University Press, 1989).

4. For a comparison of developmental strategies and debates in the Soviet Union, see Moshe Lewin, *Political Undercurrents in Soviet Economic Debates: From Bukharin*

to the Modern Reformers (Princeton, Princeton University Press, 1974). For studies
of competing strategies in China, see the introduction to Nicholas P. Lardy and
Kenneth G. Lieberthal, eds., *Chen Yun's Strategy for Development: A Non-Maoist
Alternative* (Armonk, M. E. Sharpe, 1982), pp. xi–xxxiv; Dorothy Solinger, ed.,
Three Visions of Chinese Socialism (Boulder, Westview Press, 1983); and David
Zweig, "From Agrarian Radicalism to Cooperative Commercialization: Compet-
ing Visions of China's Rural Development," in David Zweig and Steven Butler,
China's Agricultural Reform: Background and Prospects (New York, China Council
of the Asia Society, 1985).

5. Only during the heavily ideological days of the Mao cult, which reached its peak
during the Three Loyalties campaign of 1968, was there any popular support for
this radical line among the majority of peasants.

6. The Chinese argued that leftist aspects of the Dazhai movement—brigade accounting, expanded class struggle, "cutting the tail of capitalism," egalitarianism, and "equalization and transfer"—all reflected Mao's "theory of continuing
the revolution under the dictatorship of the proletariat." See the Shanxi Provincial Party Committee's "Preliminary Summation of the Lessons and Experiences of the Provincial Movement to Learn from Dazhai in Agriculture," 24
August 1980, in CC-CCP Rural Policy Research Office's Material Office, eds.,
Nongcun jingji zhengce huibian, 1978–1981 (Compendium of agricultural economic policies; Beijing, Nongcun duwu chubanshe, 1982), p. 117.

7. The Chinese differentiate among the "basic line" *(jiben luxian)*, which sets the
overall task in a given historical period and determines the issues to be resolved;
"general policies" *(fang zhen)*, which stipulate the strategies to be employed to
fulfill the tasks set by the general line; and "policies" *(zheng ce)*, the concrete
programs that are the practical outcome of both the line and the general policies.

8. Ma Yanwen, "The Bureaucratic Class and the Dictatorship of the Proletariat,"
Beijing Daxue xuebao (Beijing University journal 4, September 1976), in *Survey
of People's Republic of China Magazines* 895:18–30 (October 1976).

9. No doubt one could argue that the policy compromises between Party radicals,
military radicals, and state socialists brought about these state-centric policies.
See Edwin A. Winckler, "Dimensions of Agricultural Policy: Hebei, Jiangsu
and Guangdong in the 1970s," paper prepared for the Conference on Bureaucracy and Rural Development, Joint Committee on Contemporary China, SSRC–
ACLS, Chicago, 26–30 August 1981. This study, however, focuses solely on
the policies of what Winckler would call Party and military radicals.

10. Soviet leaders felt that to continue the transition to communism and overcome
the urban-rural gap, *kolkhozy* (collectives) must be transformed into *sovkhozy* (state
farms), thereby establishing a system of "all people's property." See James A.
Gilison, *The Soviet Vision of Utopia* (Baltimore, Johns Hopkins University Press,
1975), p. 80.

11. According to the Beidahe Resolution of 29 August 1958, "The primary purpose
of establishing people's communes is to accelerate the speed of socialist construction, and the purpose of building socialism is to prepare actively for the transition to communism. It seems that the attainment of communism in China is no
longer a remote future event. We should actively use the form of the people's

communes to explore the practical road of transition to communism." "Central Committee Resolution on the Establishment of People's Communes in the Rural Areas, August 29, 1958," in Robert Bowie and John King Fairbank, eds., *Communist China, 1955–1959: Policy Documents with Analysis* (Cambridge, Harvard University Press, 1962).

12. *People's Daily*, 14 July 1964.

13. William A. Joseph, *The Critique of Ultra-Leftism in China, 1958–1981* (Stanford, Stanford University Press, 1984), pp. 107–108.

14. See *Zhongguo nongye nianjian, 1980* (Chinese agricultural yearbook; Beijing, Nongye chubanshe, 1981), p. 5. The Soviet Union also merged collective farms in 1949, forming larger units with five to eight villages in each. Nationwide, the number of *kolkhozy* decreased by almost two-thirds. Roy A. Medvedyev and Zhores A. Medvedyev, *Khrushchev: The Years in Power* (New York, Norton, 1978), pp. 33–37.

15. Xu Dixin, "Lun qiong guodu" (On the transition through poverty), *Jingji yanjiu* 4:2–7 (1979).

16. See B. Michael Frolic, *Mao's People* (Cambridge, Harvard University Press, 1980), chap. 2.

17. Jonathan Unger, "Collective Incentives in the Chinese Countryside: Lessons from Chen Village," *World Development* 6:583–601 (1978).

18. Yu Lin County Theoretical Study Group, *Shehuizhuyi jiti suoyouzhi* (The socialist collective ownership system; Guangxi renmin chubanshe, 1976), p. 45. My translation.

19. In his study of Cuba, Silverman noted a similar dilemma: "Since all socialist revolutions have occurred in relatively backward economies, an inevitable contradiction exists between the organizational forms held to be most consistent with communist goals and the capacity to establish such an economic organization." See Bertram Silverman, "Economic Organization and Social Conscience: Some Dilemmas of Cuban Socialism," in June Nash, Juan Corradi, and Hobart Spalding, Jr., eds., *Ideology and Social Change in Latin America* (New York, Gordon and Breach, 1977), p. 238.

20. Zhang Chunqiao, *On Exercising Overall Dictatorship over the Bourgeoisie* (Beijing, Foreign Languages Press, 1975), and Hua Guofeng, *Let the Whole Party Mobilize for a Vast Effort to Develop Agriculture and Build Tachai-type Counties Throughout the Country* (Beijing, Foreign Languages Press, 1975).

21. Chen Yonggui, "Thoroughly Criticize the 'Gang of Four' and Bring about a New Upsurge in the Movement to Build Tachai-type Counties Throughout the Country," speech to the Second National Conference on Learning from Tachai in Agriculture, 20 December 1976, in *Survey of People's Republic of China Magazines* 910:79 (February 1977).

22. See *Renmin gongshe zai yuejin* (People's communes are advancing; Shanghai, Renmin chubanshe, 1974), pp. 57–64, and *Xuexi yu pipan* (Study and criticism; Shanghai), 10:7–11 (1975).

23. These categories—poor peasant, lower-middle peasant, middle peasant, rich peasant, and landlord—reflect class categories or "class labels" given by the communists since the 1920s. During land reform all peasants were given such labels

to differentiate among them according to what percentage of their income came from their own labor as compared with that which came from employing others. Although "poor" and "lower-middle peasants" had some land of their own, the fact that they had to work for others to earn a living made them reliable supporters for the communists because they had suffered "class exploitation." "Middle peasants"—that is, independent farmers—were less reliable because, although they were not "exploiters," they also had not suffered exploitation. So they were unlikely to support land reform. The difference between "rich peasants" and "landlords" is that the former did some work on their own land. These labels remained with peasants until 1979 and were seen by the radicals to have significance for the continuing battle against capitalist restoration, because presumably those who had been exploited before would continue to oppose the resurrection of class inequality.

24. *China Reconstructs* 18:23–27 (December 1969), cited in "The China Group—Reports on Rural People's Communes," unpublished data set compiled by Frederick Crook.

25. For a study of the conflict over grain, see Jean C. Oi, *State and Peasant in Contemporary China: The Political Economy of Village Government* (Berkeley, University of California Press, 1989).

26. For the concept of a "moral incentive economy," see Robert M. Bernardo, *The Theory of Moral Incentives in Cuba* (Tuscaloosa, University of Alabama Press, 1971).

27. James A. Malloy, "Generation of Political Support and Allocation of Costs," in Carmelo Mesa-Lago, ed., *Revolutionary Change in Cuba* (Pittsburgh, University of Pittsburgh Press, 1971), p. 39.

28. Fidel Castro, too, believed in the power of human will and consciousness and utilized a similar strategy in the late 1960s. See his May Day 1971 speech on creating matter from consciousness, in Bernardo, *Theory of Moral Incentives,* appendix.

29. For a study of the confrontation of traditional Confucian values, Maoist-collectivist values, and private utilitarian values, see Richard Madsen, *Morality and Power in a Chinese Village* (Berkeley, University of California Press, 1984).

30. See "Transformation of Small Production Is a Long-Term Task of the Dictatorship of the Proletariat," *People's Daily,* 17 August 1975.

31. Yu Lin County, *Shehui zhuyi jiti suoyouzhi,* pp. 47–48.

32. Ibid., pp. 60–70. The private-sector income in this study, which averaged 41.6 percent, was rather high, suggesting that the authors chose this village to make this political point because sidelines were so important here.

33. Ibid., p. 49.

34. Mao Yuanxin, Mao's nephew who was influential in Liaoning Province, tried to propagate the experience of Heertao Commune, Zhangwu County, Liaoning Province. See *People's Daily,* 9 May 1976, p. 1. For a criticism of this policy by the Party secretary of Zhangwu County, see *People's Daily,* 21 October 1979, p. 2.

35. *People's Daily,* 11 January 1968.

36. Being close to a city was seen as making a unit potentially vulnerable to "capitalist tendencies." See *People's Daily,* 3 June 1973, p. 2.

37. *People's Daily,* 24 November 1968, p. 3; Martin K. Whyte, "The Tachai Brigade and Incentives for the Peasants," *Current Scene* 7:1–13 (August 1969); and Jonathan Unger, "Remuneration, Ideology and Peasant Interests in a Chinese Village, 1960–1980," in William L. Parish, ed., *Chinese Rural Development: The Great Transformation* Armonk, M. E. Sharpe, 1985), pp. 117–140.

38. In Cuba of the 1960s they established "emulation commissions" for evaluating individual labor contributions and giving moral rewards. See Robert M. Bernardo, "Moral Stimulation and Labor Allocation in Cuba," in Irving L. Horowitz, ed., *Cuban Communism* (New Brunswick, Transaction Books, 1981), pp. 185–218.

39. In some ways this vision of the path to communism was a Chinese invention. Whereas Marxism possessed an urban bias, Mao favored the rural areas; second, the dichotomy between mental and manual labor goes back to Mencius's work and was not a critical issue for Marx.

40. "Regulations on the Work in the Rural People's Communes," rev. draft, *Issues & Studies* 15:93–111 (October 1979) and 15:106–115 (December 1979).

41. After a 1975 visit to Dazhai, a rural Nanjing cadre tried to participate in labor 300 days a year. When after several months he found it impossible to work that much and still manage the brigade effectively, he became convinced that Dazhai cadres had lied. Personal interview, 1981.

42. Maurice Meisner, "The Concept of the Dictatorship of the Proletariat in Chinese Marxist Thought," in Victor Nee and David Mozingo, eds., *State and Society in Contemporary China* (Ithaca, Cornell University Press, 1982), p. 124.

43. See Thomas P. Bernstein, *Up to the Mountains and Down to the Countryside* (New Haven, Yale University Press, 1977).

44. In her speech to the 1975 Dazhai Conference, Dazhai's Party secretary Guo Fenglian told how during a drought Dazhai allowed water to flow through its brigade to its neighbors below. Wheelright and McFarlane quote a local leader whose brigade accepted back a wild horse it had sold to another brigade and returned the money because the other unit could not train the horse. Although this type of action may reflect a selflessness among peasants, it serves above all as a method for conflict avoidance. See E. L. Wheelright and Bruce MacFarlane, *The Chinese Road to Socialism* (New York, Monthly Review Press, 1970), p. 188.

45. See Audrey Donnithorne, "China's Cellular Economy: Some Economic Trends since the Cultural Revolution," *China Quarterly* 52:605–619 (October–December 1972).

46. In 1969 teams were under severe pressure to establish local grain reserves to ensure that, in the case of war, each locality would be prepared to fend for itself. See Jean C. Oi, "The Struggle over the Harvest and the Politics of Local Grain Reserves," in Randolph Barker and Beth Rose, eds., *Agricultural and Rural Development in China Today* (Ithaca, Cornell University Program in International Agriculture, 1983), pp. 97–119.

47. Mei Fanquan, "How to Increase China's Cotton Production," *People's Daily,* 1 January 1982, p. 3, cited in Nicholas P. Lardy, *Agriculture in China's Modern Economic Development* (Cambridge, Cambridge University Press, 1983), p. 64.

48. While 3.4% of total grain produced was transferred among provinces in 1953–1956, that figure dropped to 1.5% in 1965 and to 0.1% in 1978. Lardy, *Agriculture in China's Modern Economic Development*, p. 51. Only intercounty transfers occurred in the late 1960s and 1970s. Ibid., p. 167.

49. Mark Selden, "Cooperation and Conflict: Cooperative and Collective Formation in China's Countryside," in Mark Selden and Victor Lippit, eds., *The Transition to Socialism in China* (Armonk, M. E. Sharpe, 1982), p. 58.

50. For a discussion of this issue, see Zweig, *Agrarian Radicalism*, chap. 1.

51. See *Statistical Yearbook of China 1983* (English ed. Hong Kong, Economic Information and Agency, 1984), p. 210.

52. Data collected in 1980 in my possession.

53. Steven Butler, "Field Research in China's Communes: Views of a 'Guest,' " in Anne F. Thurston and Burton Pasternak, eds., *The Social Sciences and Fieldwork in China* (Boulder, Westview Press, 1983), p. 112.

54. There the moral incentive economy also led to high rates of capital formation as well. In 1961–1963 capital formation as a percentage of GNP was 18 percent, but by 1968, when the "Revolutionary Offensive" peaked, the rate of capital formation was 31 percent. See David Barkin, "Cuban Agriculture: A Strategy of Economic Development," in Horowitz, ed., *Cuban Communism*, 4th ed., p. 64.

55. See Michel C. Oksenberg, "Policy Formulation in Communist China: The Case of the Mass Irrigation Campaign, 1957–1958," PhD dissertation, Columbia University, 1969. See also James E. Nickum, "Labour Accumulation in Rural China and Its Role since the Cultural Revolution," *Cambridge Journal of Economics* 2:273–286 (1978).

56. Data from John Loessing Buck's study, cited in Mark Elvin, "The Technology of Farming in Late-Traditional China," in Randolph Barker and Radha Sinha, with Beth Rose, eds., *The Chinese Agricultural Economy* (Boulder, Westview Press, 1982), p. 31.

57. Hua Guofeng, *Let the Whole Party Mobilize*.

58. There was also an emphasis on appropriate technologies, such as biogas digesters, rather than on highly capital-intensive technology. Thanks to William Joseph, who made this point.

59. For a more in-depth discussion of "policy winds" and the techniques of implementation, see David Zweig, *Agrarian Radicalism in China*, chap. 2.

60. Interview in suburban Nanjing, 1981.

61. Interview in Beijing with rusticated youth, 1981.

62. Similar problems occurred during the Great Leap. See Joseph, *Critique of Ultra-Leftism*, chap. 4.

63. Data collected by Vikram Seth and kindly shared with me. The "responsibility system" had not been introduced into this commune as of 1980, so the data reflect the collective period, except that collective income had probably increased owing to the 1979 rise in procurement prices for grain, a crop that this commune produced in large quantities.

64. Griffin and Saith also found that, the higher a family's dependency ratio, "the lower is collective income per head." Keith Griffin and Ashwani Saith, *Growth*

and Equality in Rural China (Singapore, International Labour Office, 1981), p. 51.

65. Anita Chan and Jon Unger found that families with more laborers benefited more from private endeavors. However, this may have depended on how important the collective sector was to their income, a factor that can vary from locality to locality. Personal communication.

66. Using a slightly different measure, Griffin and Saith found a negative correlation of − .62 for collective income per household and outside income per household. Griffin and Saith, *Growth and Equality in Rural China,* p. 51.

67. See David Zweig, "Peasants, Ideology, and New Incentive Systems: Jiangsu Province, 1978–1981," in Parish, ed., *Chinese Rural Development,* pp. 141–163, as well as Unger, "Collective Incentives."

68. See David Zweig, "Opposition to Reform in Rural China: The System of Responsibility and People's Communes," *Asian Survey* 23:879–900 (July 1983).

69. Madsen, *Morality and Power.*

70. Lardy, *Agriculture in China's Modern Economic Development.*

71. Interview with an team accountant in a brigade in southern Nanjing. See also Thomas B. Wiens, "The Limits to Agricultural Intensification: The Suzhou Experience," in Joint Economic Committee, U.S. Congress, *China under the Four Modernizations* (Washington, D.C., U.S. Government Printing Office, 1982), pt. 1, pp. 462–474.

72. See Terry Sicular, "Market Restrictions in Chinese Agriculture: A Micro-Economic Analysis," PhD dissertation, Yale University, 1983, and John H. C. Fei and Gustav Ranis, "Economic Development in Historical Perspective," *American Economic Review* 59:386–400 (May 1969).

73. See Milton J. Esman and Norman T. Uphoff, *Local Organizations: Intermediaries in Rural Development* (Ithaca, Cornell University Press, 1984), pp. 151–153.

74. Zweig, *Agrarian Radicalism in China,* chap. 7. See also Xu Lu, *Renmin gongshe suoyouzhi he zizhuquan* (The system of ownership and authority of the people's communes; Guangdong, Guangdong renmin chubanshe, 1979), pp. 12–13.

75. While suggesting that agricultural growth during the Cultural Revolution era, excluding 1967–68, was quite acceptable, Perkins argues that the labor mobilization and accumulation, which were hallmarks of this era, did not increase agricultural output very much. Dwight Perkins, "China's Economic Policy and Performance during the Cultural Revolution and Its Aftermath," *The People's Republic,* vol. xiv of *Cambridge History of China,* pt. 2 (forthcoming).

76. Dwight Perkins and Shahid Yusuf, *Rural Development in China* (Baltimore, Johns Hopkins University Press, 1984), p. 69.

Chapter 4. The Cultural Revolution as an Unintended Result of Administrative Policies by Lynn T. White III

For oral and written comments that aided the revision of this chapter, I thank David Bachman, John Fairbank, Philip Kuhn, Kenneth Lieberthal, Lucian Pye, Benjamin Schwartz, Ezra Vogel, and Allen Whiting. David Zweig and an anonymous reviewer put great work into this, for which I am grateful. For some help in the research, I thank Feng Shengping. None of these, however, is responsible for the remaining errors of fact or interpretation.

1. The 1966–1968 periodization is used here, because the official 1966–1976 era was very diverse and because some de facto reforms (in fields ranging from foreign policy to state budgets and rural industrialization) clearly began in the early 1970s. On the Russian case, see Robert C. Tucker, ed., *Stalinism: Essays in Historical Interpretation* (New York, Norton, 1977), esp. Stephen F. Cohen, "Stalinism and Bolshevism," pp. 3–29.

2. Ba Jin, *Random Thoughts* (Hong Kong, Joint Publishing, 1984), pp. xv–xvi.

3. "Here are dragons" was a common notation on medieval European maps, to indicate unknown lands. These dragons, of course, were Western.

4. Anne F. Thurston, "Victims of China's Cultural Revolution: The Invisible Wounds," *Pacific Affairs,* pt. 1 in 57:599–620 (Winter 1984–85), and pt. 2 in 58:5–27 (Spring 1985), and esp. Thurston, *Enemies of the People: The Ordeal of the Intellectuals in China's Great Cultural Revolution* (New York, Knopf, 1987).

5. See Lynn White, *Careers in Shanghai* (Berkeley, University of California Press, 1978).

6. See the suggestion in Clifford Geertz, "Deep Play: Notes on the Balinese Cockfight," *The Interpretation of Cultures* (New York, Basic Books, 1973), p. 452, that the quiet and untumultuous symbol of the Brahmana ordination ceremony is as "like Bali" as the cockfight—and might have been used by Geertz to organize an alternative essay on the culture there. The cockfight and the ordination suggest options among which Balinese choose in different situations.

7. See Lynn White, *Policies of Chaos: The Organizational Causes of Violence in China's Cultural Revolution* (Princeton, Princeton University Press, 1989).

8. Ibid. This change was "structural" in the sense used by Theda Skocpol, because it determined the resources available to alternative elites; see her *States and Social Revolutions* (Cambridge, Cambridge University Press, 1979).

9. See Lynn White, "Leadership in Shanghai, 1955–69," in Robert Scalapino, ed., *Elites in the People's Republic of China* (Seattle, University of Washington Press, 1972), esp. pp. 333–346.

10. Lucian Pye, *The Dynamics of Chinese Politics* (Cambridge, Oelgeschlager, Gunn, and Hain, 1981), for example, chaps. 4 and 5, is the academic literature's best effort to compare the relevance of functional, geographic, and generational groups with political factions.

11. See James R. Townsend, *The Revolutionization of Chinese Youth: A Study of Chung-kuo Ch'ing-nien* (Berkeley, University of California Center for Chinese Studies, 1967), p. 64—which deserves scholarly attention. In Shanghai the Young Communist League recruitment for 1965 alone was 200,000, according to *Wenhui bao* (Cultural daily), 5 May 1966. At the national level Townsend's figures imply that of the total number of League members at the end of 1965, about one-third had joined during that year; compare Gilbert Rozman, ed., *The Modernization of China* (New York, Free Press, 1981), table 9.1 (L. White), p. 275. Because a change almost as important occurred in the Party too, these figures modify an

impression of "limited recruitment" in Roberta Martin, *Party Recruitment in China: Patterns and Prospects* (New York, Columbia University East Asian Institute, 1981), pp. 66–68.

12. The May 16 Circular and Sixteen-Point Decision are available in Jean Daubier, *A History of the Chinese Cultural Revolution* (New York, Random House, 1974), pp. 289–305.

13. Robert J. Lifton, *Revolutionary Immortality: Mao Tse-tung and the Cultural Revolution* (New York, Vintage Books, 1968), p. 32.

14. Ross Terrill, *Mao: A Biography* (New York, Harper and Row, 1980), for example, p. 324 or 366.

15. *Resolution on CCP History (1949–81)* (Beijing, Foreign Languages Press, 1981), p. 46.

16. Ibid., p. 47.

17. For example, Stanley Karnow, *Mao and China* (New York, Viking, 1972), and Edward E. Rice, *Mao's Way* (Berkeley, University of California Press, 1972).

18. See Jean C. Oi, "Communism and Clientelism: Rural Politics in China," *World Politics* 37:238–266 (January 1985); and Andrew Walder, *Communist Neo-Traditionalism* (Berkeley, University of California Press, 1986).

19. Gail E. Henderson and Myron S. Cohen, *The Chinese Hospital: A Socialist Work Unit* (New Haven, Yale University Press, 1984), provides information on such authority relations in a calm period.

20. Joseph Morrison's translation of Wang Xizhe's stirring essay is in Anita Chan, Stanley Rosen, and Jonathan Unger, eds., *On Socialist Democracy and the Chinese Legal System* (Armonk, M. E. Sharpe, 1985), pp. 177–260.

21. See Harry Eckstein, "The Idea of Political Development: From Dignity to Efficiency," *World Politics* 34:451–486 (July 1982); and Clifford Geertz, *Negara: The Theatre State in Nineteenth-Century Bali* (Princeton, Princeton University press, 1980).

22. Chan, Rosen, and Unger, *On Socialist Democracy*, pp. 256–259.

23. Ibid., p. 259. Wang shows here an admirable frankness, similar to Walder's in *Communist Neo-Traditionalism*, p. 7, note 7.

24. Harold C. Hinton, *An Introduction to Chinese Politics* (New York, Praeger, 1973), p. 57.

25. Robert C. Tucker, "Does Big Brother Really Exist?" *Wilson Quarterly* 8:106–117 (Winter 1984).

26. For example, Klaus Mehnert, *Peking and the New Left: At Home and Abroad* (Berkeley, University of California Center for Chinese Studies, 1969). See also Cheng Chu-yuan, "The Power Struggle in Red China," *Asian Survey* 6:469–533 (September 1966); and Gene T. Hsiao, "The Background and Development of 'The Proleterian Cultural Revolution,' " *Asian Survey* 7:389–404 (June 1967).

27. Roderick MacFarquhar, *The Origins of the Cultural Revolution* (New York, Columbia University Press, 1974), I, 3. The second volume was published in 1983; the third is forthcoming. See also Byung-joon Ahn, *Chinese Politics and the Cultural Revolution: Dynamics of Policy Processes* (Seattle, University of Washington Press, 1966); Richard Baum, *Prelude to Revolution: Mao, the Party, and the Peasant Question, 1962–66* (New York, Columbia University Press, 1975); and Richard

Baum and Frederick C. Teiwes, *Ssu-Ch'ing: The Socialist Education Movement of 1962–1966* (Berkeley: University of California Center for Chinese Studies, 1968).

28. Parris H. Chang, *Power and Policy in China*, en. ed. (University Park, Pennsylvania State University Press, 1978), p. 2.

29. Lowell Dittmer, "The Cultural Revolution and the Fall of Liu Shao-ch'i," *Current Scene* 11:1–13 (January 1973).

30. William Hinton, *Turning Point in China: An Essay on the Cultural Revolution* (New York, Monthly Review Press, 1972).

31. K. S. Karol, *The Second Chinese Revolution,* trans. M. Jones (New York, Hill and Wang, 1974).

32. Richard Pfeffer, "The Pursuit of Purity: Mao's Cultural Revolution," *Problems of Communism* 18:12–25 (November–December 1969).

33. *China: Inside the People's Republic* (New York, Bantam Books, 1972), 72, 102–103. A most careful book in the idealistic genre is Dauber, *History of the Chinese Cultural Revolution.*

34. Leo Huberman and Paul Sweezy, "The Cultural Revolution in China," *Monthly Review* 18:1–17 (January 1967).

35. Richard D. Baum predicted such swings *before* the CR in " 'Red and Expert': The Politico-Ideological Foundations of China's Great Leap Forward," *Asian Survey* 4:148–157 (September 1964). See also Baum, *Prelude to Revolution.*

36. Michel Oksenberg, "China: Forcing the Revolution to a New Stage," *Asian Survey* 7:1–15 (January 1967); Doak A. Barnett, *China after Mao* (Princeton, Princeton University Press, 1967); and Richard D. Baum, "Ideology Redivivus," *Problems of Communism* 16:1–11 (May–June 1967). Edward Friedman also relied on development reasons, emphasizing "cultural givens of modernization" in "Cultural Limits of the Cultural Revolution," *Asian Survey* 9:188–201 (March 1969). See also Donald W. Klein, "A Question of Leadership: Problems of Mobility Control and Policymaking in China," *Current Scene* 5:1–8 (April 1967).

37. Harry Harding, Jr., "China: Toward Revolutionary Pragmatism," *Asian Survey* 11:51–67 (January 1971).

38. Liang Heng and Judith Shapiro, *Son of the Revolution* (New York, Random House, 1983), p. 118.

39. Michael Walzer, *The Revolution of the Saints: A Study in the Origins of Radical Politics* (Cambridge, Harvard University Press, 1965), pp. 8, 91, 309.

40. See Lowell Dittmer, "Thought Reform and Cultural Revolution," *American Political Science Review* 71:67–85 (March 1977).

41. Marc J. Blecher and Gordon White, *Micropolitics in Contemporary China: A Technical Unit during and after the Cultural Revolution* (White Plains, M. E. Sharpe, 1979), p. 81 and passim, gives statistical correlations to show this.

42. See Lynn White, "Workers' Politics in Shanghai," *Journal of Asian Studies* 26:99–116 (November 1976).

43. See Andrew G. Walder, *Chang Chu'n-ch'iao and Shanghai's January Revolution* (Ann Arbor, University of Michigan Center for Chinese Studies, 1977).

44. See Alfred Cobban, *The Social Interpretation of the French Revolution* (Cambridge, Cambridge University Press, 1964).

45. See Lynn White, "Bourgeois Radicalism in the 'New Class' of Shanghai," in

James L. Watson, ed., *Class and Social Stratification in Post-Revolution China* (Cambridge, Cambridge University Press, 1984), pp. 142–174.

46. See Thurston, "Victims," esp. p. 605.

47. "The Wounded" literature *(shanghen wenxue)* concerns unjust harm done to people with bad labels. See *The Wounded: New Stories of the Cultural Revolution,* trans. Geremie Barme and Bennet Lee (Hong Kong, Joint Publishing, 1979); also Perry Link, ed., *Stubborn Weeds* (Bloomington, Indiana University Press, 1983).

48. Marxist innovators (Bernstein, Kautsky, Lukacs, Gramsci, Poulantzas) try the virtues of making economically generated "classes" almost synonymous with Weberian "status groups." Policies made the CCP's classes into status groups, despite their names.

49. See Liang Heng and Shapiro, *Son of the Revolution,* and Yue Daiyun (with Carolyn Wakeman), *To the Storm* (Berkeley, University of California Press, 1985).

50. Red Guards went to rural areas where the bureaucrats whom they wished to attack had grown up, to check the accuracy of urban records in "outside investigations" *(wai diao).*

51. *Jiefang junbao* (Liberation Army news), Peking, 14 July 1984, and interviews with Cultural Revolution participants.

52. Michel Oksenberg, "Occupational Groups in Chinese Society and the Cultural Revolution," in Chang Chun-shu, James Crump, and Rhodes Murphey, eds., *The Cultural Revolution: 1967 in Review* (Ann Arbor, University of Michigan Center for Chinese Studies, 1968), pp. 1–44, distinguishes seven such occupations and assesses their respective influences on policy.

53. Hong Yung Lee, *The Politics of the Chinese Cultural Revolution: A Case Study* (Berkeley, University of California Press, 1978), pp. 302–322.

54. Stanley Rosen, *Red Guard Factionalism and Cultural Revolution in Guangzhou (Canton)* (Boulder, Westview Press, 1982), p. 147. The "Red Flags" were 74% capitalists, clerks, and professionals. The "East Winds" were 81% from approved-label families.

55. Blecher and White, *Micropolitics in Contemporary China,* p. 81. The existence of a small third faction, mostly proletarian, slightly complicated matters in this unit.

56. See White, "Workers' Politics in Shanghai," pp. 99–116.

57. Quoted from the tabloid *Xiaobing* (Little soldiers), 9 December 1967, in Rosen, *Red Guard Factionalism,* p. 235.

58. See Gordon A. Bennett and Ronald N. Montaperto, *Red Guard: The Political Biography of Dai Hsiao-ai* (Garden City, Doubleday, 1972), and Liang Heng and Judith Shapiro, *Son of the Revolution.*

59. Richard Curt Kraus, *Class Conflict in Chinese Socialism* (New York, Columbia University Press, 1981), pp. 121–122.

60. See Geof Wood, ed., *Labeling in Development Policy: Essays in Honor of Bernard Schaffer* (The Hague, Institute of Social Studies, 1985), for a critical approach to labels.

61. See Amitai Etzioni, ed., *A Sociological Reader on Complex Organizations,* 2nd ed. (New York, Holt, 1969), for many relevant articles.

62. Read Li Si, prime minister under the first emperor of China, in William Theo-

dore de Bary, ed., *Sources of Chinese Tradition* (New York, Columbia University Press, 1960), I, 136–144. Read Niccolo Machiavelli on the orderly uses of fear and cruelty in *The Prince,* introduction by Christian Gauss (New York, Mentor Classic, 1952), pp. 89–91.

63. A similar analysis, based on Etzioni's interpretation of Weber, is the classic by G. William Skinner and Edwin A. Winckler, "Compliance Succession in Rural Communist China: A Cyclical Theory," in Etzioni, *Sociological Reader,* pp. 410–438. Campaigns, monitors, and labels may well be seen as policy expressive of charismatic, traditional, and legal-bureaucratic authority types, taken in China beyond the levels at which they are most useful for adaptive change.

64. The first of these approaches implies separate factors or sectors and a systems approach; the second implies a culturalist approach to understand the motives of actors. Works like Clifford Geertz, "Deep Play," (see n. 7) can be reconciled on a practical level with functionalist or Marxist systems approaches like those by authors ranging from T. Parsons or C. A. Johnson to V. I. Lenin or Wei Jingsheng.

65. See Rosen, *Red Guard Factionalism,* for the best analysis of these immediate factors.

66. See also Lynn White, "The End of China's Revolution: An Elite Diversifies" (forthcoming).

67. See Merle Goldman, "Culture," in Steven M. Goldstein, ed., *China Briefing, 1984* (Boulder, Westview Press, 1985), pp. 21–36.

68. *Pipan zichan jieji ziyouhua sichao.*

69. See Philip Selznick, *The Organizational Weapon: A Study of Bolshevik Strategy and Tactics* (New York, McGraw-Hill, 1952), and Karl Mannheim's "ideology" or "practical ideology" as described in Franz Schurmann, *Ideology and Organization in Communist China* (Berkeley, University of California Press, 1966). Mannheim's ideas can thus describe an aggressive, nonadaptive kind of system.

Chapter 5. Factional Politics in Zhejiang, 1973–1976 by Keith Forster

I wish to express my thanks to Frederick Teiwes for the most helpful and stimulating comments and suggestions that he included in his report on my doctoral thesis. This chapter, which draws on material from the thesis, would have been all the poorer without his input. Thanks are also due to my colleague David Kelly and to two anonymous readers for their pertinent observations on the chapter.

1. Lowell Dittmer, "Bases of Power in Chinese Politics: A Theory and an Analysis of the Fall of the 'Gang of Four,' " *World Politics* 31:40–48 (October 1978).

2. See Frederick C. Teiwes, *Leadership, Legitimacy, and Conflict in China: From a Charismatic Mao to the Politics of Succession* (London, Macmillan, 1984), pp. 113–118.

3. For a description of this prolonged vendetta against alleged ultraleft Red Guards and rebels, which lasted from 1968 to 1971, see Gao Gao and Yan Jiaqi, *"Wenhua da geming" shinian shi, 1966–1976* (Ten-year history of the "Cultural Revolution"; Tianjin, Tianjin renmin chubanshe, 1986), pp. 288–294.

4. Keith Forster, *Rebellion and Factionalism in a Chinese Province: Zhejiang, 1966–76* (Armonk, M. E. Sharpe, 1990).

5. See the account of events in Shanxi Province in William Hinton, *Shenfan* (Picador, London, 1983), pt. 9.

6. See the speeches in Deng Xiaoping, *Wenxuan* (Selected writings; Beijing, Renmin chubanshe, 1983), pp. 1–34, and the Deng-inspired "Three Poisonous Weeds" trans. in Chi Hsin, *The Case of the Gang of Four* (Hong Kong, Cosmos Books, 1977), pp. 203–295.

7. For an explanation of the use of code words to attack political opponents, see Lucien Pye, *The Dynamics of Chinese Politics* (Cambridge, Oelgeschlager, Gunn, and Hain, 1981), p. 9.

8. See Ye Yonglie, *Zhang Chunqiao fuchen shi* (The rise and fall of Zhang Chunqiao; Changchun, Shidai wenyi chubanshe, 1988), pp. 279–280, 286–287; and Ye Yonglie, *Wang Hongwen xingshuai lu* (The rise and fall of Wang Hongwen; Changchun, Shidai wenyi chubanshe, 1989), p. 406.

9. See "Some Problems in Accelerating Industrial Development" (also known as the "Twenty Points") in *Zhonggong nianbao, 1977* (Yearbook of Chinese communism; Taibei, Institute of Communist Studies, 1977), V, 69, trans. in Chi Hsin, *Case of the Gang of Four*, p. 247.

10. Deng Xiaoping, *Wenxuan*, p. 14. My translation differs somewhat from the official translation in *Selected Works of Deng Xiaoping* (Beijing, Foreign Languages Press, 1984), p. 25.

11. Fujian Provincial Service, 7 August 1975, *SWB/FE/4983/BII/10–11*. See also Fujian Provincial Service, 13 July 1975, *SWB/FE/4958/BII/14–16*, for further evidence of Liao's denunciation of bourgeois factionalism.

12. Heilongjiang Provincial Service, 13 August 1975, *SWB/FE/4987/BII/1–3*. See also the *Nanfang ribao* (Southern daily) editorial of 18 August 1975, Guangdong Provincial Service, 18 August 1975, *SWB/FE/4992/BII/15–17*.

13. See the *Zhejiang ribao* (Zhejiang daily) editorials of 23 August 1975 and 14 September 1975 in *Xuexi wenji* (A collection of study documents) no. 5, 1975 (Hangzhou, Zhejiang renmin chubanshe, 1975), pp. 63–66, 67–69. I am most grateful to David Zweig for sending me this and two other editorials in the collection. David visited Hangzhou in January 1976 and recounted his experiences in "The Peita Debate on Education and the Fall of Teng Hsiao-ping," *CQ* 73 (March 1978), esp. pp. 147–148, 151–152. See also the speech by Tie Ying, secretary of the CCP Zhejiang Provincial Committee on 1 September 1975, in Zhejiang Provincial Service, 5 September 1975, *SWB/FE/5002/BII/1–2*.

14. Deng's "Twenty Points" claimed that the leadership in some industrial enterprises was in the hands of "unreformed petty intellectuals" *(meiyou dedao gaizao de xiao zhishifenzi)* and "bold elements" *(yonggan fenzi)*. *Zhonggong nianbao, 1977*, V, 68.

15. *Xuexi wenji*, pp. 63–64. The "Decision Concerning the Problem of Zhejiang," which the Central Committee and State Council had issued on 24 July 1975, went much further in detailing the activities of "counterrevolutionary revision-

ists" and "newly emergent bourgeois elements." It referred to interruptions to water and electricity supplies, disruption to production and transport and communications, raids on army units, assaults on public security offices, looting of state property, murder, arson, and poisoning of water supplies, and "counterrevolutionary riots" *(fan geming baodong)*. See *Feiqing yuebao* (Bandit affairs monthly) 18:84 (May 1976).

16. By contrast, the Yunnan first Party secretary Jia Qiyun, in a speech of October 1975, was more conciliatory and seemed to downgrade the seriousness of factional errors. Yunnan Provincial Service, 30 October 1975, *SWB/FE/5052/BII/9*.

17. Fujian Provincial Service, 13 July 1975, *SWB/FE/4958/BII/16–17*.

18. *Xuexi wenji*, pp. 70–78.

19. See *China News Analysis* 1012 (5 September 1975), 1013 (12 September 1975); *China News Summary* 579 (20 August 1975).

20. See *China News Analysis* 1012, pp. 6–7; *Far Eastern Economic Review*, 20 May 1974, pp. 14–16.

21. Teiwes, *Leadership, Legitimacy, and Conflict*, pp. 113–118.

22. This and the previous paragraph are drawn from Dittmer, "Bases of Power," pp. 48–59.

23. This phrase was used by one of Zhejiang's leading student rebels, Zhang Yongsheng, in an article that he wrote in 1969 while attending the CCP Ninth National Congress. See Beijing radio, 8 April 1969, *SWB/FE/3044/C/3*.

24. For a detailed chronological account of the politics of Zhejiang in these years, see Forster, *Rebellion and Factionalism*, chaps. 7–10.

25. In 1974 industrial production in the province had fallen by 13.6% over the previous year, and the percentage decline for important industrial goods such as steel (53.5%), pig iron (59%), cement (32%), chemical fertilizer (44%), cotton yarn (30%), and cotton cloth (27.5%) was alarming. See Zhejiangsheng Jingji Yanjiu Zhongxin Bian (Zhejiang Provincial Economic Research Center), *Zhejiang shengqing* (The affairs of Zhejiang; Hangzhou, Zhejiang renmin chubanshe, 1986), p. 1058.

26. *Zhejiang ribao*, 27 May 1969, pp. 1,2.

27. CCP Hangzhou Municipal Committee (HMC) Organization Department Criticism Group, "A gang of villains who constantly 'created havoc' thoroughly shatter the Gang of Four's bourgeois factional system in Hangzhou," *HZRB*, 17 September 1977, pp. 1,3.

28. Ye Yonglie, *Rise and Fall of Wang Hongwen*, pp. 382–386.

29. See, *Zhonggong dangshi 170 ti wenda* (170 questions and answers on the history of the CCP; Shenyang, Liaoning renmin chubanshe, 1984), pp. 308–311.

30. *Zhonggong zhongfa 1977*, no. 37, in *Zhonggong nianbao, 1979*, VIII, 35, trans. in *Issues & Studies* 15:110 (January 1979).

31. Wang may have been a lightweight on the Politburo, despised even by Yao Wenyuan, but he could throw his weight around in Zhejiang. For Yao's views of Wang as a playboy and a vain, lazy, and useless person, see Suo Guoxin, *1967 nian de 78 tian—"eryue niliu" jishi* (Changsha, Hunan wenyi chubanshe,

1986), p. 14. Large excerpts have been translated in Keith Forster, ed., "78 Days in 1967—The True Story of the "February Countercurrent," *Chinese Law and Government* 22 (Spring 1989).

32. Ye Yonglie, *Rise and Fall of Wang Hongwen*, p. 406.

33. *Zhonggong zhongfa, 1977*, no. 37.

34. *Zhejiang shengqing*, pp. 991, 994.

35. Tie Ying, "Dongyuan qilai, wei shixian xin shiqi de zong renwu er fendou" (Get mobilized and strive to realize the general tasks of the new period; Report to the sixth Zhejiang Provincial CCP Congress, 25 May 1978), *HZRB*, 1 June 1978.

36. "A Gang of Villains." See also Chu Yang, "Chedi zalan 'sirenbang' zai Zhejiangde zichanjieji bangpai tixi" (Thoroughly smash the Gang of Four's bourgeois factional set-up in Zhejiang), *ZJRB*, 21 May 1977, p. 1.

37. Andrew J. Nathan, "A Factionalism Model for CCP Politics", *CQ* 53:41, 44 (January/March 1973).

38. CCP HMC Propaganda Department criticism group, "A loyal agent of the Gang of Four in Hangzhou," *HZRB*, 21 October 1977; Zhou Feng (secretary of the CCP HMC), "Dig out the secret traitor who opposed the Party and caused trouble," *HZRB*, 24 October 1977.

39. *HZRB*, 19 November 1977; Kong Xianlian, "How did the political rumor about 'there has been no change in Zhejiang for eighteen years' get about?" *HZRB*, 26 November 1977.

40. *HZRB*, 19 November 1977; criticism group of the Hangzhou Municipal Communications Office, "Smashing the system *(kou)* and restoring the group *(zu)* was a counter-revolutionary farce," *HZRB*, 23 November 1977.

41. *HZRB*, 5 April 1978; Chen Xia (secretary of the CCP HMC), "Crimes must be accounted for, the poison cleared away—an exposure and criticism of the antiparty crimes of the two former principal responsible members of the HMC," *HZRB*, 10 April 1978.

42. Lai Keke, "Zuo beitong wei liliang jizhong huoli shenru piDeng" (Turn grief into strength and concentrate our energies on thoroughly criticizing Deng), *HZRB*, 1 October 1976, p. 6; a critique of the article by Shang Jingcai of the Zhejiang Provincial Committee Propaganda Department, *HZRB*, 28 November 1976, pp. 2–3; Shen Weicai, "Cong Gao-Rao fandang lianmengde deli ganjiang dao 'sirenbang' de zhongshi dailiren" (From a capable person in the Gao [Gang]–Rao [Shushi] antiparty alliance to a loyal follower of the Gang of Four," *HZRB*, 17 August 1977; Shen Cai, "Yimian ceng ceng jiu "zouzipai" de heiqi—pipan 'sirenbang' zai woshengde yige dailiren "jiu. sanling" fandang heiwen" (A black flag to haul out "capitalist roaders" at all levels—a criticism of the "30 September" evil article [Lai Keke's article was originally published in *Zhejiang ribao* on 30 September 1976] by the "Gang of Four's" agent in our province), *HZRB*, 27 November 1977.

43. Chu Yang, "Selling himself and frenziedly attacking the Party—an exposure and criticism of the crimes of that agent installed in Zhejiang by the Gang of Four," *HZRB*, 2 November 1977.

44. For example, Weng visited Hangzhou University on 19 April 1974 and delivered a speech in which he praised the Liaoning "model student" who handed in a blank examination paper, Zhang Tiesheng. Briefing at Hangzhou University, 19 May 1978. Weng was, to all accounts, a powerful and effective orator.

45. *HZRB,* 26 July 1978.

46. See Tie Ying's own brief reference to these events in his article "Zhou Enlai zongli jiao wo zuo jingji gongzuo" (Premier Zhou Enlai taught me to carry out economic work), *Huainian Zhou Enlai* (In memory of Zhou Enlai; Beijing, Renmin chubanshe, 1986), p. 442; Ji Yangwen, "A shocking display of opposing the Party and destabilizing the army," *HZRB,* 9 February 1977.

47. Ji Yangwen, "A shocking display."

48. "Tan Ch'i-lung—The Dominant Influence in Hangchow Labour Turmoil," *Issues & Studies* 12:103 (February 1976).

49. Union Research Institute, *Hierarchies of the People's Republic of China, March 1975* (Hong Kong, 1975); *HZRB,* 23 July 1975, p. 1.

50. Criticism group of the Zhejiang Fine Arts College, "The pipedream of the Gang of Four and that villain of our province," *HZRB,* 23 January 1977; *HZRB,* 22 March 1977, 24 March 1977; criticism group of the CCP HMC Propaganda Department, "Evidence of Zhang Yongsheng's attempt to usurp power by remote control," *HZRB,* 17 May 1977; *RMRB,* 2 December 1977, p. 2; *HZRB,* 14 August 1978, 4 April 1979; *RMRB,* 15 April 1979, p. 1.

51. See Keith Forster, "Weng Senhe—Cultural Revolution Rebel from Hangzhou," *Australian Journal of Chinese Affairs* (in press).

52. Hua Guofeng, *Speech to the Second National Conference on Learning from Tachai in Agriculture* (Beijing, Foreign Languages Press, 1977), p. 13.

53. *Zhonggong nianbao, 1979,* VIII, 36.

54. *RMRB,* 9 December 1976, p. 3.

55. *HZRB,* 2 April 1977; Shen Chuyun, "After the clearing away of the 'four pests' the Hangzhou silk complex is again making great strides," *RMRB,* 17 May 1977, p. 2; criticism group of the Hangzhou Public Security Bureau, "An extremely ferocious counterrevolutionary gang," *HZRB,* 23 June 1977; criticism group of the Hangzhou Silk Bureau, "Iron-clad proof of Weng Senhe and He Xianchun ganging up to usurp power in the silk bureau," *HZRB,* 30 June 1977; criticism group of the printing and dying workshop of the Hangzhou silk complex, "Judge the 'two rushes' from three examples," *HZRB,* 4 July 1977; Criticism Groups of the Party committees of the CCP HMC Organization Department and Silk Bureau, "From a black model see the organizational basis of counterrevolutionary bourgeois factionalism," *HZRB,* 12 August 1977; criticism group of the CCP HMC Propaganda Department, "The Gang of Four's fiendish hatchet-man Weng Senhe," *HZRB,* 7 December 1977; *HZRB,* 17 April 1979.

56. *HZRB,* 29 January 1977; Criticism Group of the CCP HMC Propaganda Department, "The new-born counterrevolutionary He Xianchun," *HZRB,* 20 June 1977; provincial core criticism study class, "An outpost to plot and seize power—an exposure and criticism of the crimes of Zhang, Weng and He in using the municipal Workers' Congress to destabilize Zhejiang," *HZRB,* 19 July 1977;

criticism group of Hangzhou Oxygen Generator Plant, "Resolutely suppress the ringleaders of beating, smashing and looting," *HZRB,* 21 June 1977, p. 3; *HZRB,* 17 April 1979.

57. I have written at greater length about this campaign in "The Politics of Destabilization and Confrontation: The Campaign against Lin Biao and Confucius in Zhejiang Province, 1974," *CQ* 107:438–462 (September 1986).

58. *HZRB,* 3 March 1977.

59. Tie Ying, "Get mobilized."

60. From May 1973, on instructions from Mao, Wang Hongwen began participating in meetings of the Politburo as a nonvoting delegate. See Hu Hua, ed., *Zhongguo shehuizhuyi geming he jianshe shi jiangyi* (Teaching materials on the history of China's socialist revolution and construction; Beijing, Zhongguo renmin daxue chubanshe, 1985), p. 312.

61. Zhai Diaoshi, "Expose and criticize the Gang of Four's heinous crimes in opposing the army and throwing it into chaos," *HZRB,* 1 February 1977; Ji Yangwen, "A Shocking display"; criticism group of the PLA Hangzhou Garrison, "Expose and criticize the crimes of the Gang of Four and its trusted follower and lackey in plotting to hold the triple plenum," *HZRB,* 10 March 1977; criticism group ZPMD logistics unit, "Those who try to destroy the Great Wall will themselves be burned," *HZRB,* 14 September 1978; *Xinhua,* 21 September 1978, *SWB/FE/*5929/BII/11–12.

62. *HZRB,* 22 February 1977; Hangzhou Garrison Investigation Group, "The epitome of the 'second armed force,'" *HZRB,* 20 May 1977; *HZRB,* 14 March 1978; briefings at the Hangzhou silk complex, 12 January 1977, 7 November 1977, 11 November 1977; briefing at the Hangzhou Oxygen Generator Plant, 4 June 1978; briefing at the Hangzhou Iron and Steel Mill, 27 May 1979.

63. "The newborn counterrevolutionary He Xianchun"; "An outpost to plot and seize power."

64. See *China News Summary* 578 (13 August 1975), p. 1.

65. See *China News Analysis* 1013, p. 4; *Far Eastern Economic Review,* 30 July 1976, p. 30.

66. *HZRB,* 27 August 1978; "Struggling for truth: Recalling the heroic deeds of CCP member Zhang Jifa in fighting against the Gang of Four," *HZRB,* 7 November 1978.

67. "A jacklike group," *HZRB,* 11 August 1977.

68. Qiu Honggen, "From my two seizures see the wolfish ambition of Lin Biao and the Gang of Four," *HZRB,* 26 November 1978.

69. "Resisting the Gang of Four, persisting in learning from Daqing," *HZRB,* 10 April 1977, pp. 1, 2; briefing at the Hangzhou Gearbox Plant, 17 July 1977.

70. Even at the silk complex the anti-Weng forces apparently could muster 30% of the work force. See David Zweig, "The Case of Weng Sengho [sic]: The Rise and Fall of a "Revolutionary Rebel," notes from an interview conducted in Hong Kong, 30 October 1980, p. 4. I wish to thank David for sending me a copy of the transcript.

71. See Keith Forster, "The 1976 Ch'ing-ming Incident in Hangchow," *Issues & Studies* 22:20–1, 28 (April 1986).

72. For his definition of clientelist ties, see Nathan, "A Factionalism Model," p. 37.
73. Dittmer, "Bases of Power," p. 55.
74. The preceding paragraphs are based on Nathan, "A Factionalism Model," pp. 42–45.
75. "The Gang of Four's fiendish hatchet-man"; Bian Wen, "What was Wang Hongwen up to in his many surreptitious visits to Zhejiang," *HZRB*, 5 December 1976.
76. *HZRB*, 28 November 1976.
77. Nathan, "A Factionalism Model," pp. 45–52.
78. See *Feiqing yuebao*, pp. 84–85.
79. According to Pye, because the question of personnel replacements touches the essence of power, it is usually settled only after policy changes have been announced. Pye, *Dynamics of Chinese Politics,* pp. 192–196.
80. T. Tsou, "Prolegomenon to the Study of Informal Groups in CCP Politics," *CQ* 65:101–102 (March 1976).
81. Keith Forster, "Repudiation of the Cultural Revolution in China: The Case of Zhejiang," *Pacific Affairs* 59:5–27 (Spring 1986).
82. Oral sources.
83. For further details, see Forster, *Rebellion and Factionalism,* chap. 8.
84. See Deng Xiaoping, *Wenxuan,* pp. 5–27.
85. Alan P. L. Liu, "The Politics of Corruption in the People's Republic of China," *American Political Science Review* 77:613–615, 619 (September 1983).
86. See Dorothy J. Solinger, "Politics in Yunnan Province in the Decade of Disorder: Elite Factional Strategies and Central-Local Relations, 1967–1980," *CQ* 92 (December 1982), esp. pp. 628–629, 660–662.

Chapter 6. Neither Plan nor Market: Mao's Political Economy by Carl Riskin

I am indebted to Richard Baum, Mark Selden, Benjamin Ward, Christine Wong, and an anonymous reviewer for helpful criticisms of an earlier draft of this chapter.

1. See Robert Michael Field, "The Performance of Industry during the Cultural Revolution: Second Thoughts," *CQ* 108 (December 1987). For an argument that the official consumption growth rate is an overestimate, see ibid., pp. 637–638.
2. Carl Riskin, *China's Political Economy: The Quest for Development since 1949* (New York, Oxford University Press, 1987).
3. This is a particular definition among several possible ones. For instance, "politicization" could instead refer to the distortion of economic policy to aid a political party; or, more positively, to the inclusion in policymaking of redistributive, environmental, moral, ethical, and other criteria ignored by the market.
4. This defense rationale for *national* self-reliance appears to have been behind the massive, centrally controlled Third Front construction projects discussed in Chapter 7 of this volume. The concentration of central efforts on a relatively small num-

ber of large-scale projects is fully consistent with a policy of local "self-reliance," as well as with the argument of this chapter regarding Mao's antipathy to central administrative planning for the economy as a whole.

5. Thomas G. Rawski, "China's Industrial Performance, 1949–73," in Alexander Eckstein, ed., *Quantitative Measures of China's Economic Output* (Ann Arbor, University of Michigan Press, 1980), p. 150.

6. While I stress here its negative derivation from the logic of rejection of both plan and market, regional and local self-reliance also had a *positive* function, namely, to mobilize resources and provide incentives for local industrialization. This aspect is explored in Chapter 9 of this volume.

7. Mao Zedong, *A Critique of Soviet Economics,* ed. and trans. Moss Roberts (New York, Monthly Review Press, 1977), pp. 102–103.

8. Jiang Yiwei, "The Theory of an Enterprise-Based Economy," *Social Sciences in China* 1:55 (March 1980).

9. Xu Jinqiang, "Hold High the Great Red Banner . . . ," in Mark Selden, ed., *The People's Republic of China: A Documentary History of Revolutionary Change* (New York, Monthly Review Press, 1979), pp. 582–591.

10. The "two-one-three" system of management: "two" refers to the "two participations"—of workers in management and of cadres in labor; "one" refers to the "one reform" of irrational rules and regulations; "three" refers to "triple combination" technical work teams consisting of workers, technicians, and administrators. See Stephen Andors, *China's Industrial Revolution* (New York, Pantheon, 1977), p. 83.

11. Selden, *People's Republic of China,* pp. 591–592.

12. *China: Socialist Economic Development,* 3 vols. (Washington, D.C., World Bank, 1983), I, 46.

13. Ibid.

14. Ma Hong, "Strengthen Planned Economy, Improve Planning," *Zhongguo caimao bao* (China finance and trade), 20 April 1982, in *FBIS,* 12 May 1982, p. K3, emphasis added.

15. Liu Guoguang, Wu Jinglian, and Zhao Renwei, "Relationship Between Planning and Market as Seen by China in Her Socialist Economy," *Atlantic Economic Journal* 7:12–13 (December 1979).

16. *China: Socialist Economic Development,* I, 89.

17. *China: Long-Term Issues and Options,* Annexes A–E (Washington, D.C., World Bank, 1985), I, 17.

18. Riskin, *China's Political Economy,* pp. 262–263.

19. Wu Xiang, "The Open Road and the Log Bridge—A Preliminary Discussion on the Origins, Advantages and Disadvantages, Nature and Future of the Fixing of Farm Output Quotas for Each Household," *RMRB,* 5 November 1980, in *FBIS,* 7 November 1980, p. L23.

20. *China: Socialist Economic Development,* I, 94–95.

21. J. C. Liu, "A Note on China's Pricing Policies," paper presented to Workshop of the Department of Economics, State University of New York, pp. 5–6. See Riskin, *China's Political Economy,* pp. 242–248, for a discussion of this question.

22. The reader should keep in mind that gross output value double-counts inter-

mediate goods and thus inflates industrial output (which contains more intermediate inputs) much more than it does agricultural output. The absolute gap
shown in Table 3 is thus exaggerated relative to one based on net value added.

23. Irma Adelman and David Sunding, "Economic Policy and Income Distribution
in China," *Journal of Comparative Economics* 11:460 (September 1987). Although
this quotation refers to a later year, the statement holds as well for the end of
the Cultural Revolution period.

24. See, for example, Wu Jinglian and Zhou Shulian, "Correctly Handle the Relationship Between Readjustment and Restructuring," *RMRB*, 5 December 1980,
in *FBIS*, 29 December 1980, p. L24, for a statement of the case against the
system of central planning, and Zhang Zhuoyuan, "Introduction: China's Economy after the Cultural Revolution," in Lin Wei and Arnold Chao, eds., *China's
Economic Reforms* (Philadelphia, University of Pennsylvania Press, 1982), pp. 19–
20, for the alternative position.

25. Liu Guoguang, "Several Questions Regarding Comprehensive Balancing," *RMRB*,
13 April 1979, in *FBIS*, 30 April 1979, p. L4.

26. Sun Yefang, "Jiaqiang tongji gongzuo, gaige tongji zhidu" (Strengthen statistical work, reform the statistical system), *Jingji guanli* (Economic management)
2:5 (February 1981).

27. Ibid.

*Chapter 7. Industrial Policy during the Cultural Revolution: Military
Preparation, Decentralization, and Leaps Forward by Barry Naughton*

This paper was written while I was a Research Fellow at the Center for Chinese
Studies, University of Michigan. I wish to acknowledge financial support from the
Mellon Foundation through the American Council of Learned Societies.

1. The "big-push" strategy has also been called the Stalinist development strategy.
This term is historically accurate but carries a burden of political implication
that is perhaps best avoided. For a good discussion of the relation between the
"big-push" strategy and other aspects of the Chinese economic model, see Robert F. Dernberger, "The Chinese Search for the Path of Self-Sustained Growth
in the 1980's: An Assessment," in Joint Economic Committee, U.S. Congress,
China under the Four Modernizations (Washington, D.C., U.S. Government Printing Office, 1982), esp. pp. 33–35, 54–59.

2. Liu Suinian and Wu Qungan, *Zhongguo shehuizhuyi jingji jianshi* (An outline
history of China's socialist economy; Harbin, Heilongjiang Renmin chubanshe,
1985), pp. 306–308; *Zhou Enlai wenxuan* (Selected works of Zhou Enlai; Beijing, Renmin chubanshe, 1984), pp. 439–440.

3. Fang Weizhong, ed., *Zhonghua Renmin Gongheguo jingji dashiji, 1949–1980*
(Economic chronology of the People's Republic of China, 1949–1980; Beijing,
Zhongguo shehui kexue chubanshe, 1984), p. 374. The initial consumption
levels projected for 1970 were production of 300 kg of grain and 24 ft of textiles
per capita. According to the recollections of Xu Yi, 70% of investment was to
go into coastal areas, 20% to inland regions, and 10% to "intermediate areas.
"On the relation between system and production structure," *Caijing wenti yanjiu*

(Studies in finance and economic problems) 1 (1981), reprinted in *Renmin Daxue fuyin baokan ziliao: Guomin jingji yu jihua* (People's University reprints: National economy and plan) 4:57 (1981). The actual plan document is not available.

4. Fang Weizhong, *Jingji dashiji,* p. 379; *Mao Zedong sixiang wansui* (Chairman Mao's Thought; n.p.), pp. 497–499.

5. Fang Weizhong, *Jingji dashiji,* p. 379; Party history research room, CCP, *Zhongong dangshi dashi nianbiao* (Chronology of major events in CCP history; Beijing, Renmin chubanshe, 1987), p. 333. On the Gulf of Tonkin and the Chinese response, see George McT. Kahin, *Intervention: How America Became Involved in Vietnam* (New York, Knopf, 1986), pp. 219–225, 339–341. Kahin states on p. 220: "By the end of 1984 there was enough evidence to establish that no North Vietnamese attack took place on August 4. What is still not known . . . is whether the president as well as Congress was misled."

6. A comprehensive description of the Third Front, including the strategic rationale behind the policy, is available in Barry Naughton, "The Third Front: Defense Industrialization in the Chinese Interior," *CQ* 115:351–386 (September 1988).

7. Cui Xinheng et al., eds., *Sichuan chengshi jingji* (Sichuan urban economy; Chengdu, Sichuan kexue jishu chubanshe, 1985), pp. 128–130, 145–146, 161–162, 177, 192, and *Guanghui de chengjiu* (Glorious achievement; Beijing, Renmin chubanshe, 1984), I, 252–253; Zhou Taihe, ed., *Dangdai Zhongguo de jingji tizhi gaige* (Economic system reform in modern China; Beijing, Zhongguo shehui kexue chubanshe, 1984), p. 591; *Guizhou jingji shouce* (Guizhou economic handbook; Guiyang, Guizhou renmin chubanshe, 1984), pp. 202–203, 212; *Guizhou nianjin 1985* (1985 Guizhou yearbook; Guiyang, Guizhou renmin chubanshe, 1984), pp. 162, 542.

8. Sun Jingzhi, ed., *Zhongguo jingji dili gailun* (Outline of China's economic geography; Beijing, Shangwu yinshuguan chubanshe, 1983), p. 94; Hubei Electric Power Industry Office, "Rapid growth of the power industry," *Hubei 35 nian* (Hubei over 35 years; Wuhan, Hubei renmin chubanshe, 1984), pp. 61–62; Henan Machinery and Electronics Office, "Henan electronics industry advancing," *Zhongzhou yicai* (The heartland's new appearance; n.p., Henan renmin chubanshe, 1984), p. 62; No. 2 Automobile Factory, "A new automotive production base," *Hubei 35 nian,* pp. 178–184; Qiu Weigang and Yi Hui, "Third Front enterprises should be brought into full play," *Jingji yanjiu cankao ziliao* (Economic research reference materials) 51:36–45 (1982).

9. Fang Weizhong, *Jingji dashiji,* pp. 396, 398–399, 479; *Guizhou nianjian 1985,* pp. 162, 488–489, 492, 520; Qiu Weigang and Yi Hui, "Third Front enterprises," pp. 36–45; *Qinghai 35 Nian,* (Qinghai over 35 years; Xining, Qinghai renmin chubanshe, 1985), pp. 46, 68.

10. No. 2 Automobile Factory, "New automotive production base," pp. 178–183; Zhou Taihe, *Dangdai Zhongguo,* pp. 346–347.

11. *Zhongguo guding zichang toui tongji ziliao 1950–1985* (Statistical materials on fixed capital investment in China 1950–1985; Beijing, State Statistical Bureau, 1987), pp. 45–49; *ZGTJNJ 1987,* p. 469; *ZGTJNJ 1988,* p. 561. Investment that cannot be allocated to any province has been excluded from the national total.

Chinese discussions frequently include Shanxi Province in statistics on the Third Front, because of the construction in that province of a secure military headquarters for the Beijing region. Overall, however, Shanxi is not characterized by the large-scale industrial investment that typifies other Third Front regions, and it has not been included in Table 1.

12. *Zhongguo gongye jingji tongji ziliao 1986* (Chinese industrial economy statistical materials; Beijing, State Statistical Bureau, 1987), pp. 230–232.

13. For further discussion of this point, see Naughton, "Third Front."

14. Fang Weizhong, *Jingji dashiji,* p. 389; Peng Dehuai, *Memoirs of a Chinese Marshall* (Beijing, Foreign Languages Press, 1984), p. 523; *Guizhou jingji shouce,* p. 212.

15. Zhou Taihe, *Dangdai Zhongguo,* pp. 589–591; *Guizhou jingji shouce,* p. 212.

16. A partial exception to this statement needs to be made for the "small Third Front" policy, in which provinces were urged to set up their own Third Front regions in remote areas within their provincial boundaries. This undertaking may have absorbed important parts of the resources of individual provinces but amounted to less than 5% of the volume of the "big Third Front." A major example was the small Third Front region set up by the city of Shanghai, which was assigned land in rugged regions of southern Anhui because Shanghai itself has no hinterland. Compare Fang Weizhong, *Jingji dashiji,* pp. 385, 433, 442; "Anhui and Shanghai remake 'small Third Front' enterprises," *RMRB,* 10 March 1987, p. 2.

17. Michael Ellman suggested several years ago that the Chinese economic system be termed "indirect centralization," in the sense that the central leadership could use political and ideological tools to ensure that local leaders implemented central government priorities even without direct management of the economy from the center. This appears feasible only in those cases where central government priorities are clear and simple. Defense preparation is just such a priority, the meaning and importance of which is easily grasped by every administrative level. See Michael Ellman, *Socialist Planning* (Cambridge, Cambridge University Press, 1979).

18. Fang Weizhong, *Jingji dashiji,* pp. 283–383; Christine Wong, "Material Allocation and Decentralization: Impact of the Local Sector on Industrial Reform," in Elizabeth J. Perry and Christine Wong, eds., *The Political Economy of Reform in Post-Mao China,* Harvard Contemporary China Series, no. 2 (Cambridge, Council on East Asian Studies, 1985), esp. pp. 260–264; Zhou Taihe, *Dongdai Zhongguo,* pp. 117–123.

19. Fang Weizhong, p. 476.

20. *China Reconstructs* 21:5 (April 1972).

21. Fang Weizhong, *Jingji dashiji,* pp. 382–383; Zhou Taihe, *Dangdai Zhongguo,* pp. 117–123.

22. Zhou Taihe, *Dangdai Zhongguo,* pp. 131, 137, 348.

23. Yu Chaoxi and Liu Tongde, "Opinions on reforming the management and structure of the labor force," *Jingji yanjiu ziliao* 11:27–29 (1981).

24. For documentation of these problems, see Naughton, "Third Front."

25. *Zhongguo dabaike quanshu: Kuangye* (Encyclopedia Sinica: mining and metallurgy;

Beijing, 1984), p. 500; *Sichuan shengqing* (The situation in Sichuan Province; Chengdu, Sichuan renmin chubanshe, 1984), pp. 383–384; *Xinhua* reports translated in FBIS, 18 October 1983, and *SWB/FE/*7350/BII/S.

26. Fang Weizhong, *Jingji dashiji,* pp. 460–464; Zhao Jian and Liu Kexun, "The twisted path of development of the steel industry," *Jingji yanjiu ziliao* 7:3–4 (1981); "Bank of Construction reports on the current situation," *Gongye jingji guanli congkan* 2:8–10 (1982); Cai Ninglin and Wu Guoxian, "Shortening construction periods," *Gongye jingji guanli congkan* 2:2–6 (1982).

27. *ZGTJNJ 1983,* p. 354; Xue Baoding, "Several questions that should be attended to in the development of capital construction," *Caizheng yanjiu* (Fiscal studies) 4:60 (1985). The average cost of large projects climbed substantially in the 1980s.

28. Zhongguo Wuzi Jingji Xuehui (China Materials Economics Society), ed., *Zhongguo shehuizhuyi wuzi guanli tizhi shilue* (An outline history of China's socialist materials management system; Beijing, Wuzi chubanshe, 1983), pp. 50–51.

29. Barry Naughton, "The Decline of Control over Investment in Post-Mao China," in D. Lampton, ed., *Policy Implementation in Post-Mao China* (Berkeley, University of California Press, 1987).

30. Christine Wong, "Ownership and Control in Chinese Industry: The Maoist Legacy and Prospects for the 1980s," in Joint Economic Committee, U.S. Congress, *China's Economy Looks Toward the Year 2000* (Washington, D.C., Government Printing Office, 1986), I, 589.

31. Barry Naughton, "Sun Yefang: Toward a Reconstruction of Socialist Economics," in T. Cheek and C. Hamrin, eds., *China's Establishment Intellectuals* (White Plains, M.E., Sharpe, 1985).

32. Liu Suinian and Wu Qungan, *Zhongguo shehuizhuyi,* pp. 385, 390; Lin Senmu and Zhou Shulian, "Reducing the overextended capital construction front," *Hongqi* (Red flag) 3:9–13 (1981).

33. Fang Weizhong, *Jingji dashiji,* pp. 505–506. This is one of the most interesting passages in this fascinating book.

34. *Shandong shengqing* (The situation in Shandong Province; Jinan, Shandong renmin chubanshe, 1985), p. 433; Chen Dunjin, "Some opinions on the choice of fiscal allocations on bank loans in capital construction investment," in Board of Editors, *Jingji yanjiu* (Economic research), ed., *Guanyu woguo jingji guanli tizhi gaige de tantao* (An exploration of the reform of our economic management system; Jinan, Shandong renmin chubanshe, 1980), pp. 151–152. See also Lin Fatang, "Key Projects During the Sixth Five Year Plan," *Beijing Review,* 9 January 1984, pp. 25–26.

35. The outcome of the decentralization policy is described especially well in Wong, "Material Allocation and Decentralization." See also Wong, "Ownership and Control in Chinese Industry."

36. Zhou Taihe, *Dangdai Zhongguo,* pp. 153–156.

37. *New China News Agency* dispatch of 13 January 1977, cited in Alan S. Whiting, "Domestic Politics and Foreign Trade in the PRC, 1971–76," in *Chinese Domestic Politics and Foreign Policy in the 1970s,* Michigan Monographs in Chinese

Studies, no. 36 (Ann Arbor, Center for Chinese Studies, University of Michigan, 1979), pp. 60f.

38. *Zhongguo gongye jingji tongji ziliao* (Chinese industry economic statistical materials; Beijing, State Statistical Bureau, 1987), pp. 230–232. The larger group of "inland" provinces from 1952 to 1978 increased their share of state fixed industrial capital from 27% to 54% but increased their share of industrial output from 29% to only 37%. *Nankai Daxue xuebao* (Nankai University journal) 1:32 (1983); Luo Ping, "Internal conditions are daily riper," *Jingjixue zhoubao* (Economics weekly), 11 August 1985, p. 2; Zhou Changqing, "Do regional distribution reform and adjustment well, bring Third Front enterprises into play," *Jingji ribao,* 28 October 1985, p. 2.

39. Zhang Biwei, "Small scale iron and steel production must be readjusted," *Jingji guanli* 5:11–13 (1979); Christine Wong, "Rural Industrialization in the People's Republic of China: Lessons from the Cultural Revolution Decade," in Joint Economic Committee, U.S. Congress, *China under the Four Modernizations* (Washington, D.C., U.S. Government Printing Office, 1982), pp. 401–402, and "Material Allocation and Decentralization," pp. 265–266.

40. Feng Shaozhou, "Reform machinery output to conserve and expand energy supplies," *Gongye jingji guanli congkan* 3:9–10 (1981); Zhou Shulian, Wu Jinglian, and Wang Haibo, *Shehuizhuyi jingji jianshe he Makesizhuyi zhengzhi jingjixue* (Socialist economic construction and Marxist political economy; Beijing, Zhongguo shehui kexue chubanshe, 1982), p. 133.

41. Luo Ping, "Internal conditions," p. 2.

42. State Economic Commission Comprehensive Transport Research Institute, "How transportation became a weak link in national economic development," *Gongye jingji guanli congkan* 4:1–3 (1981). In the case of transportation in general, and railroads in particular, decentralized investment can be expected to contribute very little to total investment.

43. For a vivid account of these problems, see Wong, "Material Allocation and Decentralization."

Chapter 8. The Maoist "Model" Reconsidered: Local Self-Reliance and the Financing of Rural Industrialization by Christine P. W. Wong

I am indebted to Penelope Prime, Carl Riskin, and Terry Sicular for helpful comments on earlier drafts of this chapter. All remaining errors and conceptual problems are naturally my sole responsibility.

1. In this chapter "rural industry" will include industrial enterprises run by people's communes and production brigades, as well as state-owned industries at the county and prefectural levels that are oriented toward agriculture.

2. Christine P. W. Wong, "Maoism and Development: Rural Industrialization in the People's Republic of China," manuscript, table 1.1.

3. Shen Xingda and Chen Zhaoxin, "Small-scale chemical fertilizer plants are scattered throughout our rural villages", *Jingji daobao* (Economic bulletin), Hong

Kong, 1 January 1976, pp. 10–13. This information was supplemented by an interview with a plant official, June 1982.

4. This estimate is derived from total fixed assets of 8.8 billion yuan in small fertilizer plants in 1979. Li Wenji, "An enquiry into the future prospects of our country's small-scale nitrogenous fertilizer industry," Master's thesis, Beijing, Chinese Academy of Social Sciences, 1981, p. 4. Although these figures apply to the 1958–1979 period, the same proportions are assumed for the CR.

5. These estimates and their derivation are presented in Wong, "Maoism and Development," chap. 5.

6. In the late 1970s critics charged that rural small plants were acting as a drag on industrial growth by competing with the modern sector for scarce resources, especially energy, which they used with great inefficiency. In spite of mounting subsidies, losses racked up by rural enterprises totaled more than 2 billion yuan in 1978, more than half of total losses of all state-owned industry. Li Yue and Chen Shengchang, "The Scale of Industrial Enterprises," *Social Sciences in China* 2(2):55 (1981). The inefficient production of farm inputs in small plants also imposed high costs on the agricultural sector. For example, fertilizers produced by the small plants cost two to three times the world market price in terms of fertilizer/grain price ratios, and their quality was so poor that they were commonly blamed for the declining yield responses to fertilizer application that plagued Chinese agriculture. The farm machinery turned out by small plants was often of shoddy quality, contributing to very low rates of machinery utilization.

7. Under this plan, ambitious targets were laid out for a fifteen-year period, to be achieved in three phases. During the first phase, which was to take five to seven years, mechanized plowing would be expanded from about 15% of farmland in 1965 to over 25%, mechanized irrigation and drainage would be expanded from 32% of farmland to over 50%, and the application of chemical fertilizers would be raised from 13.5 to about 30 *jin* per *mou* (total farmland area was about 1.56 billion *mou* in 1965). *Zhongguo nongye nianjian, 1980* (Chinese agricultural yearbook; Beijing, Agricultural Press, 1981), p. 40. The processing of agricultural produce would be basically mechanized, and transport would be semimechanized. (*Semimechanized* means the use of manually or animal-operated machines. For transport, it meant the use of handcarts or animal-drawn carts to replace shoulder poles and other means of hand carriage.) During the second phase, to be completed by 1975, one-half to two-thirds of all farmland would be mechanically plowed, 60%–65% would be mechanically irrigated and drained, chemical fertilizer use would reach 50 *jin* per *mou*, and processing and transport would be further mechanized. By 1980, at the end of the third phase, mechanization should be basically completed. Fang Weizhong, ed., *Zhonghua Renmin Gongheguo jingji dashiji, 1949–1980* (Compendium of main economic events in the People's Republic of China, 1949–1980; Beijing, Chinese Academy of Social Sciences Press, 1984), pp. 412–413.

8. Fang Weizhong, *Jingji dashiji*, p. 467. The five small industries included chemical fertilizers, farm machinery, iron and steel, cement, and energy (coal mines and hydroelectric stations).

9. Interview in Beijing, May 1982; Ministry of Agriculture, Policy Research Office, ed., *Zhongguo nongye jiben qingkuang* (The basic situation in Chinese agriculture; Beijing, Agricultural Press, 1979), pp. 51–53.

10. This is based on two estimates: first, that fixed assets totaled over 45 billion yuan for the five small industries, from Wong, "Maoism and Development"; and second, that the ratio of working to fixed capital in county-level enterprises is 42%, based on 1980 data from the Office of the Leading Group for the State Council National Industrial Census, *Zhonghua Renmin Gongheguo 1985 nian gongye pucha ziliao* (Materials from the 1985 industrial census of the People's Republic of China; Beijing, Chinese Statistical Press, 1987), VI, 216–217.

11. This designation is strictly for the purpose of distinguishing between funds specifically allocated for rural industrialization from those that were not, and should not be confused with "extrabudgetary" funds. Some of the "informal" funds are "extrabudgetary," such as the locally retained depreciation funds (see below). But others, profits and taxes diverted for use in rural industrial investment, are "informal" but not "extrabudgetary."

12. *1982 Zhongguo jingji nianjian* (Almanac of China's economy; Beijing, Economic Management Press, 1982), p. IV–30; and Zhou Taihe, *Dangdai Zhongguo de jingji tizhi gaige* (Systemic reform of the contemporary Chinese economy; Beijing, Chinese Social Sciences Press, 1984), p. 143. For an excellent account of the financial decentralization process, see Barry Naughton, "The Decline of Central Control over Investment in Post-Mao China," in D. M. Lampton, ed., *Policy Implementation in Post-Mao China* (Berkeley, University of California Press, 1987). Naughton estimates that as much as two-thirds of these funds was used for investment in new construction and expansion.

13. *ZGTJNJ 1983* (Beijing, State Statistical Bureau, 1983), p. 360.

14. Zhou Taihe, *Dangdai Zhongguo*, pp. 116–117.

15. Fieldwork in Guangdong, June–July 1982.

16. Fang Weizhong, *Jingji dashiji*, p. 411.

17. Interview in Guangdong, June 1982.

18. *New China News Agency*, 7 October 1975; in U.S. Consulate, Hong Kong, *Survey of China Mainland Press* 5960:213–214 (October 1975).

19. Fang Weizhong, *Jingji dashiji*, p. 467.

20. Zhou Taihe, *Dangdai Zhongguo*, pp. 493–494.

21. Interviews in Shandong, Guangdong, and Beijing, 1981–82. These practices were earlier reported by Carl Riskin and Jon Sigurdson; see Riskin, "China's Rural Industries: Self-reliant Systems or Independent Kingdoms?" *CQ* 73 (March 1978); and Sigurdson, "Rural Industry—A Traveller's View," *CQ* 18 (April–June 1972).

22. *RMRB*, 29 February 1980.

23. Wong, "Maoism and Development," table 1.1.

24. For an assessment of the performance of the five small industries, see Wong, "Maoism and Development." Earlier assessments were available in Christine P. W. Wong, "Rural Industrialization in the People's Republic of China: Lessons from the Cultural Revolution," in Joint Economic Committee, U.S. Congress, *China under the Four Modernizations* (Washington, D.C., U.S. Government Print-

ing Office, 1982), and Wong, "Intermediate Technology for Development: Small-Scale Chemical Fertilizer Plants in China," *World Development* 14:1329–1346 (October/November 1986).

25. The implicit comparison is with the alternative method whereby the central government collected all revenues and then allocated them for specific uses in rural industry.

26. This is of course the most important argument for centralizing management.

27. See n. 5.

28. See, for example, Alexander Eckstein, *China's Economic Development: The Interplay of Scarcity and Ideology* (Ann Arbor, University of Michigan Press, 1975), esp. chap. 8; Dwight Perkins and Shahid Yusuf, *Rural Development in China* (Baltimore, Johns Hopkins University Press, 1984), chap. 2.

29. See, esp., Wong, "Rural Industrialization."

Chapter 9. Central Provincial Investment and Finance: The Cultural Revolution and Its Legacy in Jiangsu Province by Penelope B. Prime

1. In terms of economics, the discussion of central-local relations concerns how much control the post-1949 central government has had over key economic variables relative to provincial and subprovincial governments and enterprises. A major debate on this subject was initiated by Nicholas Lardy and Audrey Donnithorne in a series of articles and comments in *China Quarterly* in 1975 and 1976 in which Lardy analyzed revenue transfers between provinces as evidence of central control after the 1958 decentralization, while Donnithorne stressed that local resource retention was increasing. See Nicholas R. Lardy, "Centralization and Decentralization in China's Fiscal Management," *CQ* 61:25–60 (March 1975), and "Reply," *CQ* 66:340–354 (June 1976); Audrey Donnithorne, "China's Cellular Economy: Some Economic Trends since the Cultural Revolution," *CQ* 66:605–619 (June 1976), and "Comment on 'Centralization and Decentralization in China's Fiscal Management,' " *CQ* 66:328–340 (June 1976).

2. *ZGTJNJ 1986* (Beijing, State Statistical Bureau, 1986), p. 611. See also Chapter 7 in this volume.

3. For example, data are not available that separate provincially run state enterprises from those run by cities and counties within the province, or that indicate the amount of industrial output contributed by small-scale, locally run state enterprises.

4. Rudong xian bianshi xiuzhi bangongshi, *Rudong xianzhi* (Rudong County records; Nanjing, Jiangsu renmin chubanshe, 1983), p. 173.

5. The provincial income figures used throughout this chapter are in current prices and come from Jiangsu tongji ju, *Guanghui de sanshiwu nian: Jiangsu sheng quom jingji he shehui fazhan tongji ziliao, 1949–1983* (The glorious thirty-five years: Statistics on Jiangsu's national economy and social development, 1949–1983; Nanjing, Jiangsu tongji ju, 1984), pp. 19–20. Provincial income includes output of goods and services of all enterprises located within the geographic boundaries of the province, including those directly managed by central ministries in Beijing.

6. The increases in the proportion of central and total investment to provincial income after 1974 probably reflect the shift in the Third Front policy, and later the coastal-led strategy of the 1980s.

7. Calculated from table 3.7, p. 58, Penelope B. Prime, "The Impact of Self-Sufficiency on Regional Industrial Growth and Productivity in Post-1949 China: The Case of Jiangsu Province," PhD dissertation, University of Michigan, 1987.

8. Li Chengrui, "Shinian nei luan qijian woguo jingji qingkuang fenxi" (Analysis of China's economic situation during the ten years of internal disorder), *Jingji yanjiu* (Economic research) 1:29 (January 1984), in *FBIS,* 7 March 1984, pp. K2–K15; and *ZGTJNJ 1984,* p. 32.

9. When decentralization occurred, most centrally run enterprises became part of the province's jurisdiction. As a result, their profits and tax payments became part of the province's collected revenues. At the same time, since data on output of goods and services are collected on a geographic basis, decentralization would not affect the measurement of provincial income. The impact of this change in accounting will be considered in this section.

10. The figures for revenue remittances in Table 8 are rough estimates calculated as the difference between total provincial revenues and total provincial expenditures. These aggregate figures give imperfect estimates since, for example, there is no way to know whether part of the revenue in a given year was surplus carried over from the previous year. More important, it would be ideal to be able to separate central subsidies to the province from strictly provincial revenue within the provincial budget. If revenues include central subsidies, however, it is likely the expenditure side does as well; thus the method used here results is an estimate closer to net remittances. When I compared my estimates with official remittance rates for the province and with estimates made directly from budgets, all the estimates were in the same ballpark, but mine were generally lower (Prime, "Impact of Self-Sufficiency," table 3.1, p. 43). This is what we would expect of net rates.

11. Some support for this is given in Nicholas R. Lardy, *Economic Growth and Distribution in China* (Cambridge, Cambridge University Press, 1978).

Chapter 10. Arts Policies of the Cultural Revolution: The Rise and Fall of Culture Minister Yu Huiyong by Richard Kraus

The preparation of this chapter was supported by a grant from the Joint Committee on Chinese Studies of the American Council of Learned Societies and the Social Science Research Council, financed in part by the Ford Foundation, the Andrew W. Mellon Foundation, and the National Endowment for the Humanities.

1. This assessment is Bell Yung's, in "Model Opera as Model: From *Shajiabang* to *Sagabong,*" in Bonnie S. McDougall, ed., *Popular Chinese Literature and Performing Art in the People's Republic of China, 1949–1979* (Berkeley, University of California Press, 1984), p. 184.

2. Biographical information about Yu is incomplete and comes mostly from his enemies. The likely year of his birth is 1932, following Jin Dongfang, "Guanyu

Yu Huiyong" (About Yu Huiyong), *Mingbao yuekan* (Mingbao monthly) 131:24–25 (November 1976).

3. "Comrade Ma Shao-po's Exposé," *Documents of the Central Committee of the Chinese Communist Party, Chung-fa (1977) No. 37, Part VI, Issues & Studies* (hereafter *Document of the Central Committee*) 15:104 (January 1979).

4. He Luting, "The Question of National Music," *RMRB*, 11 September 1956.

5. Snobbery was not limited to Shanghai. A Guangzhou music professor claimed that "the transferred children of workers and peasants cannot learn Western musical instruments, but they may study national music," and argued for a quota on such students. "Lu Zhongren choushi" (The stinking history of Lu Zhongren), Guangzhou, *Dongfeng wenyi* (East wind literature and art), 31 January 1968.

6. Yu Yuiyong, "Peng Boshan—minjian yinyue de siduitou" (Peng Boshan—sworn enemy of folk music), *Renmin yinyue* (People's music) 30:4 (August 1955).

7. Yu's next contribution to *People's Music* was much tamer, although it still bore a political edge. In 1962 Yu argued that artistic taste was socially conditioned and that musicians could not simply perform what they wanted without regard for the audience. By indirectly criticizing approaches that reduced artistic issues to the questions of inspiration and genius, Yu went against the elitist tide of the early 1960s. Yu Huiyong, "Geren yishu fengge de fazhan" (The development of individual artistic style), *Renmin yinyue* 3–4 (November 1962).

8. Yu Huiyong, "Guanyu wuoguo minjian yinyue diaose de mingming" (On the names of tonal systems used in our nation's folk music), *Yinyue yanjiu* (Music study) 2 (1959), and "Guanyu bianbie diaose wenti" (On the problem of distinguishing tonal systems) *Yinyue yanjiu* 6 (1959). Yu's work is discussed in Godwin Yuen's 1988 manuscript "Stylistic Development in Chinese Revolutionary Song (1919–1940)," pp. 65–84. See also Ding Xicai and Ju Xiufang, "Guanyu 'Yulin Xiaoqu' he Yu Huiyong qishe taoming de beilie biaoyan" (About 'Tunes of Yulin' and Yu Huiyong's base performance of gaining fame by deceiving the public), *Renmin yinyue* 4:31–32 (1979).

9. "Expose and Criticize the Counterrevolutionary Crimes of Yu Hui-yung, Sworn Follower of the Gang of Four," Beijing Domestic Service in Mandarin (9 December 1977), in *FBIS*, 14 December 1977, pp. E14–E18.

10. Hsieh Wen-ping, "A Fierce Struggle for Control of the Peking Opera Stage—The Production and Staging of *On the Docks*, a Peking Opera on a Revolutionary Contemporary Theme," in Chiang Ching, *On the Revolution of Peking Opera* (Peking, Foreign Languages Press, 1968), pp. 27–33.

11. "Jiang Qing Tongzhi dui jingju 'Haigang' de yijian" (Comrade Jiang Qing's opinions on the Beijing opera, "On the Docks"), in *Jiang Qing tongzhi lun wenyi* (Comrade Jiang Qing discusses literature and art; May 1968), pp. 112–113.

12. Shanghaishi Wenhuaju Pipanzu, "Huan Yu Huiyong de fangeming zhenmianmu" (Reveal Yu Huiyong's true counterrevolutionary face), *Renmin yinyue* 5:26–27 (May 1977).

13. "A Collection of Chou Yang's Counter-Revolutionary Revisionist Speeches," in *Selections from China Mainland Magazines* 646:14 (March 1969).

14. See "Guanyu 'xie zhongjian renwu' de cailiao" (Materials concerning "Writing

of middle characters"), *Wenyi bao* (Arts news) 8–9 (1964). The middle-characters controversy is described in Merle Goldman, "The Chinese Communist Party's 'Cultural Revolution' of 1962–64," in Chalmers Johnson, ed., *Ideology and Politics in Contemporary China* (Seattle, University of Washington Press, 1973), pp. 246–252.

15. Mao had stressed culture for workers, peasants, and soldiers in his Yan'an talks because there was no urban middle-class population in Yan'an. However, he also referred approvingly to earlier efforts to reach "students, office workers, and shop assistants" in Shanghai. See *Selected Readings from the Works of Mao Tsetung* (Beijing, Foreign Languages Press, 1971), pp. 253–254. See also my "Cultural Politics and the Political Construction of Audiences in China," in Dorothy J. Solinger, ed., *Three Visions of Chinese Socialism* (Boulder, Westview Press, 1984), pp. 58–60.

16. Yu Hui-yung, "The Revolution of Peking Opera Is a Great Victory for the Thought of Mao Tse-tung," *Hongqi* (Red flag) 8 (May 1967), in *Joint Publications Research Service* 41549–8, 26 May 1967.

17. Five of the twenty-nine articles in the *He Luting pipan wenti huibian* (Collection on the question of criticizing He Luting; Hong Kong, Yangkai shubao gongyingshe, n.d.) are from Yu's department.

18. "Exposé by Comrades Chang Li-hui and Yen Hsing," *Document of the Central Committee* 15:105–106 (January 1979).

19. Gao Gejin, "Cong Yu Huiyong de yifengxin shuoqi" (Speaking of a letter of Yu Huiyong), *Renmin dianying* (People's film) 10:9–10 (1977); "Exposé by the Party Committee of the Shanghai Institute of Music" (26 March 1977), *Document of the Central Committee* 15:104–105 (January 1979); Li Xiaoming, "Wo suo renshi de Wang Kun dajie" (The elder sister Wang Kun that I know), *Jing bao* (The mirror) 20:49 (March 1979); Xiao Ding and Xu Yin, "Yinggutou yinyuejia He Luting" (Hard-boned musician He Luting), *Jiefang ribao* (Liberation daily), 13 January 1979, reprinted in *Renmin yinyue* 10 (February 1979).

20. After his arrest Yu explained his rise as "nothing but the doing of Chiang Ch'ing and Chang Ch'un-ch'iao." "Yu Hui-yung's Account" (19 February 1977), *Document of the Central Committee* 15:106 (January 1979).

21. Xu Qian, "Zhihui zuoe, daodi miewang" (Capable only of evil, thoroughly destroyed), *Renmin dianying,* 10:6 (1977); Gao Gejin, "Cong Yu Huiyong de yifengxin shuoqi," p. 9.

22. See Andrew Walder, *Chang Ch'un-qiao and Shanghai's January Revolution* (Ann Arbor, University of Michigan Center for Chinese Studies, 1978).

23. Jiang complained to a forum of cultural workers in November 1967, "I have not been able to keep track of the plays, music and movies which you produce, as I did in the earlier years when I was together with you in the specific task of literary and artistic revolution." "Talks of Comrade Chiang Ch'ing," *CCP Documents of the Great Proletarian Cultural Revolution, 1966–1967* (Hong Kong, Union Research Institute, 1968), p. 596.

24. In questions about fine arts, Jiang similarly relied on her daughter, who once represented Jiang in seven meetings with delegates of the Zhejiang Fine Arts Academy. See "Excerpts from Speech by Comrade Chiang Ch'ing on May 19 in

an Interview with Chang Yung-sheng, Vice Chairman of the Chekiang Provincial Revolutionary Committee," Canton *Huo-chu t'ung-hsun* (Torch bulletin) 1 (July 1968), in *Survey of China Mainland Magazines* 622:6–10 (August 1968).

25. Yu Huiyong, "Huanhu Mao Zhuxi geming wenyi luxian di xin shengli" (Hail the new victory of Chairman Mao's revolutionary line in literature and art), *RMRB,* 6 July 1968.

26. "Comrade Ma Shao-po's Exposé," p. 104.

27. "Xin shidai de 'kuangren' " (The 'madman' of the modern age), Beijing *Wenyi pipan* (Literature and art criticism), 10 May 1967. See David Milton and Nancy Dall Milton, *The Wind Will Not Subside* (New York, Pantheon, 1976), pp. 232–234.

28. "Talks of Comrade Chiang Ch'ing," pp. 599–600.

29. A similar system operates in the United States, where local amateur performers are often judged on their fidelity to "official" movie or original-cast versions of Broadway shows.

30. On Tan, and Cultural Revolution arts policy in general, see Colin Mackerras, *The Performing Arts in Contemporary China* (London, Routledge and Kegan Paul, 1981), p. 20.

31. "Talks of Comrade Chiang Ch'ing," p. 599.

32. For instance, see the nearly 400-page manual for *Haigang* (On the docks) (Shanghai, Renmin wenxue chubanshe, 1972).

33. See Ellen Judd, "China's Amateur Drama: The Movement to Popularize the Revolutionary Model Operas," *Bulletin of Concerned Asian Scholars* 15:26–35 (January–February 1983). In a notorious case of 1968, a singer was shot for altering *Shajiabang.* See Perry Link, ed., *Roses and Thorns: The Second Blooming of the Hundred Flowers in Chinese Fiction, 1979–1980* (Berkeley, University of California Press), p. 111.

34. *Summary of the Forum on the Work in Literature and Art in the Armed Forces with Which Comrade Lin Piao Entrusted Comrade Chiang Ching* (Peking, Foreign Languages Press, 1968); "The General Political Department's Request for Instructions Concerning the Proposal to Revoke the Summary of the February 1966 Forum on the Work in Literature and Art in the Armed Forces" (26 March 1979), *Issues & Studies* 20:91 (September 1984).

35. Roxane Witke, *Comrade Chiang Ch'ing* (Boston, Little, Brown, 1977), p. 326.

36. "Jiang Qing tongzhi he Shanghai Wudao Xuexiao 'Baimaonu' Juzu quanti gongzhi zuotanshi de jianghua" (Comrade Jiang Qing's talk with the comrades of the "White-Haired Girl" Troupe of the Shanghai Ballet School; 25 April 1967), in *Jiang Qing tongzhi lun wenyi,* pp. 167–168.

37. Talks of 9 and 12 November 1967, *CCP Documents of the Great Proletarian Cultural Revolution, 1966–1967* (Hong Kong, Union Research Institute, 1968), p. 601. See also "Chen Boda, Jiang Qing deng shouzhang jiejian sige yangbanxi danwei de zuotan jiyao" (Summary of the conversation of Chen Boda, Jiang Qing, and other leaders in receiving four model opera units; 9 November 1967), in *Jiang Qing tongzhi lun wenyi,* p. 171.

38. Witke, *Comrade Chiang Ch'ing,* p. 451.

39. Xu Qian, "Zhihui zuoe, daodi miewang," p. 7.

40. I discuss both of these episodes in my *Pianos and Politics in China: Middle-Class Ambitions and the Struggle over Western Music* (New York, Oxford University Press, 1989), chap. 5.

41. Lowell Dittmer, *China's Continuous Revolution: The Post-Revolution Epoch, 1949–1981* (Berkeley, University of California Press, 1987), p. 198.

42. Behind the scenes Yu actively opposed facilitating television broadcast arrangements for Nixon's 1972 visit to China. When Chinese leaders met to consider the request of Alexander Haig and Ron Zeigler for aid, Yu Huiyong "took the floor first, saying we should absolutely not allow Nixon to publicize himself through television to the people of the United States and the world from China." Xiong Xianghui, "Zhou Enlai a Remarkable Statesman," *Beijing Review*, 7–13 March 1988, p. 26.

43. Chu Lan, "Keep to the Correct Orientation and Uphold the Philosophy of Struggle—Notes on Studying Chairman Mao's *Talks at the Yenan Forum on Literature and Art*," *Peking Review*, 31 May 1974, pp. 13–15; Chu Lan, "Keep to the Road of Integration with Workers and Peasants—Notes on Studying Chairman Mao's *Talks at the Yenan Forum on Literature and Art*," *Peking Review*, 20 June 1975, pp. 11–13.

44. Chu Lan, "Zai maodun chongtuzhong suzao wuchangjieji yingxiong dianxing—ping changpian xiaoshuo *Yanyang tian*" (Mold models of proletarian heroism amidst the conflict of contradictions—critique of the novel *Bright Sunny Skies*), *RMRB*, 5 May 1974, in *Xinhua yuebao* 5:197–199 (1974); Chu Lan, "Comments on the Shansi Opera "Going Up to Peach Peak Three Times," *Peking Review*, 15 March 1974, pp. 8–9, 23.

45. Ch'u Lan, "A Decade of Revolution in Peking Opera," *Hung-ch'i* 7 (July 1974), in *Survey of People's Republic of China Magazines* 785:80–88 (August 1974). Much of this article is a relatively thoughtful review of problems in implementing opera reform. Many found it distasteful for raising Jiang Qing's speech to the level of a classic, comparable to Mao's Yan'an talks.

46. The London Philharmonic played Dvorak's Eighth Symphony, Brahms' Violin Concerto, as well as music by Haydn, Vaughn Williams, Elgar, and Beethoven.

47. Hu Pai-ping and Yu Chiung, "A Political Scheme Cannot Be Covered Up with Unpleasant Noise—Commenting on the Gang of Four's So-called Criticism of Absolute Music," Peking Domestic Service, 6 November 1977, in *FBIS*, 10 November 1977, pp. E9–E10.

48. Chu Lan, "Yingdang zhongshi jiechang taolun" (We should pay attention to this discussion), in *Lun yinyue de jiejixing* (On the class character of music; Beijing, Renmin chubanshe, 1975), pp. 1–7.

49. "Grasp the Essence, Deepen the Criticism," reprinted as "Criticize the Revisionist Viewpoint in Music," *Peking Review*, 1 March 1974, pp. 18–19.

50. Chu Lan, "Shenru pipan zichanjieji de renxinglun" (Penetratingly criticize capitalism's theory of human nature), in *Lun yinyue de jiejixing*, pp. 12–23.

51. Hu Pai-ping and Yu Chiung, "A Political Scheme."

52. See Ellen Johnston Laing, *The Winking Owl: Art in the People's Republic of China* (Berkeley, University of California Press, 1988), chap. 8.

53. I examine this issue further in *Pianos and Politics in China*.

54. Han Guohuang, "The Classification of Chinese Music with Titles," *Ming bao yuekan* 165:30–33 (September 1979); Han Kuo-huang, "Titles and Program Notes in Chinese Musical Repertoires," *World of Music* 38:67–75 (1985).

55. "Chen Boda, Jiang Qing deng shouzhang jiejian sige," p. 174.

56. Hou Dezhang, "Jiang Qing yangbantuan chuguo xianchou ji" (A record of Jiang Qing's model opera troupe showing its incompetence abroad), *Zhengming* 54–55:68–71, 67–71 (April and May 1982).

57. McDougall, "Writers and Performers," p. 293.

58. Shanghaishi Wenhuaju Pipanzu, "Huan Yu Huiyong de fangeming zhen-mianmu" (Reveal Yu Huiyong's true counterrevolutionary face), *Renmin yinyue* 5:26–27 (1977).

59. McDougall, "Writers and Performers," pp. 284–285.

60. Paul Clark, remarks at the Conference on New Perspectives on the Cultural Revolution, Harvard University, 16 May 1987.

61. "Exposé and Account of Chang Po-fan, Former Responsible Person of the Writing Group of the Department of Culture," *Document of the Central Committee* 15:108 (February 1979); Wenhuabu pipanzu, "Wenyi zuopin 'duo' yu 'shao' wentishang de yichang jilie douzheng" (A fierce struggle over the question of "many" or "few" literary and art works), *GMRB,* 19 March 1977.

62. Criticism Group of the Central Broadcasting Affairs Bureau, "The 'Gang of Four' Cannot Shirk Responsibility for Their Crimes in Brutally Encircling and Suppressing the Broadcast of Literature and Art," *RMRB,* 2 February 1977, in *Survey of the People's Republic of China Press* 6300:87 (March 1977); "Song Recitals Popular in China's Cities and Countryside," *New China News Agency,* 23 May 1976, in *Survey of the People's Republic of China Press* 6107:72 (June 1976).

63. McDougall, "Writers and Performers," p. 288.

64. Ch'u Lan, "A Decade of Revolution in Peking Opera," pp. 83, 86.

65. "Chen Boda, Jiang Qing deng shouzhang jiejian sige," p. 173.

66. Witke, *Comrade Chiang Ch'ing,* p. 403.

67. Paul Clark, "The Film Industry in the 1970s," in McDougall, *Popular Chinese Literature and Performing Arts,* pp. 177–196.

68. Guo Leibu, "Jiqi jiluo di Li Desheng yinhe churen junxiao zhengwei?" (How did the up and down Li Desheng become political commissar of the Military Academy?), *Jing bao* 104:38–39 (March 1986).

69. See Revolutionary Rebel Corps and "Long Cord in Hand" Rebel Squad of Chinese Dramatists Association, "Excerpts of Sinister Words of T'ao Chu, Lin Mo-han, Ch'i Yen-ming, T'ian Han, and Yang Han-sheng at Black Canton Meeting," Peking *Hsi-chu chan-pao* (Drama combat bulletin), 24 June 1967, in *Survey of the China Mainland Press—Supplement* 203:38 (September 1967).

70. McDougall, "Writers and Performers," p. 298.

71. An excellent analysis of political infighting of the "late" CR is in Dittmer, *China's Continuous Revolution,* pp. 108–209.

72. Richard Kraus, "Bai Hua: The Political Authority of a Writer," in Carol Lee Hamrin and Timothy Cheek, eds., *China's Establishment Intellectuals* (Armonk, M. E. Sharpe, 1986), pp. 188–189.

73. Ch'u Lan, "Singing Praise for Which Educational Line?" (4 April 1974), *Document of the Central Committee* 15:98–100 (March 1979).

74. "Comrade Chang P'ing-hua's Exposé" (6 November 1976), *Document of the Central Committee* 15:102–105 (March 1979).

75. "Verbatim Record of Chairman Mao's Talks with Comrade Teng Hsiao-p'ing in Early July, 1975," *Document of the Central Committee* 15:101 (February 1979).

76. "Full Text of Chairman Mao's Written Statement of July 14, 1975," *Document of the Central Committee* 15:101–102 (February 1979).

77. *Document of the Central Committee* 15:87 (March 1979).

78. In addition, the director and scriptwriter for the film *Haixia* wrote to Mao on 25 July, complaining about their treatment by the Culture Ministry. Mao had the letter distributed to the Political Bureau. This film was backed by Deng Xiaoping and Zhou Enlai. See *Document of the Central Committee* 15:99–103 (April 1979).

79. "The Report Submitted to Chiang Ch'ing by Yu Hui-yung and Hao Liang" (10 March 1975), *Document of the Central Committee* 15:89–94 (March 1979).

80. "Record of Chiang Ch'ing's Phone Call to Yu Hui-yung on June 26, 1975," *Document of the Central Committee* 15:102–105 (April 1979).

81. "Exposé and Account of Chang Po-fan," p. 108.

82. *Document of the Central Committee* 15:94 (March 1979).

83. "The 'Gang of Four' Instigated Their Cronies Like Yu Hui-yung and Others to Dish Up Large Quantities of the So-called 'Investigation Reports' to Oppose Chairman Mao's Criticism," *Document of the Central Committee* 15:104–105 (February 1979).

84. Ch'u Lan, "Persist in Revolution in Literature and Art, Hit Back at the Right Deviationist Wind to Reverse Verdicts," *Hung-ch'i* 3 (March 1976), in *Survey of the People's Republic of China Magazines* 863:10–16 (March 1976).

85. "Yu Hui-yung's Account" (1 March 1977), in *Document of the Central Committee* 14:95–96 (September 1978).

86. Yu Hui-yung, "A Report Concerning the Arrangements for 'Writing about the Struggle Against the Capitalist-Roaders' " (20 August 1976), in *Document of the Central Committee* 14:96–98 (September 1978). See also Chen Cong and Ren Dao, "Yangmou wenyi yu Huiyong" (Conspiratorial literature and art and Yu Huiyong), *Renmin dianying* 10:2–4 (1977).

87. "Chang P'ing-hua's Speech to Cadres on the Cultural Front" (23 July 1978), *Issues & Studies* 14:92–93 (December 1978).

88. Personal interview with pianist Yin Chengzong (13 May 1987), New York.

89. Zhonggong Shanghai Yinyuexueyuan Weiyuanhui, "Ba Yu Huiyong yashang lishi de shenpantai" (Bring Yu Huiyong before the history's court), *Renmin yinyue* 5:28–29 (1977); Wenhuabu Pipanzu (Ministry of Culture Criticism Group), "Jie 'Sirenbang' sidang Yu Huiyong de laodi" (Expose the unsavory past of Yu Huiyong, sworn follower of the 'Gang of Four'), *RMRB*, 5 November 1977; Shanghai Conservatory CCP Committee, "Deepen the Exposure and Criticism of the Gang of Four; Thoroughly Settle Accounts with Yu Hui-yung," reported in Shanghai City Service in Mandarin (28 August 1977), in *FBIS*, 30 August 1977, pp. G7–G8.

90. Roderick MacFarquhar, *Contradictions among the People, 1956–1957*, Vol. I of *The Origins of the Cultural Revolution* (New York, Columbia University Press, 1974), pp. 217–273.

91. Quoted in Byung-joon Ahn, *Chinese Politics and the Cultural Revolution: Dynamics of Policy Processes* (Seattle, University of Washington Press, 1976), p. 166.

92. "There was hardly a single work of written literature produced in the 1950s and early 1960s that had a genuine claim to literary distinction. The performing arts fared slightly better, though in general the same perceptions could apply." McDougall, "Writers and Performers," p. 280.

93. See Lowell Dittmer, "Bases of Power in Chinese Politics: A Theory and an Analysis of the Fall of the 'Gang of Four,' " *World Politics* 31:26–61 (October 1978).

Chapter 11. Models and Misfits: Rusticated Youth in Three Novels of the 1970s by Richard King

1. In some cases rotating teams of propagandists criticized and cajoled recalcitrant youths around the clock until they gave way and volunteered. Personal interviews with returned Shanghainese, May 1981.

2. *Hongse jiaxin* (Red letters home; Shanghai, Renmin chubanshe, 1973) is a collection of such letters.

3. Guo Xianhong, *Zhengtu* (The journey), 2 vols. (Shanghai, Renmin chubanshe, 1973).

4. Zhang Kangkang, *Fenjiexian* (The dividing line; Shanghai, Renmin chubanshe, 1975).

5. Zhu Lin, *Shenghuo de lu* (The path of life; Beijing, Renmin wenxue chubanshe, 1979).

6. See Michael S. Duke, "Chinese Literature in the Post-Mao Era: The Return of 'Critical Realism,' " in Duke, ed., *Contemporary Chinese Literature* (Armonk, M. E. Sharpe, 1985), pp. 3–6.

7. The dilemma is so defined in *Shangshan xiaxiang hao* (Rustication is great; Shanghai, Renmin chubanshe, 1974), p. 70.

8. *Zhengtu*, p. 6.

9. Ibid., p. 125.

10. Ibid., p. 212.

11. Ibid., p. 101.

12. The model works *(yangbanxi)*, mostly in the form of modern revolutionary Beijing opera, were staged between 1966 and 1971. They are collected in *Geming yangbanxi juben huibian* (Collected libretti of model works; Beijing, Renmin wenxue chubanshe, 1974). For a discussion of the *yangbanxi*, see Richard King, "A Shattered Mirror: The Literature of the Cultural Revolution," PhD dissertation, University of British Columbia, 1984, pp. 100–135.

13. *Shangshan xiaxiang hao*, pp. 7–8.

14. Zhang Kangkang's autobiographical essay "Cong Xizihu dao Beidahuang" (From West Lake to the Great Northern Wasteland) in her *Xiaoshuo chuangzuo yu yishu ganjue* (Fiction writing and artistic feelings; Tianjin, Baihua wenyi chubanshe, 1985), pp. 140–174, includes a section on her rustication and the writing of *The Dividing Line*. Questioned about her neglect of the "marriage question" in the novel, the author explained that she was writing at a time of recovery from

a painful emotional experience and found romantic matters not to her taste. Personal interview with Zhang Kangkang, September 1987. However, when she revisited her rustication experience for her novel *Yinxing banlü* (Beijing, Zuojia chubanshe, 1986), she described in considerable detail the protagonist's marriage, childbirth, divorce, and giving away of her child, all events drawn from her own life. A translation of the novel by Daniel Bryant as *The Invisible Companion* is as yet unpublished.

15. An early element of the campaign against Deng Xiaoping was a renewed attack on Liu Shaoqi and Wang Guangmei. Criticism of the opera *Sanshang Taofeng* (Going up Peach Peak three times) appeared in 1974, as Zhang Kangkang was writing *The Dividing Line*. See Chu Lan, "Ping Jinju *Sanshang taofeng*" (Criticism of the Jinju Going up Peach Peak three times), *RMRB*, 28 February 1974, and a collection with the same title, published in September 1974 by Renmin chubanshe in Beijing. Zhang Kangkang denies that Wang Guangmei was a model for Huo Li. Far from accommodating her fiction to the current campaign, she insists, she was risking censure for creating a female villain during Jiang Qing's ascendancy. She agrees, however, that it would have been impossible not to be subconsciously influenced by the media blitzes of the day, and that her work undoubtedly shows their influence.

16. For a catalogue of the features of literary "capitalist roaders," see Shen Keding, " 'Yinmou wenyi' pipan," (Criticism of "conspiratorial literature"), *Shanghai wenyi* (Shanghai arts) 1:87–94 (October 1977).

17. *Fenjiexian,* p. 38.

18. Ibid., p. 67.

19. Ibid., p. 67.

20. Ibid., p. 158.

21. Ibid., p. 28.

22. Ibid., p. 179.

23. For an introduction to "exposure literature," see Richard King, " 'Wounds' and 'Exposure': Chinese Literature after the Gang of Four," *Pacific Affairs* 54:82–99 (Spring 1981).

24. *Shenghuo de lu,* p. 287.

25. Ibid., p. 143.

26. See "Chairman Mao's Letter to Li," in B. Michael Frolic, *Mao's People* (Cambridge, Harvard University Press, 1980), pp. 42–57.

27. Louwa's tragedy occurs in the only part of any of the three novels under discussion translated into English: "Downpour on a Leaky Roof," trans. Richard King, in Duke, *Contemporary Chinese Literature,* pp. 30–34.

28. *Shenghuo de lu,* p. 113.

29. Thomas P. Bernstein, *Up to the Mountains and Down to the Villages: The Transfer of Youth from Urban to Rural China* (New Haven, Yale University Press, 1977), p. 156: "There were 77 youths at the Daping Farm in Guiyang . . . over 80 percent of the young women were raped. The farm manager, the Party branch secretary and the *xian* committee 'played a leading role' in this regard." In Zhu Lin's short story collection *She zhentou hua* (Snake's pillow; n.p., Jiangsu renmin chubanshe, 1984), rape or attempted rape of the female protagonist occurs in

four of the ten stories. See Richard King, "Images of Sexual Oppression in Zhu Lin's *Snake's-pillow* Collection," in Michael S. Duke, ed., *Modern Chinese Women Writers: Critical Appraisal* (Armonk, M. E. Sharpe, 1989), pp. 152–173.

30. *Shenghuo de lu,* p. 26.

31. Ibid., p. 113.

32. The author's first two title proposals were *Siqu de linghun* (The dead soul) and *Juanjuan a, Juanjuan* (Oh, Juanjuan, Juanjuan). Personal interview with Zhu Lin, May 1981.

33. Qiu Shaoyun allowed himself to be burned alive rather than move and betray the location of a Communist ambush; Huang Xuguang blocked an enemy machine-gun emplacement with his body.

34. Wang Jie, Ouyang Hai, and Lei Feng were all young soldiers elevated posthumously to heroic status in the early 1960s after Lin Biao took command of the armed forces. Biographies of all three were published, Ouyang Hai's in the form of a novel by Jin Jingmai, *Ouyang Hai zhi ge* (The song of Ouyang Hai; Beijing, Renmin wenxue chubanshe, 1966). Lei Feng, "Chairman Mao's good soldier," is recalled almost every year by emulation campaigns, most strongly at times when the Communist Party wishes to stress obedience rather than initiative.

35. *Zhengtu,* p. 146.

36. *Fenjiexian,* p. 142.

37. *Shenghuo de lu,* p. 182.

38. Yu the Great, hard at work on flood prevention, passed by his home three times without entering; Wang Guofu insisted that he and his family occupy a hired hand's hut rather than build a new house; and Gao Daquan, hero of Hao Ran's *Jinguang dadao* (The golden road), 2 vols. (Beijing, Renmin wenxue chubanshe, 1972, 1974), makes the same sacrifices and more besides.

39. *Shenghuo de lu,* p. 230.

40. *Fenjiexian,* p. 17.

41. Ibid., p. 114.

42. *Shenghuo de lu,* p. 257.

43. Ibid., p. 194.

44. Ibid., p. 189.

45. Guo Xiaodong, "Muxing tuteng: Zhiqing wenxue de yizhong jingshen biange" (The totem of motherhood: A change of heart in rusticated youth literature), *Shanghai wenxue* 1:90–96 (January 1987); quotation from p. 91.

46. For a discussion of this character type, see King, *A Shattered Mirror,* pp. 124–126.

47. Derived from the *chengyu* (idiom) *yi ben wan li* (big profit from a minimal investment). See *Zhengtu,* p. 163.

48. Ibid., p. 151.

49. The butterfly lovers of Chinese legend, Liang Shanbo and Zhu Yingtai, were so called because, following their untimely and lovelorn deaths, a pair of butterflies flew out of their tomb. The violin concerto *Liang Shanbo and Zhu Yingtai,* composed in 1959 by He Zhanhao and Chen Gang, was banned during the CR.

50. *Zhengtu,* p. 446.

51. Ibid., p. 604.

52. Ibid., p. 548–549.
53. Ibid., p. 671.
54. *Fenjiexian*, p. 421–422.
55. *Shenghuo de lu*, p. 250.
56. A rape was expurgated in the revision of the CR model work *The White-Haired Girl (Baimaonü)*. In the Yan'an opera original by He Jingzhi and Ding Yi, the central character Xi'er is raped by her landlord master before fleeing and bearing her child in the hills. The model ballet has her escaping intact, thus sparing the scenarists the vexing question of how to regard a heroine who harbors the seed of an oppressor class.
57. "A Pure Woman" was the controversial subtitle of Thomas Hardy's 1891 *Tess of the D'Urbervilles*, a novel whose central figure bears a striking resemblance to Juanjuan of *Shenghuo de lu*. Both are exceptional and refined girls in lowly settings; both attract two men, a strait-laced idealist (Angel Clare/Liangzi) and a hypocrite posing as a zealot (Alec D'Urberville/Cui Haiying). Defiling by the latter makes union with the former impossible, and they are helpless before the fate that destroys them. Yet, both, though forced into compromise and deceit, are tragic heroines.
58. See, for example, scene 5 of the 1979 play *Jiaru wo shi zhende*, translated by Edward M. Gunn as "What If I Really Were?" in Perry Link, ed., *Stubborn Weeds: Popular and Controversial Literature after the Gang of Four* (Bloomington, Indiana University Press, 1983), pp. 233–239. In this scene a disillusioned farm manager says of his charges: "They're all gone with the wind, back to the city— to replace their parents at factories, or by transfer orders, or through back-door connections. They've all been let go" (p. 235).
59. Zhang Xianliang, "Ling yu rou," *Shuofang* 9 (September 1980), reprinted in several collections; translated as "Body and Soul" in *Prize-winning Stories from China, 1980–1981* (Beijing, Foreign Languages Press, 1985), pp. 59–92, and elsewhere as "A Herdsman's Story," the title of a movie made from the story (Chinese title: *Mumaren*).
60. "Body and Soul," p. 87.
61. Ibid., p. 65.
62. Ibid., p. 89.
63. Wang Anyi, "Benci lieche zhongdian," *Shanghai wenxue* 10 (October 1981); collected in *Wang Anyi zhong-duanpian xiaoshuoji* (Selected mid-length and short stories by Wang Anyi; Beijing, Zhongguo qingnian chubanshe, 1983), pp. 1–32; translated as "The Destination" in *Chinese Literature*, Autumn 1984, pp. 3–24.
64. Ibid., p. 11.
65. "Ta," *Shouhuo* 3 (May 1983); reprinted as the title work in a collection of Zhang's short novels published by Sichuan wenyi chubanshe, 1985, pp. 3–93.
66. Ibid., p. 47.
67. A reading that takes rusticated-youth fiction further into the 1980s (and thus beyond the parameters of this study) would tend to belie this despair for the rusticated-youth generation at least in one respect: some of the most creative artists now at work in China are former rusticated youths. In addition to Zhang

Kangkang and Zhu Lin, whose works are considered here, we may cite [Zhong] Acheng, author of the 1983 short novel *Qiwang* (The chess master) and film-maker Chen Kaige, director of *Huang tudi* (Yellow earth).

Chapter 12. Dramas of Passion: Heroism in the Cultural Revolution's Model Operas by Ellen R. Judd

I gratefully acknowledge the support of Canada–People's Republic of China Exchange Scholarships during the years 1974 to 1977.

1. André Malraux, *Anti-memoirs*, trans. Terence Kilmartin (New York, Holt, Rinehart and Winston, 1968), p. 360.
2. The "three prominences" are (1) among all the characters, give prominence to the positive characters, (2) among all the positive characters, give prominence to the heroic characters, and (3) among all the heroic characters, give prominence to the main heroic character. The most extensive and systematic presentation of this position and of late CR dramatic theory in general is to be found in Fang Yun, *Geming yangbanxi xuexi zhaji* (Study notes on the revolutionary model operas; Shanghai, Shanghai renmin chubanshe, 1974).
3. *Hongqi* (Red flag) 4:39 (April 1977).
4. Shanghai Jingjutuan, *Zhiqu weishushan* (Taking Tiger Mountain by strategy; Beijing, Renmin chubanshe, 1971); Beijing Jingjutuan, *Shajiabang* (Shajiabang; Beijing, Renmin chubanshe, 1970); Shanghai Jingjutuan, *Haigang* (On the docks; Beijing, Renmin wenxue chubanshe, 1974); Shandong Jingjutuan, *Qixi baihutuan* (Raid on the White Tiger Regiment; Beijing, Renmin wenxue chubanshe, 1972); Zhongguo Jingjutuan, *Hongdengji* (The red lantern; Beijing, Renmin chubanshe, 1972); Shanghai Jingjutuan, *Longjiang song* (Ode to Dragon River; Shanghai, Shanghai renmin chubanshe, 1974); Wang Shuyuan et al., *Dujuanshan* (Azalea Mountain; Beijing, Renmin wenxue chubanshe, 1975); Zhongguo Jingjutuan and Zhang Yongmu, *Pingyuan zuo zhan* (Fighting on the plains; Beijing, Renmin chubanshe, 1974); and Zhongguo Jingjutuan, *Hongse niangzijun* (The red detachment of women; Beijing, Renmin wenxue chubanshe, 1972).

   In addition, *Panshiwan* (n. pub.) was emerging as a model toward the end of the CR. It will not be given detailed attention here, but does deserve mention, especially because, in the context of this chapter, it can be seen as representing a possible solution to the problem of portraying mythic heroism in post-1949 settings. That problem was not satisfactorily resolved in either *On the Docks* or *Ode to Dragon River*. *Panshiwan* added dramatic tension and danger of suitably mythic proportions in the form of enemy agents and a dramatic confrontation with them in an underwater cave.
5. Chiang Ching, *On the Revolution of Peking Opera* (Beijing, Foreign Languages Press, 1968).
6. Ellen R. Judd, "Prescriptive Dramatic Theory of the Cultural Revolution," in Constantine Tung and Colin Mackerras, eds., *Drama in the People's Republic of China* (Albany, State University of New York Press, 1987).
7. Sherry B. Ortner, "On Key Symbols," *American Anthropologist* 75:1338–46 (1973).

8. Chu Lan, "Jingju geming shi nian," (Ten years of revolution in Beijing opera), *Hongqi* 7 (July 1974).

9. *The Red Lantern* and many of the other model operas are in good repute at present but rarely if ever performed. Actors and opera troupes have emerged from the CR with an aversion to the model operas and are unwilling to stage them. Su Shuyang (dramatist), verbal communication, 1987.

10. Joseph Campbell, *The Hero with a Thousand Faces* (New York, Pantheon, 1949).

11. Ibid., p. 388.

12. Mao Zedong, "Kanle *Bi shang Liangshan* yihou xiegei Yan'an Pingjutuan de xin," (Letter written to the Yan'an Beijing Opera Troupe after seeing *Driven up Liangshan*), in *Mao Zedong ji* (Collected writings of Mao Zedong; Xianggang, n. pub, 1975), IX, 95.

13. Robert E. Hegel, "Making the Past Serve the Present in Fiction and Drama: From the Yan'an Forum to the Cultural Revolution," in Bonnie S. McDougall, ed., *Popular Chinese Literature and Performing Arts in the People's Republic of China, 1949–1979* (Berkeley, University of California Press, 1984), pp. 197–223.

14. Abner Cohen, "Political Symbolism," *Annual Review of Anthropology* 8:87–113 (1979).

15. Hua-yuan Li Mowry, *Yang-pan Hsi—New Theater in China* (Berkeley, Center for Chinese Studies, University of California, 1973).

16. Donald J. Munro, *The Concept of Man in Contemporary China* (Ann Arbor, University of Michigan Press, 1977).

17. Mary Sheridan, "The Emulation of Heroes," *CQ* 33:47–72 (March 1968).

18. Details of the changes made in the operas during these years are highly significant, but a treatment of this issue is beyond the limits of this chapter. A summary of the changes in the original models is available in Mowry, *Yang-pan Hsi*.

19. Frederic Wakeman, Jr., *History and Will: Philosophical Perspectives on Mao Tse-tung's Thought* (Berkeley, University of California Press, 1973).

20. Mao Zedong, "Ren de zhengque sixiang shi nali laide?" (Where do correct ideas come from?) in *Mao Zedong de wupian zhexue zhuzuo* (Five philosophical essays by Mao Zedong; Beijing, Renmin chubanshe, 1963), pp. 225–228.

21. Lowell Dittmer and Chen Roxi, *Ethics and Rhetoric of the Chinese Cultural Revolution* (Berkeley, Center for Chinese Studies, University of California, 1981).

22. See ibid. for a valuable treatment of the role of disguise in the model operas and its implications regarding the problem of distinguishing hidden evil or enemies.

23. Ellen R. Judd, "China's Amateur Drama: The Movement to Popularize the Revolutionary Model Operas," *Bulletin of Concerned Asian Scholars* 15:26–35 (January/February 1983).

24. Clifford Geertz, "The Politics of Meaning," in *The Interpretation of Cultures* (New York, Basic Books, 1973).

25. Clifford Geertz, "Politics Past, Politics Present: Some Notes on the Uses of Anthropology in Understanding the New States," in *The Interpretation of Cultures* (New York, Basic Books, 1973).

26. Marshal Sahlins, *Culture and Practical Reason* (Chicago, University of Chicago Press, 1976), p. 72.

27. Antonio Gramsci, *Letters from Prison,* ed. Lynne Lawner (London, Quartet, 1979), p. 192.

28. Georges Sorel, *Reflections on Violence,* trans. T. E. Hulme (New York, Peter Smith, 1941), p. 22.

29. Ibid., p. 32.

30. Raymond Williams, "Drama in a Dramatized Society," in *Writing in Society* (London, Verso, n.d.), p. 16.

31. I am here following the definitive 1970 model version of this much-revised drama, Zhongguo Jingjutuan, *Hongdengji.*